THE CASE FOR FATHER CUSTODY

THE CASE FOR FATHER CUSTODY

By

Daniel Amneus, Ph.D.

Copyright © 1999 by Daniel Amneus
Primrose Press
2131 S. Primrose Ave.
Alhambra, CA 91803

First Printing 1999
ISBN   0-9610864-6-7

By Daniel Amneus

BACK TO PATRIARCHY
THE MYSTERY OF *Macbeth*
THE THREE *Othello*s
THE GARBAGE GENERATION
THE CASE FOR FATHER CUSTODY

THANKS TO: Richard Doyle for proofreading and saving me from many mistakes, and to John Knight and Bob Cheney for solving my computer problems.

BRIFFAULT'S LAW:

The female, not the male, determines all the conditions of the animal family. Where the female can derive no benefit from association with the male, no such association takes place.

—Robert Briffault

This book deals with the problems of:

THE FEMALE KINSHIP SYSTEM OR

MATRIARCHY OR

THE CLASSIFICATORY SYSTEM OR

MOTHER-RIGHT—

—the system of female-headed "families" which has created ghettos and barrios by encouraging women to marry the state and breed fatherless children who are eight times more likely to become delinquent.

For

CLARK

CONTENTS

FOREWORD _____ 1

I) INTRODUCTION _____ 4

II) THE SAFE DRUNK DRIVER ARGUMENT _____ 16

III) THE WAR AGAINST PATRIARCHY _____ 37

IV) THE FEMININE MYSTIQUE AND AFTER _____ 75

V) THE ASHERAH _____ 92

VI) RESTORING FEMALE KINSHIP _____ 124

VII) THE CREATION OF PATRIARCHY _____ 142

VIII) THE DOUBLE STANDARD _____ 153

IX) CHILD ABUSE _____ 178

X) ALTERNATIVE FAMILIES _____ 183

XI) EXOGAMY _____ 195

XII) THE SOCIAL CONTRACT _____ 218

XIII) NO FAULT DIVORCE _____ 230

XIV) DOMINATION VS. PARTNERSHIP _____ 236

XV) RE-DEFINING THE FAMILY _____ 250

XVI) ALIMONY AND CHILD SUPPORT _____ 270

XVII) FREE LIKE BLACKS _____ 312

XVIII) VIOLENT LAND _____ 329

XIX) HYPERGAMY _____ 336

XX) GANGBANGING AND ILLEGITIMACY _____ 346

XXI) SUMMARY _____ 375

ANNEX _____ 379

INDEX..456

FOREWORD

The female role, says Margaret Mead, is a biological fact, the male role a mere social creation. Until ten or twelve thousand years ago the function of the male was primarily to impregnate the female. He might also function, at Mom's pleasure, to provide care for her and for her offspring; but if Mom became dissatisfied with Dad, she gave him his walking papers and found a new boyfriend, as she does today in the ghetto. The male role had no stability. Children depended primarily on Mom.

In pre-mammalian reproduction (say that of a green turtle) the offspring begins its existence as an egg and never learns that it has a mother or a father. Its mother's participation in its existence consists of conceiving and gestating it and burying the resulting egg in the sand. After remaining there and maturing awhile, it emerges from the sand and waddles down to the water to find a meal—or to become a meal for some other creature. It is self-contained and lives on its own inherited resources or it dies.

In the mammalian female kinship system the offspring are born alive but are still a part of nature–they just happen. A mother cat just has kittens as a river just flows. However, mammalian mothers cherish their young, feed them from their own body, protect them, educate them. Your cat and her kittens show how meaningful mammalian motherhood is, and how irrelevant mere fatherhood is once the father has performed his minuscule sexual function. Mammalian motherhood enables the kitten to have an infancy. This is the relationship which judges understand and seek to preserve by awarding custody to mothers in divorce cases.

The kitten has no childhood. After a rather short period of helpless infancy, it becomes almost suddenly a mature adult capable of fending for itself like the infant turtle after it emerges from its egg.

The male kinship system found among humans is an extremely recent engraftment upon the female mammalian kinship system, which originated in the Mesozoic Era when the dinosaurs were young, some two hundred million years ago.

It was John Fiske, the nineteenth century American historian and philosopher, who pointed out what made human beings special—and more successful than other mammals: not only the prolongation of infancy, but the creation of a whole additional era of life, childhood, something unknown in any other species, so that human children can enjoy an enormously long period during which they are protected, cherished, educable, playful, exploratory, sensitive and aware, a period during which they can reach out and learn about and come to love the world they live in. The male kinship system, or patriarchy, is still a part of nature, but in a new sense: it depends not on biological heredity but on *social* heredity. It is a human creation, like a hydroelectric dam placed over a river to harness its power and use it to run factories and light streets. It was the great achievement of patriarchy to raise reproduction above recreation and put it to work. Man was taking charge of part of his heredity.

It is largely fatherhood which makes childhood possible. Mothers make infants but when the infants become children they are likely to be less well socialized if they have no fathers.[1] It is largely father absence which creates ghettos and gangs and messed-up kids—boys trying to find their identity through violence, girls trying to find their identity through sexual promiscuity—which generates the male violence of the next generation. They need real fathers, *sociological* fathers, not mere biological studs interested in a one-night stand or a brief or superficial relationship. Sociological fatherhood is real fatherhood. It is also what Margaret Mead called "a social invention." In the ghettos biological fathers seldom become sociological fathers, seldom amount to much, because Mom's sexual promiscuity or disloyalty—her belief in what feminists call a woman's right to control her own sexuality—denies them the role of sociological fatherhood. Lawmakers and judges fail to understand that fatherhood is a social invention, that it must be created and maintained by society. This is the main reason patriarchal society—the father kinship system—exists. They do not grasp that *social heredity has become part of biology* and that fathers are the primary means of

---

[1] Leontine Young says of mothers of illegitimate—i.e., fatherless—children: "Furthermore, her desire and her interest center in a baby almost to the complete exclusion of the child. The fact that a baby inevitably becomes a child is another of those facts that she ignores as irrelevant." (Leontine Young, *Out of Wedlock: A Study of the Problems of the Unmarried Mother and Her Child* [New York: McGraw-Hill, 1954], p. 37.)

transmitting social heredity. They suppose that humans can live like cattle, without fathers, with only the meager social heredity found in female kinship systems such as ghettos and Indian reservations. Until lawmakers and judges see that they must support the father's role *because* it is the weak biological link in the family we will have more matriarchy—along with its accompaniments: educational failure, illegitimacy, teen suicide, gangs and the rest.

I) INTRODUCTION

A Georgia superior court judge named Robert Noland always gives custody of children to the mother when he tries a divorce case. He explains:

> **I ain't never seen a calf following a bull. They always follow the cow. So I always give custody to the mamas.**

The reason Judge Noland never saw a calf following a bull is that cattle don't live in two-parent households. If we want to live like cattle, he has the right idea.

Most judges think as Judge Noland does: the mother-headed reproductive unit is natural.[1] If your cat has kittens, you realize how marginal fatherhood is. If you drive through a ghetto and see the idle males on the street corners, you realize the same thing. Apart from their function as sperm-providers, these street corner punks are so obviously unfit to be parents that if they tried to horn in on Mom's reproductive enterprise, she would do what the mother-cat would do to the father-cat—shoo him away. Leon Dash describes how it works in the Washington ghetto:

> **The pregnancy brought out feelings of possession on the part of the father of her twin boys, feelings that both frightened and angered Charmaine....The man had begun to act as if "he had [marriage] papers on me. He had got real domineering. I wouldn't stand still for it. He acted like he was more my father than my boyfriend.... I told him, 'Get your ass out of my house!'"[2]**

So he gets his ass out of her house and goes to a street corner to rap with other punks who are also unfit to be fathers and he peddles dope and becomes anti-social and so forth. This is the ghetto pattern: female sexual irresponsibility and male work irresponsibility.

---

[1]David Kirp, Mark Yudof, Marlene Franks, *Gender Justice* (Chicago: University of Chicago Press, 1986), p. 184: "80 percent of Los Angeles judges report that, despite official neutrality, they unofficially regard the mother as the appropriate parent unless she is proved unfit."
[2]Leon Dash, *When Children Want Children: An Inside Look at the Crisis of Teenage Parenthood* (New York: Penguin Books, 1989), p. 230.

Why is this black male unfit to be a father? Because his mother didn't want *his* father around any more than Charmaine wants *him* around, and he grew up not knowing what fatherhood is all about and associating responsibility with being female—a female parent, female teachers, female social workers. She married the State, which promised to take care of her. That's matriarchy.

The primary bond in nature is that which Judge Noland understands, between the mother and her offspring. The mother's bond with her sexual mate is weaker, more artificial. Men are more dependent on this artificial bond than women, and therefore more dependent on women's acceptance of sexual regulation, more dependent on marriage. It is women, not men, who write books with titles like *The Good Divorce*, *The Courage to Divorce*, *Get Rid of HIM!*, and *Learning to Leave: A Woman's Guide*.

Families are created by male intrusion into the primarily female arena of reproduction. According to "Briffault's Law," quoted at the beginning, if families are to be stable the male must have some benefit to offer the female; but females know that if they reject the sexual regulation which makes stable families possible there are welfare bureaucrats and divorce court judges like Robert Noland who will help them because they realize the naturalness of living like cattle and don't realize that civilized living is an artificial arrangement, that it requires male participation in families, and requires the social supports which will guarantee such participation.[3] It requires understanding that the welfare system and the legal system are parts of civilization, not parts of nature.

Antonia Novello, former Surgeon General of the Public Health Service, puts the woman's attitude this way:

> **How can a woman really ask for safe sex or control sexual practices when she is economically dependent on her partner? How can we expect her to speak up, and risk abandonment, when the one who abuses, neglects and infects [her] also supports the family?[4]**

Like Charmaine, she doesn't want her "partner" to be a husband, to have anything to do with "controlling sexual practices." Wives are the

---

[3]Briffault, *The Mothers* (New York: Macmillan, 1927), I, 212: "The heterosexual bond is limited and weak." Arthur Evans, *Witchcraft and the Gay Counterculture* (Boston: Fag Rag Press, 1978), p. 15: "Monogamy and the nuclear family are almost unknown in nature."
[4]*Los Angeles Times*, 29 June, 1993.

safest people in society, safer than single women and far safer than men; but it helps Ms. Novello's argument to accuse the "partner" of being an abuser, neglecter and infector, which most husbands are not. She simply prefers the ghetto pattern, where the woman, like the mother cat and Judge Noland's cows, "controls sexual practices." Society tries to find ways of giving her what she wants, of making her economically independent of males by support payments from ex-"partners," by Affirmative Action policies favoring women, and of course by welfare.

The biological marginality of fatherhood means that society must create artificial social arrangements for men which will motivate them to work, to become responsible husbands and fathers and providers for families. This artificial style of procreating and rearing children in two-parent households is called patriarchy. It depends on stable marriage—and it creates stable marriage. Women resent patriarchy because it requires their acceptance of sexual regulation. The feminist movement is a rebellion against this: a woman, feminists tell us, has a right to control her own sexuality, a right women achieve in the ghetto, where most children carry their mothers' surnames and where a third of black males are in prison or jail, on probation or on parole. Who needs them? Not black females, who can scrape by on welfare or marginal jobs which enable them to enjoy sexual promiscuity ("control their own sexuality") and reduce males to the status of boyfriends and studs.[5]

This lifestyle, where the mother heads the reproductive unit, I shall call *matriarchy*. Matriarchy properly means "government by women," which, as Professor Steven Goldberg has shown in his book *The Inevitability of Patriarchy*, does not exist and never can exist. But a convenient one-word term is required to refer to the *female kinship system* and I propose to use the term "matriarchy" to denote it.

"Patriarchies and the religions that fortify them," writes feminist Judy Mann,

are recent developments in human history. Today they are being challenged with varying degrees of vigor and success throughout the world. The rise of the women's movement in the United States is the strongest challenge ever to

---

[5]Feminist writers like to complain of the "doubly oppressed Negro woman." (Betty Millard, quoted in Daniel Horowitz *Betty Friedan and the Making of the* Feminine Mystique [Amherst: Univ. of Massachusetts Press,1998], p. 129).Cf. p. 139: Friedan "paid special attention to the role of African American women (who encountered 'double discrimination')…"

a major patriarchal system. **For this challenge to succeed, it is critically important for women and girls—and the men who stand shoulder to shoulder with them—to understand that patriarchies are recent, man-made social contrivances that draw their legitimacy from might, not divine or natural right....[P]atriarchies are neither immutable nor inevitable. They can be challenged, changed, and replaced.[6]**

Black women, says one of them,[7] cannot respect white women. They may envy them because of their affluence, because of their good looks, because of the attention and loyalty they receive from their men. They may even love them, as nannies and housekeepers. But black women cannot respect white women because white women accept patriarchy and its sexual regulation. White feminists, on the other hand, frequently praise black matriarchs for their rejection of patriarchal sexual regulation. White girls say they "don't want to live the kind of life my mother led." Black girls like Charmaine don't want to and are praised by feminists for refusing to. "While the white women often had negative perceptions of their mother's lives and rejected them as role models," writes feminist Wini Breines, "the black women were much more likely to celebrate their mothers and claim a link with them."[8] "Within segments of the African-American community," say feminists Debold, Wilson and Malave, "mothers are granted respect and authority that, by and large, non-African-American mothers are not."[9] Within segments of the African-American community, in other words, men's role is of reduced importance. This is why they are ghettos.

Since the African-American community is the site of an extraordinary amount of social pathology and since the African-American community is conspicuously matriarchal, the authority of black mothers and the lack of authority of black fathers invites further exploration. Debold, Wilson and Malave try to shed light on the black matriarchy with the following from Alice Walker's *Possessing the Secret of Joy:*

Tashi, the heroine, finds herself in a consulting room with a white male psychiatrist. "Negro women are considered the most difficult of all people to be effectively analyzed. Do you know why?" Tashi says nothing. "Negro women, the doctor says into my silence, can never be analyzed effectively

---

[6] Judy Mann, *The Difference: Growing Up Female in America* (New York: Time Warner, 1994), pp. 201f.
[7] I cannot recall who she was.
[8] Wini Breines, *Young, White and Miserable* (Boston: Beacon Press, 1992), p. 79.
[9] Elizabeth Debold, Marie Wilson and Idelisse Malave, *Mother Daughter Revolution: From Betrayal to Power* (Menlo Park, CA: Addison-Wesley Publishing Company, 1993), p. 131. The "betrayal" of the subtitle means conforming to patriarchal socialization; the "power" means rejecting it and conforming to the matriarchal socialization given ghetto girls.

because they can never bring themselves to blame their mothers." The shared comradeship of mothers and daughters in the African-American community is turned into a source of sickness by experts.[10]

Not sickness—they are just anti-patriarchal. The shared comradeship is natural, as patriarchy is artificial. To gain the blessings made possible by patriarchy, women must sacrifice this female solidarity and give their loyalty to one man in marriage, to the nuclear family. This sacrifice is the quid pro quo for the enormous rewards patriarchy bestows, the rewards which enable women to escape the ghetto and matriarchy—the female kinship system.

Black girls have *more* reason to blame their mothers—for rejecting and wrecking patriarchy and inflicting father-absence and matriarchy upon them. Black *boys* owe their predicament not to white racism but to this same female clinging to the matriarchal system which exiles males from families. The "shared comradeship" spoken of by Debold, Wilson and Malave is a comradeship in the War Against Patriarchy. Debold, Wilson and Malave write their book to encourage white girls and mothers to conform to the black matriarchal pattern which has created the ghettos.

Think how often a child's behavior is explained in terms of the mother's problems. Much of the recent discussion of "family values" is actually encoded mother blaming: families are in trouble not because of the inequities in our economic, child-care, and health-care systems but because mothers aren't doing their jobs right—often because they haven't been able to keep a man in the house....[I]n the media, as in conversations, anger and attention focus on individual mothers' inadequacies rather than on the inadequacy of our social systems[11]

Not because they haven't been able to keep a man in the house but because, like Charmaine, they don't want a man in the house or because the partial subsidizing of matriarchy by our social system enables them to get along without a man in the house. What the mothers are blamed for, and should be blamed for, is their hostility to patriarchy, a hostility which Debold, Wilson and Malave write their book to exacerbate. They would like to blame patriarchy for its inadequate support of matriarchy.

---

[10]*Mother Daughter Revolution*, p. 21.
[11]P. 22.

8

"Black women," says Peggy Orenstein, "have traditionally been a source of strength and pride for the girls in their communities."[12] But the boys have been deprived of fathers or know they might be easily deprived of them. This matriarchal pattern is rapidly spreading to the larger society, where, as Senator Moynihan tells us, "the breakup of family inevitably, predictably...will lead to the growth of large numbers of predatory males. We saw it coming. It's come."[13]

Feminists see this as progress. "For many women," says feminist Mary Ann Mason,

the route to liberation from domestic drudgery was liberation from the family. The only chance for true equality with men lay outside the patriarchal family structure....In the real world of the seventies full-time housewives were ending their careers on the rocks of divorce in astonishing numbers.[14]

It is remarkable that the social patterns of the ghettos, despite their poverty, crime, violence, ignorance, illegitimacy, drug addiction, educational failure, and demoralization, should be regarded as worthy of imitation by white feminists, but they are. These white feminists might acknowledge that they would prefer living in patriarchal Beverly Hills to living in matriarchal Watts, but they will deny that matriarchy and female sexual promiscuity have anything to do with the squalor of Watts, with the patterns which allow women to sexually de-regulate themselves, to marginalize their males and to make themselves heads of the "families" which generate the social pathology of the next generation.

We are living in what feminist Naomi Wolf calls a "postdivorce, post-sexual revolution, post-moral relativism world."[15] These three alterations of society are purposeful; they seek to overthrow patriarchy, to marginalize males and to restore the female kinship system. But they require the cooperation of the males whom they victimize. They require that men consent to allowing the legal system, responsible for enforcing contracts, to instead make marriage a fraudulent contract which guarantees husbands nothing, but guarantees wives the right to deprive husbands of their children and to use the children as Mutilated Beggars.

---

[12]Peggy Orenstein, *School Girls: Young Women, Self-Esteem, and the Confidence Gap* (New York: Anchor Books, 1994), p. 182.
[13]On "Meet the Press"; quoted in *American Rifleman*, January, 1994, p. 65.
[14]Mary Ann Mason, *The Equality Trap* (New York: A Touchstone Book, 1988), p. 120.
[15]Naomi Wolf, *Promiscuities: The Secret Struggle for Womanhood* (New York: Random House, 1997), p. 5.

"Mutilated Beggars" requires explanation. In many large cities of the East there are begging rings headed by rascals who kidnap children and mutilate them for use as beggars. The more pitiable and grotesque the mutilations, the more the beggars earn. The alms go to the owners of the begging ring.[16]

HOW MOST MATRIARCHY IS CREATED TODAY

A judge may try a divorce case in the morning and place the children in the mother's custody. He may try a criminal case in the afternoon and send a man to prison for robbing a liquor store. The chances are three out of four that the criminal he sends to prison grew up in a female headed household just like the one he himself created that morning when he tried the divorce case. He sees no connection between the two cases.

He is only doing what he has always done and what most other judges do. He sees that the biological link between the mother and the offspring is closer than that between the father and the offspring and that therefore the mother is the natural custodian of the children.

He's right in a sense. Patriarchy is artificial like everything about civilization, a shaky structure only five thousand years old, built on the firm base of a two-hundred-million-year-old mother-headed reproductive unit shared by cattle. The cattle enjoy the blessings of nature. Judge Noland thinks, as Margaret Mead thinks, that the female role is a biological fact and that fatherhood is a social invention, man-made, artificial, fragile. When the social props it requires are withdrawn society reverts to matriarchy, the pattern of cattle and the ghettos. Because other judges think as Judge Noland thinks and because they nearly always create female-headed households in place of father-headed households when they try divorce cases, the larger society, as Senator Moynihan says, is coming to take on the pattern of the ghettos.

THE FEMALE HEADED HOUSEHOLD

Female headed households are a minority of households, but they generate over seventy percent of the criminal class.

---

[16]See Chapter 5 of my *Garbage Generation* for a fuller discussion of Mutilated Beggars.

According to a study made by the Bureau of Justice Statistics, 72 percent of incarcerated juvenile delinquents grew up in broken homes, mostly female headed. Such single-parent homes are only 24 percent of all homes. The ratios of delinquency between father-headed homes and mother-headed homes show that it takes eight hundred and fifteen intact homes to generate as much delinquency as is generated by one hundred broken homes, mostly female headed.[17]

According to Getting Men Involved: The Newsletter of the Bay Area Male Involvement Network,[18]

63 percent of youth suicides come from fatherless homes, 90 percent of all homeless and runaway children are from fatherless homes, 85 percent of all children exhibiting behavioral disorders come from fatherless homes, 80 percent of rapists motivated by displaced anger come from fatherless homes, 71 percent of all high school dropouts come from fatherless homes, 75 percent of all adolescent patients in chemical abuse centers come from fatherless homes, 70 percent of juveniles in state-operated institutions come from fatherless homes, and 85 percent of all youths in prisons grew up in fatherless homes.

According to one estimate, almost two-thirds[19] of the men who marry today in the hope of becoming fathers face these statistics, face the prospect of losing their children and seeing them forced into the female kinship system by a divorce court judge who will then try to make him *pay* to have this loss inflicted on himself and his kids. More of this two-thirds figure in a moment.

Maggie Gallagher cites George Rekers, professor of neuropsychiatry and behavioral science at the University of South Carolina School of Medicine, as follows on father absence:

Both developmental and clinical studies have clearly established the general rule that the father's positive presence in the home is, in the vast majority of

---

[17]Statistics from *Los Angeles Times*, 19 September, 1988. See my *Garbage Generation* (Alhambra, CA: Primrose Press, 1990), p. 179 for a discussion of these statistics. 72 (the percentage of delinquents who are from broken homes) divided by 24 (the percentage of all homes) equals 3.0. 28 (the percentage of delinquents who are from intact homes) divided by 76 (the percentage of homes which are intact) equals 0.3684. 3.0 divided by 0.3684 equals 8.143. If the findings of this study are to be trusted *a child growing up in a single-parent home (usually female-headed) is 8.1 times as likely to be delinquent*. This study is now a decade old. The number of female-headed households has continued to increase since then.
[18]Issue 1, spring 1997.
[19]Teresa Castro Martin and Larry L. Bumpass, "Recent Trends in Marital Disruption," *Demography* 26 (1989), 37-51.

cases, normally essential for the existence of family strength and child adjustment.

Research, says Gallagher,

shows that children without fathers have lower academic performance, more cognitive and intellectual deficits, increased adjustment problems, and higher risks for psychosexual development problems. And children from homes in which one or both parents are missing or frequently absent have higher rates of delinquent behavior, suicide, and homicide, along with poor academic performance. Among boys, father absence has been linked to greater effeminacy, and exaggerated aggressiveness. Girls, on the other hand, who lose their father to divorce tended to be overly responsive to men and become sexually active earlier. They married younger, got pregnant out of wedlock more frequently and divorced or separated from their eventual husbands more frequently, perpetuating the cycle.[20]

Let's summarize it this way—this is the central argument of the present book:

The marriage contract no longer guarantees a man's right to have a family, only his obligation to subsidize its destruction and the placing of his children in a female headed household where they are eight times more likely to become delinquent, and five times more likely to commit suicide, thirty-two times more likely to run away, twenty times more likely to have behavioral disorders, fourteen times more likely to commit rape, nine times more likely to drop out of high school, ten times more likely to abuse chemical substances, nine times more likely to end up in a state-operated institution, twenty times more likely to end up in prison.[21] A father who refuses to subsidize this will be judged a rat and a Deadbeat Dad and will be pursued by the resources of government ("We will find you. We will make you pay," says President Clinton). He must perform forced labor for the benefit of another person, Mom. He must consent to give up his children, his home, his role, his property and his future income for the purpose of liberating Mom from "patriarchal oppression" and "the scourge of marriage."

Is the two-thirds figure really possible? This estimate of the number of divorces was made by Teresa Castro Martin and Larry

---

[20]Maggie Gallagher, *Enemies of Eros* (Chicago: Bonus Books, 1989), pp. 114f.
[21]*Getting Men Involved* gives as its sources the U.S.D.H.S, Bureau of the Census, Center for Disease Control, *Criminal Justice and Behavior*, vol. 14, 1978, pp. 403-26, National Principals Association Report on the State of High Schools, *Rainbows for All God's Children*, U.S. Dept. of Justice Special Report, Sept, 1988, Texas Dept. of Corrections, 1992.

Bumpass in 1989. In the following year Bumpass suggested "60% may be closer to the mark." According to Bumpass, "The *exact* level of marital disruption is much less important, however, than the fact that the majority of recent first marriages will not last a lifetime." He notes that "the underlying rate of increase in the level of lifetime divorce has been virtually constant for more than 100 years, generating the accelerating curve from 7% for marriages in 1860 to the current expectation of well over one-half."

The crucial correlation never seems to have been noticed: this increase in the number of divorces followed the switchover from automatic father custody to virtually automatic mother custody. Women are more divorce-prone than men (Briffault's Law) and their growing realization that they need not lose their children in the divorce court has been a major cause of the rising divorce rate. Switching back to automatic father custody will re-stabilize marriage and the family.

Briffault's Law says that the male must have a benefit to give the female if he is to have the privilege of associating with her. This benefit is not just his paycheck, it is his *family*, his children, his home, his wealth and status—all the good things bestowed on wives by the patriarchal system. The *family* is a patriarchal creation, though feminists wish to apply the term to non-family groupings found among animals—the mother-headed matriline which creates most of the crime and social disruption noted on pages 12ff.

It is the unwisdom of judges—or rather their weakness of character, their unwillingness to keep their oath of office and administer "equal justice under law"—which requires that father custody be made mandatory and automatic, as it was in the mid-nineteenth century, when "they were by law *his* children."

If the father were acknowledged to be the head of his family and if he could not be deprived of his children and his home and income, he would be able to provide the benefit stipulated by Briffault's Law. His wife would be grateful to him rather than divorce-prone as she is now because of the anti-male bias of the legal system. Divorce would plummet, marriage would become once again the normative expectation for both men and women. Children would be brought up in two-parent families as they ought to be.

An Ann Landers reader cites a study by Denmark's Social Research Institute which says that single fathers are calmer and less likely to punish their children than lone mothers, "who are often dogged by money problems":

> The Daily Berlingske Tidiende said yesterday a study of 1,200 children aged between 3 and 5, half living with a single mother, and half with only a father, showed that the mothers were far more stressed and depressed than the men.

> The single mothers have more psychiatric problems than fathers [continues the Danish study]. Their self-confidence is lower, and they suffer more from nightmares, insomnia attacks, the paper quoted the state-run institute as saying in a report. "Mothers have far more conflict with their children and are quicker to hit or punish their children," the report said.

> The paper quoted researcher Mogens Nygaard as saying women were not genetically more irritable than men but were under greater economic pressure, being more likely to be jobless or, if employed, generally lower paid than male workers.

> Women also perceived society as having a more favorable attitude to men caring for their children alone than for single mothers.

Ann Landers' comment:

> The study underscores the importance of providing financial support and job training for mothers.

No it doesn't. It underscores rather the importance of children having fathers. It underscores the foolishness of judges in routinely assigning custody to mothers in divorce cases. Ann Landers' is proposing more welfare, more ghettoizing of society.

THE NEED TO SAVE PATRIARCHY

The present book argues:

> That the destruction of the patriarchal system is now taking place, that the feminist movement is succeeding in altering the kinship system, and that its success explains the social and sexual chaos of present society.

Fathers could reverse this destruction, could undo the legal system's betrayal of the family and the disastrous changes of the past three decades and restore the male kinship system if they could claim custody of their children in cases of divorce.

Automatic father custody is too bad, really, for there are many bad fathers. But the anti-male discrimination of judges has gone on for over a hundred years and has—thanks to women's divorce-proneness (Briffault's Law) and their assurance of custody and support awards—is destroying marriage and the family and civilization along with them. Men (who else?) must put a stop to it. We cannot continue to live with a 60% divorce rate and a 30% illegitimacy rate.

II) THE SAFE DRUNK DRIVER ARGUMENT

Feminists will argue that even though delinquents are eight times more likely to come from matriarchal homes, still most fatherless children do not become delinquents, so there can be no objection to mother custody. Of course most fatherless boys don't grow up to rob liquor stores and most fatherless girls don't grow up to breed illegitimate children. Therefore what? Therefore we can ignore the increased *probability* that fatherlessness will create delinquency and illegitimacy? This might be called the "Safe Drunk Driver Argument": Most drunk drivers do not get in accidents. The overwhelming majority get home safely and sleep it off.

Drunks are, however, overrepresented among those who do get in accidents; and for this reason society discourages drunk driving.

The Safe Drunk Driver Argument is identical with the anti-patriarchal argument which defends the creation of fatherless households: Most fatherless children do not become delinquents; therefore creating fatherless families is OK.

Other social pathology has the same kind of correlation with female-headed households:

Most fatherless children do not become teenage suicides, but most teenage suicides are fatherless children.

Most fatherless children do not become educational failures, but most educational failures are fatherless children.

Most fatherless children do not become rapists, but most rapists were fatherless children.

Most fatherless children do not become gang members, but most gang members are fatherless children.

Most fatherless children do not become child abusers or child molesters, but most child abusers and child molesters were fatherless children.

Most fatherless children do not become unwed parents, but most unwed parents were fatherless children.[1]

Feminists understandably sense a threat to the their revolution in the obvious correlation between fatherlessness and social pathology. *Los Angeles Times* reporter Lynn Smith writes a piece called "Lack of Dad Is Not So Bad," with this:

> **Stable, two-parent families still appear to do the best job of raising kids. But when income and job status are taken into account, children raised by single mothers are nearly as likely to succeed in adulthood....**

Feminist Terry Arendell tries to make the same point:

> **The long-held view that the absence of a father adversely affects children has increasingly been challenged. For example, a study of nearly nine hundred school-aged children found that single-parent families were just as effective in rearing children as traditional two-parent families. After controlling for socioeconomic variables and matching groups of children in father-present and father-absent families, they found no significant differences between the two groups [Feldman, H., 1979. "Why We Need a Family Policy," Journal of Marriage and the Family 41 (3): 453-455]. Another scholar argues: "Studies that adequately control for economic status challenge the popular homily that divorce is disastrous for children. Differences between children from one- and two-parent homes of comparable status on school achievement, social adjustment, and delinquent behavior are small or even nonexistent" [Bane, M. 1976. Here to Stay: American Families in the Twentieth Century, p. 111].[2]**

This is like saying that pygmies are no shorter than other people *with whom they have been matched for height.* "After controlling for socioeconomic variables" means after leaving out most of the evidence. Arendell wants to limit her comparison to female-headed homes where divorce or illegitimacy does not produce economic deterioration and lowered standards of living. But half a library of feminist literature shows that divorce, father-absence and illegitimacy *do* lower the standard of living of single mothers and their children; so Arendell is saying that there is no deterioration in school achievement, social adjustment, etc., *except in almost every case.*

---

[1] See my *Garbage Generation*, pp. 215-285 for documentation.
[2] Terry Arendell, *Mothers and Divorce: Legal, Economic, and Social Dilemmas* (Berkeley: University of California Press, 1986), pp. 4f.; emphasis added. The quotation ascribed to Bane is not found on page 111 of her book.

The high crime areas of every American city are those with the largest numbers of fatherless children. No exceptions—though most of the citizens living on any ghetto street are not criminals.

The exiling of fathers from families in divorce cases is the current social policy and it is a bad policy. According to sociologist David Popenoe,

> **The negative consequences of fatherlessness are all around us. They affect children, women, and men. Evidence indicating damage to children has accumulated in near tidal-wave proportions. Fatherless children experience significantly more physical, emotional, and behavioral problems than do children growing up in intact families....[T]o reduce delinquency and violence, the child must be reared by a biological father.[3]**

According to sociologist Henry Biller

> **Males who are father-deprived early in life are likely to engage later in rigidly overcompensatory masculine behaviors. The incidence of crimes against property and people, including child abuse and family violence, is relatively high in societies where the rearing of young children is considered to be an exclusively female endeavor.[4]**

According to a recent study conducted at Exeter University in the United Kingdom, children from broken homes, as well as children with step-parents, were "twice as likely as children from intact families to have problems in all areas....Where the child experienced two or more divorces, the rate of problems rose exponentially."[5]

Why do judges routinely award custody of children to mothers? Three reasons. The first is that motherhood is more solidly based in biology than fatherhood. The second is their recognition that women, like children, are dependent creatures. This was formerly understood to mean they needed husbands, as children needed fathers. Now, in the growing matriarchal sector of society, mother custody serves to make Mom and "her" children Mutilated Beggars who are entitled to exploit the patriarchal sector—either welfare or ex-husbands. Third, they suppose they must choose between creating a fatherless household and creating a motherless one, which would be equally bad, and also unchivalrous.

---

[3]David Popenoe, *Life Without Father* (New York: The Free Press, 1996), pp. 77, 156.
[4]Henry Biller, *Fathers and Families* (Westport, CT: Auburn House, 1993), pp. 1f.
[5]Margaret Driscoll, "The True Victims of Separation," *The Medical Post*, 5 April, 1994.

But three-quarters of divorces are initiated by wives, and father custody would confront these wives with the loss of their children and the loss of Dad's paycheck—together with an accompanying loss of status—and few wives would care to forfeit these things.

Can it be doubted that the expectation of mother custody is a primary motive for divorce for women? An expectation of father custody would remove this motive and stabilize families.

Few fathers would care to face the single-parent lifestyle which traps so many single mothers with double responsibilities. Father custody would place practical and economic advantages for both the mother and the father on the side of family stability. There would be few divorces. We know this because father custody was formerly mandatory and automatic, and that was the result. There were only a few thousand divorces annually in the mid-nineteenth century when John Stuart Mill wrote "They are by law *his* children." "When divorce was rare," says feminist Lorraine Dusky, "English common law automatically gave the children to the father."[6] Automatic father custody was why it *was* rare, just as it is common today when mother custody is virtually automatic.

The feminist revolution is to be understood as a protest against female sexual regulation. Feminists say "A woman needs a man like a fish needs a bicycle"; "A woman has a sacred right to control her own sexuality"; "End human sacrifice! Don't get married!" Women's primary object, according to feminist Anne Donchin, is to create a society in which "women can shape their reproductive experiences to further ends of their own choosing."[7]

"What would it have been like," ask feminists Monica Sjöö and Barbara Mor, "if patriarchy had never happened? To get an idea, we have to comprehend the first law of matriarchy: Women control our own bodies. This would seem a basic premise of any fully evolved human culture; which is why primate patriarchy is based on its denial."[8] The first law of matriarchy excludes males from reproduction and this exclusion explains why the matriarchal areas of society are not only impoverished but violent. The first law of patriarchy, otherwise known as the Legitimacy Principle, is that children shall have fathers. The two

---

[6] *Still Unequal*, p. 336.
[7] Quoted in David Blankenhorn, *Fatherless America* (New York: Basic Books, 1995), p. 180.
[8] *The Great Cosmic Mother: Rediscovering the Religion of the Earth* (San Francisco: Harper and Row, 1987), p. 200.

laws are irreconcilable; patriarchal society is responsible for enforcing the first law of patriarchy; feminism wants to go back to the first law of matriarchy. The existing social chaos results from the betrayal of the patriarchal system (of which the legal system is a part) by the legal system itself and the resulting betrayal of the patriarchal family.

According to feminists Barbara Ehrenreich, Elizabeth Hess and Gloria Jacobs   "[Ann] Koedt's classic essay ['The Myth of the Vaginal Orgasm'] was no less than a declaration of sexual independence: women could now be sexual, fully orgasmic beings not only outside of marriage but apart from men," who, she acknowledged, now had good reason to "fear that they will become sexually expendable."[9]

Feminist Joan Kelly says, "Ours may be a historical moment...not only to 'see' how the patriarchal system works, but also to act with that vision—so as to put an end to it."[10]

According to feminist bell hooks, "Re-thinking sexuality, changing the norms of sexuality, is a pre-condition for female sexual autonomy; therefore sexuality and by implication 'sexual freedom' is an important, relevant issue for feminist politics."[11]

Women have always resisted patriarchy. Feminist Eva Keuls tells us:

"Many passages in Greek literature reveal an underlying fear of women getting out of hand, and taking control over their men and their own lives. Evidently the Athenian Greeks perceived their wives and daughters as caged animals, temporarily subdued but ready to strike out if given the slightest chance."[12] Feminist Linda Wagner-Martin says "Escaping control of the patriarchy has long been a central theme in writing by contemporary women."[13]

Book titles like *Get Rid of HIM, Once Is Enough, Young, White and Miserable, Mother Daughter Revolution, The War Against Women* reveal the feminist program to get rid of the patriarchal system. This program is succeeding. It is making marriage meaningless. "Family law," says

---

[9]Barbara Ehrenreich, Elizabeth Hess and Gloria Jacobs, *Re-Making Love* (New York: Anchor Press/Doubleday, 1986), p. 70.
[10]*Feminist Studies*, 5, 1979, p. 225.
[11]bell hooks, *Feminist Theory From Margin to Center* (Boston: South End Press, 1984), p. 148.
[12]Eva Keuls, *The Reign of the Phallus* (Berkeley: University of California Press, 1985), p. 321.
[13]Linda Wagner-Martin, *Telling Women's Lives: The New Biography* (New Brunswick, N.J.: Rutgers University Press, 1994), p. 23.

feminist Brenda Hoggett, former British law commissioner responsible for family law,

> no longer makes any attempt to buttress the stability of marriage or any other union. It has adopted principles for the protection of children and dependent spouses which could be made equally applicable to the unmarried. In such circumstances, the piecemeal erosion of the distinction between marriage and non-married cohabitation may be expected to continue. Logically we have already reached a point at which, rather than discussing which remedies should now be extended to the unmarried, we should be considering whether the legal institution of marriage continues to serve any useful purpose.[14]

This shows that this woman—and she speaks for legions of women—doesn't believe in marriage or the family. She believes marriage should give the husband no rights—though marriage or cohabitation still requires ex-husbands and ex-boyfriends to "protect" ex-wives and children, which is to say subsidize them. She thinks the wife is privileged to take the husband's children from him and impose slavery on him—the performance of forced labor for another person, herself. These are the "principles for the protection of children and dependent spouses" to which Ms. Hoggett refers. " The courts have abandoned the concept of justice and the obligation to enforce contracts. She does *not* say the wife has any obligations towards the husband. She says rather this:

> The courts have abandoned the concept of breach of matrimonial obligations— and their powers of adjustment of property interests in the long term are now so extensive that ordering one spouse from his own home no longer seems so drastic. Far from ordering spouses to stay together, courts are increasingly able and willing to help them separate.[15]

THE BETRAYAL OF CIVILIZATION BY THE LEGAL SYSTEM

Let's understand what this means. Courts are participating in—or rather *organizing*—the destruction of the patriarchal family, and the social system which supports it, and switching over to matriarchy, or mother-right, or the classificatory kinship system, destroying the father-headed family and replacing it with the mother-headed matriline. The "one spouse" who is ordered from "*his* own home" is the male, who gets

---

[14] Quoted in John Campion and Pamela Leeson, *Facing Reality: The Case for the Reconstruction of Legal Marriage* (London: The Family Law Action Group, 1994), p. 5.
[15] *Ibid.*

separated off into limbo to make way for Mom's boyfriends. This is the ghetto system or matriarchy. It requires ignoring the concept of justice and the significance of the marriage contract. The courts insist on their power to order the husband out of the home built by his labor.

What Ms. Hoggett describes is the "natural" condition of the ghettos, of Indian reservations, of the Republic of Haiti. It implements Anne Koedt's "Declaration of sexual independence: women could now be sexual, fully orgasmic beings not only outside of marriage but apart from men"—who now had to fear that they would become "sexually expendable." This means abandoning patriarchy's use of sex as the organizing principle of society and going back to the system of unregulated sexuality found among dogs, cats and cattle. It means abandoning sexual law-and-order.

"Is there really a new woman?" ask Sam and Cynthia Janus. They answer:

Yes there is! She is seriously involved in her career; she is also a lover and a mother. Her sense of empathic identification with men can bridge the gap between men and women. She is autonomous, has relationships of parity, is able to express herself sensually, and appreciates her network of women friends. For too long, sexist stereotypes substituted for reality; women are no longer pinups—they live, breathe, have opinions, and can take charge of a wide range of personal and professional situations.[16]

This woman is unmarriageable. She's not "new" at all. She is the autonomous, pre-patriarchal Stone Age woman, sexually emancipated, who refuses to form a permanent relationship with a man upon which he—or her children—can depend. She doesn't need a man and she repudiates the principle of hypergamy. A man would be a fool to marry such a woman.

Feminists like her are so gleefully frivolous in contemplating their sexual independence that they suppose men ought to be equally gleeful about their own "sexual expendability." But for men sexual marginality is not a joke. The whole system of patriarchy is intended to de-marginalize him, to make him co-equal with his wife. *Unlike* Haitian males, the males on Indian reservations, ghetto males. Men must realize

---

[16]Sam Janus and Cynthia Janus, *The Janus Report on Sexual Behavior* (New York: John Wiley, 1993) p. 55.

that their Money Card and the efforts he puts out to earn the money (efforts which shorten his life by seven years) is the only means for doing this and they must refuse to relinquish it.

This is why "He shall rule over thee"—why he *must*, since (as the Annex shows) she will not otherwise submit to sexual law-and-order, which is a *male* idea. The deadly message of feminism is that females mean to once again take reproduction into their own hands and marginalize males. Men must wake up and understand this. The male must take charge of his family not only for his own sake but also for the sake of his children and for his *wife's* sake. "Sex," as Barbara Ehrenreich says, "is a fundamentally lawless creature, not easily confined to a cage."[17] But it must be confined—otherwise matriarchy.

Aside from divorce, thirty percent of today's children are born out of wedlock. Few teenage girls, the principal breeders of illegitimate children, realize or care that they are ghettoizing society and returning it to the kinship system of the Stone Age. Nor do judges think about this consequence when they create fatherless families in their divorce courtrooms. They do not understand that they are the principal creators of the crime, delinquency and illegitimacy of the following generation.

FATHER CUSTODY: A BOON FOR MOTHERS

It is the *supposed* willingness of mothers to sacrifice career to children that supplies the traditional reason for awarding them custody. Father custody would allow them to do what the Sam Januses[18] say they want to do, put their careers first. Mother custody is an albatross for mothers, a leading cause of the feminization of poverty.

The male must be able to offer a woman a sufficient benefit to induce her to accept the sexual regulation required for family stability— he must "settle into a stable long-term job," must become a family provider. But he must also have society's guarantee that when the woman does accept sexual regulation by entering a marriage contract the contract will be enforced. The legal system is not responsible to create motherhood; it is responsible to create fatherhood and to support it. This is the primary reason it exists. The fathers' rights movement must

---

[17] Dust wrapper of Heyn's book.
[18] Sam Janus and Cynthia Janus, *The Janus Report on Sexual Behavior* (New York: John Wiley, 1993), p. 336.

make judges and lawmakers understand this. Only in this way can the male's non-biological contribution to marriage be made equivalent to the female's biological contribution. Only in this way can men have stable families. Only in this way can marriage be made meaningful.

The means whereby marriage is being made meaningless—the means whereby the female kinship system is being restored—is explained by feminist Susan Faludi in discussing the anti-abortion movement:

> **As resentment over women's increasing levels of professional progress became mixed with anxiety over the sexual freedoms women had begun to exercise, they developed a rhetoric of puritanical outrage to castigate their opponents.**
>
> **For public consumption, the spokesmen of the militant anti-abortion movement called feminists "child-killers" and berated them for triggering "breakneck abortion rates." But more revealing was what they said under their breath: their whispered "whores" and "dykes" were perhaps their more telling epithets. Sexual independence, not murder, may have been the feminists' greater crime....The real change was women's new ability to regulate their fertility without danger or fear—a new freedom that in turn had contributed to dramatic changes not in the abortion rate[19] but in female sexual behavior and attitudes. Having secured first the mass availability of contraceptive devices and then the option of medically sound abortions, women were at last at liberty to have sex like men, on their own terms.[20]**

The men she refers to who "have sex on their own terms" are George Gilder's "naked nomads," the sort of men who made the West wild and the ghettos violent. But women who "have sex on their own terms" are more dangerous than these men and must be consigned to the margins of society, as they formerly were. The derelictions of these women are (in Ms. Faludi's view) *offset* by their changes in "sexual behavior and attitudes," which permit them to live "on their own terms" apart from families, thus undermining the male kinship system and ghettoizing society. She wishes her readers to suppose that a woman's sexual loyalty, rather than being her principal contribution to her marriage, is of no greater importance than a man's sexual loyalty.

The point is crucial. A woman's primary contribution to the marriage is her sexual loyalty, without which there is no family.

---

[19]Yes, of course in the abortion rate, as is acknowledged two lines below. This quote is further discussed on page 229.
[20]*Backlash*, p. 403.

Women's sexual disloyalty creates matriarchy and ghettos. The patriarchal system is made possible by the woman's acceptance of the obligation of chastity which enables her husband to have a family. The feminist demand for "sexual equality," for the right "to have sex like men, on their own terms," destroys women's bargaining power, destroys what entitles her to be supported by her husband. Women are dependent creatures who need husbands and women's demand for economic independence from husbands is wrecking the whole patriarchal system and returning society to matriarchy. Ms. Faludi is as aware of this as anyone. She says:

> **The Roper Organization's survey analysts find that men's opposition to equality is "a major cause of resentment and stress" and "a major irritant for most women today." It is justice for their gender, not wedding rings and bassinets, that women believe to be in desperate short supply.[21]**

The women whom Ms. Faludi celebrates who want sex "on their own terms" are entitled to no bargaining power at all, for they will use it, as she acknowledges, to undermine patriarchy and restore matriarchy. "*Women* were at last at liberty" she says, oblivious to the distinction between chaste and unchaste women, women willing to give a man a family and women who marry in contemplation of divorce and subsidization by an ex-husband, women who accept patriarchy and women who want to restore matriarchy. "As a result," she continues,

> **in the half century after birth control was legalized, women doubled their rates of premarital sexual activity, nearly converging with men's by the end of the '70s....By 1980, a landmark sex survey of 106,000 women conducted for *Cosmopolitan* found that 41 percent of women had extramarital affairs, up from 8 percent in 1948.**

It is women's loyalty to the male kinship system and to their families which entitles them to the benefits bestowed by patriarchy on good women. The female sexual disloyalty which Ms. Faludi advocates is incomparably more threatening and damaging to civilized society than men's philandering. It makes the man's role in reproduction meaningless and reduces the woman's role in reproduction to what it is in the matriarchal ghetto. It forfeits the woman's right to subsidization by the man within marriage. It forfeits her right to subsidization following marriage. It forfeits her claim to custody of the children.

---

[21]*Backlash*, p. xvi.

Ms. Faludi takes over feminist Lenore Weitzman's argument about the wife's right to an equal share of the "assets of the marriage," complaining that "judges were willfully misinterpreting the statutes to mean that women should get not one-half but *one-third* of all assets":[22]

The concept of "equality" and the sex-neutral language of the law, Lenore Weitzman writes,

have been] used by some lawyers and judges as a mandate for "equal treatment" with a vengeance, a vengeance that can only be explained as a backlash reaction to women's demands for equality in the larger society.[23]

As Ms. Weitzman says elsewhere, "Our major form of wealth comes from investment in ourselves—our 'human capital'—and in our careers. This is true in marriage too. Husbands and wives typically invest in careers—most particularly in the husband's education and career—and the products of such investments are often a *family's* major asset. But despite the ideology of *marriage* as a partnership in which both partners share equally in the fruits of their joint enterprise, the reality of divorce is quite different. When it comes to dividing family assets, the courts often ignore the husband's 'career assets'—a term I coined for the array of tangible and intangible assets acquired as part of a spouse's career."[24]

These feminists suppose that going through a marriage ceremony not only entitles the wife to the husband's children, his home, his furniture and appliances, his future earnings, but also his tangible and intangible career assets *because she has custody of his children and makes her demands in their name.* And the law agrees—agrees that marriage is without significance for its original purpose, the creation of a patriarchal family. Its purpose is now said to be rather that of enslaving the husband and restoring matriarchy.

Ms. Weitzman's plea is that *divorce* should benefit the woman equally with marriage. This makes divorce attractive for women. The wife could reason, "I don't need a husband since I can exchange him for an ex-husband who can be compelled to subsidize me. My contribution of going through a marriage ceremony is equivalent to his contribution of getting an education and acquiring status in his field of work." Ms. Weitzman is really pleading that the wife's non-assets ought to be

---

[22]P. 25.
[23]P. 25.
[24]*Ms.*, February, 1986.

considered as assets as long as she can cling to "her" children and make her demands in their name. The wife needs to know that her greatest asset is having a husband; Ms. Weitzman's program for shafting ex-husbands by punitive divorce awards will deprive a very large number of women of husbands by frightening men away from marriage in the first place.

Ms. Weitzman wants us to suppose the ex-husband's previous earning ability was made possible by his ex-wife's previous services to him. But obviously the withdrawal of these services must cripple him just as the providing of them formerly benefited him—especially if their withdrawal is accompanied by the deprivation of his children, the chief "assets of the marriage" from his point of view. What she calls assets of the marriage are really assets of the husband, the chief inducement he had to offer his wife to marry him.

The liabilities of the marriage need to be discussed along with its assets. Ms. Faludi and Ms. Weitzman claim for the ex-wife the privilege of de-motivating her ex-husband by her claim to share his "assets" apart from marriage, thus making his chief asset, his motivation, into a liability, while at the same time perpetuating her dependence on him— foregoing the feminist goal of standing on her own feet "without sexual favor or excuse," as Ms. Friedan says.[25]

Ex-wives and their lawyers are privileged to victimize the *employers* of ex-husbands as well as the ex-husbands themselves. The *Los Angeles Times* of 27 August, 1985 reports a $24,000 out-of-court settlement from an employer who fired an ex-husband whose salary he was ordered to garnish:

> **Allred [a feminist attorney] said a court ruling, made while the case was pending, established that ex-spouses and children have the right to sue companies for firing their breadwinner: This "will serve as a warning to employers that the wage assessment law was passed for the protection of children."**

Such judgments will make ex-husbands less desirable as employees. Being a breadwinner formerly made a man more desirable because he was more highly motivated. Fathers like this one will find the mother's claim to the "assets of their marriage" has made him less

---

[25]*The Feminine Mystique*, p. 346.

employable. Children will be victimized. His ex-wife's asset (being able to sue his employer) is *his* liability, a "negative asset" which, in the interests of justice, should be shared by the wife.

The wife's major asset, by which she places the husband under obligation to her, is her sexual loyalty, which guarantees him a family and legitimate children. Divorce, if the wife gets custody of the children, deprives him of this guarantee and therefore deprives the ex-wife of her claims on him by depriving him retroactively of the *imagined* security he thought he had prior to the divorce. It demonstrates that he never really had this security (which he had paid for, however). It's like an insurance policy issued by an unsound company which never would have paid the benefits it promised, but which accepted premiums month after month in return for a promise. A wife enters into a marriage contract which promises the husband a lifetime loyalty and inalienable offspring. Then, following the breaking of the contract the husband loses the most important assets, the children, and is faced with the demand for the surrender of his earnings on the ground that they are needed by the wife who has taken his children from him.

The husband's major contribution to the marriage is irrevocable. It cannot be removed retroactively: he has supported his wife, paid her bills, given her a home, raised her standard of living by 73 percent.[26] But the wife's major contribution to the marriage, the gift of a family, *is* removed retroactively in over half of marriages and threatened with removal in all: She never really gave him the family which was the quid pro quo for his supporting her. The husband discovers in the divorce court that what motivated him to get married and to labor during the years of the marriage had no permanent existence—it was not a gift but only a loan backed by a woman's promise—and unbacked by the law. He discovers that the law which must enforce contracts interprets the most basic contract as not binding on his wife, only on him, and it therefore deems it just to deprive him of his most precious possession, his children, probably also of his home and his future income.

A society which hopes to remain civilized must motivate its men to become providers for families; otherwise it will become a matriarchy. The divorce rate combined with mother custody instructs men that they cannot depend on marriage. In the words of David Hartman, since "you

---

[26]This is Dr. Lenore Weitzman's celebrated statistic, frequently quoted in feminist literature. See Chapter 8 of my *Garbage Generation* for a discussion of it.

get less of what you tax and more of what you subsidize, the percentage of individuals living in traditional families is in a continuing and alarming decline, while government subsidized 'alternate lifestyles' proliferate....[M]arriage has severely declined, falling from three out of four households in 1960 to slightly above half of all households in 1994."[27]

Feminists rejoice in women's freedom to divorce while remaining subsidized—their freedom to superimpose the lower matriarchal tier of society on the higher patriarchal tier and claim subsidization from it, to claim sanctity for the Motherhood Card and deny sanctity to men's Money Card.

---

[27]*The Family in America*, July, 1997.

A Canadian publication, *Everyman: A Men's Journal,*[28] gives the following information on the lower tier: "What Do We Know About Children from Single Mother Families?"

Rates of [children's] problems from single-mother vs. two parent families (%).

Problem	Single-mother	Two-parent	Relative Odds
Hyperactivity	15.6	9.6	1.74
Conduct disorder	17.2	8.1	2.36
Emotional disorder	15.0	7.5	2.18
Behavioral problems	31.7	18.7	2.02
Repeated grade	11.2	4.7	2.56
Current school Problems	5.8	2.7	2.22
Social impairment	6.1	2.5	2.53
Social problems	40.6	23.6	2.21

This says that children of single mothers are 2.21 (221%) times as likely to have one or more social problems than those from two parent families, twice as likely to have emotional disorders previously mentioned.

Feminists have a tediously repeated rationale for ignoring such statistics. It is thus stated by Lynette Triere:

> **Parents who stay with each other "because of the children," then subject them to the misery of their lives together, are doing a favor to no one. By now, it is almost a cliche to observe that divorce is better for children than continuing in a bad marriage.**[29]

Divorce is not better for children; it is better for Mom because it is accompanied by mother custody, support payments, and the massive transfer to her of "the assets of the marriage." Psychologists Wallerstein and Blakeslee know it is not better for children. So does Dr. Rex Forehand, of the University of Georgia:

---

[28]Issue 27, September/October, 1997.
[29]Triere, p. 285.

[C]hildren in high-conflict divorced families did the worst, considerably worse than children who remained in homes where their mother and father fought constantly.[30]

The anti-male bias of the courts is the principal reason why most divorces are initiated by wives, why they say "The day of the kept wife is over," why they say, "For parents to stay in an unhappy relationship is to teach the children that they have no options in life," why they say "I have to do this for myself,"[31] why they say a woman ought to "*put yourself first.*"[32]

The implied corollary—in feminist thinking—is that fathers must be decent chaps and hand everything over to Mom "for the sake of the kids," though exiled mothers are almost never expected to do this. (A minuscule token number of mothers are ordered to pay minuscule support money to custodial fathers. The sums are small and the delinquency rate nearly double that of "deadbeat dads." Such "deadbeat moms" are following; Ms. Triere's advice to "put yourself first.") This explains why most divorce actions are initiated by wives and helps to explain why increasing millions of men have lost interest in marriage and why so many women ask "Where are the men?"

Part of the father's role is to socialize his sons to become fathers themselves when they grow up. Will Marcia Clark's sons, whom Marcia (of O. J. Simpson fame) deprived of their father; will lesbian feminist Adrienne Rich's sons, whom Adrienne deprived of their father; will tens of millions of other father-deprived sons, learn how to be fathers? Or will they think of a father the way feminists encourage them to think, as a leftover from the discarded patriarchal system? Will these sons wish to live the kind of life their father lived and have a temporary family followed by exile and not-so-temporary support payments? Feminist Lynette Triere gives the feminist answer for Moms:

There is no reason that a woman should be bound for life to a mistaken choice she made at age eighteen, twenty-four, thirty-three or forty-one. It is an unreasonable demand....[T]he issue of freedom is important for women. There is joy in freedom....Perhaps a woman should take seriously the philosophic truism that she is endowed with certain inalienable rights, that among these

---

[30]Quoted by Maggie Gallagher, *Enemies of Eros*, p. 200.
[31]Triere, p. 272.
[32]Triere, p. 75; emphasis in original.

are life, liberty, and the pursuit of happiness. For many *women*, the act of leaving is truly a declaration of independence.[33]

The woman may correct a mistaken choice. Lucky she. The man may not. His choice to be a provider was irrevocable. Besides which he enjoys the "freedom" of surrendering his children and his property. Without this, the woman will be denied her independence, her "joy in freedom," her right to stand on her own feet.

If the male has no Money Card, or if the female doesn't think his money is worth the trouble of her submitting to sexual regulation, or if she can get his money, or enough of it, without having to submit to sexual regulation, or if she can get enough of the taxpayer's money to keep her afloat and to subsidize her in sexual promiscuity, the male can forget about having a family. The result will be the female kinship system.

A female who desires sexual independence may think, as a friend of feminist Natalie Gittelson thinks:

Lily, my engaging hostess, set the psychological tone of the day. On the verge of legal separation from her husband...Lily said dryly, "Right now, I'm free as a bird. A little adultery here, a little adultery there." She laughed. "What's the dif? I'm not emotionally involved."[34]

Or as feminist Linda Hirschman thinks:

They force women into marriage with social pressures such as the withdrawal of welfare.[35]

Welfare, in other words, is preferable to marriage. The Id is talking, demanding freedom from responsibility and regulation. Never mind the cost, especially the cost to her husband and her children and the taxpayer. Economics is talking. The more economically independent the woman is the more divorce-prone she is: if she has economic independence she doesn't need a man and they both know it. (Only "independence" bears considerable resemblance to *dependence*.) Then Brifffault's Law swings into action. She doesn't want to be under

---

[33]Lynette Triere, *Learning to Leave: A Woman's Guide* (New York: Warner Books, 1982), pp. 20f.; emphasis added.
[34]Natalie Gittelson, *The Erotic Life of the American Wife* (New York: Delacorte Press, 1972), p. 114.
[35]*Los Angeles Times*, 25 September, 1996.

obligation to him, she wants to be economically and therefore sexually independent—or only indirectly dependent, without reciprocal responsibilities and loyalties. This is why she says "I don't want to live the kind of life my mother led," why she says, "A free disposition over one's own person is an original right in a matriarchal society,"[36] why she speaks of "the right of a woman to control her own body and reproductive processes as her inalienable, human, civil right, not to be denied or abridged by the state or any man,"[37] why she rejects the *Great Evil*, the "tyranny of sexual monopoly,"[38] the "association of sex with male domination and control" which makes the two-parent family possible. Her real complaint is against accepting sexual law-and-order. Much better that her ex-husband should get out and give her support money. The judge understands.

This is what feminism is all about: Women's reproductive independence—matriarchy—means getting rid of the two-parent family ("the way my mother lived"), reducing fatherhood to meaninglessness by a sixty percent divorce rate and a thirty percent illegitimacy rate. Free at last.

Men have not yet woken up to what this means to them and to their children—a change in the kinship system from father-right to mother-right, a return to Stone Age arrangements. Ms. Friedan thought that "Society asks so little of women." Why should the triflingness of women's services be rewarded not by the husband who receives the trifles, but by the ex-husband who is deprived of them?[39] Ms. Hewlett quotes a report by a British Law Commission:

Society has no special interest in permanently maintaining the legal shell of a marriage that has failed, and the role of the law in such cases is to manage the dissolution process with the minimum human cost.[40]

The minimum cost to Mom. The cost to Mom is minimized by increasing the cost to Dad. This is held to be justified by Mom's privilege of making Mutilated Beggars out of the kids and appealing to the judge's

---

[36]Helen Diner, *Mothers and Amazons* (New York: Anchor Books, 1973), p. 31.
[37]Betty Friedan, *It Changed My Life*, p. 122.
[38]Miles, *The Women's History of the World*, p. 48.
[39]Ms. Friedan quotes one of them, *Feminine Mystique*, page 63: "By 8:30 A.M., when my youngest goes to school, my whole house is clean and neat and I am dressed for the day. I am free to play bridge, attend club meetings, or stay home and read, listen to Beethoven, and just plain loaf." She is also able to contemplate the sort of mischief suggested by Dalma Heyn or Barbara Seaman or a hundred other encouragers of female promiscuity.
[40]Hewlett, p. 136.

magnanimity on their behalf. It is presumed that this has no cost for society. One major cost is the destruction of male motivation needed to support families. The British Law Commissioners deem the "real marriage" to be the emotional bonds uniting the man and the woman and deem the marriage contract itself to be a mere piece of paper, a "legal shell." This illustrates the difference between marriage in the matriarchal and patriarchal systems. In the former, it is, as Marilyn French says "casual, informal," as in the Stone Age. The later patriarchal age made fatherhood non-casual and non-informal, made fatherhood equally important with motherhood and equally responsible. Today's legal system is working full bore to restore the Stone Age system, to re-marginalize husbands in conformity with the feminist program, even to let women have children "without having a man around." Making the marriage contract a legal shell turns society over to matriarchy, since, as Robertson Smith says, "a want of fixity in the marriage tie will favour a rule of female kinship."[41]

Civilized society must be "a man's world," since the woman's world is the ghetto; but the law now works to destroy the man's world by destroying the father's motivation and role, telling the mother she is entitled to chuck the marriage if she feels like it and the law will minimize the damage to *her*, since she has custody of the children.[42]

In the early years of the feminist movement it was a commonplace of feminist propaganda that the destruction of the patriarchal Sexual Constitution and the abandoning of the sex role socialization upon which it is based would liberate not only women but men by getting rid of the stereotype that a woman was dependent on a man. Feminism, it was asserted, would make a woman stop "preying upon her husband"[43]—the husband driven into a seven-year earlier grave by her parasitism. "Doing it for *ourselves*," said Ms. Friedan, "is the essence of the women's movement: it keeps us honest, keeps us real, keeps us concrete."[44] They would no longer try to earn their way in the world by being doll-wives. They would stand on their own feet. Only, of course, they didn't mean it.

---

[41]W. Robertson Smith, *Kinship and Marriage in Early Arabia* (London: A. and C. Black, 1903), p. 78.
[42]For example: *Los Angeles Daily News*, 18 December, 1996: "The case at hand involved a woman who allegedly hid her two children from her ex-husband for more than seven years. She then sued for overdue child support while their children still were minors.
   "Regardless of the wife's conduct, the ex-husband must pay what he owes, because child support is for the benefit of the child, not the parent, the [California State Supreme] court said in its unanimous decision Monday."
[43]*The Feminine Mystique*, p. 308.
[44]*It Changed My Life*, p. xviii.

They still expect the alimony and child support that go with mother custody—how else could they stand on their own feet?

III) THE WAR AGAINST PATRIARCHY

The most fundamental fact about a society is its kinship system—whether the reproductive unit is headed by the male or the female. Americans are fortunate in being able to compare the two systems. In every large American city there is an area where the female kinship system predominates—the ghettos, where most households are headed by women. These are the high crime, high delinquency, high illegitimacy, high poverty areas, the areas where the "First Law of Matriarchy" prevails: "Women control our own bodies"[1]—where "adultery is a human right," where "you have a right to your own morality," to take off your mask of the Perfect Wife, of the Angel in the House, the area where Mom is enormously in charge of her life and can say "I don't care. I have to do something about my own life."[2]

Women don't like to live in these areas, but they prefer the lifestyle which creates them, where they have "sexual options," and independence from men. Ehrenreich, Hess and Jacobshave been quoted on the welfare system which keeps these areas afloat: "[O]ne reason for the stigmatization of welfare, and hostility to it, is undoubtedly that *it offers women independence from individual men* and hence a certain measure of potential sexual freedom." This creates "male fears of women's sexual independence."[3]

Feminist Evelyn Reed, looking nostalgically back to the Stone Age, complains how the patriarchal system which created civilization also imposed sexual regulation on women:

Dispossessed from their former place in society at large, they were robbed not only of their economic independence but also of their former sexual freedom.[4]

They lost some of their *poverty* ("economic independence") by acquiring male providers, who raised their standard of living, but who

---

[1] Monica Sjöö and Barbara Mor, *The Great Cosmic Mother: Rediscovering the Religion of the Earth* (San Francisco: Harper and Row, 1987), p. 200.
[2] *It Changed My Life*, p. 324.
[3] Barbara Ehrenreich, Elizabeth Hess and Gloria Jacobs, *Re-Making Love: The Feminization of Sex* (Garden City, N. Y., 1986), p. 197; emphasis added.
[4] Evelyn Reed, *Woman's Evolution: From Matriarchal Clan to Patriarchal Family* (New York: Pathfinder Press, 1975), p. 24.

insisted in exchange on their sexual loyalty, what Engels called "the world-historic defeat of the female sex."[5] "Many women," says feminist Alix Pirani, "want to be liberated from stifling male domination, want greater sexual freedom and self-determination, but have yet to realize fully what is happening when they grant that to themselves, what the meaning of that freedom is."[6] They have to realize that acceptance of sexual law-and-order is the price they must pay for the economic and status advantages conferred by patriarchy. Linda Hirschman has been quoted: "They force women into marriage with social pressures such as the withdrawal of welfare"[7]—implying that society should subsidize alternatives to marriage so that women can afford to be promiscuous.

This sexual de-regulation is what Betty Friedan means when she speaks of "break[ing] through sex discrimination and [creating] the new social institutions that are needed to free women from their chains." Especially from the chains of marriage when it is stable, when it permits men to have families. This really does require the "chaining" of women— requires them to keep their marriage vows as it requires men to keep theirs. Women who can't endure the chains can't be kept from leaving, but they can be kept from taking their children with them. Feminists would like us to think that motherhood is sacred but wifehood is "sex discrimination," which hangs chains on them. The chains need to be replaced by "new social institutions"—female promiscuity and its corollary, state subsidization. "Adultery is a human right," we are now told,[8] a claim which when made in behalf of women eliminates their major contribution to marriage, destroys the legitimacy of children, undermines the security of property and the motivation of men's labor. Briffault's Law—that women will not associate with men—will therefore feel free to be promiscuous—in the absence of a male-supplied benefit— is why society must guarantee the stability of the father's role.

A different view of women's sexual obligation was formerly stated in the *Book of Common Prayer*. The bride was asked to *give* her troth, while the groom was merely asked to *pledge* his. Feminist Bishop Spong, makes it a grievance against the patriarchalism of his Episcopal Church

---

[5]Friedrich Engels, *Origin of the Family, Private Property and the State.*
[6]Alix Pirani, *The Absent Father: Crisis and Creativity*, p. 37
[7]Linda Hirschman, "Against the Possibility of Equality," *Los Angeles Times*, 25 September, 1996.
[8]By a speaker at the Second International Conference on Health and Human Rights at Harvard University in October, 1996. Reporter Jim Sedlak "saw most heads nodding in agreement." (*Human Life International Reports*, Dec., 1996)

that this distinction continued to be made well into the 1970s.[9] The woman's greater gift made the family possible—her acceptance of greater sexual responsibility, that which entitled her to be provided for. The husband cannot claim a right to be supported by his wife on the ground that he pledges his troth not to procreate offspring with other women. In marriage she gives the greater gift—but in divorce she retracts her greater gift. If she gains custody of the children, the usual case, she not only retracts her troth, she retracts *the whole shtick*. She reveals that in promising to give her husband a family she was waving a fraudulent contract at him. Her offer of a family would have had value only in a patriarchal society where the law supports the male kinship system and guarantees the father he cannot be deprived of his children. So the wife didn't *give* her troth after all, only pretended to. But the husband is not privileged to withdraw his "pledged" troth; his pledge has to be worth more than his wife's gift; he must keep giving support money—otherwise the judge would not place the children in the mother's custody—would not, in other words, support the female kinship system.

MEANINGLESS SEX

Ehrenreich, Hess and Jacobs tell us that "Early writers on sex, Barbara Seaman and Shere Hite among others,"

insisted, at least implicitly, that sex should have no ultimate meaning other than pleasure, and no great mystery except how to achieve it. They realized that for women to insist on pleasure was to assert power, and hence to give an altogether new meaning to sex—as an affirmation of female will and an assertion of female power.

For *men* to insist on responsible sexual behavior is to assert that sex does have a meaning beyond pleasure, that its regulation is needed to preserve the patriarchal two-parent family and ordered society. This is to recognize that those women who seek to affirm female will and female power are enemies of patriarchal society.

The old meaning, which in one form or another was always submission to male power, could be inverted.

---

[9]John Shelby Spong, *Living in Sin?* (San Francisco: Harper and Brothers, 1988), p. 56.

These are no small achievements—the re-making and the reinterpreting of sex....The more decisively sex can be uncoupled from reproduction, through abortion and contraception, the more chance women have to approach it lightheartedly and as equal claimants of pleasure.[10]

They believe women can and should behave less responsibly—and thereby marginalize men. Bishop Spong feels the same way. "Twentieth century innovations in birth control—what Madonna Kolbenschlag calls 'the great emancipator' of women—doomed the old sexual economy":

With the resulting equalization of the sexes, what was sauce for the gander became sauce for the goose. All of those outlets that male-dominated society had set up to protect and control the female, while accommodating the male's desire for additional sexual outlets, were called into question....The woman, having been imprisoned for centuries inside a male-dominated system, discovered sexual freedom and socio-political equality simultaneously.[11]

Equality, the feminist shibboleth. How unfair that women are paid less than men. How unfair that women are held to a higher sexual standard than men. Only when these two disadvantages are removed will feminists cease their clamors. This will be when men have no role, when patriarchy is abolished, when women are married to the state. "The changes necessary to bring about equality," says Ms. Friedan,

were, and still are, very revolutionary indeed. They involve a sex-role revolution for men and women which will restructure all our institutions: child rearing, education, marriage, the family, medicine, work, politics, and economy, religion, psychological theory, human sexuality, morality, and the very evolution of the race.[12]

They involve, in other words, a return to matriarchy, a ghettoizing of society, the adoption of feminist Carolyn Shaw Bell's program for "a special tax to pay for the total welfare benefits of families headed by women, and sufficient to increase these benefits so as to wipe out the income differential between poor children with only a mother and well-off children with two parents. The tax would be leveled on all men."[13] In other words patriarchy ought to finance its own destruction by paying

---

[10]*Re-Making Love*, pp. 195f.

[11]*Living in Sin?*, p. 51

[12]*New York Times Magazine*, 4 March, 1973.

[13]Carolyn Shaw Bell, "Alternatives for Social Change: The Future Status of Women," in *Women in the Professions* (Toronto: D. C. Heath, 1975), p. 133.

women to breed fatherless families—the ghetto pattern, but with higher payments.

Bishop Spong can hardly contain his glee when he contemplates the destruction of the patriarchy:

> **The sexual revolution was on. The forces of change gathered, the pace accelerated, the tide became inexorable. Women's suffrage; increased educational opportunities for women; coeducational colleges that refused to oversee private behavior;...the social mobility, assisted by ever-improving transportation systems, which increased anonymity; the entry of women into the work force; the opening of executive and professional ranks to women—all these combined with effective birth control to change the shape of history. These were the forces that dismantled the patriarchal control system, and the reasons why the moral norms of a bygone era are not holding.**[14]

These developments are reasons why the male kinship system requires to be reinforced by mandatory father custody. Bishop Spong, like all feminists, wants to get rid of this "imprisoning of women inside a male-dominated system." But this "imprisoning" is what creates the two-parent family, fatherhood, the male role and patriarchal civilization. *Unless women accept this "imprisoning" they have no claim on men, and men must not allow them to have custody of their children.* "By godly decree," Spong says,

> **the role of woman in the past was clear. She was to be the keeper of the hearth, the rearer of children, obedient and loyal to her husband. If she did not marry she was viewed as a failure, called pejoratively "an old maid" and generally pitied. Before marriage, at least in the dominant strand of the social order, she was expected to be chaste. Elaborate control or chaperone systems were developed to guarantee that chastity.**[15]

To guarantee their chastity—and therefore their bargaining power and therefore their place in "the dominant strand of the social order," where they want to be and where their families want them to be, and where other less chaste and less fortunate women envy them for being. This strand of the social order became dominant because it regulated sexuality, thus assuring that males belonging to this strand had families. The woman's loyalty to her husband is the sine qua non for the husband's meaningful participation in reproduction, and for his

---

[14]*Living in Sin?*, p.51.
[15]P. 43.

transmission of his achievements and his estate to his children. Without his status as family head he is in danger of becoming a drifter and a beachcomber and disrupter of society. As a family head he has a motive to become a stable and productive member of society and to raise his wife's and children's standard of living by 73 percent. As a family head he will be able to bequeath his entire estate to his children rather than dissipating it in supporting an ex-wife who will clamor for an ever greater share of his assets—called (after there is no marriage) "the assets of the marriage."

The legal system views the wife's sexual loyalty to her husband ambivalently: (1) it is of such trifling importance that its withdrawal deprives the husband of nothing; (2) it is of such portentous importance that even its *former presumed (not actual)* existence creates a permanent obligation upon the ex-husband to continue subsidizing the ex-wife so she can afford to deprive him of his children, home, et cetera, and live (if she chooses) in matriarchal promiscuity.

Bishop Spong fails to see that women's claim to this bargaining power depends on her chastity and on patriarchal society's enforcing of this chastity, without which her man is cut off from meaningful fatherhood. Woman's virtual free ride ("Society asks so little of women") is given her not in return for her waxing the floors and making peanut butter sandwiches for the Cub Scouts (trifles upon which Ms. Friedan appropriately poured ridicule) but for her sexual loyalty to her husband (upon which Bishop Spong *inappropriately* pours *his* ridicule) and that when she withdraws her loyalty by divorce or sexual promiscuity she should forfeit not only her free ride but the custody of the children whose father has hitherto paid her bills in the mistaken belief that her loyalty was trustworthy and that she was actually giving him the family she is now taking away. Divorce and automatic mother custody destroys the father's family; it ought to destroy the mother's bargaining power. Automatic father custody will restore the patriarchal family and make women realize that their bargaining power within the patriarchal system depends mostly on their sexual loyalty.

Without father custody the woman is not really *giving* her husband anything. If she can revoke her apparent gift, as she now does in sixty percent of marriages, the gift's value is reduced to zilch. Today's society is betraying patriarchy by trying to convince women that they don't need

41

bargaining power because they can rely instead on the state's power to coerce their ex-husbands ("We will find you. We will make you pay.")

For men to share in the reproductive function of women's bodies they must have some benefit to offer women, as indicated by Briffault's Law. It is one purpose of the institution of marriage to secure this benefit for the woman. Feminists think that merely taking marriage vows secures this benefit and that prolonging the marriage serves no additional useful purpose, such as providing children with fathers or such as providing fathers with motivation.

GHETTOS AND PROMISCUITY

The emancipation of women is the reason why the ghettos live in squalor and violence. As George Gilder says:

> **The key problem of the underclass—the crucible of crime, the source of violence, the root of poverty—is the utter failure of socialization of young men through marriage.**[16]

Bishop Spong thinks otherwise: "The patriarchal assumption that everyone needs to be married," he says, "has become inoperative, and the single population has risen dramatically in our time."[17] So has the prison population, consisting largely of single males who are the offspring of single females. So has the number of "children who grow up in divorced families [and] are not climbing the economic ladder as high as their parents did." The larger society is beginning to follow the matriarchal ghetto pattern where, as Jared Taylor says, "Young blacks are half as likely to be working as young whites."[18]

The spread of this pathology to the larger society is aided by males who make themselves superfluous by subsidizing the destruction of their families through alimony and child support payments to ex-wives, thus liberating them from sexual regulation by accepting slavery for themselves. The liberated women are not grateful. Neither are the children. William Tucker cites a recent experience of David Blankenhorn talking to "an ordinary school in Indiana where 30 percent of the graduating class was pregnant with illegitimate children":

---

[16]*Wall Street Journal*, 30 October, 1995.
[17]*Living in Sin?*, p. 42.
[18]Jared Taylor, *Paved With Good Intentions*, p. 11.

> When he began counseling an auditorium full of students about the virtues of intact families he met a wall of animosity. Boys complained their fathers had never been around to help them. Girls solemnly proclaimed themselves capable of raising babies without men. Each of these declarations was met by thunderous applause from the assembled teenagers.
>
> If nothing else, Blankenhorn's experience shows how, once the culture of illegitimacy gains a foothold, it is difficult to control.[19]

Mothers' imagining themselves capable of raising babies without men is why fathers are never around to help. The boys who complained of their fathers' absence are at least aware that they have fathers, though they are unaware that their absence is probably owing to their mothers' desire to be sexually unregulated like their female classmates.

Most women chafe against and resist the confinements of marriage and sexual law-and-order. "Suddenly," says Gloria Steinem,

> there are no more excuses for all the prejudices, injustices and rigid social stereotyping that women face every day in every part of our lives. Those wrongs traditionally have been defended because someone thinks they're "good" for the economy, or the family, or the nation's social fabric. But nobody can claim that they're good for the women who are damaged and demeaned by them.
>
> What's good for women must be defined by women themselves... particularly the fundamental right of reproductive freedom.[20]

She writes as though reproduction is something affecting only women, not men, not children. Women do not yearn to impose sexual law-and-order on men; many of them yearn to get rid of it and claim their "fundamental right" to be promiscuous. As Ehrenreich, Hess and Jacobs say on page 128, women will tolerate ghetto poverty in preference to sexual regulation. Listen to feminist Madeline Lee complain about "trying to overcome in a single generation the accumulated weight of ages of repression, double standards, and antisex, antiwoman thinking":

> I'm sure there are women who have truly integrated their feminist understanding with their unruly psyches and successfully sloughed off the remnants of repressed childhoods [read: sloughed off patriarchal socialization]

---

[19]William Tucker, "The Moral of the Story," *The American Spectator*, October, 1996, p. 22.
[20]Letter circulated by the Ms. Foundation for Women, October, 1988.

but the women I spoke with were not among them. Nevertheless, what rang clear and consistent through all their individual stories was the determination that they were not going to be responsible for transmitting repression and confusion [read: transmitting patriarchal socialization]. Even if it's difficult, they feel they should be open about their own bodies, tolerant of sexual diversity, encouraging of their daughters' explorations.... *You have a right to your own morality.*[21]

When she speaks of mothers' "eagerness to free our daughters from old constraints and limitations," she is talking about getting rid of the patriarchal system and stable marriage. Gilder imagines women try to impose these on men. He says:

For in general, civilization evolved through the subordination of male sexual patterns—the short-term cycles of tension and release—to the long-term female patterns.[22]

Women have had to use all their ingenuity, all their powers of sexual attraction and restraint to induce men to become providers. Society has had to invest marriage with all the ceremonial sanctity of religion and law. This did not happen as a way to promote intimacy and companionship. It happened to ensure civilized society.[23]

"The problem," says Gilder, "resides in the nexus of men and marriage. Yet nearly all the attention, subsidies, training opportunities and therapies of the welfare state focus on helping women function without marriage. The welfare state attacks the problem of the absence of husbands by rendering husbands entirely superfluous."

In order to relieve the pain of the poor, says Gilder,

our society must come to recognize that their problem is not lack of jobs or lack of money but moral anarchy originating with the establishment and most sorely victimizing blacks.[24]

OK, but the moral anarchy does not originate with the establishment; it originates with liberal women, motivated by a desire to get rid of patriarchal control and get back to the "natural" kinship system in which the reproductive unit is headed by the female. The establishment is merely their willing handmaiden. The greatest share of

---

[21]*Ms.* May, 1982; emphasis in original.
[22]George Gilder, *Sexual Suicide* (New York: Quadrangle/N.Y.Times Book Co, 1973), p. 86.
[23]P. 78.
[24]*Wall Street Journal*, 30 Oct 95.

the establishment's culpability belongs not to the welfare system but to the legal system, whose divorce courts routinely replace father-headed families with mother-headed ones. Most of these female headed households result not from promiscuous girls breeding illegitimate children but from the demands of wives who feel, with Ms. Friedan, "I don't care, I have to do something about my own life":[25]

> **Ordinary women—wearing masks so they wouldn't lose custody of their children, or be faulted for speaking out in divorce cases still in the courts— spoke their full bitterness at the reality of the divorce crisis.[26]**

Ms. Friedan had become a best selling author and had assured custody of her children, so she could afford to let it all hang out. Ordinary women were obligated to keep up the pretense expected by Gilder and the judges—that they still believe in "the family"—the pretense of Mrs. Thatcher and Dr. Blankenhorn that it was usually the husband who "abandoned" the family.

Ms. Friedan scorns the "masks" women wear to perpetuate the feminine mystique,

> **the benign-destructive masks of pseudo- and real power that women acquired in the modern American family, hiding their socioeconomic dependency...role-playing and the torturous stifling masks imposed by that excessive dependence...see through those old masks and feel the burden, and want the out that equality could give you before it is too late...what a relief to take off my surgical mask!...her economic dependence, her denigration of herself...her own real feelings behind that mask of superficial sweet, steely rightness....They took it out on themselves and covertly on husbands and children....Locked in those iron masks, we finally choke with impotent rage...[27]**

One senses the powerful feeling behind this—Ms. Rich's "enormous potential counterforce." This is why we have a sixty percent divorce rate. The swallowing of this rage is the burden which patriarchy imposes on women for the benefit of children and men and civilization. There is no other way in which the male can be intruded into reproduction, no other way of bringing about the switch from the female headed matriline of dogs, cats and cattle to the patriarchal family. The human male who cannot offer his female a benefit in exchange for her acceptance of sexual

---

[25] *It Changed My Life*, p. 324.
[26] P. 317; emphasis in the original.
[27] *The Second Stage*, pp. 96, 313, 99, 56f; *It Changed My Life*, p. 232.

regulation must either give up hope of having a family or must impose "Islamic discipline" on her. If, as is the case in America and Western societies, the legal system refuses to recognize that it is part of the patriarchal system and supposes instead that it ought to go along with the feminist program because it is more "natural," there will be matriarchy and its pathology. Briffault's Law will operate to destroy families if females think the benefit offered by males is insufficient, or if females suppose they can make themselves economically independent of males, or suppose that the legal system will deprive the male of the benefit and award it to the female without his consent—by giving her custody of the children. The evidence offered for this in the Annex of this book is but a small portion of what could be given.

Ms. Friedan rattles on:

The bitterness, the rage underneath the ruffles, which we used to take out on ourselves and our kids and finally on the men in bed, is out in the open now, scaring us in its scorching intensity, goading men to exasperation and despair. And now the men are letting it hang out too: how they really feel about female parasites, the dead weights, alimony, the sexual nothingness of the manipulated breadwinner.

Isn't that precious? She wants her readers to suppose that ex-husbands who are coerced into sending support money to Mom are *beneficiaries* of the feminist revolution, since they are no longer manipulated breadwinners. She believes that.

Ms. Friedan's "masks" are the roles which society expects men and women to adopt, which make civilized living possible. A judge is expected to behave like a judge, a soldier is expected to behave like a soldier, a wife and mother is expected to behave like a wife and mother. Acceptance of such roles requires discipline, and immature and irresponsible people dislike discipline. This is the attraction of matriarchy.

Ms. Ehrenreich shares this dislike. She writes on the dust wrapper of Ms. Heyn's *Erotic Silence of the American Wife* that "women are sexual beings and that, for women as well as men, sex is a fundamentally lawless creature, not easily confined to a cage." Therefore what? Therefore we must either let it run wild or we must impose regulation upon it. The former is the feminist program, the latter the patriarchal program, which attempts to channel sex and reproduction within families. Gloria Steinem writes on the same dust wrapper, "Because patriarchy has restricted women's bodies as the means of reproduction—and then assumed these restrictions to be 'natural'—we have little idea what female sexuality might really be. Dalma Heyn shows us a new reality and a tantalizing hint of the future—and neither women nor marriage will ever be the same."

Removing Ms. Ehrenreich's "cage" does exactly what she says it is intended to do: it makes women "fundamentally lawless creatures." This means women will no longer share their reproductive lives with men—and this is why fathers must have custody of their children.

THE NATURALNESS OF MATRIARCHY; THE ARTIFICIALITY OF PATRIARCHY

The restrictions are *not* "natural"; they are artificial, like the internal combustion engine. The female kinship system is natural, like the flow of a river. It just happens. The male kinship system, like a hydroelectric dam, harnesses the power of sex, "confining it to a cage." "Everything connected with civilization," as Lord Raglan says, "is highly artificial,"[28] nothing more so than confining reproduction within patriarchal families. It was this innovation, made only a few thousand years ago, which made patriarchal civilization possible. The "natural" system of reproduction, as Judge Noland understands, is the earlier female-headed reproductive unit of the barnyard.

The feminist movement, let it be said again, is an attempt to restore this female-headed arrangement—by appealing to the Mutilated Beggar principle—by arguing that the mess it creates is so great that it must be offset by a government Backup System for aiding single mothers, for discriminating against males and patriarchal families for the benefit of females and matriarchal "families."

OTHER MASKS

How about the "masks" worn by lady firepersons who are incapable of lifting a ladder or a two-hundred pound man or climbing a six-foot fence and who prove their upper body strength by performing push-ups from their knees rather than from their toes as men are required to do?

---

[28]Lord Raglan, *Jocasta's Crime: An Anthropological Study* (London: Watts and Co, 1940), p. vii.

Why aren't these masks—besides being incapable of duping anyone, besides being a threat to the public safety, besides demoralizing the men who must accept the increased risks and responsibilities imposed by working alongside incompetent females—why aren't they just as much "playacting" as the masks worn by the Perfect Wife or the Angel in the House?

The demoralization in the armed forces and service academies is notorious. "In the past ten years," acknowledged Ms. Friedan in 1981, "more than half the West Point graduates have resigned as army career officers, as the first women graduated from West Point in 1980, take up careers as army officers."[29] If women are capable of soldiering, soldiering confers no status on men.

Phyllis Schlafly speaks of the "mountain of evidence that women are not performing equally with men in military service today," evidence acknowledged even by West Point spokesman Col. Patrick Toffler, who was supposed to testify that sexual integration was a success. "During five hours of cross-examination under oath," says Mrs. Schlafly, he revealed a lot of things that West Point has heretofore concealed."

> Col. Toffler admitted that West Point does not require the same physical performance of female cadets that it requires of male cadets. He admitted that West Point has dual standards for males and females, that women cadets do not pass the same physical tests as men, and that if they perform the same task, the women are given higher grades. Female cadets are allowed to hold leadership positions based on their padded scores....

> Col. Toffler admitted that West Point has a sexual quota system for the admission of women cadets and for their assignment after graduation (such as to the engineers). "Those quotas have got to be met," he said. The women cadets do not compete with the men, but compete only against each other for designated female quota slots....Military policy permits no negative comment about the performance of women.[30]

A later piece by Mrs. Schlafly quotes a woman soldier: "We can't carry as much or stand up to the pressures and conditions. Whoever tells you we can, don't believe him." "Those who tell you we can" are military spokesmen like Col. Toffler who are compelled to speak through the preposterous "masks" assigned by politically correct pols and

---

[29]Betty Friedan, *The Second Stage* (New York: Summit Books, 1981), p. 133.
[30]*Human Events*, 15 June, 1991.

bureaucrats to proclaim the feminist party line which they know to be untrue. Mrs. Schlafly quotes an Israeli general as saying: "We do not do what you do in the United States because, unfortunately, we have to take war seriously."[31]

The reply to the Israeli general might be: "In the United States, there is another war which politicians must take seriously, the War Against Patriarchy. This war must be fought by falsifying what everyone knows to be true and asserting what everyone known to be false."

Ms. Friedan's attempted evasions are worthy of comic opera:

Now one woman cadet interrupted with a question for the male cadet: "Tell the truth, do you really want to go into combat? Does anyone really want to go into combat? she asked with a quiet passion. "You do what you have to do. It's your duty, it's miserable and awful and terrifying and you'd be crazy to want to do it. But you've had the training, you can be trusted to do what has to be done. You can trust yourself to do the job."[32]

Talk about masks. This female cadet is putting on an Emperor's-New-Clothes performance bordering on the grotesque. The man "does what he has to do" because his failure to do so will brand him a coward and get him court-martialed. The woman knows she doesn't have to do what the man does because timidity is feminine—and her commanders know it and won't place her where she will have to "do her duty." The pretense (when it is a matter of winning a parlor intellectual argument rather than winning a battle) is not just less honest than a woman's pretense of being a Perfect Wife or an Angel in the House; it is destructive of the whole purpose of the military. Ms. Friedan knows this as well as everybody else, but she doesn't object to masks when they serve the bad purpose of undermining the patriarchal system.

On August 18, 1976, [writes Brian Mitchell], a detail of American soldiers was pruning a tree in the Joint Security Area separating North and South Korea when they were suddenly attacked by a truckload of axe-wielding North Korean guards. Two officers were killed. Nine other soldiers were wounded.

Major General John Singlaub, chief of staff of U.S. forces in Korea, decided to take limited military action. United Nations forces in the South prepared for

---

[31]*Human Events*, 13 July, 1991.
[32]*Second Stage*, p. 185.

the worst. Forces moved into positions and air forces were called in from Alaska and Japan.

As soon as it became clear that the alert was no ordinary training exercise, commanders throughout Korea were flooded with requests from female soldiers for transfers to the rear. War was more than these women had bargained for when they had joined the Army. Most fully expected to be evacuated in the event of hostilities, but when the question was raised at higher headquarters, Singlaub nixed the idea immediately and ordered all soldiers to their posts.

Later, when the emergency was over, Singlaub learned that his order had not been strictly obeyed. Many women had abandoned their posts near the border and headed south on their own. Some turned up later in units well to the rear. Others reported for duty with dependent children in tow, since their arrangements for child-care did not cover the event of war. In some instances, male noncommissioned officers had left their posts temporarily to tend to the safety of their wives and girlfriends in other units.[33]

Was anyone surprised? Of course not. Everyone knows that women soldiers are a joke, like women policemen and women firemen. The male future soldiers at West Point and the Citadel and The Virginia Military Institute and The Citadel actually enjoy playing their roles and many, perhaps most wives and mothers actually enjoy playing at their maternal roles, as they did when they were children and played house and played with dolls.

"Since women are not without aggression," says sociologist Steven Goldberg, "it is necessary...that they be socialized away from depending on aggression to attain their ends."[34] Otherwise they will face too much frustration. But besides this there is "the need for societal efficiency":

Men are not stronger and more aggressive than women because men are trained to be soldiers, nor do women nurture children because girls play with dolls. In these cases society is doing more than merely conforming to biological necessity; it is utilizing it....Societies conform their institutions and socialization to the sexual directions set by physiological differentiation, first because they must and second in order to function most efficiently.

---

[33]Brian Mitchell, *Women in the Military: Flirting with Disaster* (Washington D.C.: Regnery, 1998), pp.77f.
[34]Steven Goldberg, *The Inevitability of Patriarchy* (New York: William Morrow, 1973), p. 117.

An army made up of women soldiers or even one diluted with a relatively small number of them as ours is, is inefficient. Everyone knows this. The purpose of making these women "soldiers" is to enable politicians to buy the women's vote. They function as taxpayer-supported camp-followers and comfort girls.

A predictable consequence of the success of the feminist program is an increase in violence. Richard Gelles and Murray Straus, who specialize in the study of violence, write: "One skeptical reader of our study noted that he was seeing more child abuse now than ten years ago. Since he also reported that he sees a largely minority, single-parent, and poor population, this is not surprising."[35] The matriarchal areas are the areas of high crime, high violence and high child abuse. Confucius said that problems ought to be settled by patriarchal authority exercised within the family. Patriarchal authority is what feminists hate. They have discovered that they can earn their own money, withdraw their loyalty from their husbands, and make their appeals to judges instead, knowing that the judges, co-opted into the War Against Patriarchy and timid about offending feminists, will do right by them. Unfortunately, Gelles and Straus buy into this feminist phutzing:

Our own research has found that paid employment of married women helps rectify the imbalance of power between spouses, and provides women with the economic resources they need to terminate a violent marriage.[36]

Also to terminate a so-so marriage or a boring marriage or a marriage like Marcia Clark's in which the husband is insufficiently stimulating intellectually, or a marriage less attractive than an adulterous adventure such as Ms. Heyn's heroines have their fun with.

Rectifying the imbalance means destroying hypergamy, destroying the husband's economic provider role, undermining his motivation, perhaps provoking him into anti-social behavior. Gelles and Straus say "Violence is less common when the wife is at home than when she works,"[37]—when the balance is *not* rectified.

If she becomes an ex-wife she needs him to make "compensatory payment" so that she may remain dependent on him without being under

---

[35]Richard Gelles and Murray Straus, *Intimate Violence: The Causes and Consequences of Abuse in the American Family* (New York: Simon and Schuster, 1988), p. 112.
[36]Page 113.
[37]Page 88.

obligation to him. This enables her to remove her mask and, as the saying is, to stand on her own feet.

Removing the mask reveals beneath it a second mask—that of the helpless little lady whom *somebody* (a judge?) must help. "As long as women have less power," writes feminist Professor Ira Reiss,

they will feel the need somehow to please and attach themselves to those more powerful creatures called men, and sex will serve as a commodity in that pursuit.[38]

As long as women have less power they will support the family and the patriarchal system. "Many women," says Reiss, "have learned that they can be free sexually but will still not be treated equally by men."[39] Of course not. To be "free sexually" is to be promiscuous, of value only to men who want a superficial relationship. "Several feminist writers," he continues, "have noted the clash between sexual equality and inequality in social power." If women gain the right to "equality"—the right to be equally promiscuous—they will be treated as the "bad" women they are, and will lose much of their "social power." He quotes Ehrenreich, Hess and Jacobs:

For women, sexual equality with men has become a concrete possibility, while economic and social parity remains elusive.[40]

Their "sexual equality" (= promiscuity) removes the bargaining power which the acceptance of sexual regulation entitles them to by enabling them to offer men families.

"Where there is inequality of power," says Reiss, "men can pressure women into sexual encounters and sex can be easily used by women as a lure and a means of trying to balance power differences that exist."[41] Reiss uses "equality" to mean equal promiscuousness, as though promiscuity were a privilege men coveted for themselves and denied to women. If women are promiscuous men can more easily pressure them into sexual encounters because they have little to lose. But a chaste woman has a great deal to lose and cannot easily be pressured into sexual encounters. Chastity gives her power.

---

[38] Ira Reiss, *An End to Shame* (Buffalo, N.Y.: Prometheus Books, 1990), p. 97.
[39] Reiss, p. 96.
[40] Ehrenreich, Hess and Jacobs, p. 9.
[41] P. 97.

"A woman who behaves as a sexually and economically free person," says feminist Riane Eisler with truth, "is a threat to the entire social and economic fabric of a rigidly male-dominated society." And she adds with equal truth: "Such behavior cannot be countenanced lest the entire social and economic system fall apart."[42] Men have thus far supposed that the sex war can be ended by appeasement—by paying support money to ex-wives, by giving women men's jobs and men's wages so they can "support their families"—which is to say so they can deny families to men.

One feminist book after another reflects women's resentment of the patriarchal regulation which makes families possible. Feminist Dalma Heyn is fascinated by this resentment:

I am now more than ever interested in the extraordinary power of transgression for women. And extramarital sex...is the single most emphatic form of transgression against a historical framework that has defined and confined women, and still does.

This is the big grievance. They want to be freed from the "historical framework" of patriarchal marriage. Ibsen's Nora felt the same, but in the age of Victoria it was inappropriate to say she wanted to be promiscuous, so she talked about going away to find herself, to "grow" as the saying is. Ms. Heyn's heroines are more straightforward:

After many years of marriage, women feel "old" but not "adult"—while in their affairs, they feel "adult" but not "old."...Stepping out of the role of wife, with its implications of selflessness and obligations to fill others' needs, into the role of a sexually joyous and self-interested person—risking societal pressure and the possibility of hurting a beloved husband—infused these women immediately with a sense of competence and satisfaction, as though they had emerged from a trance to find that their personalities had been returned to them.[43]

This is the triumph of the female kinship system—in the words of Ms. Eisler, gaining "sexual independence: the power to freely choose how and with whom to mate." Their personalities are returned. They are sexually joyous. A happy ending.

---

[42]Riane Eisler, *The Chalice and the Blade: Our History, Our Future* (San Francisco: Harper and Row, 1987), p. 97.
[43]Heyn, *The Secret Erotic Life of the American Wife* (New York: Turtle Bay Books, 1992), pp. 31, 87.

"[T]here is no society in the world," said Margaret Mead, "where people have stayed married without enormous community pressure to do so."[44] Ms. Heyn is doing her bit to advance the feminist program of wrecking marriage.

Feminist political scientist Jane Mansbridge says she found in interviews with low income welfare mothers that they prefer AFDC over dependence on men, and don't view welfare as dependence because it gives them and their children independence from the control of men who were not good for them.[45] More to the point it gives them and their children independence from men who were *good* for them, as the statistics on pages 12ff. indicate

It is worth reminding ourselves of the process by which patriarchy was created, thus described by feminist Gerda Lerner:

The appropriation by men of women's sexual and reproductive capacity occurred prior to the formation of private property and class society....Surpluses from herding were appropriated by men and became private property. Once having acquired such private property, men sought to secure it to themselves and their heirs; they did this by instituting the monogamous family. By controlling women's sexuality through the requirement of prenuptial chastity and by the establishment of the sexual double standard in marriage, men assured themselves of the legitimacy of their offspring and thus secured their property interest.[46]

On what better, more socially useful motives could men act? They sought to benefit their children (also their wives) by insisting on the Legitimacy Principle, that children must have fathers, that women should accept sexual regulation and live in families. Men sought to secure their property to themselves *and their heirs*—to benefit their children. Divorce deprives the children of most of this benefit in order to confer a portion of it on the ex-wife and to de-control her sexuality. This is the purpose of the feminist/sexual revolution—to get rid of stable marriage and return to the female headed reproductive unit.

---

[44]Quoted in Wallerstein and Blakeslee, *Second Chances*, p. 297.
[45]*The Liberator*, October, 1995, citing as source WOMEN/POLITICS, Newsletter of the Organized Section for Women and Politics Research of the American Political Science Association, Vol. 7, No. 2, August, 1995, p. 3.
[46]Gerda Lerner, *The Creation of Patriarchy* (New York: Oxford University Press, 1986), pp. 8, 22.

FATHER'S DAY

Dear Abby similarly and regularly contributes to the undermining of patriarchy. Here is a letter she receives from a father named Thomas Mulder:

DEAR ABBY: I was so moved, and felt such appreciation for your Father's Day column. I would like to acknowledge what a valuable message it carried. You said:

"A 21-gun salute to the divorced father who has never uttered an unkind word about the mother of his children (at least to the children) and who has always been johnny-on-the-spot with the support check."

Abby, those words brought tears to my eyes as I sat quietly reflecting on the seventh year I have celebrated Father's Day without my children. It struck me as amazingly sad that in seven years of being there for my children—and always providing child support—I've never received a thank-you. My morale has been worn down over the years by the stereotyping of divorced fathers as "deadbeat dads."

Abby, if I never get a "thanks," I'll survive. Reading the public thanks in your column for a principle I've upheld not only for the sake of my children, but for the sake of fathers and children everywhere, is a powerful remedy for the sadness I have carried. For any recipient of support out there who has thought of saying "thanks," but never did—I'd bet it wouldn't hurt.

May I offer a sincere "you're welcome" from a loving, supportive dad?

THOMAS MULDER

Abby's reply:

DEAR THOMAS: You may—and thank you for the thank you. How sad that those unsung heroes—divorced dads who never miss a payment—are all too often unappreciated. It would be so easy to just walk away and not fulfill the responsibilities to their children. Yet you, and many like you, sacrifice to see that your children are fed, clothed and educated.

You are to be commended for loving your children enough to be a responsible father.[47]

---

[47]*Los Angeles Times*, 15 August, 1995.

All so magnanimous. Thomas Mulder speaks of "the principle I've upheld." What he has upheld is matriarchy, to which he has contributed his children and his income. All he gets is the satisfaction of being a wind-up toy for feminism, imagining himself to be a great guy. He is being masochistic and it is the knowledge on the part of judges that the world is full of beautiful, noble, magnanimous—and masochistic—men like Thomas Mulder that causes them to routinely discriminate against them. If Thomas Mulder is so noble and magnanimous, why didn't the judge place his children in Thomas Mulder's custody? He didn't because he knew he could depend on Thomas Mulder's magnanimity and he couldn't depend on his wife's magnanimity to perform corresponding services for *him* and the kids if he placed them in *his* custody. The wife would simply have laughed at him. Thomas Mulder asked for what he got, which was injustice in the service of the War Against Patriarchy. The judge replaced his father headed family with a mother headed one because he supposed it was *natural* to do so. Also the easy thing, the thing that all judges do and have done for a century. The judge probably knows that families headed by fathers produce better behaved, higher achieving children but he can't see that he ought to keep the father as family head rather than promote the female kinship system.

Thomas Mulder's ex-wife's support check depends on Mulder's belief that he is doing the right thing. But the use of children of divorce as Mutilated Beggars has become so obviously exploitive, so clearly a means of enabling Mom to throw off sexual law-and-order and expel her husband, so manifestly a makeshift for enabling judges to continue ignoring the damage they inflict on children and society that fathers like Mulder ought to realize that their true responsibility is to end this family destruction by taking custody of their children. He should be thinking "You don't own me!—I'm tired of wearing the chains hung on me by my ex-wife and her weakling catspaw judge." Gloria Steinem tells women they are female impersonators. Fathers who send support money to their ex-wives are father impersonators clinging to a fragment of the male role. "Women," says Betty Friedan, "have outgrown the housewife role." Men have outgrown the ex-husband role which accepts and finances automatic mother custody.

"I would die," said feminist Susan B. Anthony, "before I will give up the child to its father."[48] Why might not Thomas Mulder say "I will die before I will give up my children to their mother and pay her so she can afford to hold them as hostages?" "The male legal ownership of children," says Phyllis Chesler, "is essential to patriarchy."[49] Quite so; and since patriarchy is essential to civilization, Thomas Mulder is betraying his children, patriarchy and civilization when he contributes his kids and his money and his loyalty to the female kinship system.

"Our culture," says Wade Horn, "needs to replace the idea of the superfluous father with a more compelling understanding of the critical role fathers play in the lives of their children, not just as 'paychecks,' but as disciplinarians, teachers, and moral guides. And fathers must be physically present in the home. They can't simply show up on the weekends or for pre-arranged 'quality time.'"[50]

Daughters say they don't want to live the kind of lives their mothers led. What will Thomas Mulder's sons say—or Marcia Clark's or any of the millions of other sons deprived of their fathers? If they have any sense they will say that they don't want to live the kind of life their fathers led. Thomas Mulder's case is one more victory in the War Against Patriarchy, a war partly fought and lost on the battlefield of Thomas Mulder's own mind. He imagined himself to be doing a good thing in paying for the wrecking of his family, much as Indian wives once regarded *suttee* as a good thing: it was an honor to immolate themselves on the funeral pyres of their dead husbands. The custom ended when the widows woke up to the silliness of what they were doing and when society stopped expecting it.[51]

Why should fathers give up their children, and pay to do so, as they are now expected to do? So that Dear Abby and President Clinton will approve of them? So that society can continue its roller coaster ride into matriarchy? Father custody is the only way to give society the three things it most needs, the stability of families, the restoration of fatherhood and the restoration of childhood, whose loss is now herding kids into gangs and delinquency and premature sexuality.

---

[48]Quoted in Phyllis Chesler, *Patriarchy: Notes of an Expert Witness* (Monroe, Maine: Common Courage Press, 1994), p. 38.
[49]*Ibid.*, p. 47.
[50]*Imprimus*, June, 1997.
[51]Suttee is foolishness, but in support of a good cause, patriarchy; Mulderism is foolishness in support of a bad cause, matriarchy.

Relief agencies in third world countries are given the Thomas Mulder treatment. According to the *Los Angeles Times*, "Relief groups face crises of conscience as more and more workers are attacked. When food and supplies meant for the needy are stolen by warring gunmen, agencies must ask if they're doing more harm than good."[52]

One relief worker puts it this way:

> **"A Liberian warlord said to me one day, 'I can starve a village until the children die, and then you will come with food and medicine which I will take, and no one can do anything about it,'" recalled American aid worker Martha Carey. He was right, said Carey, who was stunned to find one village in which children had starved, families had been massacred, and survivors begged: "Don't bring food, don't bring anything, it makes things worse. Just go and leave us alone."**

No one can do anything about it, says the warlord, who is in the driver's seat, as Thomas Mulder's ex-wife is in the driver's seat. How about men raising their consciousness? How about the Thomas Mulders of America waking up and putting a stop to the silliness of paying their ex-wives to destroy their families and drag their children into the female kinship system and ghettoizing society?

> **Juveniles [says Horn] are the fastest growing segment of the criminal population in the United States. Between 1982 and 1991, the rate at which children were arrested for murder increased 93 percent; for aggravated assault, 72 percent; for rape, 24 percent; and for automobile theft, 97 percent....The teen population is expected to grow by 20 percent over the next decade, and this is precisely the generation most likely to be reared without fathers. The prospect has led many sociologists, criminologists, and law enforcement agencies to conclude that shortly after the turn of the century we will see an adolescent crime wave the likes of which has never been seen before in this country.**

Feminists regard the reversion to matriarchy as progress. Female de-regulation in one generation means poorly socialized children in the next, troublemaking boys and promiscuous girls and second generation illegitimacy. This will continue as long as judges suppose mothers ought to have custody of children and fathers like Thomas Mulder are willing to pay for it.

---

[52]25 January, 1997.

"Today things have changed," says feminist Lynette Triere:

Not only is the neat, assured definition of marriage being questioned, but more broadly, women are reexamining the boundaries of what they have been taught to expect out of life.[53]

What they now expect, she says, is not merely "new depth" but also "new breadth," which must be interpreted to mean more of the sexual promiscuity which characterizes the female kinship system:

Despite the continuing media emphasis on adolescent male sex fantasies, mature women are finding new depth and breadth in their sexual experience. Discarding tired molds that required accepted behavior at designated ages, women are discovering their own individual time clocks whose accuracy depends on how they feel about themselves. They are learning to express their wants and need no apologies. Many have found that their original choice of a partner[54] **all those years ago no longer works out. If it was not wrong at the beginning, it certainly is now.**[55]

This mystification about "tired molds that required accepted behavior" and "individual time clocks whose accuracy depends on how they feel about themselves" is simply a declaration of female independence from the male kinship system. Ms. Triere is saying the same thing as Dalma Heyn's adulteresses, who are reborn and released. The same thing as Riane Eisler when she says women have begun to reclaim their own sexuality—by de-regulating themselves. "Women during the last three decades have not only been talking and writing more openly about sex; as women have begun to gain more personal, economic, and political power, they have also more openly, and far more actively, been engaging in sex."[56]

This, says Ms. Eisler, is a "struggle against the assertion of male entitlement to their bodies...the right to be seen by oneself and others as belonging to oneself rather than someone else...the right to self-determination."

Male entitlement, she says, without indicating whether the male is a husband or a non-husband, thus implying (as Ms. Hoggett implies)

---

[53]Lynette Triere, *Learning to Leave: A Woman's Guide* (New York: Warner Books, 1982), p. 13.
[54]In feminist discussions seeking to undermine the male kinship system "husband" and "marriage" are replaced by "partner" and "relationship."
[55]*Ibid.*, p. 14.
[56]*Sacred Pleasure*, p. 282.

that marriage is meaningless, that society operates under the female kinship system. If marriage is meaningless, there is no basis for a female claim to entitlement to the male paycheck. If marriage is meaningful and the sharing by the male in the reproductive life of the female ("male entitlement to their bodies") has as its quid pro quo the sharing of the female in the male's paycheck, then the withdrawal by the female of her sharing implies the withdrawal by the male of his. His sole obligation is to the children he has procreated, who accordingly belong in his custody.

THE KEPT WOMAN

"The day of the kept woman is over," says Ms. Triere.[57] The kept woman is the woman who accepts sexual regulation, who allows a man to have a family, allows her children to have a father. The kept woman is entitled to be subsidized by a husband. If she repudiates her kept status, she makes a family impossible and, properly, denies to herself the benefits of the patriarchal system. If she is given these benefits anyhow by a divorce court judge, Briffault's Law comes into operation: the male can no longer give her the benefit he formerly gave her, since she has already taken it from him; accordingly "no association takes place."

"Women's reproductive freedom" now is interpreted to mean freedom to take a man's children and paycheck. It must be re-interpreted to mean the loss to women of their children and the benefits patriarchy bestows on good women, "kept" women.

Since the 1960s feminists have been assuring us that divorce and illegitimacy didn't mean "the family" was breaking down—it was merely undergoing development, adapting to social changes such as feminism. There are, they explained, many forms of "family." When President Carter called a White House Conference on the Family, the first thing the feminists attending it did was to re-name it the White House Conference on *Families*—meaning that the female kinship system is just as good as the male kinship system, meaning that a lesbian getting herself impregnated with a turkey baster is entitled to the same status and benefits as any other "family."

---

[57]P. 145.

60

THE HETHERINGTON CASE

The case of William Hetherington illustrates how far the legal system will go in capitulating to the feminist war against patriarchy. Hetherington's wife deserted him and their children to run off with a boyfriend. Later she broke up with the boyfriend and, facing the prospect of losing custody of her children and losing the status accompanying such custody, she proposed to Hetherington that they should be reconciled. The reconciliation provided her with the opportunity of accusing him of marital rape, of which he was duly convicted. Hetherington has now languished in prison for over eight years for a "crime" of which he is innocent. The prolongation of Hetherington's incarceration serves only the bad purpose of saving the reputation of the judge, Thomas Yeotis, from the exposure of his weakness of character and his wish to play shabby chivalric games.

Judge Yeotis said he wanted to make Hetherington "a symbol to all mankind"—by demonstrating that a wife who *accuses* her husband of marital rape must be a victim in need of rescuing. Before such a politically correct judge all the woman needed to do was dab her eyes with kleenex and wonder what a poor little weak woman like herself would do if she didn't have a big strong judge like Yeotis to protect her. The big strong judge's chivalry didn't cost him a thing. He passed that cost on to Hetherington in the form of a sentence of 15-to-30 years in prison for the crime of having had sex with a wife who had deserted him and their children to run off with; a boyfriend—and then proposed a reconciliation.

The message Judge Yeotis sent to all mankind was not that rape was a bad thing but that judicial genuflecting to feminist pressure was a good thing, that he hungered for feminist approval and was willing to ignore his oath of office to get it.

Until recently in rape prosecutions it was customary for the judge to read Sir Matthew Hale's admonition that the jury ought to "view the woman's testimony with caution. Rape is an accusation easily to be made and hard to be proved and harder to be defended by the party accused though never so innocent." No more. Feminists tantrumed at the suggestion that a woman might commit perjury, and the legal system, always their obedient servant, suppressed Sir Matthew Hale's commonsense admonition. "Woman," said Blackstone, "is the favorite of the law."

"In the struggle for survival wc tell lies," says feminist Adrienne Rich, "to bosses, to prison guards, the police, men who have powers over us, who legally own us and our children, lovers who need us as proof of their manhood." [58]

In 1987, Joseph Gallardo of the state of Washington raped a ten-year-old girl, was convicted and sentenced to three years in prison, after which he was deemed to have paid his debt to society and was released. There is a difference between a sentence of three years and a sentence of 15-to-30 years, a difference suggesting that Hetherington's offense is five to ten times more serious than Gallardo's.

The marriage contract has always been understood as a sex contract. If it were not, marriage would be meaningless—which is perhaps the real intention of the feminists who clamored for the new law outlawing marital rape. [59] It was Hetherington's misfortune that he came to trial at a time when the issue of "marital rape" was being publicized by feminists as a grievance against the patriarchal family and men in general. One result of this agitation was the passing of a law which, in effect, declared that marriage gave husbands no right to cohabit with their wives. *Black's Law Dictionary*, a standard reference work, calls rape "the act of sexual intercourse committed by a man with a woman not his wife and without her consent." The new law has the effect of removing the words "not his wife" from this definition, thus making the status of the husband identical with that of a non-husband.

This is a logical corollary to the often-stated feminist demand that a woman has the right to control her own sexuality—in other words that not only does a husband have no more right to have sex with his wife than any other man, but that the wife has the right to cohabit with a non-husband (commit adultery) regardless of her marriage contract. Such an interpretation of marriage makes it meaningless and strikes a deadly blow at the core of civilized society.

---

[58]*Woman and Honor*, quoted in *off our backs* Jan., 1978. "Women," said Schopenhauer, "commit perjury far more frequently than men in courts of law. It is even doubtful whether they should be sworn as witnesses at all."
[59]It is evidently the intention of British feminist law commissioner Brenda Hoggett, who questions whether marriage serves any useful purpose.

The new law is anti-male, of course. It is also anti-marriage, anti-family and anti-woman. The woman's primary contribution to the marriage is her willingness to share her reproductive life with her husband and thereby enable him to have a family. The woman's willingness to make this offer and the man's willingness to make the complementary offer to love, honor, protect and provide for the resulting family are what make civilization and social stability possible. The condition of the ghettos shows what happens when the marriage contract becomes meaningless or irrelevant. The new Michigan law tells the woman that she may renege on her marriage vow at any time. It makes her incapable of entering into a stable and enforceable marriage contract on which a man—and children and society—can depend. Granting the woman the right to renege on her contract makes the contract worthless and deprives the woman of most of her bargaining power in the marriage marketplace. It is hard to imagine anything more damaging to society—or to women.

The contract is worse than useless. If it had not been for the contract Hetherington would be a free man. If it had not been for the contract Judge Yeotis would not have put on his grandstanding. It would hardly be an exaggeration to say that since the passage of this law the most dangerous place for an American husband to be is in the marital bed.

A mere adulterer like President Kennedy or President Clinton or Dalma's ladies, or a mere rapist like Joseph Gallardo would never be treated as Hetherington has been treated—adultery is no longer against the law (is it?) just as sex with one's wife is now against the law if the wife wishes it to be.

The Book of Common Prayer formerly declared that marriage was (among other things) "a remedy against sin." One must wonder whether the lawmakers who hurriedly passed the law under which Hetherington was condemned considered what its consequences would be in terms of family breakdown, divorce, adultery, incest and domestic violence, consequences which include the sins against marriage was formerly deemed a remedy.

The injustice of the treatment given Hetherington is acknowledged by the offer made to him to commute his sentence to time served if only he would admit guilt by plea-bargaining—and thus save face for Judge

Yeotis and "the system." This is what the case is now all about—covering up the sleaziness of what has been done to Hetherington in the hopes that the public will become bored with hearing about it or that it will somehow go away.

THE SATURDAY NIGHT BASH

Feminist Barbara Seaman thinks that "the sexual morality of an *individual* is and should be a private matter, for it has no bearing on the general welfare if *she* conducts herself responsibly."[60] The de-regulation of the female, the repudiation of patriarchy and the replacement of sexual regulation and marriage by matriarchal promiscuity and divorce or adultery are the real feminist goals. Ms. Seaman thinks that women will start taking charge of their own sex lives—will, in other words, transfer society from patriarchy to matriarchy. Ms. Heyn has the same idea. She focuses on the personal, but the political is in the background:

> **I am saying that for all these women I interviewed, sexually exclusive marital relationships were made joyous only when they first killed off that Perfect Wife, and shattered this rigid institutional cage in which she flourished and which imprisoned their sexual selves.**[61]

The cage is patriarchy. They were joyous only when the goal of matriarchy is to be achieved, when they were *no longer* sexually exclusive, when "women control our own bodies," when "you don't own me," when, as Byllye Avery says, "the definition of 'family' must change,"[62] when it is acknowledged that "a woman's right to have a baby without having the father around is what feminism is all about."[63]

Ehrenreich, Hess and Jacobs have the same idea. How they hate sexual regulation, marriage and family and long-term commitments upon which children and fathers and society must depend. Thus speaks the eternal feminine. "You don't own me! You don't own me!"

These writers tell us: "We are drawn, *as women have been for ages* [emphasis added], to the possibility of celebrating our sexuality without the exclusive intensity of romantic love, without the inevitable

---

[60]*Free and Female*, p. 207.
[61]Heyn, p. 285; emphasis added.
[62]On Bill Moyers' program, L. A.'s Channel 28, 7 September, 1989.
[63]Quoted in the 1996 Defense of the Family Survey.

disappointment of male-centered sex, and without the punitive consequences."[64]

Of course. The Saturday night bash, the Oktoberfest, the New Year's Eve party,[65] the Mardi Gras—escape from responsible sexuality, especially from the regulation of female sexuality upon which the whole fabric of patriarchal society depends. They want no male-centered sex— no sex in which the male has *any* meaningful role. No sentimentality about children. Sex without much reference to reproduction.

In Greek antiquity, women's hatred of regulation was manifested (among other ways) by their worship of the god Dionysus, an importation from Thrace. Hear the *Oxford Classical Dictionary*:

> [Thracian religion] was crude and barbaric before Greek influences transformed it. There is evidence of primitive animal-worship, human sacrifice, magical ceremonies, orgiastic rites....Dionysus was their greatest god and their chief contribution to Greek religion. He was a god of vegetation and fertility, worshipped in wild, ecstatic rites....[T]he Thracian and Macedonian women were especially devoted to his orgia. The cult swept over Greece like wildfire....The cause was its ecstatic character which seized chiefly on the women. They abandoned their houses and work, roamed about in the mountains, whirling in the dance, swirling thyrsi and torches; at the pitch of their ecstasy they seized upon an animal or even a child, according to the myths, tore it apart and devoured the bleeding pieces. [The maenads who worship Dionysus] roam through mountains and woods and lead the life of animals. They are beyond all human concerns, conventions and fears. Dionysus inspires them with strength so that they can uproot trees and kill strong animals. They also hunt animals and devour their raw flesh....(pp. 764, 288, 528)

More about these wild Id-forces in Chapter V. Patriarchy bottles up these forces in women in order that males may be equal sharers in reproduction, may create families, the institution which puts the power of sex to work. But the wild forces are always roiling, surging and striving to surface. It is especially necessary to control them in women, who must accept the burden of sexual regulation if children are to have a second parent. Therefore God says to Eve "He shall rule over thee." The contemporary feminist movement is a manifestation of the same women's passion to get rid of the hated patriarchal regulation and the second

---

[64] *Re-Making Love*, p. 199.
[65] Large numbers of illegitimate children are born at the end of September, nine months after New Year's Eve. *Los Angeles Daily News*, 18 October, 1993.

parent. The worship of Dionysus which swept over Greek women like wildfire three millennia ago manifested women's passion to get rid of the same hated patriarchal regulation. Today they have the law and its machinery on their side, supporting the female kinship system—buying the women's vote—attempting arduously to create through public policy some inevitably inadequate substitute for the real thing—from day care, to the WIC program, to programs "to make 'deadbeat dads' come across with the monthly check." But no law can "compel the enormous sacrifices, from working overtime, to taking a second job, to mortgaging the house to pay for college, that married fathers routinely make for their children, but which divorced fathers seldom do."[66] The law cannot handle the problem by seeking alternatives to the family. Wayne Doss, director of the Bureau of Family Support for the Los Angeles District Attorney's Office, is "concerned that if custodial mothers are allowed to sue state and county agencies for failing to collect their support money from deadbeat dads it will quickly become an unmanageable program."[67] *Anything* to replace the family is unmanageable. Wives must accept sexual regulation and husbands must refuse to subsidize wives or ex-wives who refuse to—and take custody of their children themselves. "In California and nationally," says the *Los Angeles Times*,[68] "increasing enforcement of child support orders is a major part of the effort to reduce welfare rolls." It won't work. It will increase welfare by increasing divorce and it will increase male rolelessness and demoralization and crime and dope-addiction and the rest of the pathology mentioned on pages 12ff.

"The crackdown on non-custodial parents who fail to support their children," says the *Times*,[69] is immensely popular politically":

The President's denouncement of such parents during his State of the Union Address met with the loudest cheers of any of his proposals that evening.

[According to Clinton] The government will "say to absent parents who aren't paying their child support: 'If you're not providing for your children, we'll garnish your wages, suspend your license, track you across state lines and, if necessary, make some of you work off what you owe,'" Clinton said. "People

---

[66]Gallagher, *Abolition of Marriage*, p. 43.
[67]*Los Angeles Times*, 11 May, 1996.
[68]2 May, 1997.
[69]17 April, 1994.

who bring children into this world cannot and must not walk away from them."

Do the deadbeat dads walk away or are they expelled? Mostly the latter. If Clinton's program is put into practice, it will be easier for wives to expel more of them. What is Clinton saying to a young man who contemplates marriage and the creation of a family? What does he say to a wife who is getting bored with her husband and who reads in Ms. Heyn and Ms. Bakos about the attractions of promiscuity and adultery and a woman's sacred right to control her own sexuality? He tells both of them that if a woman goes through a marriage ceremony she is thenceforward entitled to a free ride at her husband's or ex-husband's expense. He is also telling single promiscuous women that they need not go through the marriage ceremony at all—that their unchastity is all that is required to qualify them for the free ride. He is making war on patriarchy and the family and promoting the female kinship system. This is why he is "immensely popular."

Despite marked increases in establishing paternity [continues the *Times*] child support collections from fathers whose children receive welfare benefits have stayed constant or increased only gradually in most states.

In 1992, state governments collected child support payments from only 832,000, or 12%, of the 6.8 million absent parents whose children received Aid for Families With Dependent Children. Comparatively, the collection rate in 1988 was 11%, or about 621,000 of 5.7 million absent parents.

The collection rate increases by 1% while the number of absent fathers increases 34%. Is it not obvious that the way to save families and money is to stop exiling fathers? Telling mothers that they are entitled to the fathers' money and that the government will collect it for them will increase the amount of family breakdown, female unchastity, illegitimacy and the social pathology indicated on pages 12ff.

When custodial parents are on welfare [continues the Times] the child-support enforcement system collects directly from the non-custodial parent and gives the custodial parent $50 a month—in part to encourage them to cooperate in naming and tracking down the other "parent." The rest of the money is used to offset the welfare payment.

So the father has the satisfaction of knowing he is also subsidizing the Welfare System which promotes matriarchy and makes fathers like himself superfluous. The woman's cooperation will make men more leery of commitment, will exacerbate the War of the Sexes. The message is "Women are dangerous." They no longer need share their reproductive lives with a man in order to lay a claim on his money. The government now works to subsidize and to compel men to subsidize matriarchy and the Promiscuity Principle, illegitimacy, marital breakdown, family destruction and the rearing of children in fatherless homes.

The idea is to make males more responsible; the effect is to make females less responsible:

To be eligible for AFDC, the government requires mothers to name the father so they can track him down and order him to pay child support. But many mothers claim that they do not know the father's identity—or they give a false name.

In South Carolina, in the first 11 months of 1993, for example, 37% of the 2,840 fathers named were excluded by genetic testing.

The females have gained the feminist goal of living in the female kinship system; but their sexual promiscuity is incompatible with civilized living. Government ought not to encourage it and fathers ought not to subsidize it.

The wild Id-forces in men are also dangerous, also in need of discipline. The family has hitherto been the means for imposing this discipline, but women, correctly seeing the family as *their* disciplinarian too, their enemy, the creator of the hated patriarchal system, are willing that men should be liberated from all family restraints other than economic obligations. Today, as feminist Carolyn Heilbrun says, women "have to a great extent stopped internalizing the [patriarchy's] idea of what women's lives should be."[70] Meaning women have got rid of the internal restraints formerly imposed by the patriarchal family. Her idea is that while women emancipate themselves from the sexual loyalty which gives men their role as fathers, men will maintain their patriarchal discipline and keep performing their provider role. The result, beginning in the 1960s, might have been predicted: an explosion of moral anarchy, divorce, illegitimacy, and sexual confusion, educational failure, drug culture, the 1992 Los Angeles riots, Central Park wildings by fatherless boys.

---

[70]*Los Angeles Times Magazine*, 18 July, 1992.

Freud thought women had little sense of justice, this being, he supposed, "connected with the preponderance of envy in their mental life."[71] To this opinion feminist Betty Friedan attempted the following reply:

Victorian culture gave women many reasons to envy men: the same conditions, in fact, that the feminists fought against....[They were] denied the freedom, the status and the pleasures that men enjoyed....She would, of course, have to learn to keep her envy, her anger, hidden: to play the child, the doll, the toy, for her destiny depended on charming man. But underneath, it might still fester, sickening her for love. If she secretly despised herself, and envied man for all she was not, she might go through the motions of love, or even feel a slaving adoration, but would she be capable of free and joyous love?[72]

Ms. Friedan speaks of high-aspiring women who envy high-status men for their conspicuous achievement. Such men are also envied by most other men. Apart from such overachievers, Ms. Friedan might see much reason *not* to envy men. Speaking of men in general, Katherine in *The Taming of the Shrew* has this: He "cares for thee and for thy maintenance, commits his body to painful labor both by sea and land to watch the night in storms, the day in cold, whilst thou liest warm at home, secure and safe, and craves no other tribute at thy hands but love, fair looks, and true obedience, too little payment for so great a debt."[73]

"Her destiny depended on charming men," depended, in other words, on "love, fair looks, and true obedience," which Ms. Friedan thinks undignified and insincere. Women should not have to put on such a show to "earn" the economic and status advantages men confer. Why cannot women stand on their own feet, earn their own economic security and status and thereby be enabled to love "freely and joyously" rather than in exchange for conferred economic benefits doled out by a man?

She could earn her own economic security, but she would find it hard to find a man interested in being the recipient of her free and joyous love outside of one-night stands, because the man would have no domestic security with her, no bargaining power. He would know she

---

[71]Quoted in Betty Friedan, *The Feminine Mystique*, p. 116.
[72]*The Feminine Mystique*, p. 117.
[73]Katherine's speech at the end of *The Taming of the Shrew*.

could dump him when she was no longer in heat, when she no longer felt like giving her love freely and joyously. Then, as the fivefold-greater divorce rate of employed women shows, she might exercise her privilege of discarding him as Betty discarded Carl, as Adrienne Rich discarded Alfred, as Marcia Clark discarded Gordon. What do such high-achieving women need husbands for?

IV) THE FEMININE MYSTIQUE AND AFTER

Society today is less energized than it was during the era of the Feminine Mystique following World War II, when America's industrial plant, already the wonder of the world during the war, *doubled* in just twenty years, when the GNP grew 250 percent and per capita income increased 35 percent between 1945 and 1960.

Those were the years of which Joseph Satin said "Never had so many people, anywhere, been so well off"—the pre-feminist years, when families were stable, before "they redesigned our concepts of sexuality and gender equality."

Of these years sociologist David Popenoe writes:

For a short moment in history, fatherhood again became a defining identity for many men....For many American citizens, the fifties were an enormously peaceful and satisfying period. The future looked bright indeed....

Yet the era suddenly ended, the birthrate plummeted, and the dramatic "social revolutions" of the three decades following the fifties— the sexual revolution, the divorce revolution, and the women's liberation movement—were launched. All three of these revolutions had as their primary aim the de-regulation of female sexuality, in other words the undermining of the male role and patriarchy. Women's achieving, or partially achieving, economic and sexual independence wrecked the patriarchal golden age, a wrecking abetted by the divorce courts which deprived millions of men of their families.

"As women went into the labor force," continues Dr. Popenoe,

young men in large numbers rejected domesticity and even the masculine ideal. The laid-back and family-rejecting hippie became a model for many men and all "rigid gender roles" became something to be eschewed at all costs. Marriage fell out of fashion, replaced by the rapidly growing

phenomenon of living together outside of marriage. After an historical moment of glory, the modern nuclear family came apart at the seams.[1]

"Compared with their children, moreover," writes Barbara Dafoe Whitehead,

the postwar generation had much lower levels of divorce. Thus divorced baby boomers may benefit by drawing upon the social and emotional capital generated by these unions over forty or fifty years. However, Generation Xers, the children of the divorce revolution, may not be able to count on a similar lifeboat from their parents.[2]

THE PRIMARY CAREGIVER

The ongoing feminist victory over patriarchy hinges on automatic mother custody in divorce. Mom is the "primary caregiver." This is true while the baby is allowed to gestate unaborted within Mom's womb—though the pro-life bumper sticker truly reminds us: "The most dangerous place in America is a mother's womb." Mom is responsible for all abortions and most infanticides, intentional or unintentional. "If the mother is unmarried, the risk of death to her infant more than doubles," says Maggie Gallagher.[3] The law supposes that if it gives Mom custody and *if Dad keeps paying the bills* things will work out—and besides there's welfare.

Mom functions best as caregiver when the children are infants. But infants become children—who need Dad more and Mom less. Take another look at page 42, where Dr. Blankenhorn tries to persuade the fatherless Indiana schoolchildren to grow up. They stomp their feet and refuse to listen. They "grow up" to be Clintons and Lewinskys, both father-deprived, both trying to "play adultery," as little kids play house. Think of Princess Diana, who yearned to be "The Queen of Hearts"—continually seeking sympathy with suicidal gestures, continually seeking advice from her astrologers, her fortune-tellers, her New-Age mystics, her tarot card readers, her mediums and psychics and clairvoyants—another messed-up kid, abandoned by her mother, strung out on eating disorders, bingeing and purging. Poor kid.

---

[1]David Popenoe, *Life Without Father: Compelling New Evidence that Fatherhood and Marriage Are Indispensable for the good of Children and Society* (New York: The Free Press, 1996), pp. 128ff.
[2]*The Divorce Culture*, p. 175.
[3]Gallagher, *The Abolition of Marriage*, p. 42.

Think of the most famous of all feminist tracts, Ibsen's *Doll's House*, about a wife named Nora who walks out on her husband. Mother Nora knows that her husband will continue to take care of the children: "How am I equipped to bring up children?" she asks her husband Torvald. When Torvald indignantly says, "Before all else, you're a wife and a mother!" she replies: I don't believe that anymore." She leaves carrying no obligations with her: "I won't look in on the children. I know they're in better hands than mine":

NORA: Listen, Torvald—I've heard that when a wife deserts her husband's house just as I'm doing, then the law frees him from all responsibility. In any case, I'm freeing you from being responsible. Don't feel yourself bound, any more than I will. There has to be absolute freedom for us both. Here, take your ring back. Give me mine.

To the modern reader this seems to mean *You don't need to feel yourself responsible to provide for me—or for the children.* "There has to be absolute freedom for us both" seems to mean that a family consists of two people without children. But this is not Ibsen's meaning. Taking back the rings does not de-procreate the children. The children belong with their father: Ibsen accepts the nineteenth century legal axiom that "they are by law *his* children," that the father, not the mother, is the primary caregiver. Women have come a long way since Ibsen's time. Torvald loses his wife. Today he would also lose his children, probably his home, any meaningful father's role, his income, and much of his property.

A Doll's House is properly considered a feminist breakthrough, a pioneer statement of women's right to independence. But few Victorian women would have imitated Nora, since it was obvious that she would be unable to pay next month's rent. It was necessary for the wife not only to gain sexual independence, but to regain economic *dependence* either on her ex-husband or on the taxpayer, through welfare or through "earned income tax credit" or some other means. In other words, it was necessary to get rid of the patriarchal system and switch over to the matriarchal system, in which the mother takes custody of the children. It is this custody which entitles her to subsidization.

Unlike today's husband who loses everything, Torvald loses only his wife. He is still the head of what is left of his family. Ibsen still accepts the patriarchal family, based on the male kinship system.

Today's feminist might look back on *A Doll's House* as a breakthrough for the feminist movement but Ibsen still accepts the father-headed family. More about this in Chapter IX.

STELLA PAYTON

"Nonresidential fathers," says Barbara Dafoe Whitehead,

tend to lose their incentive to put more money in their children's household. Some may actually reduce their workloads or refuse opportunities for better jobs, either out of resentment at the postdivorce arrangements or out of a sense that their extra earnings would not result in more time or better relationships with their children. Thus far, stricter legal control and enforcement of paternal obligations have not been very successful in putting more money in children's family households; during the 1980s intensified federal, state and local government efforts to boost child support payments increased the percentage of women receiving payments by less than 3 percent.[4]

Society must persuade its young men to assume the responsibilities of fatherhood by guaranteeing to them the rewards of fatherhood. Judge Noland must be made to realize that the biological marginality of the male role in reproduction is not a reason for discriminating against males, not a reason for depriving them of their children, but a reason for strengthening their role and thereby strengthening the family—strengthening it principally against its most powerful enemy, women's hatred of patriarchy, women's resistance to sexual regulation, women's preference for the female kinship system, a preference expressed most commonly as the demand for economic independence from men.

Stella Payton, a black woman, writes a defense of welfare for mothers because "all welfare mothers have children." In an essay titled "First, Take Care of the Children," she has this:[5]

I never thought I'd be on welfare. I am an articulate, intelligent, college-educated woman. I had many plans for my life. Being on welfare was not on the list. But getting there is easier than you think.

---

[4]*The Divorce Culture*, p. 159.
[5]*Los Angeles Times*, 1 February, 1997.

It's easier because sexual promiscuity and the female kinship system are easy, are *natural*—and patriarchy, which would have kept her off welfare, is artificial and women hate it because it makes them behave themselves.

> **In 1992, my life took a turn with an unplanned pregnancy. When I refused to have an abortion, my son's father vanished. After Alex was born, I started looking for work again. I had no idea finding a job in my field would be virtually impossible....With no child support, affordable child care or insurance, and only part-time work, I had to go on welfare.**

Single women ought not to have pregnancies. Pregnancies ought to take place within marriages. Ms. Payton needs a husband and Alex needs a father, but this would interfere with her right to control her own sexuality—her right to be promiscuous. If her boyfriend had been a husband and had had what Ms. Eisler calls "inflexible lifelong sexual bonds" with her, there would have been no welfare problem. Ms. Payton's unchastity marginalized her boyfriend and he knew it—knew he could not be a real husband or a real father and therefore he "vanished." Sensible of him; but Ms. Payton wants her readers to think it was a rotten thing for him to do—getting a poor female pregnant and then abandoning her. It would have been a rotten thing if she had been willing to give him a stable family, but what she wanted was what Ms. Eisler calls a "healthy amount of spontaneity and sexual experimentation," which resulted in a fatherless child. Ms. Payton asks society to "take care of the children"—so she and moms like her will not need husbands. Result: Alex becomes a Mutilated Beggar.

> **Welfare reform is easier when everyone becomes responsible. Let's form partnerships to provide safe, nurturing and affordable environments for our children and at the same time rebuild community relationships between government, families, churches and businesses.**

The partnership which would provide the responsibility, safety and nurturing environment is marriage; but her real plea is not that "everyone becomes responsible" but that she may be irresponsible, privileged to live in the female kinship system where marriage is interchangeable with cohabitation and single motherhood, where fathers are not heads of families but where mothers are heads of families entitled to tell the fathers to get out of her (or his own) house—and who are obligated to send support money to keep Mom off welfare. Ms. Payton, in other words, doesn't want a husband around to share parenting with her, and since she is female, and since "children belong with their mother," she is the boss, in charge of her kids, married to the state, a ghetto matriarch. She wants to deprive her son of a father by making "everyone"—everyone besides herself—responsible, so that she need not put up with a husband. The "families" she speaks of are fatherless ghetto matrilines whose men President Clinton promises to hunt down ("We will make you pay"). The "partnership" she wants is not a family but a means for getting along without a family, of financing a fatherless family, a network where "everyone" becomes responsible. Everyone except the father. Alex's father didn't "vanish"; he knew, like Charmaine's boyfriend, that he had to get out of Stella's house because in the matriarchy where Stella wanted to live fathers have no authority.

The two people who really need to be responsible, her boyfriend and herself, refuse to be; she wants no part of the chains of marriage and he knows he cannot be a father with an unchaste woman. So Alex will go through life with no father and will face the problems listed on pages 12ff. of this book.

This is matriarchy. This is why we have ghettos. Getting there is easier than you think.

Judges must be made to realize that the biological marginality of the male role is not a reason for discriminating against males, not a reason for depriving them of their children, but a reason for strengthening their role.

Marriage is less romantic than economic. It is held together not by what Betty Friedan calls "free and joyous love"—code language for the female kinship system—but by the husband's willingness to work and the wife's willingness to work things out, by her sexual loyalty based on (among other things) her realization that the custody of her children and her sharing of her husband's paycheck are at stake. If wives want to feel "reborn," to "see things in color," to experience "this feeling of being awake rather than asleep," to believe that sex was "a creative thing...a talent—like, I don't know, painting or writing. You develop your talent, that's all. You don't let it languish—that's what our parents did"[6]—if wives want this excitement—and don't have to pay the price of losing

---

[6]Heyn, p. 82.

their children and Dad's paycheck to get it—they will have a powerful motive for adultery or divorce. This is why the divorce rate is sixty percent and the illegitimacy rate thirty percent, why Ehrenreich, Hess and Jacobssay "All the old prohibitions and taboos would have to give way to the needs of the sexually liberated woman."[7]

If Carl Friedan believed that Betty married him to experience "free and joyous love," he discovered that such love was unstable when Betty walked out with his children. Tens of millions of other American men have discovered the same. Let's "take off the masks," as Ms. Friedan likes to say: the notion that marriage ought to be based on free and joyous love is an affectation made so that one of the spouses, usually the wife, can later complain that love has vanished and that its absence justifies doing what Betty Friedan did to Carl.

Free and joyous love between a man and a woman is an undependable basis for a child rearing institution. One of Ms. Friedan's promiscuous friends illustrates:

> **She is currently involved with two married men in two different cities. Over the last week she has seen both, spent two intense days with one, several with the other, but does not quite know when she'll see either one again. This has been going on for several years. Neither has any interest in leaving his wife, nor would she really want to marry either one of them.[8]**

She just wants to experience free and joyous love, like Dalma's ladies.

One of the great gifts of patriarchy to women was the feminine mystique, thus described by George Gilder:

> **This intuition of mysterious new realms of sexual and social experience, evoked by the body and spirit of woman, is the source of male love and ultimately marriage. In evoking marriages love renders the woman in a way transparent: the man sees through her, in a vision freighted with sexual desire, to the child they might have together.[9]**

Gilder understands the idea of Briffault's Law—that the male must supply the female with a benefit if he hopes to associate with her:

---

[7] *Re-Making Love*, p. 71.
[8] *It Changed My Life*, p. 239.
[9] *Men and Marriage*, p. 14.

This vision imposes severe social conditions, however. For it is a child that he might have only if he performs a role: only if he can offer, in exchange for the intense inner sexual meanings she imparts, an external realm of meaning, sustenance, and protection in which the child could be safely born.

He fails to see, however, that society is failing to create the supports which will allow the male to perform his role and be an equal participant in reproduction:

In the man's desire, conscious or unconscious, to identify and keep his progeny is the beginning of love. In a civilized society, he will not normally be able to claim his children if they are born to several mothers. He must choose a particular woman and submit to her sexual rhythms and social demands if he is to have offspring of his own.

But if he chooses a particular woman by marrying her he has only a forty percent chance of having offspring with her,[10] since he faces a sixty percent divorce rate and the assurance that the judge will award custody of his children to his ex-wife. Gilder understands that all societies are built on the tie between parents and offspring. But whereas biology informs the female that her tie is dependable in any sort of society with any sort of sexual arrangements, and that accordingly women need not have the long-term sexual horizons Gilder claims for them, both biology and experience inform the male that his tie is precarious and requires that he both take long-term views and also create a society which guarantees his role by guaranteeing the legitimacy and inalienability of his children. American men are now discovering that this guarantee, once dependable, has been removed and that society is abandoning the male kinship system and returning to matriarchy. It is returning likewise to the patterns of short-term, compulsive sexuality which Gilder associates with males, but which are in fact associated with matriarchy and savagery, with Indian reservations, ghettos and the barnyard. "The central truth of marriage," says Gilder is "that it is built on sex roles."[11] Gilder also knows that while the female role is a fact of nature, the male role is a social creation, which society must support. Our society refuses that support and Gilder goes along with society's refusal:

[H]e is sexually inferior. If he leaves, the family may survive without him. If she leaves, it goes with her. He is readily replaceable; she is not. He can have

---

[10]It was about fifty percent when Gilder wrote.
[11] *Men and Marriage*, p. 14.

a child only if she acknowledges his paternity; her child is inexorably hers....The man's role in the family is thus reversible; the woman's is unimpeachable and continues even if the man departs.[12]

No, no, and no. Gilder is describing and uncritically accepting the female kinship system. The male kinship system—patriarchy—rests on the following contrary principle, stated by (though protested by) John Stuart Mill:

They are by law *his* children.[13]

Gilder can't take this seriously and supposes no one else can. But the rejection of this principle is what the whole sexual crisis is about—it's really a conflict over the kinship system. It is only a slight exaggeration to say that the law in patriarchal society exists to make fathers heads of families—for imposing patriarchy. It is the law's betrayal of the family by its failure to do this which has created the existing sexual mess. Lawmakers and judges get things backwards: they suppose that a biological fact requires their services and a social creation such as fatherhood does not. Their mistake is why we have a sixty percent divorce rate, why our families are in ruins.

Gilder tries to blame men for the existing mess, accusing them of disloyalty to marriage. Men do not initiate three-quarters of divorce actions. Men do not write books with titles like *The Good Divorce*. They do not proclaim, with Ehrenreich, Hess and Jacobs, that "the symbolic importance of female chastity is rapidly disappearing....It is not only that women came to have more sex, and with a greater variety of partners, but they were having it on their own terms, and enjoying it as enthusiastically as men are said to."[14]

Kathleen Hall Jamieson quotes Supreme Court Justices O'Connor, Kennedy and Souter's defense of abortion: "The ability of women to participate equally in the economic and social life of the Nation has been facilitated by their ability to control their reproductive lives," and comments: "At issue is whether women will be able to decide whether and when to conceive and carry to term. When women have that option, enshrined in law, and accessible without financial risk or social stigma,

---

[12] *Men and Marriage*, p. 13.
[13] J. S. Mill, *The Subjection of Women* (Cambridge, MA: M.I.T. Press, 1970; original publication, 1869), p. 32.
[14] *Re-Making Love*, p. 2.

the hold of this bind will have been broken."[15] Broken for the woman, but her husband will bear a fivefold greater risk of divorce and loss of his children, a risk that can only be removed by a guarantee of father custody.

The family must be stabilized. Society cannot live with a sixty percent divorce rate and a thirty percent illegitimacy rate. Feminists think it can. The Annex to this book, the frenzy of the Greek women worshipers of Dionysus (page 65), Dr. Mary Jane Sherfey's warning that all women are potential nymphomaniacs who must be controlled by rigid family bonds if civilization is to exist (page 309)—these things prove the naturalness of the yearning of many women to be liberated and promiscuous, a yearning which only patriarchal socialization keeps them from acknowledging. They are convinced that the feminist movement will bring about their liberation by altering the kinship system from patriarchy to matriarchy, thus freeing them to be as sexually indiscriminate as other mammalian females.

THE BIRMINGHAM LADIES

Patriarchy requires women to accept sexual regulation. Feminism requires them to reject it. Feminist Lynn Segal has recorded a significant episode in women's conflict to achieve this rejection. Here is how the conflict between the two kinship systems appears to feminists:

> [T]here was also, by this time [early 1980s], an equally strong belief that women's own sexuality was "crippled" and "denied" by men's imposition of "compulsory heterosexuality." The turning point in the adoption of this new feminist analysis of sexuality in Britain was when the Birmingham National Women's Liberation Conference in 1978 passed (against such fierce opposition that it terminated all future national conferences) the motion to make "the right to define our sexuality the over-riding demand of the women's movement, preceding all other demands. Men's sexual domination of women, which prevented the emergence of women's self-defined sexuality, was now being formally accepted as the pivot of women's oppression. A prevailing "political lesbian" or sexual separatist ideology was growing stronger within the women's movement....The old feminist message that "the personal is political" had been inverted to become "the political is personal" and the personal is sexual.[16]

---

[15]Kathleen Hall Jamieson, *Beyond the Double Bind* (New York: Oxford University Press, 1995), p. 61.
[16]Lynn Segal, *Is the Future Female?* (New York: Peter Bedrick Books, 1987), p. 96. See page 82 for other women who dislike their maternal functions. And see the Annex.

There is no indication whether this self-defining of women's sexuality is outside marriage (where nobody ever denied it to women, though such unchaste women were formerly de-classed) or within marriage, which would wreck the family and the patriarchal system and deny to women the right to enter a contract to share their reproductive lives with men. Probably these women are unaware of the difference. Men, to whom the difference is crucial, will either continue permitting the de-regulation of sexuality and the destruction of patriarchy or they will enforce father custody. It remains to be seen whether men will awaken to the necessity of father custody in time.

"*The* over-riding demand of the women's movement, preceding all other demands." These Birmingham women understood the reality behind the feminist movement: it is a war against patriarchy. Women's refusal to accept sexual regulation means a refusal to make a meaningful contract of marriage at the time of life when they are young and nubile and when their bargaining power is greatest. Their refusing regulation means that they give to men the right not only to be promiscuous themselves but to discard older wives for younger women. A bad deal for women.

Ms. Hoggett (page 21) may suppose that there is no difference between marriage and shacking-up, that the law has—REALLY— "adopted principles for the protection of children and dependent spouses which could be made equally applicable to the unmarried"—in other words Mom and "her" children are protected by Dad's obligation to perform forced labor for Mom even if Mom performs no services for Dad. But the "principles" to which Ms. Hoggett refers are incapable of providing equally well for women and children. These principles have demoralized countless men and made them underachievers, unwilling or unable to provide for families. They are undermining marriage, returning society to the female kinship system, creating the feminization of poverty and herding children into it.

ADRIENNE RICH AND PRESIDENT CLINTON

Lesbian feminist Adrienne Rich turns down an award from President Clinton, blaming him for "his lack of political convictions" in refusing "to protect poor women and children" from poverty.[17] Most of

---

[17]*Los Angeles Times*, 13 July, 1997.

these women and children are poor thanks to Ms. Hoggett's "principles"—because the women have rejected patriarchy by breeding fatherless children or making them fatherless by divorce. Ms. Rich wants President Clinton to perform as father-surrogate for these poor women and children, which he is incapable of doing, however much he wants the women's vote. The kids need fathers, and placing them in their fathers' custody would enable them to be fathers and enable the mothers to get jobs. There is no realistic substitute for patriarchy—for letting fathers have families, letting them participate meaningfully in the biological, social, and spiritual continuity of the race. Human evolution has reached the point where fathers have become necessary if society is not to ghettoize itself. Ms. Rich doesn't want to understand this because it means society must accept "compulsory heterosexuality" as normative and she wants to get rid of compulsory heterosexuality along with patriarchy. It's to be hoped that heterosexuality and patriarchy are here to stay—but this will require placing the most powerful bond in nature— that between the mother and her offspring—on the side of family stability by guaranteeing fathers custody of children. It worked in the nineteenth century. It will work today and nothing else will.

CLAIMING VICTIMHOOD

"There is," says lesbian feminist Lillian Faderman, "a good deal on which lesbian-feminists disagree....But they all agree that men have waged constant battle against women, committed atrocities or at least injustice against them, reduced them to grown-up children, and...a feminist ought not to sleep in the enemy camp."[18] This claiming of victimhood is to be understood as a cover for claiming the right to reject patriarchal socialization. No women were ever less victimized than American women at the time feminists launched their movement. After World War II, wrote Margaret Mead in 1959, "something did happen to men as fathers. The GIs came home to be the best fathers—from the standpoint of their young children—that any civilized society has ever known."[19] They also created the greatest prosperity any society has ever known. This was prior to the unleashing of the sexual revolution, which,

---

[18]Lillian Faderman, *Surpassing the Love of Men: Romantic Friendship and Love Between Women from the Renaissance to the Present* (New York: William Morrow, 1981), p. 413; quoted in Ira Reiss, *An End to Shame: Shaping Our Next Sexual Revolution* (Buffalo: Prometheus Books, 1990), p. 102.
[19]*New York Times Magazine*, 10 May, 1959; cited in David Blankenhorn, *Fatherless America: Confronting Our Most Urgent Social Problem* (New York: Basic Books, 1995), p. 106.

as Ehrenreich, Hess and Jacobs inform us (truly) was a revolution in the sexual behavior of women.

"A feminist ought not to sleep in the enemy camp." In primitive matriarchal society this goal is achieved by *exogamy*, which will be discussed in Chapter XI and which is thus interpreted by Sjöö and Mor:

> **In the early small kin-group structures, the custom of exogamy had led women to take mates from outside the mother-clan, so the childbearing women were always the cohesive group within the community—their mates tended to be visitors, blood-strangers to the matrifocal group.[20]**

Elise Boulding tells us that "Evidence from some of the earliest [Neolithic] village layouts suggests that adults lived in individual huts, women keeping the children with them. Marriage agreements apparently did not at first entail shared living quarters....He could easily be sent away if he didn't please his wife, or his wife's mother. Older men (and sometimes young men) would have a thin time if their wives sent them away and they could not persuade any other woman to take them in."[21]

Just like the Washington, D. C. ghetto, where Charmaine tells the father of her twins to get out of her house. Just like sixty percent of today's marriages, where wives hire lawyers at their husbands' expense to have a divorce court judge like Robert Noland do the same.

It is to prevent this female exercise of power that patriarchy makes the father the head of the household and strengthens his family ties. Exogamy minimizes the father's ties to his family. Women like it; it permits them to be unchaste, to reject patriarchy and sexual regulation, to make the exiled boyfriends sexually second-class citizens. More about this in Chapter XI.

According to Bruno Bettelheim, all men's initiation rites were originally based on men's desire to imitate, to participate in, women's mysteries—menstruation and childbirth, overwhelming magic events (magic because of their periodicity as well as their blood-power). "*Nowhere*," say Sjöö and Mor, "can we find any rites or mysteries in which women have tried to imitate a male process or function; this alone

---

[20]Sjöö and Mor, p. 184.
[21]Elise Boulding, *The Underside of History* (Boulder, Colorado: Westview Press, 1976), p. 119.

tells us about the source of original *mana* or power. All blood rituals derive from the female blood of menstruation and childbirth."[22]

The feminine mystique. At the level of biology men envy women. It is the genius of patriarchy to put this envy to work, to use it to make men overachievers and producers of wealth and civilization. In a successful patriarchal culture, such as ours formerly was during the era of the Feminine Mystique, this creativity and productivity of males became so spectacular that the envy was reversed and feminists like Betty Friedan told women they should envy men, emulate male-style achievement and not just "live through their bodies."[23] So now we *do* have "women trying to imitate male process or function"—lady soldiers, lady policepersons, lady firepersons making themselves at least as ridiculous as males practicing *couvade*.[24] The intrusion by females into the Citadel and the Virginia Military Institute is a very feminine attempt to prove that "Women are not inferior." Males are forbidden to laugh at them.

Feminists Sjöö and Mor, unlike Ms. Friedan, believe that women ought not to imitate men and *should* live through their bodies. "For over two thousand years," they say,

Western biblicized women have been undergoing conditioning out of our natural powers and wisdoms; we grow up learning to disregard the effects of our own rhythms, which are cyclic like the moon's, the tides, the seasons. We learn the habits of ignoring them, denying them, trying to forget or overcome them, as we live under the rule of the man (without and within), who conceives of time as something that can be ordered and processed in mental-mechanical categories, regardless of the body's or the earth's phases.[25]

Talk about the feminine mystique! "Women's menstrual blood," they say,

always was, always is of the essence of the creative power of the Great Mother. Blood is the physical counterpart of the mystical life force spiraling

---

[22]Sjöö and Mor, loc cit.

[23]*The Feminine Mystique*, p. 140.

[24]Webster's New International, 2d ed.: "A custom, among primitive peoples in many parts of the world, in accordance with which when a child is born the father takes to his bed as if he himself had suffered the pains of childbirth, cares for the child, or submits himself to fasting and purification." Feminists resent the idea of women's being deemed "unclean" after childbirth and needing to go through purification (the "churching of women") before being re-admitted to the congregation. This uncleanness is part of the feminine mystique which generates male awe and is therefore imitated in *couvade*.

[25]Sjöö and Mor, p. 351.

throughout the cosmos, nourishing the universe, sustaining its breathing in and out, its manifestations and dissolutions....[W]e now have no menstrual ceremony of any kind. Menstruation is just each woman's private affliction, or annoyance; it has no positive value or function. We cannot withdraw into contemporary menstrual huts, to listen to our bodies, minds, and needs, to establish contact with our cyclic and primal cosmic selves, to experience ourselves as sacred animals.[26]

Ms. Friedan's pitch was the opposite: "Don't you want to be more than an animal?" A better way to spend a life, she tells her readers, is "mastering the secrets of the atoms or the stars, composing symphonies, pioneering a new concept in government or society...splitting atoms, penetrating outer space, creating art that illuminates human destiny, pioneering on the frontiers of society."[27]

"Men know that women are an overmatch for them," said Dr. Johnson. Hypergamy (women marry up, men marry down) and the feminine mystique give them a status which men must earn, ordinarily by work and self-discipline and high achievement. This is why men earn more money than women. Let's say it again: The male's willingness to earn something he can offer the female in exchange for her sexual loyalty is what creates families, creates the wealth of society, and its stability. Patriarchal civilization depends on the male's ability to buy a woman's sexual loyalty. Too many men today lack this ability and remain underachievers ("*Me?* Marry *him?*"). "Marrying a man with an unstable work history or low wages is not a good formula for avoiding welfare," say Christopher Jencks and Kathryn Edin. "More than half the women who marry such a man can expect their marriage to end in divorce and to collect little child support."[28]

Patriarchal civilization also depends on society's ensuring that the contract binding the woman's sexual loyalty to the man's economic loyalty is enforceable. The law presently permits the woman to rob the man of his money card on the grounds that it is less essential than the woman's motherhood card and that she is accordingly privileged to

---

[26]Sjöö and Mor, p. 186. Employers should perhaps be made to provide time for this withdrawal to menstrual huts?
[27]*The Feminine Mystique*, pp. 247, 239.
[28]"Do Poor Women Have a Right to Bear Children?" in *The American Prospect*, Winter, 1995.

revoke her sexual loyalty. This is how matriarchy is created—when the woman can love "freely and joyously," where she is in control of her own sexuality and need not share it with one man in a stable marriage.

V) THE ASHERAH

THE CONFLICT OF THE KINSHIP SYSTEMS

In Old Testament times, the struggle to impose the patriarchal system was projected into the conflict of religions in Palestine, a conflict between the older worship of the Great Mother and the newer worship of Yahweh or Jehovah. According to Bishop Spong,

> **Yahweh's principal rival was identified most frequently in the Bible by the name Baal. Baal was the male consort to the female deity Asherah. The religion of Asherah-Baal was a nature religion—a fertility cult tied to the cycles of the seasons and the fecundity of the soil and womb. This goddess-god couple was worshiped in local shrines with explicitly sexual liturgies that included both male and female prostitutes....Baal worship...was intensely sexual, with the vital power of reproduction honored as the source of life. In the Yahwist tradition the masculinity of God was all important—Yahweh had created nature and was the Lord of nature.[1]**

This is untrue, and Bishop Spong knows it to be untrue. The Bible nowhere represents God as having gender, as a sexual being like the Great Mother. Bishop Spong speaks of "the biblical insistence on the totally masculine nature of God and the corresponding assignment of divine (i.e., male) prerogatives to men, who alone, the myth argues, are created in the image of this God."[2] God's image, in which humanity is created, is not male but *male and female* (Genesis 1:27; 5:1-2). It is not the masculinity, but the asexuality or androgyny of God which is emphasized. This is in fundamental contrast to the Great Mother who was *really* sexist, as Rosalind Miles explains: "We think today of a number of goddesses, all with different names—Isis, Juno, Demeter—and have forgotten what, 5000 years ago, every schoolgirl knew; no matter what name or guise she took there was only one God and her name was woman."[3]

The female deity [says Spong] was identified with nature and sought to call people into harmony with nature.

---

[1] Spong, pp. 119f.
[2] Spong, p. 125.
[3] Miles, p. 20.

Part of this harmony has been described by Ms. Miles: "the immortal mother always takes a mortal lover, not to father her child but essentially in exercise and celebration of her womanhood."[4]

The female kinship system had the support of religion. The reproductive unit was female-headed, as in today's ghettos, a sexual imbalance against which the patriarchal religious system of Yahweh directed itself:

> Given the intense rivalry of these two traditions, it stands to reason that the Hebrew Bible, written by the Yahwists, would have an overwhelmingly male bias. If the followers of Yahweh were engaged in a struggle to destroy the fertility goddess, who was Yahweh's primary rival, would they not be prone to denigrate any value or contributions that might be associated with a female deity? Would not women, vital to a fertility religion as representatives of the mother goddess, also be devalued by the Yahwist tradition? This is exactly what happened, and it is out of this struggle that the biblical writers adopted the pervasive anti-female bias that permeates every page of their Scriptures. This anti-female bias not only won the day among the Hebrews but also passed uncritically into Christianity. Through Christianity that male bias has spread throughout the Western world.[5]

Bishop Spong asks "Does this sexist prejudice in the Bible reflect the mind of God?" He answers by appealing to the opposite sexist prejudice of the Stone Age and early civilizations:

> Anthropologists seem certain that the first deity worshiped by human beings was a goddess, not a god. Reverence was given to the deity as the mother of all things living, and she was identified with the earth or the soil....The primary analogy by which these creatures understood human life was sexual, and for that reason the woman, the obvious bearer of the new life, was primary....Men were quite secondary. Out of the womb of the earth mother came plants and the other gifts of life. Into the womb of the earth mother at burial went her children and her products; the vital life force of the divine mother had ceased to be present in them. Because the connection between sexual intercourse and childbirth had not yet been discerned, the women of the tribe held the real power.[6]

"Women held power." "Men were quite secondary." Talk about sexism. Bishop Spong has no objection to the sexism of the rival matriarchal religion he writes about, where "God was conceived in

---

[4]Miles, p. 25.
[5]Spong, p. 120.
[6]Spong, p. 121.

primarily female images,"[7] and he doesn't want his readers to know
about the Great Mother's unladylike behavior, thus described by Ms.
Miles:

> **In her darkest incarnation the bad mother did not simply wait for people to
> die, but demanded their deaths. The Persian Ampusa, her worshippers
> believed, cruised about the world in a blood bubble looking for something to
> kill. Here is the Hindu Great Mother Kali:**
>
> > **She is luminous-black. Her four limbs are outstretched and the hands
> > grasp two-edged swords, tools of disembowelment, and human
> > heads. Her hands are blood-red, and her glaring eyes red-centered,
> > and her blood-red tongue protrudes over huge pointed breasts,
> > reaching down to a round little stomach. Her yoni is large and
> > protuberant. Her matted, tangled hair is gore-stained and her fang-
> > like teeth gleam. There is a garland of skulls about her neck; her
> > earrings are the images of dead men and her girdle is a chain of
> > venomous snakes.[8]**

These Mother Goddesses go by different names, but they are all
really one, "the female deity...identified with nature [who seeks] to call
people into harmony with nature." They all reject the "overwhelming
male bias" of the new God Yahweh. In Canaan her consort Baal was
worshipped with "horrible orgies of unrestrained sensuality"[9] and the
invasion of this worship into the temples where Yahweh was worshipped
explains the "sexist" prejudice which Bishop Spong complains of.[10]

Ms. Miles continues:

> **Overemphasis on the good mother, procreative and nurturing, also denied the
> bad mother, her dangerous, dark and destructive opposite.... Wedded as we are
> to an all-loving, all-forgiving stereotype of motherhood, it is at first sight
> difficult to reconcile [the] terrifying image of bad mother with the good. But
> both "life" and "death" sides of the Goddess come together without strain in
> her primary aspect, which is in fact not motherhood pure and simple, but her
> sexuality. As her primary sexual activity she created life; but in sex she
> demanded man's essence, his self, even his death.[11]**

---

[7]Spong, p. 121.
[8]Quoting Allen Edwardes, *The Jewel in the Lotus*, pp. 58f.
[9]W. Robertson Smith, *The Old Testament in the Jewish Church* (London: Adam and Charles Black,
1892), p. 350.
[10]A similar invasion of Bishop Spong's own church is described in *Penthouse* magazine, December,
1996. See below, p. 251.
[11]Rosalind Miles, *The Woman's History of the World* (New York: Harper and Row, 1988), pp. 23f.

Bishop Spong makes his pitch to feminists and homosexuals, so he has no reason to emphasize these not-so-nice things.

Ms. Miles again:

> Here again the true nature of the Goddess and her activities have fallen victim to the mealymouthed prudery of later ages. Where referred to at all, they are coyly labeled "fertility" rituals, beliefs or totems, as if the Great Goddess selflessly performed her sexual obligations solely in order to ensure that the earth would be fruitful. It is time to set the historical record straight. The fruitfulness of crops and animals was only ever a by-product of the Goddess's own personal sexual activity. Her sex was hers, the enjoyment of it hers, and as all these early accounts of her emphasize, when she had sex, like any other sensible female, she had it for herself.

Sexual promiscuity, in other words, was part of the matriarchal system, and this had the consequence of cutting men off from meaningful participation in reproduction: "men were quite secondary." As Judge Noland tells us, children belong with their mother. The only way men can get themselves into the act is if every mother is a wife and marriage is a binding contract. Today's feminists fight against allowing marriage to have this meaning—or much meaning at all: a woman has the right to control her sexuality regardless of contract. Too bad the divorce courts agree with this. This is the difference between patriarchy, which allows children to have fathers, and matriarchy, which permits Mom at her pleasure to get the father out of *her* house and let her boyfriends in. "The suddenness with which marriage has been overthrown," says Maggie Gallagher, "is breathtaking."[12] This means the suddenness with which the male kinship system has been overthrown.

> In every culture [continues Ms. Miles], the Goddess has many lovers. This exposes another weakness in our later understanding of her role as the Great Mother. That puts a further constraint on the idea of the good mother....[S]he was always unmarried and never chaste. Among the Eskimos, her title was "She Who Will Not Have a Husband."[13]

"Women," says Spong, "are discovering they are free to leave a destructive marriage." Also free to leave a boring marriage in which no fault is even alleged. Also free to take the Old Boy's children, his home and his paycheck and to create a destructive female headed household

---

[12]Gallagher, *The Abolition of Marriage*, p. 5.
[13]Miles, p. 24.

generating the pathology listed on pages 12ff. She is free to leave the patriarchal system and enter the matriarchal system with her children. Patriarchy denies women this freedom because abundant experience proves they misuse it. Their ordinary motive is not to escape a destructive marriage but to escape from sexual regulation. This is the significance of the most emphasized feminist slogan: "a woman's right to control her own sexuality." Consider the fury with which the Birmingham women make this demand. Glance at the Annex of this book. Perpend Barbara Ehrenreich's words: "[F]or women as well as men, sex is a fundamentally lawless creature, not easily confined to a cage."[14]

It must be confined to a cage if children are to have two parents, which overwhelming evidence shows to be the best arrangement for them. Society's major purpose, compared to which everything else is almost trivial, is the proper procreation, rearing and socializing of children. Spong says he is "no longer willing to acknowledge the claim that morality has been frozen in an era that primarily served the dominant male."[15] It primarily served those whom Spong never bothers to mention—children. Male dominance is universal[16] and male headship of families is made necessary by the marginality of the male role. Nature formerly made the female the head of the reproductive unit but social heredity, we now realize, has in the human species become a part of nature. This is a new evolutionary development and women don't like it, don't like to be deprived of their monopoly of parenthood. Patriarchy has given us civilization, has transformed the world for the better. Ms. Boulding may express her admiration of the freedom of Indian squaws, but she wouldn't care to live on a reservation. Feminists admire the self-sufficiency of black matriarchs, but they wouldn't like to live in the ghetto. Their preference for the lifestyle which creates the ghetto is the reason why they must be regulated, why "He shall rule over thee," why fathers must have custody of children in divorce. Patriarchy must deny women the freedom to ghettoize society.

"Does the group of people for whom marriage is an asset," asks Spong, "have the right to impose the standard that enhances their lives upon those people who have chosen a different path?"[17] *Yes.* The group

---

[14]Quoted on the dust wrapper of Heyn's *Erotic Silence of the American Wife.*
[15]Spong, p. 66.
[16]As Steven Goldberg shows in *The Inevitability of Patriarchy.*
[17]Spong, p. 65.

of people for whom marriage is an asset are most importantly children. Children must not be made the victims of parents, especially mothers, using the magic-wand argument, "It's better for the kids to go through a divorce than to live in a home where parents fight all the time." In most cases the home with fighting is better for children than the female headed home which replaces it. This is the view of both children themselves and of sociologists. Social policy, like laws, ought to be framed for the general case, not the hardship case. Hard cases make bad law and bad social policy. "Children," say Wallerstein and Blakeslee, "can be quite content even when their parents' marriage is profoundly unhappy for one or both partners. Only one in ten children in our study experienced relief when their parents divorced."

> **[Children] have a very primitive, very real fear of being left on their own. A child's immediate reaction to divorce, therefore, is fear. When their family breaks up, children feel vulnerable, for they fear that their lifeline is in danger of being cut. Their sense of sadness and loss is profound. A five-year-old enters my office and talks about divorce with the comment "I've come to talk about death." Children feel intense loneliness....Children do not perceive divorce as a second chance, and this is part of their suffering. They feel that their childhood has been lost forever.[18]**

Women are free to leave a destructive marriage "without ruining *their* lives." Because women hate patriarchy and because the legal system rewards them with custody and everything else the chivalrous judge can screw the husband for, women choose divorce more often than men; but it is a choice which still causes not only their children but themselves a lot of suffering because, as Wallerstein and Blakeslee say, "divorce places an extraordinary if not terrifying burden on mothers."[19] But regardless, they are too much concerned with their own lives, too little concerned with their children's. "In our study," they say,

> **about 10 percent of the children had poor relationships with both parents during the marriage. This number jumped to a shocking 35 percent of children at the ten-year-mark. These children were essentially unparented in the postdivorce decade, and in fact many of them were called upon to take care of their parents.[20]**

---

[18]*Second Chances*, pp. 12f.
[19]*Ibid.*, p. 187.
[20]*Ibid.*, p. 200.

Hatred of patriarchy leads many women to suppose shaking it off through divorce means they will be better parents:

Unfortunately, many women in unhappy marriages assume that divorce will enable them to become happier, better mothers. But I find little evidence of that. Mothering does not improve by virtue of divorce. In only a few families did the mother-child relationship in the postdivorce family surpass the quality of the relationship in the failing marriage. As a matter of record, the opposite occurred more frequently. At the ten-year mark, over a third of the good mother-child relationships have deteriorated, with mothers emotionally or physically less available to their children.[21]

Bishop Spong would rather not hear such facts, because he knows feminists don't want to hear them, and because he is taking a ride on the discontents of these feminists. "Further," he says, "women who want children may opt to raise them as a single parent. Marriage is no longer the universal vocation."[22] This is the feminist party line: rebellion against patriarchy and the Legitimacy Principle. "Should they be forced by the expectations of society into marriage for the sake of companionship and for the gratification of sexual needs?" Yes, they should. Otherwise they deny their children fathers and they deny higher status to "good" women who accept regulation and give men a meaningful role. Spong is writing of educated and economically independent women who "have it all" and therefore need no husbands. Briffault's Law makes them unmarriageable unless the man has assurance of custody. Without this assurance, he is likely to be uncommitted and irresponsible. With it, the mother becomes marriageable and is motivated to be responsible, to accept the two-parent patriarchal system necessary for children.

Here's feminist Judy Mann, who rejects patriarchy:

In recent years, much of the anti-feminist drumbeat has been the attempt to regulate women's reproductive freedom.[23]

Not just recent years. This has always been the central idea of patriarchy: without the regulation of women's reproductive freedom there is no responsible male role and society reverts to matriarchy.

---

[21]Wallerstein and Blakeslee, p. 187.
[22]Spong, p. 64.
[23]Judy Mann, *The Difference: Growing Up Female in America* (New York: Time Warner, 1994), pp. 12f.

> Somewhere in adolescence [says Ms. Mann], our daughters are silenced....They become uncomplaining and compliant. They learn to wait. Carol Gilligan and her associates describe how girls drive their perceptions of reality underground. The work of these researchers evokes a powerful image of a turbulent subterranean river in women's psyches while their surface behavior adapts to the social imperatives to "be nice" and not to be "rude" or "disruptive."

This turbulent subterranean river is always working to undermine the patriarchal system, to get men out of the house so women and girls can be free. But as feminism brings this counterforce to the surface there is a problem with the reaction of the threatened male:

> All-pervasive cultural influences such as rap music trash women and celebrate male dominance over them. But how many adult women have listened to this music and found out what our daughters and sons are listening to? How many of us have had the energy at the end of a working day to vet the musical tastes of children? I am speaking of both boys and girls here for a very good reason: The recurring themes of violence against women in this music send a destructive message of permission to boys as well as a message of submission to girls.

It is a crude message, but it comes from the heart. We must pay attention to it.

> Consider the lyric from the rock group Guns 'N Roses in which they sing of murdering a former lover and then burying her in the backyard so they will not miss her. Should anyone be shocked that a fourteen-year-old boy who listens to sadistic lyrics about women turns into a fraternity house gang-bang rapist a few years later?

A lot of male energy is mis-channeled into hostility. Better it should be put to work to create families and pursue the arts of peace— but that would be patriarchy.

> Violent themes against women are a Hollywood staple. Violence against women is the norm on many television shows and rental videos. Our daughters and sons still come of age listening to an obbligato of primitive violence directed against women. Would we tolerate this kind of culturally sanctioned violence against African-Americans?[24]

---

[24]Mann, p. 14.

One wonders whether Ms. Mann has read *From Reverence to Rape,* describing the treatment of American women in the movies coincident with the rise of feminism. Aside from which much of such violence comes *from* African-Americans, males who have been denied a more civilized outlet for their energies, a fact which feminists (and their hangers-on like Bishop Spong) don't wish to be told. These African-American males are the most obvious victims of the matriarchal system—though with the progress of feminism they are being joined by "the coming white underclass."

"Mandatory economic dependency for women, as a class, has ended," says Bishop Spong. There is no feminist movement to abolish mandatory support obligations on ex-husbands, however, nor is there anything mandatory about getting married. It was formerly supposed to be mandatory to stay married—to keep marriage vows. Bishop Spong now assures women that this keeping of vows has become non-mandatory: a woman's vows need not be taken seriously. He imagines that this deprivation of bargaining power benefits women.

Shame and guilt have less influence on women's sexual behavior than they used to. A woman need worry less about her "reputation." But this means that her offer to share her reproductive life with a man is less valued. Formerly, her sexual loyalty was her principal offering, that which enabled her husband to have a family and her children to have a father. So Bishop Spong and the feminists who celebrate women's independence are de-valuing the most valuable thing a woman has to offer a man.

Betty Friedan tells her readers that "Women have outgrown the housewife role" and that more of them ought to want "a real function in our exploding society"—meaning more ought to have elitist careers.[25] "The main barrier to such growth in girls," says Ms. Friedan, "is their own rigid preconception of woman's role, which sex-directed educators reinforce, which they refuse either explicitly or by not facing their own ability, and responsibility to break through it."[26]

The main barrier, in other words, is not patriarchal oppression: "[A]ll the rights that would make women free in society, were won on paper long ago....I say the only thing that stands in women's way today is

---

[25]*Feminine Mystique,* pp. 308, 162.
[26]p. 163.

this false image, this feminine mystique, and the self-denigration that it perpetuates. This mystique makes us try to beat ourselves down in order to be feminine, makes us deny or feel freakish about our own abilities as people. It keeps us from moving freely on the road that is open to us."[27]

Ms. Friedan's elitist feminism and Sjöö and Mor's ecofeminism agree on the grand goal, that women shall be sexually independent of men—which, however, leaves men in limbo and creates a matriarchal ghetto. This is progress.

The Bible has been called the most patriarchal book ever written. As pointed out above, it reflects the struggle between the two kinship systems, projected onto two religious systems, the patriarchal one worshiping the Hebrew god Jahweh or Jehovah, the matriarchal one worshiping the goddess Asherah and her consort Baal. "The *asherah*," say Sjöö and Mor,

> **was the Neolithic Goddess (Inanna-Ishtar, Astarte-Ashtoreth-Asherah) or the symbol of the Goddess. It was a conventionalized or stylized tree, perceived as she, and planted therefore at all altars and holy places. The *asherah* represented the Goddess as Urikittu, the green one, the Neolithic mother-daughter of all vegetation, of agricultural knowledge and abundance. Yahweh's absolute hostility to the *asherah* was the political hostility of the nomadic-pastoral Hebrew people, or their priesthood at least, to the settled matriarchal cultures and their Goddess beliefs. It became a psychological hostility to the entire living earth, doctrinalized in the biblical texts:**
>
> > You must completely destroy all the places where the nations you dispossess have served their gods: on high mountains, on hills, under a spreading tree. You must tear down their altars, smash their pillars, cut down their sacred poles [*asherahs*], set fire to the carved images of their gods, and wipe their name from that place. (Deuteronomy 7:5ff.)[28]

This is how the male kinship system made war against the female kinship system in Old Testament times. The target was not primarily altars, pillars and trees but the licentious worship associated with them, the anarchic female kinship system and its promiscuous, orgiastic and meaningless sexuality, the lifestyle which tried to keep sex shallow and merely recreational, an endless series of Saturday night bashes rather than the organizing principle of society which made stable families and

---

[27] *It Changed My Life*, pp. 62f.
[28] Sjöö and Mor, p. 269.

96

permanent fatherhood necessary. "The constant fight against matriarchal religion and custom," say Sjöö and Mor, "is the primary theme of the Old Testament. It begins in Genesis, with the takeover of the Goddess's Garden of Immortality by a male God, and the inversion of all her sacred symbols—-tree, serpent, moon-fruit, woman—into icons of evil."[29]

The war between the two kinship systems has never ended. There was a time before the war a few thousand years ago when Mom was in charge and Dad a mere boyfriend. The creation of patriarchy elevated the boyfriend to fatherhood and made fatherhood permanent. It was a turning point not just in history but in evolution. The human race was henceforth to be propagated by two parents rather than one or one-and-a-half. The male parent must be more than a boyfriend if children are not to be disadvantaged. Society must be organized to ensure that children have the second parent-—must be organized patriarchally.

Feminists want to change back to the matriarchal system. As Helen Diner says, "A free disposition over one's own person is an original right in a matriarchal society."[30] "The Great Mother," says Ms. Miles,

originally held the ultimate power—the power of the undisputed ruler, that of life and death. Where woman is the divine queen, the king must die. Mythologically and historically, too, the rampant sensuality of the Great Goddess and her taste for blood unite in the archaic but undisputed practice of the killing of the king. "King" is in fact an honorary title for the male chosen to have intercourse with the Queen-Goddess in a simple reenactment of the primal drama subsequently described by historians and anthropologists as "the sacred marriage," with the male "acting as divine consort" to the Goddess.

Making Mom the primary caregiver weakens the male provider role and produces the consequences noted on pages 12ff. It attacks one of patriarchy's traditional supports, religion. According to feminist Riane Eisler, what the religious right "would impose on us is a religious form of fascism in which the ultimate strong man is a wrathful divine father who countenances neither freedom nor equality [and] would also impose on us...strict and, if 'necessary,' violent control over women and women's

---

[29]Sjöö and Mor, pp. 264f.
[30]Helen Diner, *Mothers and Amazons* (New York, 1973, Anchor Books) p. 31.

sexuality, since this control is both a symbol and a linchpin for all other forms of domination and control."[31]

The control is seldom violent, but it is good PR to represent it as threatening to become so. The alternatives are accordingly said to be sexual fascism on the one hand (Chinese foot-binding, female circumcision, chadors) and on the other hand total sexual de-control of women. Ms. Eisler describes this alternative as follows:

> **But if we succeed in completing the cultural shift from a dominator to a partnership social and ideological organization, we will see a real sexual revolution—one in which sex will no longer be associated with domination and submission but with the full expression of our powerful human yearning for connection and for erotic pleasure.[32]**

This de-control, or "free love," or recreational sex is the motivator of the female kinship system, as the desire for families is the motivator of the male kinship system. It has, as Ms. Eisler says, its own religious dimension. In Old Testament times it provided the attraction of the Canaanite worship on the High Places, denounced by the Hebrew prophets ("horrible orgies"). It provides the attraction of Bangkok's brothels and the gay bath houses in San Francisco's Castro District. It was one of the attractions of early Christian Gnosticism. "Orgiastic sex rites," says homosexual Arthur Evans, "appeared among some Gnostics and scandalized traditional Christians. Roman authorities used these practices to discredit Christianity as a whole. Traditional Christians consequently condemned the Gnostics and denied any connection with them."[33]

In the fourth century Ms. Eisler's "real sexual revolution" was represented by Messalianism: "The Messalian doctrines were the extreme expression of the longing to comprehend mystical revelation through sensual experience."[34]

"Women were the chief priests of the old religion," says Evans. "The material substructure of the old religion was a matriarchal social

---

[31]*Sacred Pleasure*, p. 199.
[32]*Ibid.*
[33]Arthur Evans, *Witchcraft and the Gay Counterculture* (Boston: Fag Rag Books, 1978), p. 51.
[34]*Ibid.*, p.52, quoting Milan Loos, *Dualist Heresy in the Middle Ages* (The Hague: Martinus Nijhoff, 1974), p. 72.

system that reached back to the stone age."[35] "In Asia Minor," he continues,

> we find "the Great Mother of the Gods," who was associated with animals, sex and nature....Her priests were both women and men. The men castrated themselves, grew long hair, and wore the clothing of women....The Great Mother of the Gods was worshipped with sacred orgies. Participants of the rituals played flutes, castanets, cymbals, and drums, calling these the "strings of frenzy."...Homosexual and heterosexual acts of all kinds took place at these rituals. As one academic (a tight-assed homophobe) puts it, there were "revolting sensual rites, the presence of the hermaphroditic element."...A man who wanted to become a priest of the Great Mother attended the orgies, and in an ecstatic and frenzied trance, castrated himself....This castration was entirely voluntary, and was undertaken only by those who wished to be initiated as priests.[36]

It's all so beautiful, so meaningful. But does it create a stable society? The sexually marginal male will never be more than a drifter or a mere boyfriend unless society gives him a family to head, to channel his energies into. Ms. Eisler writes interminably about "partnership," but her term excludes the partnership essential to the patriarchal system, that which gives fathers their role, stable marriage.

She says:

> I should clarify that by sexual empathy, caring, responsibility, and respect I do not mean inflexible lifelong sexual bonds....[S]ex in lifelong marriages has all too often been marked by lack of respect, empathy, responsibility, and caring. And what we today call serial monogamy (that is, a series of committed relationships rather than a single exclusive relationship till death) along with a healthy amount of spontaneity and sexual experimentation, are not inconsistent with caring, empathic, and mutually responsible sexual relations.[37]

It goes without saying that in such "spontaneous" arrangements the mother retains custody of the children and the father retains responsibility to subsidize her. What Ms. Eisler describes is matriarchy. The objection to which is that it damages children and denies males a role. According to the National Health and Education Consortium,

---

[35] Evans, p. 79.
[36] Evans, p. 22.
[37] P. 200.

A majority of children from broken homes suffer from limited cognitive development and psychological and physiological disturbances, and are unable to form close attachments.[38]

According to Valerie Riches, Director of Family and Youth Concern, Oxford,

The fact is that the files of relevant government bodies are bulging with evidence that broken homes mean more battered children. Research has shown that it is 20 times more dangerous for a child if the natural parents cohabit rather than marry. It is 33 times more dangerous for a child to live with its natural mother and her boyfriend than with the natural parents in a marriage.[39]

"The sacred status of womanhood," says Ms. Miles,

"lasted for at least 25,000 years—some commentators would push it back further still, to 40,000 or even 50,000. In fact there was never a time at this stage of human history when woman was *not* special and magical."[40]

Mythologically, the ritual sacrifice of the young "king" is attested in a thousand different versions of the story. In these the immortal mother always takes a mortal lover, not to father her child (although children often result) but essentially in exercise and celebration of her womanhood. The clear pattern is of an older woman with a beautiful but expendable youth—Ishtar and Tammuz, Venus and Adonis, Cybele and Attis, Isis and Osirus....The lover is always inferior to the Goddess, mortal where she is immortal, young where she is ageless and eternal, powerless where she is all-powerful, and even physically smaller—all these elements combine in the frequent representation of the lover as the Goddess's younger brother or son. And always, always, he dies.

This is ancient history which we read about in *The Golden Bough.* It is also the eternal feminine, though since the triumph of patriarchy, it has gone underground and become the "enormous potential counterforce" always at work to undermine the male kinship system and to restore the female kinship system where Mom occupies the driver's seat and is "enormously in charge of her life."[41]

---

[38]*Los Angeles Times*, 17 December, 1996.
[39]*London Daily Telegraph*, 28 December, 1996.
[40]Miles, p. 21.
[41]Adrienne Rich's words. See page 264.

Historic survivals of the killing of the king [continues Ms. Miles] continued up to the present day. As late as the nineteenth century, the Bantu kingdoms of Africa knew only queens without princes or consorts—the rulers took slaves or commoners as lovers, then tortured and beheaded them after use....[W]hen God was a woman, all women and all things feminine enjoyed a higher status than has ever been seen since in most countries of the world.[42]

This is sexism. What a triumph for the new patriarchal system of Yahweh that it was able to deconstruct it and control the "rampant sexuality of the Great Goddess and her taste for blood"—*to put sex to work*, as the hydroelectric dam puts the power of the river to work. This is the great achievement of patriarchy, which is based on female chastity and meaningful marriage which enables men, hitherto marginal, to participate as equals in reproduction. The great achievement of women's liberation is to return to the unregulated sexuality of the Stone Age and the Canaanite High Places. This achievement has been made possible by the acceptance of female promiscuity ("a woman's right to control her own sexuality") and by the incomprehension of divorce court judges who mindlessly reiterate that "the children belong with their mother."

The Old Testament is the Jewish record of the patriarchal victory, which today's woman's liberation movement is reversing. "[W]hat does it mean," asks Bishop Spong,

"in the midst of a sexual revolution, when people call on the church and world to return to the sexual morality of the Bible? Both the religious and ethical directives of the Bible were formulated out of a patriarchal understanding of life, with the interests of men being primary. Are we willing to return to these destructive definitions of both men and women? Do we desire to hold up the biblical image of dominance and submission as the Christian model for male-female relations in our time?"

Emphatically, yes. The "enormous potential counterforce" of women's resistance to sexual regulation must be contained or there will be matriarchy and the pathology of the ghettos. "He shall rule over thee" because otherwise women will not submit to sexual law-and-order.

Throughout the course of evolution the female has headed the reproductive unit. But *human* evolution has reached the point where a second parent is necessary if the pathology of matriarchy is to be avoided. The father's role is the weak link in the family *biologically*—if

---

[42]Miles, p. 27.

biology is interpreted to exclude social heredity. The meaning of the patriarchal revolution is that social heredity has become part of biology and that the role of the father who transmits much of this social heredity must be stabilized by being given social, legal and religious support. This is why patriarchal society exists. Much of this support is artificial, even trivial, but the father needs all the help he can get. Hence male headship of families. Hence the transmission of the father's surname to the wife and children. Hence "Mr." Precedes "Mrs." on the envelope, followed by the husband's given name and not the wife's. And so forth—the things which feminists condemn as "oppression."

Male dominance is universal, and most women want their men to be more dominant, not less. According to the psychologist Karl Menninger for every woman who complains to her shrink that her man is a brute, there are a dozen who complain that he is a wimp—incapable of acting like a father who takes charge, accepts responsibility and gets things done.

"What does it mean to return to the sexual morality of the Bible?" It means putting a stop to the sexual revolution. It means restoring the stability of marriage—making it something more than cohabitation. It means giving children fathers who cannot be exiled by judges who haven't the foggiest notion of the suffering they inflict.

Bishop Spong asks,

"If the Bible has nothing more than the letter of literalism to offer to our understanding of human sexuality today, then I must say that I stand ready to reject the Bible in favor of something that is more human, more humane, more life giving, and, dare I say, more godlike. I do believe, however, that there is a spirit beneath the letter that brings the Bible forward in time with integrity."

In other words, forget the plain patriarchal message of the Bible and read into it the contemporary feminist flim-flam. After all, we are "in the midst of a sexual revolution." Why fight it? Bishop Spong points out correctly, that the Bible is filled with reflections of the ancient war between the old fertility religion and the newer patriarchal religion of Yahweh, and he points out some of the consequences of the victory of the latter:

A shift from the deification of the land to assigning man the responsibility for subduing it.

The dawning of human self-consciousness, of separation from the co-consciousness of savage mentality—-the beginning of human thought and therefore human history.

The achieving of a new level of humanity in which had replaced instinct as the primary motivator of human behavior.

Emergence of the ego that "dared to stand against...instinct."

Freedom from "total immersion in nature," symbolized by the journey of Abraham.

The understanding that the deity is not exclusively female, that God was no longer circumscribed by the reproductive processes of nature.

The creation of most of the major religious systems—"direct by-products of this process of re-definition."

The abolition of human sacrifice.

The regulation of female sexuality, which makes responsible male sharing in reproduction possible.

Emphasis on the cultural as opposed to the merely biological significance of religion.

An end to tribalism.

The origin of reflective thought and history.

Following this, Bishop Spong triumphantly asks whether "in the midst of a sexual revolution," we want to go back to *this*? Of course we do. The contemporary sexual revolution is undermining all these accomplishments, which is why we must get rid of it. Bishop Spong calls these accomplishments "destructive." They are destructive only of things which need to be destroyed: unregulated sexuality, fertility orgies, sacred prostitution, co-consciousness and mindless reduction of human life to the merely biological level where it functioned during the half million years of childhood known as the Stone Age. They are *constructive* of the patriarchal system, the greatest of all human creations, the great cultural fabric built on the firm biological foundation of female sexuality, once that sexuality is made to submit to the regulation that enables males to participate in it as equals.

Women's sexuality must be regulated because men must be made partners in reproduction. A glance at the Annex shows that women do not submit willingly to such regulation. Hence the joy of Ms. Heyn's adulteresses, their sense of release in getting rid of "those nice-girl games," of being re-born, of doing bad and feeling good, of feeling adult but not old in their affairs, rather than feeling old but not adult in their marriages. Hence the sixty percent divorce rate. Hence the books by feminists encouraging women to divorce.

Bishop Spong says "Divorce has become part of the cost that society must pay for the emancipation of women."[43] Women should not be emancipated; they should be regulated, as men should be. Emancipated women are divorce-prone, adultery-prone, likely (with present divorce arrangements favoring mother custody) to drag their children into the female kinship system and inflict its pathology on them. Emancipated women are ghettoizing the larger society as their black sisters have created the ghetto of the inner city.

"An early reversal of the high divorce rate," says Spong, "would require, I believe, suppression of the growing equality between the sexes."

"Equality" refers to men's superior earning ability: men earn more than women. President Clinton and his rabble of bureaucrats. campfollowers and hustlers, wants to buy the women's vote by *conferring* benefits upon women—making them "firepersons" and such foolishness.[44] Spong has the same idea. In patriarchy men earn more because *patriarchy puts sex to work to motivate men to earn more*. This is the genius of patriarchy: putting sex to work. Men have to earn more or they aren't in the running for the women. Men have to confer on women the benefits required by Briffault's Law—and keep conferring them.

---

[43]Spong, p. 64.
[44]"President Clinton and numerous women's and labor groups are supporting tougher enforcement. When he presents his budget Monday, Clinton will ask Congress for $14 million to hire more staff to enforce equal pay laws. Clinton has raised the pay equity issue several times recently…." (*Los Angeles Times*, 30 Jan., 1999)

Hypergamy (women marry up, men marry down) will make men losers if they can't offer their women a paycheck larger than their own—or if the woman can depend on the dear good judge to award her a slice of her ex-husband's paycheck along with custody of the children. Their greater earning is what gives men their role as family providers. In the ghettos, where women support themselves or are supported by Welfare State Feminism, women are promiscuous and men are roleless. Only men's superior earning power makes them winners—makes them able to supply their women with the benefits required by Briffault's Law. Clinton's and Spong's conferring "equality" on women makes men losers—makes women say "I don't need that man." Men's superior earning power is what stabilizes society. The judge's depriving men of this superior earning ability is what, more than anything else, destabilizes society by giving the judge rather than the father control over the father's paycheck. The absence of the father's superior earning power destroys the male role and creates the chaos of the ghettos and barrios. Men's greater earning power is why women marry them and form families. Women who earn as much as their husbands make poor wives, want few children or none, are divorce-prone and adultery-prone.

If Spong were asked to show that women living in a patriarchy are less than equal he would probably compare the earnings of women and men *within the patriarchy.* What he should compare is the living standards of women in the patriarchy and the living standards of women in the matriarchy, in a female-headed household—compare the living standard of wives which has been raised 73 percent by marriage with the living standard of ex-wives which has been lowered 73 percent by divorce. Spong thinks divorce contributes to the "growing equality between the sexes." Where is the equality for the woman facing the "feminization of poverty," for the woman tied to humiliating dependence on support payments from an ex-husband or from welfare? "Women with young children, according to Wallerstein and Blakeslee,

> **especially if they are driven into poverty by divorce, face a Herculean struggle to survive emotionally and physically. The stress of being a single parent with small children, working day shift and night shift without medical insurance or other backup, is unimaginable to people who have not experienced it. No wonder some women told us that they feel dead inside.[45]**

---

[45]Judith Wallerstein and Sandra Blakeslee, *Second Chances* (New York: Ticknor and Fields, 1989), p. 301.

A *wife* might claim she is entitled to "equality" on the grounds that her services to her husband were equal to those of him to her. An ex-wife can make no such claim. Her demands are based on her status as a Mutilated Beggar—and the like status she inflicts on her children thanks to automatic mother custody.

Woman's yearning to be back in the driver's seat is shown by the Annex to this book. The matriarchal forces will never give up their war against patriarchy, against evolution. There will always be feminists and their allies—sexual anarchists and homosexuals, ACLU types in the Law, Bishop Spong types in the Church, Kinsey types in schools and universities, Murphy Brown types in the media—making war against sexual law-and-order and the father-headed family. Today's feminism is to be understood as matriarchy's counterattack against patriarchy and the family. Its program is to sexually de-regulate women in the name of "equality," "pluralism," and "multiculturalism," to destroy the family and restore the female kinship system. The sixty percent divorce rate and the thirty percent illegitimacy rate means this program has already succeeded, most of its success having occurred in just the last three decades. The responsibility of patriarchy now is not just to hang on, but to reclaim its lost territory, to re-establish the family as the reproductive unit of society by re-establishing the father as its head.

In this war the enemy's primary weapon is female sexual disloyalty—adultery or divorce-with-mother-custody.

Dalma Heyn prefaces her book with the following passage from Hawthorne's *Scarlet Letter*.

[Hester] assured them, too, of her firm belief that, at some brighter period, when the world should have grown ripe for it, in Heaven's own time, a new truth would be revealed, in order to establish the whole relationship between man and woman on a surer ground of mutual happiness.

This surer ground will be supplied by the contemporary feminist/sexual revolution and its recognition of the naturalness of sexual promiscuity and the breeding of fatherless children. Thus will women regain the status they lost by giving up sole parenthood to share parenting with fathers. Free at last.

The era when Hawthorne was writing *The Scarlet Letter* was the era when Alexis de Tocqueville was visiting America and writing his classic *Democracy in America*, in which he said that "In America, a single woman can undertake a long journey in safety," as indeed Hester and Pearl do in Hawthorne's narrative. Today, now that feminism and the de-regulation of female sexuality have created the ghetto and are re-creating the larger society in the image of the ghetto—the brighter future Hester and Hawthorne and Ms. Heyn and feminists yearn for—a single woman cannot jog in Central Park in safety. If she tries, she may find herself beaten and gang-raped by a posse of fatherless punks who grew up in matriarchal homes created by the sexual de-regulation of their mothers.

"What we have here," says Ms. Heyn in her promotion of female sexual de-regulation,

is women saying again and again that their sexuality, which had been so disempowering inside the confines of conventional goodness [read: inside the patriarchal family] had, outside it, become empowering. They are saying that their love, inside marriage, had made them feel disconnected and devitalized, while outside it, in relationships they created for pleasure alone, they felt neither idealized nor debased. Their sexuality had "come alive" as surely and inexorably as they themselves had.[46]

For pleasure alone. Not for the proper procreation and socializing of children in two-parent homes. Ms. Heyn provides the explanation of women's hatred of the sexual regulation which patriarchy requires of them. They *empower* themselves by escaping from the patriarchal rules. Feminist psychologist Carol Tavris thinks women are victims of "socially imposed low self-esteem" by being taught to imagine that "whatever's wrong is women's fault—sick, diseased women at that. Until women begin to look outward to the roles, obligations and financial realities that keep them stuck instead of always looking inward to their own faults and failings, their low self-esteem is bound to continue. And so will comforting theories that blame women's problems on sickness rather than powerlessness."[47]

Ms. Heyn's solution for these women—adultery—is "empowering" because it makes women's sexuality "for pleasure alone," thus striking a

---

[46]P. 191.
[47]*Los Angeles Times*, 5 March, 1990.

deadly blow at procreative sex, the stability of families, the enemy, patriarchy. The Erotic Silence of the American Wife means her adultery.

Ms. Heyn cites Carolyn Heilbrun's *Writing a Woman's Life* as complaining that a woman's story ends with her wedding:

> **But examine the romance plot closely and you will see that after you cut to the chase—marriage—it is Mr. Right's story that continues, not our heroine's. After her implicit goal of becoming a wife is reached, her story is over. Once inside the little cottage, the moment after becoming a wife, as Carolyn Heilbrun points out, "the young women died as a subject, ceased as an entity," was left there languishing on the page, without a voice, hardly a heroine at all, relegated to a plot that cannot thicken. This story that goes nowhere for her is, nevertheless, the only plot written for a woman's life, just as happily ever after (that is, monogamous marriage) is the only ending that certifies her success as a woman in this society.[48]**

It is Mr. Right's story that continues. In other words maternity and woman's maternal functions are an anti-climax which interferes with Mom's making a *real* contribution to society such as men make, such as Mr. Right makes. Ms. Heyn thinks women might make a better contribution by forgetting their marriage vows—then they don't "die as a subject" but keep on having adventures, all the more fun if they are forbidden.

"The plot cannot thicken" because the plot makes very little sense apart from children and family, apart from the patriarchal system which gives it meaning. Elizabeth Adams, the Hollywood madam, defended her call girl business not on the grounds that it gave her girls an alternative to marriage—to dying as a subject and ceasing to be an entity—but because she was educating her girls so that they qualified themselves to make excellent marriages into the best families. Bernard Shaw made the same defense of Mrs. Warren's profession, which enabled the whore-mother to give her daughter a superior education and qualify herself for success in patriarchal society. Most of the call girls working for Sydney Biddle Barrows, the Mayflower Madam, "looked forward to being married someday."[49]

Ms. Heyn thinks it too bad that adulterous wives in literature come to a tragic end—Anna Karenina, Tess, Hester, Madame Bovary: "Unlike

---

[48]Heyn, P. 11.
[49]Sydney Biddle Barrows, *Mayflower Madam* (New York: Ivy Books, 1986), p. 205.

the classic tragic hero, whose pride or folly dictate a suffering which then redeems him, the tragic heroine need not have a fatal flaw to warrant her tragic ending: Tess is neither proud nor foolish; neither is Anna. Their suffering comes from without rather than from within; it arises out of the insistence of a social order rather than from any character defect."[50]

The social order is called patriarchy and it makes civilization possible. These adulterous women are violating its rules, designed to safeguard the family and the reproductive role of fathers—remote considerations, in feminist thinking, in comparison with their desire to get out of the patriarchal system and get back to the matriarchal system which de-regulates them.

It is highly advantageous to a woman to *be* a sex object and for society to have her be, for it is thus that men are motivated to be achievers and to create wealth and social stability and to benefit their children—and their wives. But the advantages can best be derived from a husband whose stable motivation (and therefore work performance) is assured. The focus on what sexual adventures the wife desires is irrelevant to the man's motivation—except as it works to undermine it. For a woman to seek sexual pleasure marks her as an easy lay, which is too threatening, too disruptive to patriarchy, which must channel male sexuality into marriage, thereby getting society's work done and giving children two parents and the best home environment. Society gets no work out of men (or women) by making *men* into sex objects. A woman cannot be motivated to support a family adequately because she loves a man or has a sexual adventure with one. But society can use the woman as a sex object to motivate a man to support a family, to pay taxes, to buy real estate, to create a stock portfolio—to contribute to society rather than disrupt it. It is for this reason that female sexuality must be regulated.

This regulation breaks down if the man loses control over his paycheck and loses custody of his children, as happens in the divorce court, or when the woman marries the state and lives off welfare and affirmative action benefits. Many women prefer this, and (this needs to be repeated) will accept a drastic lowering of their (and their children's) standard of living to gain this sexual freedom. Ehrenreich, Hess and

---

[50]P. 14.

Jacobs have been quoted on women's preference for even "penurious" sexual freedom over "marriage and dependence on one man."[51]

Virtually automatic mother custody explains most of women's divorce-proneness, the ongoing erosion of marriage and the plight of children, their sexual confusion, their miserable educational performance, their turning to violence and drugs. They see the destruction of so many families and fear they have little hope of families of their own. They fear commitment and their fear is realistic.

Feminists view the attaining of sexual independence for women as a proper object of social policy. But it would be a disaster for women—as well, of course, as for men and children. Women need reminders of how they benefit from patriarchy—how breaking its rules will result in economic suffering and loss of status. In spite of which, many women will choose to break the rules. Ms. Heyn tells of Amanda:

> **Amanda, living alone and talking about the "mess" she made of her life as a result of her affair, tries to figure out why she is not depressed about it:**

> **I'm alone. I'm not seeing either man. I have no money. And what I feel—I feel released. I know I should feel regret, but what I really feel is reborn.**

And Paula:

> **I did the worst thing in the world, the worst thing for a woman in this entire culture. And you know what? It was the best thing I ever did. It opened my eyes to so much...it opened my heart.**

The women began seeing everything "in color" and feeling more "alive."[52] This is the way women are—or anyway too many of them. This answers Freud's question, "What does a woman want?" Ms. Heyn thinks "that women don't really know what they want, or don't say what they need, or don't say what they mean, or don't mean what they say":

> **Those who have noticed the difficulty women have in speaking about what is most precious to them—love and sex—may also suggest that the silence is not cultural but inherent; that women, even when they know what they want, will not speak of it because they are "secretive" or "manipulative" or "tricky."**

---

[51]*Re-Making Love*, p. 196.
[52]P. 269.

They not only lack a voice, these explanations imply, they lack much more: a morality; a self; a soul.[53]

They lack *patriarchal* morality, civilized morality, morality which can be the basis of family life. Some of them seek meaning in a puerile revival of cults of the Stone Age Great Mother. According to Riane Eisler, "a new genre of women's writings about sex is gradually beginning to emerge: writings that link sex with a full-bodied spirituality imbued with erotic pleasure....What they deal with is the reclamation of nothing less than women's ancient sexual power—and with this the powerful archetype of the prehistoric Goddess....Most invoke the ancient Goddess as the source of erotic power, although a few like Carter Heyward, still write of her as God. But whatever term they use, their focus is on resacralizing both woman and the erotic—which they define as inclusive of, but not exclusive to, sexuality—and on the erotic as empowering."[54]

Feminist Dr. Mary Jane Sherfey tells us that "To all intents and purposes the human female is sexually insatiable...."[55] Dr. Sherfey believes, according to feminist Barbara Seaman, "that every girl born has the capacity to become a veritable nymphomaniac."[56] Even if Sherfey is right, however, continues Ms. Seaman,

I think that most of the women who opt for marriage and family life will continue, sedately and perhaps a little sadly at times, to "will themselves" satisfied. A mother's attachment to her young is very strong and not easily jeopardized.

This is why father custody will stabilize the family and society.

On the other hand, there is no question that a new life-style is emerging for educated women in civilized countries. The world is pretty well filled up, and the men who rule it are coming to view babies as a threat to their own survival. The pressures on women to marry and reproduce are rapidly diminishing, at the same time as their solo economic position is improving.[57]

Seaman wrote in 1972, when overpopulation was the big scare. Today "civilized countries" suffer from a below-replacement level

---

[53]P. 18.
[54]Eisler, *Sacred Pleasure*, p. 284. Ex-husbands hounded for support money for ex-wives will be relieved to learn that "The power these women speak of is not the power to dominate and control others through fear and force" (p. 285).
[55]Quoted in Barbara Seaman, *Free and Female*, p. 44.
[56]Seaman, p. 45.
[57]Seaman, p. 45.

birthrate. Men in them don't view babies as a threat to their survival;
their fear is that they can't have families—that women, with the help of
the divorce courts, are imposing a matriarchal society upon them. If
men knew that every woman is a potential nymphomaniac, and if she
could become economically independent with the help of affirmative
action policies, he would know the improbability of his becoming a
breadwinner for a family. He would be in danger of becoming a
demoralized underachiever (like the young men of the ghettos, like the
young men described by Judith Wallerstein on page 411). What men are
really afraid of is that women are willing to forfeit the advantages
patriarchy has hitherto bestowed on them in exchange for their
acceptance of patriarchal regulation. According to Ms. Seaman,

> **Anthropologists have clarified that in some cultures, even today, the vast
> sexual capacity of the female is taken for granted. Their field work in
> primitive cultures lends extremely convincing support to the historical thesis
> that the forced suppression of female sexuality was somehow necessary for
> the development of "higher civilizations."[58]**

Ms. Heyn speaks of women

> **being thrown into the central dilemma of relationship they had encountered
> both at adolescence and in marriage: how to speak honestly about their
> deepest feelings but not be "bad"; how to say what they desired without
> sounding "wrong" to desire it; how to speak about sex without displeasing me
> and being punished somehow.[59]**

Such women would do well to keep quiet about their "deepest
feelings" since speaking honestly about them would reveal that they are
enemies of the patriarchal system upon which they depend. They *are*
bad; their real, albeit unexpressed, aim is to reject patriarchy. Their
deepest feeling is a yearning to be promiscuous and to employ this
promiscuity as a means to restore the female kinship system and
mother-right—"a woman's right to control her own sexuality" and
therefore her right to disregard her marriage contract.

The success of feminism has caused this "right" to be taken for
granted. Formerly a woman had the right to contract to *share* her
reproductive life with a man who depended on the contract and on
society's enforcing of it. Today, women insist that they also have the

---

[58]Seaman, p. 38.
[59]Heyn, pp. 173f.

right to break the contract, to deprive the man of the children procreated under it. They see the corollary of a woman's right to control her own sexuality as her further right to demand that the law shall nullify her obligations under the contract while still enforcing the man's economic obligations under it. How long will men continue to permit this subversion of their marriages and their families?

Ms. Heyn probably sees herself as promoting the liberation of women. She might consider the condition of women in Eastern lands, where, as William Robertson Smith says, men cannot trust them[60] and accordingly impose *purdah* on them or wrap them in black cloth and keep them out of sight. Sexual liberal Dr. Alex Comfort, suggests that there is a strong case for treating sexuality as Indian and Arabic works have treated it, like ballroom dancing.[61] The regulation of female sexuality in Indian and Arabic societies is far more strict, indeed cruel, because of the lack of inner controls of shame and guilt such as Ms. Heyn and Dr. Comfort wish to remove. The Arabic and Indian controls, Dr. Comfort says, are the result of treating sex like ballroom dancing. Arabic and Indian societies don't practice ballroom dancing; they practice belly dancing. Ballroom dancing is found where there is a presumption of female chastity and the relations between the sexes are permitted to be sexually stimulating without undermining the patriarchal Sexual Constitution. Belly dancing is calculated to arouse and inflame the passions of lustful men—but its complement is harsh external restraints on females. Dr. Comfort may imagine Arabic and Indian women relish the Joy of Sex but he would not care to live in a society where women wear veils.

"The passion of love," says Jacob Burckhardt of the Arabs,

"is indeed much talked about by the inhabitants of towns, but I doubt whether anything is meant by them more than the grossest animal desire. No Arabian love poetry takes account of any other aspect."[62]

"Convinced that [Saudi Arabian] women have no control over their own sexual desires," says feminist Jean Sasson,

---

[60]William Robertson Smith, *Kinship and Marriage in Early Arabia* (London: Adam and Charles Black, 1903), p. 167.
[61]Alex Comfort, *Sex in Society* (Secaucus, N.J.: The Citadel Press, 1963), p. 155.
[62]Quoted in Briffault, *The Mothers*, II, 152.

it then becomes essential that the dominant male carefully guard the sexuality of the female. This absolute control over the female has nothing to do with love, only with fear of the male's tarnished honor.[63]

Let's say only with the male's fear of matriarchy, a justifiable fear, which Americans ought to share.

It is the argument of the present book that men should ensure sexual law-and-order, not by imposing purdah upon women, not by wrapping them in black cloth, but by guaranteeing fathers custody of their children. The popularity of scores of books like Ms. Heyn's and Dr. Comfort's proves that feminists and parlor intellectuals seek to get rid of sexual regulation and restore matriarchy and sexual anarchy.

Feminist Dr. Sherfey, was cited earlier as saying that women have as insatiable a sex drive as certain female primates:

Having no cultural restrictions, these primate females will perform coitus from twenty to fifty times a day during the peak week of estrus, usually with several series of copulation in rapid succession. If necessary, they flirt, solicit, present and stimulate the male in order to obtain successive coitions. They will "consort" with one male for several days until he is exhausted, then take up with another. They emerge from estrus totally exhausted, often with wounds from spent males who have repulsed them. I suggest that something akin to this behavior could be paralleled by the human female *if her civilization allowed it.*[64]

The emphasized words mean *in the absence of patriarchal control,* the control lacking in Old Testament times when the fertility worship at the Canaanite high places involved "horrible orgies of unrestrained sensuality."[65] This is what Ms. Eisler wishes to revive. She calls it "the reclamation of nothing less than woman's ancient sexual power—and with this the powerful archetype of the prehistoric Goddess." This is being promoted by "a new genre of women's writings about sex...writings that link sex with a full-bodied spirituality imbued with erotic pleasure."[66]

The Hebrew prophets denounced this unregulated sexuality under the comprehensive term "idolatry." "What," asks Bishop Spong, "was the

---

[63]Jean Sasson, *Princess: A True Story of Life Behind the Veil in Saudi Arabia* (New York: Avon Books, 1992), p. 6.
[64]Seaman, p. 36; emphasis added.
[65]William Robertson Smith, *The Old Testament in the Jewish Church,* 2d ed. (London: Adam and Charles Black, 1892), p. 350.
[66]*Sacred Pleasure,* p. 284.

appeal of what the Bible calls idolatry? Wherein lay the power of this religious tradition that Yahwism never fully succeeded in suppressing?...If these traditions were in fact 'nothing,' as the words of the Yahwists asserted, why did the followers of Yahweh seem so threatened by them?" Answer: Asherah and Baal were a matriarchal sex cult; Jahweh was a patriarchal cult which channeled sex through families. Asherah and Baal made the mother the head of the reproductive unit, de-regulated female sexuality and encouraged sexual license; Jahwism made the father the head of the reproductive unit and imposed patriarchy. It's the same difference which separates feminists and anti-feminists today.

One problem is that people like Bishop Spong do *not* feel threatened. On page 251 of this book reference will be made to a *Penthouse* article describing same-sex marriage ceremonies and homosexual orgies in front of the altar in St. Gabriel's Church in Brooklyn in 1996. It was like old times—like the orgies at the Canaanite high places.[67]. It might have given Bishop Spong pause but it probably didn't.[68]

It is the purpose of patriarchy to prevent this sort of sexual foolishness and to channel the energy it represents into the creation of families. This channeling is a primary responsibility of churches and the legal and educational systems—all of which are betraying it for the bad purpose of de-regulating sexuality and restoring matriarchy and its anti-social twin, homosexuality.

Debold, Wilson and Malave's *Mother Daughter Revolution* is part of the attack on the patriarchal socialization of girls. "In the shadow of the wall," they say,

girls see the injustices in their worlds but have no recourse and few allies. The dawning realization of women's subordinate position within the culture becomes more and more clear to them.... The unspoken threat is abandonment and exclusion.... By shutting off what they know and feel, these

---

[67]See page 245.
[68]One learns with relief that *Penthouse* has retracted its December 1996 article: "A report issued last year after an investigation conducted on behalf of the diocese found that 22 of the 38 allegations in the *Penthouse* article were completely untrue or unproved and nine more were largely untrue, reported Episcopal News Service." (*L.A. Times*, 4 July, 1998)

girls buy continued closeness with their mothers and the other women in their lives. But as they do so, they know and feel that it is not fully real.[69]

They gain the benefits patriarchal society bestows on good women. Of course it's "not fully real." The female role is an eminently artificial thing, like the male role. So is civilization. Accepting the patriarchal scenario privileges women to belong to the upper tier of our two-tiered society. Patriarchal socialization converts female resentment into feminine charm and male violence into constructive labor. Both are artificial; their complementariness makes civilized life possible. Feminists suppose that women can withdraw their contribution to this entente and men won't withdraw theirs. It hasn't worked.

---

[69]P. 44.

VI) RESTORING FEMALE KINSHIP

Barbara Katz Rothman writes a book called *Recreating Motherhood*[1] which begins with this:

> I recently had the interesting experience of trying to put together a very short family photo album for a celebration of the Bar Mitzvah of my son, Dan. A colleague had just done one for his daughter, and it seemed to be a lovely idea to copy.
>
> My colleague began his with a family tree. I started but it got complicated, messy: we had divorces, deaths, remarriages, too many convoluted branches somehow.

The "flat generational lines" didn't represent family to her, "So I scratched the tree idea, and went straight to the photos."[2]

> They were nurturing pictures, one after another. It wasn't by lineage that I saw Dan's first thirteen years, but by nurturance: people holding, greeting, caring, tending, teaching.
>
> For me, the idea of nurturance as mattering more than genetics, loving more than lineage, care more than kinship, is not just an intellectual fancy. It's really there, in my heart....I am not alone in this. More and more of us are choosing to live our lives this way, putting together families by choice and not by obligation.

The "new definition of motherhood, of relationships, of parents and of children" is the familiar feminist nonsense. She has rediscovered the female kinship system and regards it as a wonderful new revelation. Ms. Rothman's problem in putting together the photo album reflects the difficulty in describing "family" relationships in a society where family and fatherhood are rapidly becoming meaningless. Louis Henry Morgan was the discoverer of this alternative way of describing kinship, which he called the "classificatory system." Webster's New International, second edition defines it this way:

---

[1] New York: W. W. Norton, 1989.
[2] P. 17.

classificatory system. *Anthropol*. A primitive system of reckoning kinship, found among American Indians, Australasians, etc., according to which all the members of any single generation in a given line of descent (as in a clan) are reckoned as of the same degree of kinship to all the members of any other generation. The system is contrasted with the descriptive system, in vogue among civilized peoples, which discriminates degrees of individual kinship in each generation.

The Descriptive System is found among civilized peoples, where families are headed by fathers. The Classificatory System is found among uncivilized peoples, whose "families" are headed by mothers—like the American Indians, the people of the Australian bush and the American ghettos, societies based on the female kinship system, where females reject sexual regulation. The latter is what Ms. Rothman is describing. It excludes males from meaningful sharing in reproduction. It is rapidly becoming the system of all American society as women liberate themselves from sexual norms and divorce court judges automatically give mothers custody.

Ms. Rothman favors the female kinship system because of its "nurturance," as feminists Sjöö and Mor do: "it creates a silent dialog of love and union between the mother and child....This is done by all animal mothers"—including of course Judge Noland's cows. "The child's bond with the mother," they say, "is both erotic and mystical, and thus a challenge to established power."[3] A challenge, that is to say, to the sexual regulation imposed by patriarchy. It creates a silent dialog of love and union between mother and child but does nothing to create a similar dialog of love and union between father and child.

Maintaining sexual regulation is also a form of nurturance, as is paying the bills, these being fathers' responsibilities—poorly performed in the female kinship system, which is why it requires more support from society's Backup System–welfare, delinquency control, drug programs, affirmative action programs.

Feminists imagine this "new definition of motherhood" and the sexual revolution which brought it about are really new, a breakthrough

---

[3]*The Great Cosmic Mother*, pp. 220f. These writers cite the Nayars of southern India as a matriarchy which enjoys these blessings and which therefore has, among other good things, "no prostitution." As Elie Reclus says of matriarchal societies including the Nayars "all the women belonged to all the males of a tribe without distinction," such societies being "still in existence amongst most savage or semi-barbarous peoples." ("The Nairs" in *Primitive Folk* (London: Walter Scott, n.d.), p. 157.)

achieved only since the feminist/sexual revolution, something which
finally liberates women to the attainment of equality, freedom and
justice. "I choose to live my life this way," says Ms. Rothman. Men
cannot choose, not if women reject sexual regulation and have the
support of judges in doing so. The genealogies Ms. Rothman mentions
have no significance in ghettos, or in clans or on Indian reservations.
The social system based on mothers' "nurturance" is what creates
ghettos, where fathers are allowed to hang around if they behave
themselves. If Mom gets tired of them, they leave and pursue other
girlfriends.

"Putting together families by choice and not by obligation," she
says. *But it is the mother who does the choosing.* If she chooses, she gets
rid of the father and takes his kids. Her choice "puts together" a family
by dissolving it or preventing its formation. Two problems with this
pattern are, in the present generation, paying the bills, in the following
generation building enough prisons.

"In a mother-based system," says Ms. Rothman, "a person is what
mothers grow—people are made of the care and nurturance that bring a
baby forth into the world, and turn the baby into a member of society."[4]
Ms. Rothman thinks of herself as a feminist, but her emphasis on
women's maternal functions is the old feminine mystique which Ms.
Friedan's feminism wanted to get rid of. Ms. Rothman and Sjöö and Mor
and the ecofeminists have brought feminism full circle back to women's
maternal functions.

**I believe [says Ms. Rothman] it is time to move beyond the patriarchal
concern with genetic relationships....[W]e need to value nurturance and caring
relationships more than genetic ties....Stripped of all the social supports, is
that genetic tie sufficient to define a person?[5]**

Nobody would say it was. What is claimed is the desirability
(proved by the resulting social stability and productivity and improved
quality of life) of maximizing the importance of the tie to the father. This
tie is biologically tenuous, which is why it is important to emphasize its
significance by titles, patrilineal surnames, ancestor worship, the
patrimony, the landed estate—by creating the social heredity which

---

[4]P. 35.
[5]P. 40.

fetalization, paidomorphy and neoteny have made necessary if the human offspring is to have a childhood, or a decent one.

Money is part of this social heredity. The father's Money Card is one reason for the legal system to support the father in cases of divorce. The father's role is the one for which biology does the least and therefore the one for which society must do the most. The *primitive* idea of kinship, says William Robertson Smith is "that those who are born of the same womb and have sucked the same breast share the same life derived from the mother....[T]he fact that *rahim*, womb, is the most general Arabic word for kinship shows clearly enough that the...kinship through the mother [is] the earliest and universal type of blood relation." Smith has been quoted previously concerning not only the Arabs but equally with "other races which have once had a rule of female kinship: Everywhere *as society advances* a stage is reached when the child ceases to belong to the mother's kin and follows the father."[6]

The reverse is likewise true: when a society is, like our own, in a state of retrogression there is likely to be a social pattern of the child ceasing to belong to the father and becoming solely attached to its mother. Which is to say, there is a correlation between social pathology and female headed households.

"In a better world," says Ms. Rothman,

in the world I would want us to have, there would be virtually no women giving up babies: contraception, abortion, and the resources to raise her own children would be available to every woman.[7]

Ms. Rothman, like Ms. Eisler and the rest of the feminist crowd—like Barbara Seaman, like Betty Friedan, like Elise Boulding, like Lorraine Dusky, like Stephanie Coontz, like Dalma Heyn, like Merlin Stone, like Rosie Jackson, like Mary Daly, like Gerda Lerner like Judy Mann—like all these writers of bad books, many now entrenched with tenure in academe—is once again dusting off the hoary feminine kinship system and presenting it as a wonderful discovery; and all the parlor intellectuals and media people are rushing to agree with her—writing about equality and progress and pluralism and multiculturalism and

---

[6]William Robertson Smith, *Kinship and Marriage in Early Arabia* (London: A. and C. Black, 1903), pp. 177, 37; emphasis added.
[7]P. 133.

modernity and the rest. How sad that returning to the classificatory kinship system should be regarded as progress. How sad.

She is saying the same thing liberals and parlor intellectuals were saying a century ago. George Bernard Shaw spoke of "every woman bearing and rearing a valuable child receiv[ing] a handsome series of payments, thereby making motherhood a real profession as it ought to be."[8] This is an AFDC program, but with more generous payments to women breeding fatherless children. Shaw was well aware of women's hatred of the patriarchal system:

> **My own experience of discussing this question leads me to believe that the one point on which all women are in furious secret rebellion against the existing law is the saddling of the right to a child with the obligation to become the servant of a man.[9]**

Let's say the saddling of the right to a child with the obligation to share the possession of that child with a father. Like the black woman on the Donahue show a few years ago: "We want the right to have children without having husbands." They don't think of husbands as providing benefits, so they don't want to associate with them. Briffault's Law. It's natural for taxpayers to pay their bills, they suppose—this is what taxpayers are for. It's natural for judges to destroy families and to deprive children of their fathers and to jail ex-husbands for not sending them support money. This is what judges are for. Shaw thinks it is unnatural for women to be made servants of men, but judges don't think it unnatural for ex-husbands to be servants of ex-wives. Or rather *slaves*, for a servant must be paid, and an ex-husband can be compelled to perform forced labor without pay. That's what ex-husbands are for. It's natural because while women must be privileged to say "You don't own me," men must say to their ex-wives "You do own me; I have a natural aptitude for the servile condition." A black woman, an unwed mother, is quoted by Rickie Solinger: "If your old man has been like my old man, you wouldn't think not having him around was any great loss."[10]

That old man lacked the social support to make him a sociological father. Fatherhood is a *social creation*, not a biological fact. Judges like

---

[8]Preface to *Getting Married*; *Prefaces by Bernard Shaw* (London: Constable and Company, 1934), p. 15.
[9]*Ibid.*
[10]Rickie Solinger, *Wake Up, Little Susie*, p. 79.

Robert Noland can't grasp that fatherhood requires *their support*. We have allowed these enemies of patriarchy into the chicken coop and we must get them out by making father custody once again automatic and mandatory.

More in accord with the spirit of the female kinship system is not to marry at all but to shack up with a stud-provider who if he misbehaves can be told to get out of the house. Either way, men have no rights. The ex-husband, especially if he earns a steady paycheck which can be garnished, may be kidded into supposing he is obligated to subsidize his ex-wife's sexual independence. To the woman this is natural ("This money is certainly a reasonable and fair thing to expect"[11]) as stable marriage is not ("You have legitimate human needs that are not being fulfilled in this marriage. You are totally justified in using that as the reason for your desire to leave."[12]). More and more men will drift from the role of husband and ex-husband into the less threatening, less responsible role of stud.

More and more unsocialized women prefer things this way; fewer and fewer women are being properly socialized. This change manifests the "enormous potential counterforce" which energizes the women's movement. It is what feminist Mary Ann Mason means when she says "For many women the route to liberation from domestic drudgery [is] liberation from marriage." This is what feminist Robin Morgan speaks of when she says "I want a woman's revolution like a lover. I lust for it." It is what feminist Margaret Sanger meant by saying "marriage is the most degrading influence in the social order." Because many women hate patriarchy, hate its regulation. They think that the worst thing for them to be is a "good girl,"[13] one who accepts the patriarchal system, one who allows a man to share her reproductive life, one who allows her children to have a father.

Women discovered that the weakness of character of judges was an exploitable resource. Every judge thinks with Britain's Lord Lane that "the law doesn't seem to be about justice; the needs of children have to

---

[11]Triere, p. 154.
[12]Triere, p. 46.
[13]Heyn, p. 81.

come first"[14]—and the children must not be separated from their mothers.

Can we go back to that happy era when women were willing to be wives and mothers, to perform maternal functions as their grandmothers did, when the resulting family stability made more people more well off than they had ever been?

No, we can't—for the reason explained by a woman named Angela Franco, writing on the Internet. She asked,

Are you trying to suggest that women should revert back to the behavior of the oppressed women in the past, be docile and quiet, let men do the working while we stay home and clean and take care of the kids? Because if that's what you are suggesting, let me enlighten you a bit—it's never going to happen.[15]

It's never going to happen as long as men continue to submit to the anti-male bias of the divorce courts and consent to seeing the institution of the family destroyed and society returning to matriarchy as the ghettos have done.

It's never going to happen, but something else is going to happen, and the sooner the better. The men who get married believing that marriage will give them families are going to rub their sleepy eyes and realize that marriage has become a fraudulent contract which gives men no security of having families and children. They are going to realize that Ms. Hoggett speaks for the American as well as the British legal system when she says marriage has become meaningless. They are going to realize that the wife's withdrawal of her primary contribution to the marriage, her sharing of her reproductive life with her husband, removes his reciprocal obligation to support her; and that since the purpose of this support was to benefit his children, the children belong with him, not with her. They are going to realize that the anti-male bias of divorce court judges cannot be removed by appeals to their integrity or their oath of office. It's never going to happen as long as men consent to seeing their families destroyed and society returning to matriarchy.

---

[14]Lord Lane, a former Lord Chief Justice, cited in John Campion and Pamela Leeson, *Facing Reality: The Case for the Reconstruction of Legal Marriage* (Cross Winds/Carron Lane, Midhurst, West Sussex, 1994), p. 35.
[15]10 September, 1995.

But what is required is perfectly obvious: father custody of the children of divorce, as was automatic and mandatory in the mid-nineteenth century. This will permit men to have families and children to have fathers. It will restore male motivation. It will make women understand the value to themselves of the double standard and of their sexual loyalty, the things which formerly gave them their bargaining power in the patriarchal system.

"The Greeks, and most humans before our smug twentieth century," writes Professor Bruce Thornton, "knew that the power of woman was the power of eros, and the power of eros was the creative and destructive power of nature itself, the forces that both men and women must strive to order and control for civilization—and human beings—to exist."[16]

The order is imposed by patriarchy and its sexual discipline. Nothing else will impose it. "Puritanism," says Alain Danielou, "is totally unknown in the primitive or natural world."[17] That is why it is primitive and natural, like the matriarchal ghettos.

Feminist Elise Boulding, impressed with the inner peace of sexually unregulated women in the matriarchal ghettos and on Indian reservations, asks, "Where does their serenity and self-confidence come from? What do they 'know'?...This is a time for the rest of us, especially middle-class Western women, to 'go to school' to those of our sisters who have the unacknowledged skills, the confidence, the serenity, and the knowledge required for creative social change."[18] This serenity is what Ms. Heyn calls "a deeply comfortable internal persona." It comes from their sexual irresponsibility, which is the essence of the matriarchal system, which inflicts alcoholism on so many of their men and fetal alcohol syndrome on so many of their babies. According to the *Journal of the American Medical Association*, thousands of American Indian and indigenous Alaskan teen-agers inhabit a world so filled with alcoholism, violent death and personal despair that by the end of high school 1 out of 5 girls and 1 out of 8 boys have attempted suicide. According to Michael

---

[16]Bruce Thornton, *Eros: The Myth of Ancient Greek Sexuality* (Boulder, Colorado: Westview Press, 1997), p. 98.
[17]Alain Danielou, *Gods of Love and Ecstasy: The Traditions of Shiva and Dionysus* (Rochester, Vermont: Inner Traditions, 1979), p.17.
[18]Elise Boulding, *The Underside of History: A View of Women Through Time* (Boulder, Colorado: Westview Press, 1976), p. 790.

Resnick, an epidemiologist and co-author of the survey, "This is the most devastated group of adolescents in the United States."[19]

The "creative" social change Ms. Boulding supposes to be taking place is that from patriarchy back to matriarchy, where women enjoy the confidence and serenity she thinks middle-class Western women ought to enjoy. This would mean an end to fatherhood and the legitimacy of children:

> **One of the anomalies of the child's role in industrial society [says Ms. Boulding] is the absurd stigma of illegitimacy for children born to unpartnered women. This type of labeling will disappear as all societies return to practices once universal in tribal society; the legitimization of a child's existence through the recognition of the birth itself.[20]**

"There is no such thing as an illegitimate child" means, among other things, "We must not distinguish between good and bad women— must not reward the good ones and de-class the bad ones." This is the way things are done in "tribal society." The child is legitimate because it has a mother and therefore, so Dr. Boulding thinks, needs no father. In a society where there is no fatherhood, females and males will be equally entitled to irresponsible sex, thus giving women the equality they clamor for.

Discussing what she calls girls' "freedom envy," feminist Judy Mann offers this: "The physical penis is not the object of envy. Far more likely, girls are envious of what it represents: freedom."[21] They have the idea that males are freewheeling lechers and they resent not sharing their happy lifestyle.

In matriarchy children are presumed not to be disadvantaged by father deprivation. But fatherless children really are disadvantaged, and not only by reason of their economic predicament. The principal "right" of children is the right to have a father and to grow up in a two-parent home—the right to live under the patriarchal system.

The squaw's calm self-assurance comes from the naturalness of her life-style. Like Ms. Heyn's adulteresses, she just does what comes easy: the squaw never did submit to patriarchal regulation, the adulteresses

---

[19]*Los Angeles Times*, 25 March, 1992.
[20]P. 787.
[21]Judy Mann, *The Difference*, p. 47.

have learned they can reject it since the marriage contract no longer has the support of the law and religion and the mores of society. The squaw pays the price of living in poverty on a reservation; the divorced wife may pay the price of a lower standard of living. But what a relief to get rid of patriarchy and its artificial regulation of female sexuality. Free at last: "You don't own me! You don't own me!" "I am better at this," says one of Ms. Heyn's adulteresses, "than I am at marriage."[22] She is at home in the female kinship system.

Patriarchy tries to make women sexually responsible and men financially responsible—to support families. Feminism and its backup-- the clambering politicians hungering for the feminist vote, from President Clinton down to District Attorneys and office seekers in virtually every city—want fathers to suppose that in supporting ex-families they are supporting their families rather than destroying them—are the enemy. The rejection of sexual responsibility, by women and by office holders who want the women's vote, is what feminism is all about. They will get what they want unless their rejection of sexual responsibility is understood to forfeit their claim to custody of their children.

It's never going to happen—the restoration of meaningful fatherhood and the two-parent family—until men realize that the anti-male bias of divorce court judges is so total that the only solution is to take all discretion out of their hands and to return to the nineteenth century practice of automatic and mandatory father custody.

According to Betty Friedan, "Only economic independence can free a women to marry for love, not for status or financial support, or to leave a *loveless, intolerable, humiliating* marriage, or to eat, dress, rest, and move if she plans not to marry."[23] The real meaning of this is revealed by leaving out the verbiage intended to help the rationalization along: "Only economic independence can free a woman to leave a marriage. Get your ass out of my house. I want to live under the female kinship system. Economic *dependence* might induce a woman to marry, but economic independence can free a woman to leave a marriage." No "association" need take place if Mom doesn't need the benefit of economic dependence Dad bestows. If the ex-husband can be made to contribute to Mom's

---

[22]p. 187.
[23]Betty Friedan, *The Feminine Mystique*, 10th anniversary edition (New York: W. W. Norton. 1973), p. 371; emphasis added.

economic "independence" so much the better—serves him right for being male.

A husband is valued for achievement, responsibility, status. The boyfriend is valued for "what his body was like, his smile, his credentials as a friend and lover and nurturer; whether he treated her respectfully and kindly, and as an equal." This threatens and punishes high achieving males, and rewards underachieving ones. It is the husband who provides the economic base for her game-playing and he must be a responsible achiever with status, but, in feminist thinking, must have no bargaining power. What, then, is his motive for being a high achiever? How can he protect his family and himself without a guarantee of father custody? He can't. Her guaranteed custody makes her "feel competent and sure-footed, at once frighteningly out of control and, strangely, very much in command." If she is a competent adulteress, she is excited to be not only cheating on the husband who seeks to control her but to be winning a skirmish in the War Against Patriarchy. It's fun because it is forbidden:

> **And this forbidden experiment begins to become surprisingly rewarding....[S]he begins to create something new, something she could not have experienced even before marriage, no matter how many relationships she had.**

It's less fun when there is no husband to betray. The woman, says Ms. Heyn,

> **is free to create an unusual entity—a sexual relationship in which she has no prescribed role....It will be she who decides if this relationship will take place, where, when, how often, and just what her part in it will be. She does not have to win a man, because she already has one;[24] she does not have to plan the future, which is already planned with someone else; she does not have to worry about whether the relationship will end, nor if all her needs will be filled. She does not have to worry about whether she will have a date for Saturday night. She has one. She has a life. It will be day by day, this friendship; its only goal is mutual pleasure, without which it has no reason for being....The women spoke about how revolutionary this arrangement felt.[25]**

It is the ultimate revolution: the change of the kinship system from patriarchy to matriarchy, from sex as procreation-centered and child-

---

[24]Actually two—D.A.
[25]Heyn, pp. 162f.

centered to sex as recreation-centered, from sex as a motivator of achievement to sex for fun. Its only goal is mutual pleasure, and if Hubby doesn't like it, let him leave and pay alimony and child support. Children, fatherhood, social stability can wait while Mom plays her games. For children it is a long wait. According to child psychologist Judith Wallerstein, "There was no transition, no cushioning of the blow. Their loneliness, their sense that no one was there to take care of them, was overwhelming.... Such are the core memories of these adults 25 years later."[26]

This is matriarchy. Free at last. It is more than game playing: there are few better ways for the "enormous potential counterforce" bottled up in women to be released, for the War Against Patriarchy to be fought and won.

"Love" is introduced into such feminist scenarios for the purpose of lamenting its absence, which is understood to invalidate the marriage contract. An economically independent woman is privileged to get out of a bad marriage—or a boring one. This is why economically independent women have the highest divorce rate and why sensible men would be well advised to avoid marriage with them—unless custody is given to fathers.

Their demand for economic independence makes no sense except as a demand for sexual independence. As feminists Ehrenreich, Hess and Jacobs say:

> **The young office worker who earns barely enough to rent her own apartment, the married woman who brings in her own share of the family income, even the single mother on welfare, have more sexual options than a "kept" woman, married or not. In fact, one reason for the stigmatization of welfare and hostility to it, is undoubtedly that it offers women independence from individual men and, hence, a certain measure of potential sexual freedom. Male fears of women's sexual independence are at least partly responsible for the cruelly inadequate level of support available.[27]**

Think of Clinton's rising popularity at the very time the Lewinsky scandal was breaking. He has no idea of the torrent he is unloosening but he knows he has the women's vote, the homosexual vote, the vote of

---

[26]Quoted in *Human Events*, 11 July, 1997.
[27]Barbara Ehrenreich, Elizabeth Hess and Gloria Jacobs, *Re-Making Love: The Feminization of Sex* (Garden City, N. Y.: Anchor Press/Doubleday, 1986), p. 197.

every sexual anarchist. The "certain measure of potential sexual freedom" signals the unleashing of woman's "enormous potential counterforce," which—as the ghettos prove—will result in the wholly realistic "male fears." Men do not want to be told to get out of women's houses, much less out of their own. They don't want to lose their children. And they have an uneasy feeling that their Money Card is their only card and they don't want to lose that card to their wives or to judges who don't care about exercising a little chivalry at their expense. Civilization, once again, is built on female chastity, far more than male chastity. Female chastity permits children to have fathers and enables men to have families. This is the big thing—that women allow men to share in reproduction. Men are properly afraid of women's sexual independence, their unchastity. Unchaste women and feminists deem it cruel of men not to subsidize women's unchastity by giving ex-wives more of the economic "benefit" which is the male's principal bargaining chip—it is cruel of men not to marginalize themselves like Thomas Mulder. They think it would be nice for men to subsidize women's "sexual options" so that they wouldn't need marriage or husbands. "Perhaps most of all," they say, "women's sexual revolution was made possible by women's growing economic independence from men." "Independence, even in straitened and penurious forms, still offers more sexual freedom than affluence gained through marriage and dependence on one man." They will prefer semi-impoverished independence with promiscuity to affluence with chastity. "You don't own me! You don't own me!" "The right to define our sexuality is *the* over-riding demand of the women's movement, preceding all other demands." Sexual freedom (read: the female kinship system) is the goal for these irresponsible women, as marriage and family is the goal for responsible men. (Quite a reversal of the traditional view, is it not?—showing that marriage really is an economic institution.) It is a woman's voluntary renunciation of sexual independence which makes a family possible. And this is what women most want to get rid of, their over-riding demand. Can anything other than automatic father custody bridle this demand now that women have tasted blood—now that they have President Clinton on a string and every District Attorney? It's not going to happen, and the sex war will rise to frightening levels. Bachofen warned us.

A wife's willingness to renounce her sexual independence is the reason why a husband is willing to subsidize her. When she insists on her right to sexual independence and implements this "right" by adultery or divorce, she loses her right to subsidization and custody of her husband's children. But men must be able to play their Money Card.

The crucial question is, Should the woman's renunciation of her sexual independence be "voluntary"? Yes. But it must also be irrevocable—"for better for worse, for richer for poorer, in sickness and in health, forsaking all other"—with no lawyer talk or feminist weasel words about "no reason a *woman* should be bound for life to a mistaken choice *she* made at age eighteen, twenty-four, thirty-three, or forty-one" being "an unreasonable demand," and legally unenforceable whereas the man's financial obligations to the woman *are* legally enforceable and if he doesn't think so he is a deadbeat dad and the President (who needs the women's vote) will feed his social security number into the computers and make him pay up.

Only fathers can enforce female chastity. Fathers must be made to see how essential female chastity is. Fathers must be made to see that the Money Card is virtually their only bargaining chip, the benefit promised to wives by Briffault's Law. They must not be intimidated or jollied into supposing that they are being decent chaps when they sell off their children's birthright by acquiescing to pay child support and "spousal" support to ex-spouses. Judges must be made to see that they are properly part of the patriarchal system which pays their salaries and that they forfeit their salaries by selling out to the female kinship system.

We have seen (page 7) how feminists are attracted to the lifestyle of black matriarchs. Wini Breines is one of these :

> **While the white women often had negative perceptions of their mothers' lives and rejected them as models, the black women were much more likely to celebrate their mothers and claim a link with them....Black mothers were often pillars of their families, and their strictness, repressiveness even, could be seen as strengths because of the burdens of racism and poverty. The written record suggests that the white daughters were less able to be empathic or experience solidarity with their mothers than were black daughters. What was commendable for one group of women was a source of tension and ambivalence for the other.[28]**

Debold, Wilson and Malave comment on this same "superiority" of black females:

---

[28]Wini Breines, *Young, White and Miserable: Growing Up Female in the Fifties* (Boston: Beacon Press, 1992), p. 79.

Many African-American girls manage to hold on to their voices and their belief in themselves in adolescence, more so than white or Latina girls. To do so, they draw on strong family connections and communities, and on the role that women play in those families and communities (although these communities have suffered in the last decade or so as fewer resources have come their way).[29]

They hold on to their voices and their belief in themselves. This gives them the self-assurance, lacking to white and Latina girls. But they tell their boyfriends or their husbands to get their asses out of the house. So they live in a matriarchy where males seek a masculine role not by supporting families but by the compulsive masculine rituals which make their part of town a high crime, underachieving area. The cost of the girls' high self-esteem is paid by boys and taxpayers. Debold, Wilson and Malave and Wini Breines choose not to see that the socialization of white girls is what makes patriarchy work, what gives white boys their role. This is another way of saying that the male kinship system is a second story built on the female kinship system, and requires women's acceptance of sexual regulation.

Let me repeat. It requires that men be able to give women the benefit spoken of in Briffault's Law. The black girls prefer to reject the benefit and to enjoy their self-esteem. They can do this because they marry the government and live off welfare and affirmative action. This is the motivation that keeps the ghetto alive and functioning. It's the natural way for girls and women to live. Patriarchy requires white girls to make the following inner adjustment:

At adolescence, a girl first becomes aware of an inner, authentic voice that struggles to articulate who she is in relation to others in her world, particularly in relation to her mother....Girls begin to see that life is complicated and that they can safely reveal only certain layers of what they know. This leads them to wonder who they are and who they really knows them. "Their courage seems suddenly treacherous, transgressive, dangerous," notes Annie Rogers. "But the 'true I' lives on in an underground world waiting and hoping for a sign that she may emerge whole, and open herself again."[30]

"Transgressive"—against the patriarchal system which is their best friend if only they knew it, but which they hope to destroy by their sexual rebellion. This is what makes them dangerous. Feminism and the

---

[29]Debold, et al., p. 14; emphasis added.
[30]Debold, et al, p. 112f.

mother daughter revolution wish them to be dangerous, to restore the natural society of the ghetto matriarchy. The "inner authentic voice that struggles to articulate who she is" is the voice of nature, the voice of her mammalian genes who say to her that reproduction is the business of the female; males have no business monkeying with it: "Get your ass out of my [or your] house."

Dr. Joyce Brothers makes the same point—equally missing the connection between the higher culture and greater affluence of patriarchy and the lower culture and lesser affluence of the ghettos, where, however, females feel more at home:

> **A recent survey by the American Assn. Of University Women found that while a majority of girls are confident and assertive in the lower grades, by the time they reach high school fewer than a third feel really good about themselves.**

Black girls don't have this dip in self-esteem and self-assurance.

> **Janie Victoria Ward of the University of Pennsylvania theorized that one factor might be that black girls are surrounded by strong women they admire.[31]**

They feel good about themselves because they deny men (other than taxpayers) their provider role. All it requires (besides affirmative action benefits) is that they refuse to accept the sexual regulation which makes their white sisters "young, white and miserable."

Feminist professor Stephanie Coontz makes the same pitch about black matriarchs:

> **But many African Americans have also managed to pull positive lessons out of their hardships. African-American working women, for example, have made the largest income gains relative to men of any ethnic group, producing new options for women both inside and outside of marriage. Many black women are models of strength, courage, and independence.... These examples suggest that there are sources of solidarity and strength even in the experience of extreme adversity—and growing numbers of white working-class Americans may have to seek those sources in the next decade.[32]**

---

[31]*Los Angeles Times*, 17 April, 1992.
[32]Stephanie Coontz, *The Way We Never Were: American Families and the Nostalgia Trap* (HarperCollins, 1992), p. 254.

Ms. Coontz sees no connection between the marginalizing of black males and the "hardships" and "extreme adversity" of black females and the pathologically large numbers of female-headed households. She thinks these are the "positive lessons" that whites ought to learn from blacks so that they too can ghettoize themselves. That's what she is teaching her students at Evergreen State College in Washington.

A wife may be glad to have a husband who washes dishes and mops floors; but she is also glad to think "I don't need that man."

If the sexual regulation of women were not what makes civilization possible by permitting men to be fathers and children to have fathers, it would be an absurdity. But the sexual regulation of women *is* what makes civilization possible by permitting the creation of families and by permitting males to participate in reproduction, by making sex something more than one-night stands, more than recreation—by channeling male energy into being providers, by creating fatherhood. Accordingly, the sexual de-regulation of women, now taking place under the aegis of the sexual revolution, attacks patriarchy at its core by its withdrawal of female sexual loyalty to the family and to marriage. This is what feminism is all about.

VII) THE CREATION OF PATRIARCHY

The creation of patriarchy just a few thousand years ago was an *evolutionary* development, comparable in importance to the aeons-long creation of motherhood beginning some two hundred million years ago in the Mesozoic Era. We are used to thinking of Evolution as Charles Darwin thought of it, as something which *changes bodies* slowly, gradually and continuously, something operating over grand divisions of geologic time. The idea that evolution can also operate by *social*, not just by biological, heredity is unfamiliar and scary. The idea that *man can now control his own evolution* fills us–or should–with an awesome sense of responsibility.

Even Betty Friedan senses this, though she gets things backward:

"If, indeed, these phenomena of changing sex roles of both men and women are a massive evolutionary development, as I believe they are."[1]

She sees patriarchy as a male scheme for depriving women of freedom, status and pleasure. I have quoted her as saying "Victorian culture gave women many reasons to envy men...[but deprived her] of free and joyous love?"[2]

Black women *don't* envy their men and this explains the condition of the ghettos. "I don't need that man" and "Get your ass out of my house" are the sort of things heard when women don't envy their men. They are the sort of things heard when government agencies intervene massively on Mom's side by decreeing mother custody for Mom and support payments for Dad, by promoting "equality" for women, by giving them quotas and affirmative action benefits. Giving up free and joyous love (=sexual promiscuity) is the price women pay for the ordered sexuality on which patriarchal culture is based. It was a good trade-off, benefiting women as well as men, creating the modern world. We have tried feminism for a third of a century and it doesn't work. It's destroyed families and messed up our kids. The linchpin in the feminist program is mother custody following divorce. Pull that pin, held in place by men's

---

[1] *The Second Stage*, p. 142.
[2] P. 54.

money, and the feminist structure collapses. If men understand that their responsibility is not to create motherhood but to create fatherhood and to keep their children in the male kinship system where they have their best chance to thrive, they will refuse to pay child support to ex-wives. That's all it would take.

Woman's principal weapon in the War Against Patriarchy is her enormous motivation to get rid of the seemingly irrational regulation of her sexuality, which allows men their reproductive role. Man's principal weapon is his love of his children and his understanding that they belong in the male kinship system.

Many (not all) women want to return to the female kinship system, its sexual freedom, its promiscuity, what Betty Friedan calls "its freedom, status and pleasures." This is why Charmaine wants her boyfriend to get his ass out of her house. This is why Freud thought woman was the enemy of civilization, which she is when she can *afford* to get her way and ignore the benefits of Briffault's Law. This is an important reason why she clamors so insistently for economic independence and for *conferred* benefits.

"The male," says feminist Barbara Seaman, "is 'in trouble,' or 'endangered,' comparatively speaking, from the moment he is conceived, for more males than females die in the womb, in the birth canal, and at every subsequent step along the way":

> **It is now believed, although the whys and wherefores are not yet clear, that the greater vulnerability of the male may be related to the fact that his embryonic development is less autonomous and more chancy. There are more opportunities for things to go wrong—in his body and in the male circuits of his brain....The male may be larger, on the average, and better able to lift weights, but let us not allow appearances to deceive us any longer. In many respects, including staying power, we must correctly be called the first and the stronger sex. One writer enumerated some of the female's biological advantages: "more efficient metabolism, the more specialized organs, the greater resistance to disease, the built-in immunity to certain specific ailments, the extra X chromosome, the more convoluted brain, the stronger heart, the longer life. In nature's plan, the male is but a 'glorified gonad.' The female is the species."[3]**

---

[3]Barbara Seaman, *Free and Female* (New York: Coward, McCann and Geoghegan, 1972), pp. 26f., quoting Elizabeth Gould Davis, *The First Sex* (New York: G. P. Putnam's Sons, 1971), p. 329.

How ridiculous, then, for women to envy male achievement. How unfair to try equaling it by quotas, affirmative action and comparable worth programs to discriminate against men. Why not give a little cheer for the poor male cripple who succeeds in making the superior female envious, making her declare "Women are *not* inferior," making Betty Friedan shame her sisters by telling them "Society asks so little of women"?

But this superior male achievement which makes females envious is based on male participation in reproduction, on men being heads of patriarchal families and women's acceptance of sexual regulation. Unmarried males are conspicuously underachievers, earning scarcely half of what married men earn. Women need to understand that they benefit from having a husband and a family. If they can receive the same benefit, or even a part of it, from a divorce court judge rather than from her husband, the arrangement breaks down and society returns to matriarchy.

Dr. Mary Jane Sherfey puts it thus: "The human mating system, *with its permanent family and kinship ties,* was absolutely essential to man's becoming—and remaining—man":

The forceful suppression of woman's inordinate sexual drive was a prerequisite to the dawn of every modern civilization and almost every living culture. Primitive sexual drive was too strong, too susceptible to the fluctuating extremes of an impelling, aggressive eroticism to withstand the disciplined requirements of a settled family life....It could well be that the "oversexed" woman is actually exhibiting a normal sexuality—although because of it her integration into her society may leave much to be desired....[T]his hypothesis will come as no great shock to many women who consciously realize or intuitively sense their lack of satiation.[4]

This is paraphrased by Ms. Seaman: "All hell could break loose" if women realized their vast sexual capacity. "The magnitude of the psychological and social problems facing mankind is difficult to contemplate."

Two obvious inferences: 1. Women's sexuality requires regulation; 2. Women will resist this regulation—a glance at the Annex will show how intense this resistance is.

---

[4]Seaman, p. 36.

Small wonder that women resist, that there is a war of the sexes—of which the contemporary women's movement is a manifestation. Biology makes the female the head of the reproductive unit. It is an astonishing *cultural* achievement for the human male not merely to have intruded himself into this biological unit but to have made himself the head of it.

The significance of this is that culture—social heredity—has become part of biology. Previously, fatherhood had been (as feminists never tire of telling us) a mere matter of providing sperm for Mom, a matter of elemental biology, as with dogs and cats and Judge Noland's cattle, following which Mom was privileged, if she chose, to tell him to get his ass out of her house. This is what most American wives are privileged to tell their husbands, thanks to the law's siding with the wife.

With the creation of patriarchy, the human male became a *sociological* father, taking responsibility to love, honor, protect and provide for the new creation, *his* family. The role of the sociological father was a cultural creation and biologically precarious; and the female, while valuing the benefits of having a male provider and his money, understandably resented being de-throned from her exalted status as sole head of the reproductive unit. Feminists frequently remind us of women's higher status during the Stone Age, and lament what Engels called the world historic defeat of the female sex by the creation of the patriarchal family. Maintaining the stability of the male's new status meant changing the organization of society, of which the most basic feature is the kinship system. "Originally," writes William Robertson Smith, "there was no kinship except in the female line, and the introduction of male kinship was a kind of social revolution which modified society to its very roots."[5]

The contemporary women's movement aims to end male headship of families and to restore the female-headed reproductive unit. This destruction of the family and alteration of the kinship system is nearly complete in the ghettos and is far advanced in the larger society with its thirty percent illegitimacy rate and sixty percent divorce rate combined with virtually automatic mother custody. The growth of the female kinship system is the explanation of the growth in social pathology which has so drastically accelerated during the last thirty years. It is the

---

[5]William Robertson Smith, *Kinship and Marriage in Early Arabia* (London: Adam and Charles Black, 1903), p. 213.

consequence, as Ehrenreich, Hess and Jacobs say, of changes in the sexual behavior of women, not of men. Men have not yet figured out what is happening.

Suppose an animal trainer were to attempt the absurd experiment of creating a cat-family by training the male cat to perform support obligations for his "partner" and his kittens in a "relationship" and train the female cat to accept his support. It wouldn't work. The mother cat would chase the male cat away as Charmaine chased away the father of her twins. Mother mammals have gotten along without husbands since the Mesozoic Era. They don't need males any more than fish need bicycles. They see no reason to share their kitten-rearing with a male.

It is not at all surprising that the female human feels Adrienne Rich's "enormous potential counterforce" against male intrusion into her realm of reproduction. And yet human evolution has accelerated so rapidly that the human female does need a helper, whether she is willing to accept him or not. The two-parent family works better, produces better children.

"*The American Journal of Sociology* in 1987 published an article in which Robert J. Sampson and W. Byron Groves analyzed data from a study involving hundreds of British communities. This analysis established "a direct link between single parenthood and virtually every major type of crime."[6].... Still other studies show that a majority of members of terrorist teenage gangs come from female-headed households. New York Senator Daniel P. Moynihan in a January 1987 issue of *Time* wrote:

> **A community that allows a large number of young men to grow up in broken families, dominated by women, never acquiring any stable relationship to male authority, never acquiring any set of rational expectations about the future—that community asks for and gets chaos. This is what we got—chaos.**

The sisters of these young men make their contribution to the chaos by breeding a disproportionate share of the next generation of fatherless boys and girls. They understand what Judge Noland understands, that the role of the female is central, that the role of the male is marginal. They do not understand, and Judge Noland does not

---

[6]Nicholas Davidson, "Life Without Father: America's Greatest Social Catastrophe," *Policy Review*, 1988).

understand, that *this is why society must support the male role, the weak link in the family.* Society might provide this support, as some societies do, by purdah, gynaecea, foot-binding, by denying women liberty and the vote. Or it might confer the benefits stipulated by Briffault's Law through a contract of marriage, in which the male agrees to be a provider for the female and their children in return for the female's acceptance of the sexual regulation which permits the male to be a father and his children to have a father.

But the contract must be binding, must repress the urges of the female to claim her freedom and sing "You don't own me," as she did "when God was a woman," when she could be promiscuous and dismiss her boyfriends at pleasure and acquire new boyfriends. She feels, as Dalma Heyn's adulteresses feel, that the contract oppresses her, takes the fun and adventure out of her life. She will collect grievances against the patriarchal society which creates and enforces the contract. She will feel, with Susan B. Anthony, that "By law, public sentiment and religion, from the time of Moses down to the present day, woman has never been thought of as other than a piece of property, to be disposed of at the will and pleasure of man."[7]

"When God was a woman" women *were* free and promiscuous and men had little meaningful role in reproduction. Then children belonged to Mom. Today, once again, they belong to Mom—and have an eight times greater likelihood of becoming delinquent.

Mom will rebel even though the benefits of the marriage contract might be so great that feminists complain of being insufficiently challenged: "society asks so little of women"—or like Ibsen's Nora in *A Doll's House* complain that "You've always been so kind to me...[but] you've never understood me. I've been wronged greatly, Torvald—first by Papa and then by you...I'm going home—I mean home where I came from."

She will leave her husband's home and return to her father's home in order that she may be independent of a man. "It's a great sin" that her husband gave her a free ride and pampered her, expecting little other than that she will bear his children and give him creature comforts and moral support.

---

[7] Quoted in Merlin Stone, *When God Was a Woman*, p. 236.

Her real reason for walking out on Torvald is the same as Betty Friedan's reason for walking out on Carl: "I don't care. I have to do something about my life....I want out." She can't stand the regulation patriarchal society imposes on women. She feels with the women of Birmingham that "the right to define our sexuality" is "*the* over-riding demand of the woman's movement, preceding all other demands."

THE IRRECONCILABILITY OF THE TWO KINSHIP SYSTEMS

This is the female kinship system. The male kinship system says the opposite: "He shall rule over thee." There is no way of reconciling the two systems. Either women are in charge of reproduction or men are. In the mid-nineteenth century men were and the law sided with men: "They are by law *his* children." Today's law has returned to mother custody—with a few token exceptions.

It must be obvious to men, though it is not obvious to these feminists, that this female autonomy, which denies men all reproductive rights, greatly reduces the possibility of using the family as a system for motivating males. This is said by Sjöö and Mor (correctly) to be the state of things "if patriarchy had never happened."

The purpose of the feminist movement is to change the kinship system. Patriarchy was created to guarantee males a secure role in the families they provide for. The present chaos arose because the legal system of the society responsible to create the male role has become the chief enemy of that role. The fathers' rights movement must stop what that legal system has been doing for a hundred years, with dizzying acceleration for the last thirty years, using patriarchal marriage to subvert patriarchy itself, by letting women go through the marriage ceremony, then repudiating the marriage but taking custody of the children and claiming the benefits of marriage in their name.

The changeover to the female kinship system is facilitated by the ease of obtaining casual sex under it. "A youth boiling with hormones," say historians Will and Ariel Durant,

will wonder why he should not give full freedom to his sexual desires; and if he is unchecked by custom, morals or laws, he may ruin his life before he matures sufficiently to understand that sex is a river of fire that must be

banked and cooled by a hundred restraints if it is not to consume in chaos both the individual and the group.[8]

This was written in 1968, before the cresting of the feminist revolution. Being "consumed in chaos" is now the fate of thirty percent of children brought into our society by the ease of obtaining sex under matriarchy. Today the Durants would see reason to reverse the gender of the pronouns and return to the double standard.

How can patriarchy defend itself? How can it put the river of fire to work to create wealth and stabilize society? By stabilizing marriage. By making marriage vows mean what they say. By allowing men to play their Money Card. By restoring father custody.

This sounds simple and it is. But it is opposed by the feminists who have taken over the churches and the educational system and made them vehicles for feminist propaganda, and by the media and the entire judiciary and legislative bodies, the entire political system and the welfare system—and made society itself a massive instrument for destroying patriarchy and returning to the female kinship system.

This is the significance of the feminist revolution and the mother daughter revolution—an astonishing accomplishment brought about mostly in just three decades.

The problem is that matriarchy is so natural, patriarchy so artificial. Matriarchy has a two hundred million year biological backup, patriarchy a five thousand year backup.

The problem is not to end the discrimination of divorce court judges against fathers. This is not going to happen. Judges are cowards who will continue to do what they have been doing for over a century because they don't know what else to do and because they suppose the docility of the American male is without limit. The problem lies with fathers themselves. Fathers have to wake up to what is happening—*a change in the kinship system.* Fathers have to realize that if women are released from their sexual loyalty to husbands ("You don't own me!"), men must be released from their vow to provide for them ("You don't own me either!") and must accept the corollary by claiming custody of their children. The fathers' rights movement will be helpless until it

---

[8]Will and Ariel Durant, *The Lessons of History* (New York: Simon and Schuster, 1968), pp. 35f; emphasis added.

understands the necessity of this, of playing their Money Card, their only bargaining chip. Claiming Joint Custody won't do it—it will merely perpetuate the destruction of families and still leave fathers saddled with support obligations.

Marriage is an economic institution and it is being betrayed not only by judges' destruction of families but by the fathers' consenting to subsidize this destruction with alimony and child support money and by consenting to pay the legal fees of their wives' lawyers, by vacating their homes and turning them over to their wives to install the female kinship system in them, by consenting to have their families wrecked by three members of an odious profession, men with no concern for their welfare or that of their children, men who will even deny them the right to due process, the two lawyers and the judge retiring into chambers to facilitate the carving up of his family, to prevent a record being kept which might serve as the basis of later appeals, and, not incidentally, to save lawyers' time, so that more cases may be processed and more fees generated. Fathers must regard such shuffling as what it is, mere bluff to get them out of the home built with their labor.

Bachofen told us that changing the kinship system meant violence. Fathers must recognize that they and their children are the victims of the violence resulting from the destruction of patriarchy. A return to patriarchy will no doubt mean further violence, though this can be moderated by showing women the relevance of Briffault's Law. Most women are not feminists. They will accept patriarchy when they see its benefits, when they see that a husband has more to offer them than lawyers and bureaucrats. But the husband must have custody of the children and secure possession of his property. If women can see a way of getting these by finagling through lawyers and bureaucrats many of them will do so. Only father custody can put a stop to it.

MARRIAGE: AN ECONOMIC INSTIUTION

The central truth that marriage is an economic institution is concealed by representing it as a romantic institution, properly begun and held together by a set of agreeable sensations called "being in love," and therefore properly terminated when these agreeable sensations are no longer experienced or are experienced with diminished intensity. "Only economic independence," says Ms. Friedan, "can free a woman to marry for love." If the wife has assured custody of the children in addition to economic independence, the husband is at her mercy: she will transfer herself and her children to the female kinship system, the goal of the feminist movement. She can repudiate her marriage vows and she knows that the judge will collapse the family and expel her husband because he supposes that the female kinship system is more natural than the male kinship system, which it is—unless social heredity is also recognized as part of nature, which it is.

When the husband is expelled, the economic realities underlying marriage come to the surface and force realization of the fact that the judge has placed the children (also Mom) at risk. The only way the judge can offset (but only partially) the damage he inflicts on the kids and Mom is to enslave Dad. Otherwise he would have reason for placing the children in the father's custody. Otherwise, let's say, the judge would have reason for keeping his oath of office, for administering equal justice under law, for enforcing the marriage contract as he enforces other less important contracts, for stabilizing the institution of the family, which is fundamental to patriarchy and incompatible with matriarchy.

The replacement of the economic institution of marriage by the romantic institution can be carried a step further by getting rid of the romance. In 1963, Betty Friedan made her appeal to "free and joyous love." Ehrenreich, Hess and Jacobs, writing after public opinion had been softened up by two decades of preparation, could afford to be more realistic: "We are drawn, as women have been for ages, to the possibility of celebrating our sexuality without the exclusive intensity of romantic love...."[9] This means they want to be promiscuous. No price tag for sexual irresponsibility or sexual disloyalty. They don't need any romantic nonsense to justify it. No phony pretense like Betty Friedan's "Only economic independence can free a woman to marry for love."

It remains for fathers to see the inference: Economic independence and the assurance that judges will allow mothers custody of their children when they demand sexual independence are enabling women to wreck the patriarchal system.

---

[9] *Re-Making Love*, p. 199.

VIII) THE DOUBLE STANDARD

The hated double standard, which feminists see as the core of women's oppression, should rather be seen as the source of their bargaining power. The repudiation of the double standard and consequent de-regulation of female sexuality deprives children of fathers and men of families, and hence of motivation to provide women with the benefit stipulated by Briffault's Law , which says that a woman will not associate with a man who has no benefit to offer her. Women must be made to see that men's loss of the motive to provide them with a benefit deprives *women* of their bargaining power with men. Perpend the following from one of Dear Abby's readers:

> **What really makes me mad are these sex-loving guys who want to marry virgins! I feel if a guy wants to marry a virgin, he should be one, too. Guys should wait for sex, just like girls are supposed to do. I have talked to both men and women about this. Most of them agree with me. Abby, what do you think?"**

This is Abby's half-baked reply:

> **The attitude you have described is called a double standard, which is defined as "a set of principles applied more rigorously to one group than another." There would be less hypocrisy in the world if we all held ourselves to the same standards we expect others to observe."** [1]

The double standard demands more of *men*. A man's virtue is his integrity, his courage, his honesty. Not so with women. "The habit of calling a woman's chastity her "virtue," says Archbishop Richard Chenevix Trench,

> **is very significant. I will not deny that it may in part be indicative of the tendency, which we many times find traces of in language, to narrow the whole circle of virtues to some one upon which peculiar stress is laid; but still in the selecting of this peculiar one as the "virtue" of woman, there speaks out a true sense that this is indeed in her the citadel of the whole moral**

---

[1] *Los Angeles Times*, 18 May, 1998.

being, the overthrow of which is for her the overthrow of all—that it is the keystone of the arch, which being withdrawn, the whole collapses and falls.[2]

Destroying the double standard destroys the male kinship system. A man has no motivation for subsidizing and giving his name to another man's child. Marriage is patriarchy's way of securing the benefit of the man's paycheck to the woman, and of securing the family to the man. Cohabitation or divorce or adultery are the three common ways of releasing women from the double standard—releasing the woman from the marriage contract, but not the man. The woman might introduce confusion of progeny into her own household, the man does not (though he may introduce it into somebody else's). In the female kinship system, illegitimate children are the same as legitimate ones. If the father doesn't care whether the child he holds in his arms is his, he is accepting the female kinship system and rejecting the patriarchal family and his responsibility to it. But the male kinship system tries to elevate marriage above cohabitation and elevate legitimate children above illegitimate children, in order to motivate fathers to be stable providers, in order to assure them that fatherhood is essential. This requires the double standard. The single standard creates matriarchy, which fails to motivate males.

"A girl is watching," Debold, Wilson and Malave say. "What is she learning about being a woman?"[3] She should be learning (but nobody will teach her) the advantages of accepting the double standard and the patriarchal sexual regulation which entitles her to the benefits offered by patriarchy to chaste women—including a stable family, higher status and a higher standard of living.

Let's try this: "A boy is watching. What is he learning about being a man?" Patriarchy has until recently taught boys they should expect to become providers for families. What is he learning when he hears a feminist teacher tell the girl sitting next to him "You need to have a career of your own, so you won't have to depend on a man"? What is he learning when the girl is told by Joycelyn Elders that she ought to carry a condom in her purse when she goes on a date? The boy is learning that patriarchy, family, sexual loyalty and fatherhood are irrelevant to females—which is to say that the female kinship system is normative. The more there is of this sort of thing, the more necessary father custody

---

[2]Richard Chenevix Trench, *On the Study of Words* (London: Routledge and sons, n. d.), p. 68f.
[3]P. 117.

becomes as the only way to save patriarchy and the two-parent family and the male role. What do boys learn from seeing their fathers expelled from their families and coerced into subsidizing their ex-families? What will they learn even from fathers who still retain their status within families yet live under the threat of divorce with virtually no chance of equal justice in the divorce court? The motivation of such boys will come increasingly to resemble the motivation of boys of the inner cities, where most of the children carry their mothers' surnames and where they seek some sort of meaning by scrawling graffiti, by wearing earrings, by recreational sex, by buying lottery tickets and hoping for a windfall, by taking dope or selling it. The boys—and girls—will find themselves increasingly drifting into the matriarchal/ghetto lifestyle.

Maggie Gallagher thinks it strange that men are no longer socialized to create wealth and social stability by forming families. What's strange? They know that if they marry they have a sixty percent chance of losing their children, their role and their future paychecks. They are coming to realize that a woman who proclaims her right to control her own reproduction is proclaiming her unwillingness to share it with a man, which is what marriage and family and patriarchy are all about. They are coming to realize that a liberated woman is likely to be a disloyal wife. They must come to realize as well that what is needed to make her a loyal wife is the law's support of the father's role. Until then men must remain afraid of women, of marriage, of feminism, of the divorce court judges who have made themselves good soldiers in the War Against Patriarchy.

Marcia Clark divorced her husband Gordon Clark because she "no longer found him intellectually stimulating." The judge gave her custody of Gordon's two young sons and ordered him to pay her support money. Before she signed her book contract for 4.2 million dollars, she already earned almost twice as much as Gordon, but she asked the court to increase his support obligation so that she could buy more clothes and make a better impression on TV audiences.

What is she teaching her sons about becoming men, about marrying, starting families and becoming providers for them?

"Psychotherapists report," according to Debold, Wilson and Malave, "that while men often express the wish to be more like their fathers, women more commonly express the desire to be different from their mothers and struggle not to be like them in any way....Being like our mother is almost terrifying."[4] Is not Marcia Clark teaching her sons that if they try to have families, as their father did, they may lose them—whether or not they are intellectually stimulating. That they may find the *Playboy*/adolescent/bachelor lifestyle more congenial, less threatening, than being a family provider. That if they do marry, they had better not marry a brainy and liberated woman like their mother. That the divorce court judge is no friend of fathers or of families. That he does not believe in equal justice under law—not justice for fathers. That he is—or at least wants to seem—an excellent friend of mothers and of women's liberation—which is to say he regards himself as a supporter of the Female Kinship System. Gordon Clark's sons will doubt that fatherhood is what David Popenoe deems it to be, "a critical component in the evolutionary success of our species."[5] They may think that a woman needs a man like a fish needs a bicycle—though she also may want his money for new clothes. They may accept rolelessness as the proper condition of the male and the precondition for the liberation of the female. They may join the "40 percent of the young men [who] are drifting—out of school, unemployed [or join the] 60 percent of the youngsters...on a downward educational course."[6] Anyhow, they will not want to lead the kind of life their father lives. "Father loss," says Barbara Dafoe Whitehead, "narrows and darkens children's horizons. Deprived of a father's sponsorship, many children lose confidence in themselves and their futures. Children from middle-class divorced families have lower expectations for college and future employment than their counterparts in intact families."[7] The kids (and of course their fathers) pay the costs for the benefits reaped by their mothers, thus described by feminist Constance Ahrons: "Today, record numbers of women have options for the first time in their lives. One enormous option is to leave a marriage that doesn't meet their needs."[8]

David Courtwright concludes his book *Violent Land* with the appeal that "we should not doubt...the social utility of the family, the institution best suited to shape, control, and sublimate the energies of young men."[9]

---

[4]*Mother Daughter Revolution*, p. 24.
[5]*Life Without Father*, p. 165.
[6]Hewlett, *When the Bough Breaks*, p. 141.
[7]*The Divorce Culture*, p. 158.
[8]Constance Ahrons, *The Good Divorce* (HarperCollins, 1994), p. 35.
[9]Courtwright, p. 280.

Would a return to the family mean we must return to the hated Double Standard? Emphatically, yes. A woman who rejects the double standard is refusing to offer a husband a family, "the institution best suited to shape, control, and sublimate the energies" of men, young or old. A man who marries such a woman is placing his future children at enormous risk of growing up in the matriarchy.

THE TWO-TIERED SOCIETY

Society consists of two tiers which are becoming defined with increasing sharpness—an upper patriarchal tier whose men are higher achievers, whose women accept the double standard, and whose children grow up in stable two-parent nuclear families; and a lower matriarchal/plebeian tier whose women reject the double standard and whose men and children live in, or are in danger of falling into, the female kinship system. Welfare and the legal system and the Backup System which replaces fathers are the bulwarks of the lower tier. Father custody is the means of strengthening the upper tier.

"IS THIS ALL?"

Feminists will recall Betty Friedan's celebrated opening paragraph in *The Feminine Mystique*, ending with the despairing *cri de coeur*, "Is this all?" Let's try reversing the genders:

> **The problem lay buried, unspoken, for many years in the minds of American ex-husbands. It was a strange stirring, a sense of dissatisfaction, a yearning that men suffered at the end of the twentieth century in the United States. Each ex-husband struggled with it alone. As he vacated the house made possible by his labor, turned over the furniture and appliances and the good car to his ex-wife, took on her debts, paid her attorney's fees so that she could afford to divorce him, rented a bachelor's apartment, shopped for household appliances and furniture at thrift stores, looked forward to spending 36 hours with his kids twice a month—if his ex did not interfere with his visitation— moonlighted at a second job so that he could make his support payments. As he fell asleep alone he was afraid to ask even of himself the silent question— "Is this all?"**

The "success" of the feminist movement depends on this willingness of men to continue putting up with these deprivations. Maybe someday men will get the idea that this paying for the destruction of their families is a bad idea. The ex-wife sees nothing wrong with it:

148

"ordering one spouse from *his* own home no longer seems so drastic," says Ms. Hoggett. "Women, despite initial pain and income loss, tend almost immediately to feel that they benefit from divorce." "A 1982 survey found that even one year after a divorce a majority of women said they were happier and had more self-respect than they had in their marriages."[10]

This hostility of women to marriage explains why there must be a double standard, why mothers must not see their children as potential Mutilated Beggars whose victimization by father-deprivation can be made to yield Mom's support income. Many women, despite the feminist slogan that they don't want to be dependent on a man, very much want to be dependent on ex-husbands who receive no reciprocal services. The standard of living is lower, but the psychological satisfactions are enormous. Sexual freedom, as emphasized by Dalma Heyn, Barbara Ehrenreich, Elizabeth Hess and Gloria Jacobs, is the main goal, besides which there is an end to role-playing games, or rather their replacement by a different set of games in which Mom is a combination of heroic rebel and Mutilated Beggar and pitiable victim, but nevertheless "enormously in charge of my life."

As women increasingly cut themselves off from the patriarchal system by illegitimate breeding or divorce, politicians try harder to make the displaced men responsible for the mess. This further emancipates women and makes the women's vote more deliverable to politicians.

Fathers ought to see this as reason for demanding custody of their children. Growing female irresponsibility must be offset by increasing male responsibility, but not the kind feminists want—subsidizing the female irresponsibility. Father custody benefits not only children and fathers themselves, but society. There is a vast difference between the productivity and stability of a real father and that of a "putative father." When the law reinforces the father's role by giving him his children it makes them real fathers and family providers. When the law assures fathers of custody, the powerful psychological bond between mother and offspring becomes a prop for family stability rather than, as now, a justification for family dissolution.

---

[10]Coontz, *The Way We Never Were*, p. 224.

Evolution has worked out a new reproductive format which makes human males essential, and accordingly (since women don't like this new format) "He shall rule over thee"—society must impose father headship of families, the male kinship system, including the hated double standard. Most women will see the advantages of this patriarchal system, but there will be objectors. George Sand's biographer Andre Maurois tells us what she wanted for women:

> **Not the right to vote nor to sit in parliament, but the enjoyment of equality with men in Law and in Love. She believed that where the husband holds the wife in subjection, married happiness is impossible, that it can exist only in an atmosphere of freedom. Women would make no demands if they were loved as they wished to be. "As things are, they are ill-used. They are forced to live a life of imbecility, and are blamed for doing so. If they are ignorant, they are despised, if learned, mocked. In love they are reduced to the status of courtesans. As wives they are treated more as servants than as companions. Men do not love them: they make use of them, they exploit them, and expect, in that way, to make them subject to the law of fidelity."**

They are not forced to live a life of imbecility—certainly not in America today, where there are more women than men in college, where Ms. Friedan *complains* that "Society asks so little of women" and tells them that they have already won on paper all the rights they are entitled to and need only get rid of the hated *image* that holds them down. Women can and do prepare themselves for re-entry careers and use their abundant leisure as they choose. They need not play bridge and golf. They can prepare themselves to be brain surgeons. All that should be required of them is that they not drag their children into matriarchy by depriving them of their fathers.

> **That [continues Maurois] was her main grievance: that was the cry which, first uttered in her girlhood, echoed through every one of her books. In the name of what Justice, human or divine, could a woman be bound by a code of loyalty which a man refused, in his own case, to regard as other than empty and ridiculous? Why should a woman remain chaste while a man was free to wander at will, and indulge the coarse tastes of a libertine?**

Why should a woman not be as coarse as a libertine too? The man's coarseness, however regrettable, doesn't deprive him of his bargaining power because he still functions as father and provider. The man should, of course, behave like a gentleman, but feminists want to reject the corollary—that the woman ought to behave like a lady because this would enslave the woman. If she chooses instead to be as coarse as a libertine she forfeits her bargaining power, since she signals her unwillingness to perform her primary functions as wife and mother.

What Sand wanted was to see restored to women those civil rights of which they were deprived by marriage, and to have repealed a law which exposed the adulterous wife to degrading penalties—"a savage law, the only effect of which is to make adultery a permanent feature of our society, and to increase the number of cases in which it is committed."

She could see but one remedy for the injustices which were rampant in all matters connected with the union of the sexes—freedom (in her day non-existent) to divorce and re-marry.[11]

She is not deprived of rights by marriage; she voluntarily renounces them when she marries and agrees to let a man share her reproductive life—to give him children and a family. It is to gain children and a family that the man marries her and provides for her and their children. If the law permits her "to divorce and re-marry" why should this permit her to deprive him of his children—and then in addition deprive him of his property on the ground that the children must not be impoverished?

She wants freedom to divorce and re-marry and to take her children with her. This is matriarchy, where the female heads the reproductive unit and the father is a stud—as is also the man she re-marries. If the father retains the children, patriarchy is preserved: the father continues to head the family.

It is a stable reproductive family unit based on economics, not a recreational arrangement based on temporary exhilaration, which can be repudiated as a "legal shell" when the exhilaration subsides.

The campaign to replace fathers with computers which will search for fathers is incompatible with the institution of the family. Stuart Miller explains why the computers fail:

Of the 30% of child support payments not collected a significant number are owed by fathers who are imprisoned. A high percentage of prisoners have child-support obligations, and as many as one-third of the inmates in many county jails are there in the first place because of child support noncompliance.

---

[11]Andre Maurois, *Lelia* (New York: Harper, 1953), pp. 324f.

Many of the other delinquent fathers are addicts, alcoholics, disabled, mentally incapacitated, unemployed, or otherwise unable to pay pre-set child support amounts.[12]

Many of these fathers are victims of despair induced by the shabby treatment they have received from the divorce court which destroyed their families and the motivation provided by these families. "But the largest number of all delinquents," says Miller, "are those who simply don't exist":

Recently, the Florida Department of Revenue, the agency responsible for child support enforcement in that state, sent out 700,000 notices to allegedly delinquent fathers. The summonses demanded immediate payment or the recipient would be incarcerated. Subsequently, officials acknowledged that probably 500,000 of those notices were sent to individuals who actually did not owe child support. One of those recipients, Daniel Wells, died eight years ago in a traffic accident, but the state still wanted him to cough up $160,000 in past-due child support! (About the same amount of money Florida wasted on postage for the notices.)

Nor is this an isolated case. The General Accounting Office found in 1992 that as many as 14% of fathers who owe child support "cannot afford to pay the amount ordered."

Miller speaks of "the inherent unfairness in taking something away from people and then making them pay for it":

Most fathers are deeply committed to their children, yet a 1991 Census Bureau study found that about half of fathers receive no court-ordered visitation. When fathers do receive visitation, almost 80% pay all of their child support. When fathers receive joint custody, the compliance rate jumps to more than 90%.

According to Miller, much of the problem is created by mothers themselves. He cites Wallerstein and Kelly's *Surviving the Breakup* as showing that half of the mothers see no value in the father's continued contact with the children. According to Sanford Braver, a University of Arizona psychologist, who confirms this, 40% of mothers interfere with Dad's relationship with the children.

The abuse heaped on deadbeat dads obscures the key fact: fathers are more responsible—which is why they are *expected* to pay. The

---

[12]*Wall Street Journal*, 2 March, 1995.

judge's knowledge that the father is more likely to pay is one reason he gives the mother custody. If he gave custody to the fathers the mothers would contribute little or nothing, but with mother custody the children have a parent and a half, for most fathers will continue to subsidize Mom. Miller cites a study made by the federal Office of Income Security Policy in 1991:

> **[L]ess than 30% of custodial fathers receive a child support award, whereas almost 80% of custodial mothers do. Yet about 47% of those mothers who are ordered to pay support totally default on their obligation. In the interest of fairness, if nothing else, policy makers should make an effort to collect child support from both delinquent fathers and mothers.**

No they shouldn't. All alimony and child support should be abolished. Why should mothers (any more than fathers) be obligated to perform forced labor for the benefit of ex-spouses who perform no reciprocal services? Miller is assuming that divorce courts are *just* in awarding support awards to mothers. There is no justice and no intention of being just. The judge wants to pretend that he is concerned only for the best interests of the children, which in his thinking means giving them to the mother and expecting the father to share his income with her, which is what he usually does. Lord Lane tells us, "the needs of children have to come first,"[13] but what Lord Lane refuses to see is that the children's primary need is for the father himself. The law should provide them with fathers rather than exiling them, provide them with a stable reproductive family unit based on economics, not a recreational arrangement based on temporary exhilaration.

If the divorce court judge placed the children with the father, he would seldom be exiling the mother because there would seldom be a divorce. Marriage would be stabilized. We know this because in the mid-19th century, when fathers automatically got custody there were only a few thousand divorces annually. There were a lot of unhappy marriages, but fewer than today, with Mom in the driver's seat and Dad riding in the sidecar.

But would not the switchover to father custody deprive the mother of most of her bargaining power? *That's the idea.* That confirms Briffault's Law—and applies it to our problem. Mom has too much bargaining power, Dad too little. Mom's bargaining power has been

---

[13]See page 61.

pressed into her hands (at her own insistence) by muddleheaded politicians and judges who haven't the fuzziest notion of the harm they are doing by permitting women to throw their husbands out, take custody of the children and bring them up in the female kinship system. Let's put it this way: The massiveness of the present family destruction is changing the kinship system from patriarchy to matriarchy, from the descriptive to the classificatory system. Women hate patriarchy, which depends on female chastity. Without female chastity men cannot be fathers. Today's feminists have discovered that they can destroy patriarchy by refusing their sexual loyalty to men—and they know the judges will side with them when they refuse. The day of the kept woman is over, and with it the family.

But so is the day of the free ride for disloyal women. So is the day of using the children as Mutilated Beggars. So is the day of judges plundering ex-husbands. Women are dependent creatures, as is sufficiently proved by their attempts to screw ex-husbands, to screw AFDC, to screw Affirmative Action programs for conferred benefits. Society is giving them what they want at the cost of destroying its families and reverting to matriarchy. Father custody will not solve the problem of illegitimacy—only women's and girls' acceptance of the double standard will do that—but it will solve the problem of runaway divorce.

Ibsen's Norway and America in the 1950s bribed women to behave themselves, leading to such protests as *A Doll's House* and *The Feminine Mystique*, with their pleas that women must be allowed to grow, to be self-actualizers, to share men's burdens. It is sufficiently clear by now that what women really wanted was not growth and self-actualization, but de-regulation.

Here, as described by feminist Marilyn French, are two ladies from the subcontinent of India who are *not* in rebellion against the feminine mystique and the infantilizing of women:

Two women gather seaweed on the Indian coast near Ahmadabad: they bend and rise, bend and rise, pulling up the greens, adding them to their pile. When they have as much as they can carry, they lug the pile up the beach to a wagon pulled over on the side of the road, dump it in the wagon, and return for more. They continue in this for hours, until the wagon is full. All the while, a man sits in the wagon, head nodding in the sun, holding the reins of his horse. He does nothing....Farm women in Africa (and India) are the most overworked humans in the world, working ten to fifteen hours a day at a host

of jobs. **A typical Zimbabwean woman's day begins at 3:00 A.M. Every day she goes to the river for water, weeds the fields (breast-feeding her baby as she works), chases animals away from crops, pounds grain into flour, prepares meals, and gathers wood (steadily walking farther with these heavy loads because drought and overcutting have depleted fuel wood).[14]**

Could there be a greater contrast with the suburban housewives described by Ms. Friedan as suffering from "the problem that has no name"? ("Not too much was asked of them but too little....Society asks so little of women."[15]) But Ms. Friedan doesn't hold up Amerindian squaws or Indian women of the subcontinent or Zimbabwean women as exemplars for her middle-class readers. Her exemplars are American men:

But the husbands of the women I interviewed were often engaged in work that demanded ability, responsibility, and decision. I noticed that when these men were saddled with a domestic chore, they polished it off in much less time than it seemed to take their wives.[16]

The thought suggests itself: Perhaps the poor seaweed gatherers are so overworked because of the lack of motivation of their men. The signature of "developing" countries—the backward, impoverished squalid countries, where slavery,[17] cannibalism, bride-burning, human sacrifice[18] and female circumcision are still known, are those which have not yet discovered how to make men work to support families. "Women in developing countries," says Ms. French, "work harder than men."[19] This is one reason why they are "developing"—backward, impoverished, usually matriarchal. Perhaps the Indian *men* suffer from "the problem that has no name" as they doze in the sun, idle their time away and expect to be served by their women.

---

[14]Marilyn French, *The War Against Women*, pp. 29, 34.
[15]Betty Friedan, *The Feminine Mystique* (New York: W.W. Norton, 1963), pp. 252, 328.
[16]*Ibid.*
[17]David Aikman, "Slavery in Our Time," *The American Spectator*, February, 1997: "Take Sudan, for example. Eyewitness reports and interviews with escaped slaves, slave-traders, and captured slave-raiders have been collected by human rights groups (particularly Amnesty International and Human Rights Watch Africa), by Sudanese Roman Catholic bishops and Protestant clerics and missionaries, and by numerous international reporters for several years....Slaves could be purchased or sold in Sudan, readers and viewers learned, for as little as $15. If they were female and nubile, the price could be as much as several hundred dollars. Before that happened, many slave-owners would subject their human chattel to forcible genital mutilation."
[18]Alain Danielou, *Gods of Love and Ecstasy: The Traditions of Shiva and Dionysus* (Rochester, VT: Inner Traditions, 1984), p. 170: "In Shivaism, human sacrifice, which is the culmination of animal sacrifice, was practised in the rites of both Skanda and the goddess. Today, it is rare."
[19]P. 33.

Suppose Freud's question "What does a woman want?" had been put to such a Zimbabwean or Indian woman, what would her answer be? Perhaps: "I want to live in America, that women's paradise, to have a loving father who would care for me, buy me nice things, send me to a posh women's college like Smith, where I could get a superior education and meet interesting people. After college I would want to marry a nice husband who would buy a suburban home for me, and a car and would protect me with life insurance and health insurance and let me go shopping with his credit cards and allow me to play golf and bridge in the afternoons when I didn't shop. In America I would need to spend only 3 percent of my time on my maternal functions.[20] In America I would live such an easy life that I would survive my husband by seven years (unlike in India, where men outlive women). Or I could divorce him and take *my* children and *his* house and compel him to continue supporting me. I could join a feminist group and complain of how oppressed I was. I might live in Maryland or Ohio, where the nice governors have issued blanket pardons to all wives who murder their husbands."

Thus (perhaps) the yearning of the Indian or Zimbabwean woman, dreaming of the good life, as feminists like Ms. Boulding dream of the good life of Indian squaws and third world women, their serenity and quiet sureness.

Suppose Freud's question were asked of an American housewife, someone like Ms. Friedan before she liberated herself by divorce. She would reply that while she suffered from *acedia*, the problem that has no name, she did not at all wish to live the life of the squaw or the Zimbabwean peasant woman or the seaweed gatherers of Ahmadabad or the life of early nineteenth century women such as Lucy Stone, whose mother exclaimed when she was born "Oh, dear! I am sorry it's a girl. A woman's life is so hard."[21] When Ms. Friedan complained that "society

---

[20]Dorothy Dinnerstein, *The Mermaid and the Minotaur: Sexual Arrangements and Human Malaise* (New York: Harper and Row, 1976), p.25: "Another generous average estimate is that each birth might remove a woman from her normal sphere of activity for at most six months. This assumes, of course, that except for lactation—which is also optional—the responsibility for child care is shared equally by men, and that working hours are short and flexible enough to make this possible. Both of these conditions are so well within our technical means that the problem is to explain why they do not now exist (that is, to understand the societal and psychological patterns that block their overdue development)."

Six months times three is a year and half. Thus to be physically a mother should in principle, for a woman who chooses this option, require *at most* about 3 percent of the fifty-year period of adult vigor between the ages of fifteen and sixty-five.

[21]*Feminine Mystique*, p. 88.

asks so little of women" or when Ibsen's Nora in *A Doll's House* complained that her husband's pampering and coddling kept her from growing up and being a high achiever (like men) she was thinking of helping to share men's work in the Senate, in corporate offices, university classrooms, medical clinics, or research laboratories—the sort of thing feminist Dr. Gerda Lerner is thinking of when she says, "What the cost was to society in general through the loss of talent and intellectual work of half the population cannot be estimated."[22] Dr. Lerner isn't thinking of seaweed gathering. She is thinking of the superior performance of males under patriarchy, a performance not matched by males under matriarchy. She is really complaining (though without realizing it) that civilization is a male creation.

Would some Indian philosopher-playwright like Ibsen sympathize not (as Ms. French does) with the female seaweed gatherer but with her husband sitting idly on the wagon all day holding the reins of his horse— and allow *him* to complain (as Ibsen's Nora does) that he was suffering a "great evil" by being deprived of meaningful labor, perhaps driven, like some of the husbands of the squaws described by Ms. Boulding, to alcoholism or suicide?

Like Ms. Boulding's reservation Indians, like the ghettos, like the Tierra del Fuegians who don't wear clothes and the, Australian aborigines who don't build shelters. Like the Veddhas of Ceylon, like the Jivaros of Ecuador, like the Nairs of the Malabar Coast, beloved of feminists for not even having marriage and families, like the tribes of the Orinoco, like the Khyougtha of the Chittagong; like most other societies that nobody has ever heard of, like the Lycians spoken of by Herodotus, like the Seri Indians , and every other matriarchal culture. It's *natural.* Look at your dog and your cat. The judge knows this. He doesn't want to listen to an anthropological lecture on kinship systems. He just wants to do what he and his fellow judges have done for a hundred and thirty years—give the mother custody and hit the father with support obligations. It's that simple. But the sixty percent divorce rate is making payments hard to collect. Men are beginning to wonder whether getting married and starting a family is worth the acceptance of slavery. Their reluctance to pay is creating a new class of politicians like President Clinton and Los Angeles' District Attorney Gil Garcetti who cultivate

---

[22]Gerda Lerner, *The Creation of Feminist Consciousness* (Oxford: Oxford University Press, 1993), p. 30.

female voters by villainizing "Deadbeat Dads" who don't feel like subsidizing matriarchy.

If the genders were reversed, women would not submit to what men now submit to. If lawmakers did to women what they routinely do to men—if they deprived them of their children, their homes, their property, their role, and compelled them to work and share their income with their ex-husbands, those lawmakers would be torn to pieces by mobs of frenzied women—and they know it and that's why they don't do it. Lord Lane knows it and that's why he prefers to strike up a pose about his concern for the welfare of the children whom he victimizes by ignoring justice and depriving them of fathers.

What is mostly needed to end the ongoing massacre of families is the raising of men's consciousness. Men must realize they are not being honorable gentlemen in consenting to have their children taken from them. They are betraying and abandoning them.

"Joint Custody is the cure," says Stuart Miller.[23] *No it is not;* and Miller's reason for supposing it to be—"When fathers receive joint custody, the child-support compliance rate jumps to more than 90%"—is the worst possible "justification" for it. Miller is saying that joint custody makes the destruction of the family *workable.* Families ought not to be destroyed; they ought to be strengthened. Father custody will accomplish this, joint custody will not. Joint custody will only strengthen divorce.

Father custody would benefit women. According to *Ms.* Magazine, "divorced women have the lowest household incomes of any group of women surveyed....One reason that divorced women are in the worst economic situation is that their income decreases markedly when their marriages end and they are able to save much less than single or married women....Single women without children have a greater measure of economic freedom than the rest."[24] Single women without children, in fact, earn slightly more than single men.

According to a report by the Carnegie Corporation, "The percentage of families with only one parent or with two parents who work out of the home has soared from about 40% in 1970 to almost 70% 20 years later":

---

[23] *Wall Street Journal,* 3 February, 1995.
[24] *Ms.* May, 1978.

"The problems have gotten worse," says David Hamburg, president of the Carnegie Corp of New York.

"Young teens engage in more and more risky behavior. Things that used to be tried out in later adolescence are much more commonly occurring earlier—drugs, sex and violence. The risks have gotten higher—from somewhat risky to very risky."

"Altogether, nearly half of American adolescents are at high or moderate risk of seriously damaging their life chances," the report states. "The damage may be near-term and vivid, or it may be delayed, like a time bomb set in youth."[25]

(Nearly half! Why do we tolerate it?)

"The juvenile crime rate," says Max Vanzi, has outpaced the adult crime rate in recent years....Meanwhile, as overall crime rates are dropping in California, juvenile arrests have been rising, totaling more than 255,000 in 1995. Those arrests can be expected to continue upward as the youth population increases...."[26] According to a report issued by several federal agencies, mortality among black males 15 to 19 has risen from 125.3 deaths per 100,000 in 1985 to 234.3 per 100,000 in 1994, an increase of 87 percent in nine years.[27] According to Malcolm Klein, USC professor and author of *The American Street Gang*, gang violence has proven to be intractable and has grown worse.[28] According to Mary Ridgeway, a gang probation worker in Los Angeles, the most alarming trend is the increasing youth of armed gang members. Two decades ago, the shooting was done by 16- to 19-year-olds. Now, more shootings are committed by 13- to 15-year-olds.[29]

Los Angeles Times writer Bettijane Levine, says, "It is not a media mirage: Statistics confirm that more horrendous crimes are being committed by increasingly younger children....A recent analysis of data in California cities showed that homicide arrest rates for juveniles were increasing faster than for any other age group. Between 1980 and 1990, the homicide arrest rate for youngsters ages 10 through 17 increased 65%."[30]

---

[25]*Los Angeles Times*, 12 October, 1995.
[26]*Los Angeles Times*, 21 April, 1997.
[27]*Los Angeles Times*, 3 July, 1997.
[28]*Los Angeles Times*, 29 September, 1995.
[29]*Ibid*.
[30]*Los Angeles Times*, 6 September, 1995.

According to Irwin Garfinkel and Sara McLanahan, "The biggest differences in the performance of schoolchildren appear in teacher evaluations—such as grade point averages and behavioral assessments—both of which show substantially lower scores for children from one-parent families."[31]

Ms. Friedan cites a pair of public-opinion polls made in 1968 and 1971 by Daniel Yankelovich. In the first of these seventy percent of college students answered Yes to the question, "Do you believe that hard work will always pay off?" In the second, 67 percent said No. Quite a change in three years—years which witnessed the cresting of feminism. Ms. Friedan's comment:

As we go into the 1980s, Yankelovich is finding that a majority of adult American men no longer seek or are satisfied by conventional job success. Only one out of every five men now says that work means more to him than leisure. More than half of American men say that work is no longer their major source of satisfaction.[32]

Of course. The reward for working was formerly that it gave a man a family. Now more than half of them are deprived of their families and the others are threatened with the same deprivation. In 1981 Ms. Friedan quoted Bernard Lefkowitz's report of a 71 percent increase in working-aged men who have left the labor force since 1968 and who are not looking for work.[33] Society cannot motivate these men to be family providers as it motivated their fathers and grandfathers during the era of the feminine mystique. Society has destroyed their work ethic by destroying their families or their hope of having families. Women, according to Ms. Friedan, are complaining that increasing numbers of men are turning to homosexuality or celibacy.[34]

She tells us, "I've suspected that the men who really feel threatened by the women's movement in general or by their own wives' moves toward some independent activity are the ones who are most unsure of their women's love."[35] They would be fools not to be, since marriage is an economic arrangement in which the man supports the woman and their children in order to have a family.

---

[31]*Single Mothers and Their Children*, p. 28.
[32]*The Second Stage*, P. 134.
[33]*The Second Stage*, p. 136.
[34]P. 138.
[35]*The Second Stage*, p. 155.

Such a man often worries that his wife has married him only for economic security or the status and vicarious power he provides. If she can get these things for herself, what does she need him for? Why will she continue to love him? In his anger is also the fear she will surely leave him.

She doesn't need him and they both know it, even if they haven't seen the statistics or read Nickles and Ashcraft's *The Coming Matriarchy*. If the man imagines marriage is held together by "love" he will find out differently from her demands for post-marital subsidization, like those Ms. Friedan tried to collect from her ex-husband. "Most men," she continues,

sense they are really dependent on women for security and love and intimacy, just as most women learn, after the old resentment-making imbalances are out of the way, that they are dependent on men for these same qualities.

They are dependent on men for these same qualities *and for financial support*, as their clamors in the divorce court prove. "The resentment-making imbalances" refers to the man's money, which gives him his bargaining power. Ms. Friedan thinks of men's money as a love-spoiler "which our movement for equality between the sexes would change."[36] Meaning women can be made economically independent of men by political agitation and Affirmative Action, by admitting women to the armed services academies and the Virginia Military Institute and by making women firepersons and policepersons and pretending that they can perform such jobs. A 1991 Navy study revealed that 65 percent of enlisted women in the pay grades E-4 and below became pregnant while on sea duty. "It's killing our [combat] readiness...all across the boards," says the Navy spokesman.[37] And their mostly fatherless kids will be deprived also of their mothers and cared for by low-paid child care workers with high turnover rates. Many of these kids are headed for the underclass.

With women economically independent, we can, says Ms. Friedan, "open up alternative lifestyles for the future, alternatives to the kind of marriage and nuclear family structure that not only women but men want out of today."[38]

---

[36] *It Changed My Life*, p. 224.
[37] *Los Angeles Times*, 28 July, 1992.
[38] *It Changed My Life*, p. 113; see p. 147 supra.

This was written in 1976. We are now seeing that future. We are in a position to compare Ms. Friedan's glowing anticipation of it with the reality. "What surprises are in store for men," she exclaimed,

> **and for us, as we give up some of that manipulating control of the family we once used to keep them emotional babies, dependent on us—protecting them from the grounding, warming, human realities of daily life?...And even if we no longer need men to take care of us, to define our whole existence as in the past—just because we are no longer that dependent, can't we now more freely admit that we still need and want men to love, to have babies with, to share parenting and chores and joys and economic burdens and adventures in new kinds of families and homes?**[39]

The big surprise in store for the man is divorce and getting wiped out when the lady no longer feels like bestowing her love freely and joyously. The big surprise is the triumph of the Promiscuity Principle (a woman's right to control her own sexuality), the destruction of the Legitimacy Principle (every child must have a father) and the undermining of patriarchy and the nuclear family. Feminist Dorothy Dinnerstein tells us her intention "is to help make sure that the eruption turns out to be part of a genuine revolution: a fundamental reorganizing event embodying the clearest possible insight into the process that is being reorganized: a revolution conceived in such a way that it will not reverse itself."[40] Feminist Sandra Schneiders speaks of "a deep, abiding, emotionally draining anger that, depending on a woman's personality, might run the gamut from towering rage to chronic depression."[41]

Ms. Friedan is right that there are growing numbers of men who "want out"—men increasingly fearful of commitment, as the costs of commitment grow and the rewards of commitment dwindle. According to Frank Pittman, Atlanta psychiatrist and family therapist, "We have a society full of men who are not really interested in being fathers."[42] We had better believe these people. The patriarchal system is artificial; it must be imposed. It is accepted by women only because of its advantages—money, stability and high status for good women. Feminist rhetoric tells women they can gain these advantages for themselves. Feminist rhetoric has the backup of the legal system which properly owes its loyalty to the patriarchy which created it, not to the matriarchy.

---

[39]*The Second Stage*, pp. 122f.
[40]Dorothy Dinnerstein, *The Mermaid and the Minotaur* (New York: Harper and Row, 1976), p. 125.
[41]Sandra Schneiders, *Beyond Patching* (New York: Paulist Press, 1991), p. 98.
[42]*Los Angeles Times*, 12 June 12, 1992.

Fathers have yet to discover this. George Gilder writes of women's long-term sexual horizons. How can *men* have similar long-term horizons when they face a sixty percent divorce rate, which makes possessing such horizons a nightmare for them?

"Not only," says Nigel Davies, "has the institution of marriage...become more fragile, its nature also has been transformed. Until recent times, marriage even in the West was based on the idea of the wife being a form of property. But among other factors, the female-headed household has destroyed this notion."[43] It has destroyed this notion by making the ex-husband (or the taxpayer) a form of property, using the justification that the children (in Mom's possession, naturally) are *her* property.

The ghettos show what is in store for us. Gail Stokes's essay *Black Woman to Black Man* "accurately expresses the rage of some working black women who have equated manhood with the ability of their husbands to be the sole economic provider in the family and who feel cheated when black men refuse to accept the role":

Of course you will say, "How can I love you and want to be with you when I come home and you're looking like a slob? Why white women never open the door for their husbands the way you black bitches do."

I should guess not, you ignorant man. Why should they be in such a state when they've got maids like me to do everything for them? There is no screaming at the kids for her, and whether her man loves her or not, he provides...provides...do you hear that, nigger? PROVIDES![44]

She understands that marriage is an economic institution. If she acquired economic independence together with an education, she might think otherwise, like elite feminists. She would then find herself in the group with the highest divorce rate. The economic "resentment-making imbalances" are what hold marriages together; and when women earn their own way, they can do something about their resentment—they can skip into the female kinship system, as Ms. Friedan did, as ghetto matriarchs do.

---

[43]Nigel Davies, *The Rampant God* (New York: Morrow, 1984), p. 275.
[44]Gail Stokes, *Black Woman to Black Man*, quoted in Victoria King, *Manhandled: Black Females* (Nashville, TN: Winston-Derek, 1992), p. 61.

It's the same everywhere. In Egypt, "Women's growing economic power—with more of them now working and increasing their education—is another frequent source of tension," says Suzanne Fayad, a psychologist at the El Nadccm Center for Violence Victims.[45] The "epidemic of violence against women...is fueled...by poverty, male frustration and a rising tide of Islamic extremism that often seems directed at curtailing women's choices...."

Margaret Mead tells us that "Somewhere at the dawn of human history, some social invention was made under which males started nurturing females and their young":

We have no reason to believe that the nurturing males had any knowledge of physical paternity, although it is quite possible that being fed was a reward meted out to the female who was not too fickle with her sexual favors.[46]

Here is the economic basis of marriage: the female gives the male a family; the male gives the female economic support. But now the feminist revolution, exploiting women's resentment of patriarchal regulation, offers to make the women economically independent or semi-independent, and thus make men superfluous or semi-superfluous, and make marriage meaningless. The divorce rate is approaching the breaking point. Patriarchy and stable marriage are no longer functioning as a means for organizing society. Women have withdrawn their sexual loyalty and men must do something about it. Why not father custody?

"Human society," says feminist-anthropologist Helen Fisher, rejoicing over women's new sexual freedom, "is now discovering its ancient roots....Men and women are moving toward the kind of roles they had on the grasslands of Africa millions of years ago."[47] True. Women's yearning for the primeval freedom of the African grasslands is identical with the "enormous potential counterforce" which animates the feminist movement.

Yet it must be a man's world. The woman's world was when they enjoyed their freedom back on the African grasslands, the world they enjoy in the ghettos and on Indian reservations and in subsidized housing tracts where women and children live on welfare and food stamps.

---

[45]*Los Angeles Times*, 3 May, 1997.
[46]Margaret Mead, *Male and Female* (New York: William Morrow, 1949), p. 189.
[47]*U.S. News and World Report*, 8 August, 1988.

Margaret Mead has been quoted on the need of the male to provide food for some female and her young—if he wants to be a full member of society. It would be nice if women were not dependent creatures, if they could earn their own way. "Women, after all," says Ms. Friedan, "are fighting for an equal share in the activities and the power games that are rewarded in this society."[48] She means the activities pursued by successful males, activities which most women, however, are incapable of pursuing. And now the high status formerly awarded to women's maternal functions has been largely lost. Women who rely on these functions are "just housewives."

Men are losing their motivation, as shown by Judith Wallerstein's study mentioned on page 112. According to Sylvia Ann Hewlett cited on page 33.

A full 60 percent of the youngsters in her sample are on a downward educational course compared with their fathers, and 45 percent are on a similar downward course compared with their mothers.[49]

Father-loss, says Ms. Hewlett, causes children to lose confidence in themselves. They drift because they have rejected the male "double standard of work" which depends on the female acceptance of the double standard of sexuality. Female unchastity deprives men of the role of family provider, the only role capable of civilizing most men. Many of these men had been deprived of *their* fathers by Mom's divorcing them. The sons will in turn be poor role models for *their* sons.

Betty Friedan told us a third of a century ago that sex roles were obsolete, that we should take off our "masks." We now see the resulting rolelessness and see that the roles or masks performed a useful function, like a judge's robes. Now we have bewildered men adorning themselves with earrings and freaky haircuts and bewildered girls adorning themselves with nose rings or eyebrow rings or clamoring to be soldiers, policemen and firemen.

"Wallerstein," says Hewlett, talks about the "sleeper" effects of marital disruption, problems of commitment and attachment that may surface many years after parental divorce. According to Wallerstein, when it comes to forming relationships in adult life, "it helps enormously to have imprinted on

---

[48]*The Second Stage*, p. 147.
[49]*When the Bough Breaks*, p. 141.

one's emotional circuitry the patterning of a successful, enduring relationship between a man and a woman." This is what most children of divorce lack....There is...a great deal of new evidence showing that the breakup of a marriage can trigger severe emotional and intellectual problems for children, many of which center on the fact that the children of divorce see very little of their fathers.[50]

The worst results are found in the ghettos, where, according to Professor Steven Goldberg, "the few blacks who today commit vastly disproportionate numbers of violent crimes suffer not from emotions too powerful to resist, but from a lack of conscience itself (owing in large part to the absence of a father)."[51]

The white pattern described by Wallerstein increasingly resembles the black pattern thus described by Ms. Richmond-Abbott: "Many young blacks postpone marriage. When they do marry at a later age, it is often an impulsive decision and there may be only a tentative commitment to the marriage."[52]

Like it or not, civilized society depends on women's acceptance of patriarchal sexual regulation, without which there cannot be families. It is not "little" that society asks of women, as Ms. Friedan would have us believe—this sexual loyalty which allows men families. Without it society becomes matriarchal.

---

[50]Hewlett, pp. 115, 113.
[51]"Black Murder," *Chronicles*, January, 1995.
[52]Marie Richmond-Abbott, *Masculine and Feminine: Sex Roles Over the Life Cycle* (Menlo Park, CA: Addison-Wesley Publishing Company, 1983), p. 286.

IX) CHILD ABUSE

A disproportionate amount of child abuse is committed by mothers even in two-parent homes (this is a dirty little secret feminists don't want you to know), but the amount of abuse increases enormously when the mother becomes single. According to Patrick Fagan and William FitzGerald, "The person most likely to abuse a young child is the child's own mother....The most dangerous place for a women and her child is an environment in which she is cohabiting with a boyfriend who is not the father of her children. The rate of child abuse may be as much as 33 times higher."[1] According to Ronald Tansley, "In Oregon last year [1994] 33 children were killed as a result of child abuse. Mothers were killers in 27 of these cases."[2] In Milwaukee County in 1989 there were 1,050 reported cases of child abuse. Eighty-three percent of these cases occurred in households receiving AFDC. In other words in mostly female-headed households.[3]

According to Maggie Gallagher, "The person most likely to abuse a child physically is a single mother. The person most likely to abuse a child sexually is the mother's boyfriend or second husband....Divorce, though usually portrayed as a protection against domestic violence, is far more frequently a contributing cause."[4]

The fiction that fathers are the principal child abusers is promoted not only by feminists and the media and politicians seeking the feminist vote, but by otherwise respectable scholars. Thus Richard Gelles:

Mothers, because they spend more time with their children and have a greater responsibility for child care, are more likely to use physical discipline than fathers are.

Gelles then goes on to compare *mothers* not with *fathers* but with *males*, lumping fathers with the second greatest abusers (after mothers), mothers' boyfriends (who may become stepfathers):

---

[1]Patrick Fagan and William Fitzgerald, *The Child Abuse Crisis: The Disintegration of Marriage, Family and the American Community."*
[2]*Transitions*, July/August, 1995.
[3]*The Family in America: New Research*, December, 1989.
[4]*Abolition of Marriage*, p. 36.

But males, although they spend less time with children and have less overall responsibility for child care, are more likely than females to injure or kill children....A child's mother is more likely to kill or injure him than his stepmother is. Male offenders tend to be more distantly related to their victims. A child's stepfather or the boyfriend of his mother is more likely to kill or injure him than his father is.[5]

Male offenders, in other words, tend not to be fathers—fathers tend not to be offenders. Gelles says (if the reader takes the trouble to winkle out the meaning) that the biological father is the child's best protector, not only against the stepmother but against the mother, who is far more likely to abuse or kill the child than the father, and who is especially abusive and murderous if she becomes single—i.e., if she and the judge exile the child's best protector, the father.

The father protects the child better against the stepmother than the mother protects the child against the boyfriend or stepfather. How many readers will understand this truth behind Gelles's coyly evasive predication about the distantness of the "male offender"?

Sociologist Ira Reiss cites the findings of Diana Russell of Mills College, who "studied sexual abuse of children with emphasis on father/daughter incest":

Russell found that 2 percent of those growing up with a natural father were sexually abused as were 17 percent of those growing up with a step-father.[6]

The child is thus eight and a half times safer with a father than with a stepfather. David Finkelhor cuts Russell's estimate of danger from fathers in half:

Sociologist David Finkelhor, [a specialist in child sexual abuse] has estimated that for the country as a whole about 1 percent of women are sexually abused in some fashion by their fathers....Finkelhor's 1 percent amounts to about one million American women aged eighteen and over who have been sexually abused by their fathers! If these estimates are anywhere near the mark, father/daughter incest is far from a rare phenomenon.

---

[5]Richard Gelles, *The Book of David: How Preserving Families Can Cost Children's Lives* (HarprCollins, 1996), pp. 75f.
[6]Ira Reiss, *An End to Shame: Shaping our Next Sexual Revolution* (Buffalo: Prometheus Books, 1990), p. 52.

But why the emphasis on the threat of the father rather than on the far greater threat of the stepfather or boyfriend, who enters the picture once the father is exiled? Reiss cites Freud's skepticism of women's reports of father incest:

Almost all of my women patients told me that they had been seduced by their father. I was driven to recognize in the end that these reports were untrue and so came to understand that the hysterical symptoms are derived from fantasies and not from real occurrences.

Reiss's comment:

Today there are many who, like Freud, still prefer to deny the reality of such incest; however, the evidence is overwhelming. Unfortunately, father/daughter incest is a reality, not a fantasy.

But if *almost all* of Freud's female patients accused their fathers and if only two percent of them (Russell's estimate) or one percent of them (Finkelhor's estimate) were actually molested then "almost all" of them *were* mistaken and Freud was right.

The same *suggestio falsi* is found everywhere in the press and the media. Thus Carla Rivera in the *Los Angeles Times* of 15 November, 1996:

Mothers, who were the largest single category of perpetrators, were involved in 20 of the slayings. In 17 of the cases, death came at the hands of a boyfriend, stepfather or other caregiver. The report found that 62% of the assailants were men, most frequently either a father or the mother's boyfriend, stepfather or other caregiver.

Again the fathers are lumped with the mothers' boyfriends and other caregivers to make up the 62 percent of male villains.

A recent study based in Sacramento County found that abused children are 67 times more likely than non-abused ones to run afoul of the law.

Based on the results of its study [says the Los Angeles Times of 20 June, 1997], the Child Welfare League of America challenged President Clinton to veto bills pending in Congress that would earmark federal funds for new juvenile prison facilities. Instead the league...urged the federal government to funnel more money to such programs as preschool for low-income kids, home

visits for teenage mothers, enrichment and mentoring programs in high school and family counseling for first-time juvenile offenders.

According to the *Times*, "the arrest rate for abused children was 60 children per 1,000, compared with a rate of 0.89 for non-abused children." It quotes Buffalo Police Commissioner Gil Kerlikowske, as saying "If Congress is serious about fighting crime, it won't pretend that just building more jails is going to solve the problem. Those of us on the front lines know we'll win the war on crime when Congress boosts investment in early childhood programs and Head Start, health care for kids, after-school and mentoring and recreational programs."

If the child's principal abuser is the mother and the next worst abuser is the mother's boyfriend, why invest in either juvenile prisons or "early childhood programs" rather than protect the child from abuse by allowing his best protector, the father, to remain in his home?

Health and Human Services Secretary Donna Shalala calls on "all Americans" to help stop the growing harm inflicted on the country's children, over a million of whom were victims of substantiated child abuse in 1994, an increase of 27 percent since 1990.[7] "All Americans" includes divorce court judges—but they are the ones who most frequently place children where they are at greatest risk, in female headed households. Ms. Shalala seems not to know that children are safest in a father-headed family and that the single mothers and mothers' boyfriends in whose care judges place so many of "the country's children" are the principal abusers. "All Americans" includes President Clinton, who tells ex-husbands "We will make you pay"—pay to subsidize the singleness of the mothers who commit most of the abuse—pay these mothers so that they can afford to expel *them* and drag their children into the Female Kinship System. "All Americans" includes Ms. Shalala herself who tries to implement President Clinton's policy of compelling ex-husbands to subsidize the abusive arrangement which excludes them and thereby increases the amount of abuse.

The National Committee to Prevent Child Abuse issues a list of ten ways to prevent child abuse. All ten are irrelevant to the major causes: "Support activities...Volunteer at a local child abuse program...Report suspected abuse or neglect...Advocate for services to help families...Speak up for non-violent television...Make a contribution...Help

---

[7] *HHS News*, 1 April, 1996.

a friend, neighbor or relative...Help yourself...Support and suggest programs...Promote programs in schools."

Let's say, the National Committee to Prevent Child Abuse is a screen organization which pretends concern about the abuse in order to disguise the fact that its program perpetuates and exacerbates abuse. There is no hint in its proposals that the best means to protect children is to keep the father in the home.

X) ALTERNATIVE FAMILIES

"Most Americans," says feminist Stephanie Coontz, "support the emergence of alternative ways of organizing parenthood and marriage. They don't want to reestablish the supremacy of the male breadwinner model, don't want to have male overachievers or to define masculine and feminine roles in any monolithic way."[1]

Ms. Coontz sounds like *Cosmopolitan*, which has been quoted: "The woman we're profiling is an extraordinarily sexually free human being" whose new bedroom expressiveness constitutes a "break with the old double standard."[2] These women are the "most Americans" Ms. Coontz speaks of—those who want to get back to matriarchal promiscuity. They are making patriarchy and the family seem obsolete and making matriarchy seem modern and normative. This portentous change will continue until fathers realize the threat posed by the female kinship system and insist on the custody of their children.

There is no comprehension by Ms. Coontz or at *Cosmopolitan* or among lawmakers and judges of how this female promiscuity attacks the male role and therefore removes the husband's economic responsibility to the wife or ex-wife, of how it removes both "the male breadwinner model," and the grounds for mother custody. "I have met men," says Ms. Coontz,

> who tell angry stories about having been tricked by a woman into thinking it was "safe" to have sex. "Why should I have to pay child support?" demanded one. "Doesn't that just encourage women to have babies outside of marriage?" It is, of course, totally unethical for a woman to assure a man that sex is "safe" when it isn't. But what is the alternative? If a man could get off the hook by claiming "she told me it was safe," no unmarried father would pay child support.[3]

The alternative is patriarchy, based on chastity and the double standard. No unmarried father *should* pay child support—which subsidizes the alternative to patriarchy and bribes women to be "totally

---

[1] Stephanie Coontz, *The Way We Really Are* (Basic Books, 1997), p. 77.
[2] Cosmopolitan, September, 1980, quoted in Susan Faludi, *Backlash*, p. 404.
[3] Coontz, p. 88.

unethical." Society does not need "family diversity." It needs patriarchal families. "Family diversity" is undermining society. If mothers can get support money from men without submitting to the regulation imposed by marriage, why should they accept regulation and give husbands a role and a family? This necessity for males to have a role and a family is why wives must submit to husbands. To say that an unwed mother is entitled to be supported is to deny that chastity gives a woman bargaining power. Removing the double standard frightens responsible men away from marriage.

WOMEN YOU SCREW

"There are women you screw and women you marry." If all women are willing to screw, there are none to marry. Feminists don't want to understand this. Ms. Coontz, for example, says "The 'traditional' double standard...may have led more middle-class girls to delay sex at the end of the nineteenth century than today, but it also created higher proportions of young female prostitutes."[4] Of course. These are the "women you screw." Patriarchal society puts these women to work as part of its program to regulate sexuality. They are an essential part of the system, but men do not marry such women since it is impossible to have a family with them.

Following World War II, when India became independent of British rule, a number of legal innovations were proposed, including the abolition of prostitution. Prime Minister Nehru was sympathetic to the idea but was dissuaded from supporting it by a group of learned Brahmins who pointed out to him that where there are no brothels every home becomes a brothel. In such a society there would be no rules regulating female sexuality: women would have, as Ms. Friedan puts it, an "inalienable human right to control our own bodies."[5]

This is the essence of the female kinship system. Her right is inalienable—regardless of the marriage contract. The meaningfulness and enforceability of that contract are essential to the patriarchal system and since the law now refuses to enforce it—since the legal system will not support the family—it is necessary to remove all discretion from that system and make father custody automatic. The present situation, with

---

[4]*Coontz*, p. 2.
[5]*It Changed My Life*, p. 153.

men having to trust women and lawyers, is too threatening to men. Ms. Friedan speaks for millions of women when she says women have a right to disregard the marriage contract. Judge Noland speaks for most judges when he says human reproduction ought to be modeled on that of cattle. It is no wonder so many men are afraid of marriage, no wonder so many men are afraid of judges willing to do the bidding of disloyal wives— judges whose weakness therefore encourages wives to be disloyal. No wonder the proportion of single adults has skyrocketed from 21% in 1970 to 41% in 1992, no wonder so many children have no fathers.

In 1992, the quincentenary of Columbus's discovery of America, it was the fashion among parlor intellectuals to condemn the great explorer for the bad things he did, one of these being the introduction of prostitution into America. Where sex was free, as it was in tribal America, women were liberated and prostitutes would have starved because they had nothing to sell. Where sex is free wives have nothing to sell either, so men have no stable families and no motivation to become high achievers. Women offer their love "freely and joyously"—but only temporarily. This is the female kinship system.

American men are slowly realizing that this kinship system is now taking over our own society, preventing men from having families, preventing prospective wives from having anything to sell, because the marriages they offer men (thanks to the legal system's betrayal of the family) are based on a contract whose fraudulence is becoming obvious. American men have yet to realize that there is only one solution to this breakdown—automatic father custody.

Ms. Coontz thinks Charles Murray is cruel for wanting to deny child support to women who bear illegitimate children:

> **Charles Murray of the American Enterprise Institute...advocates denying child support to any woman who bears a baby out of wedlock. Girls, he declares, need to grow up knowing that if they want any legal claims whatsoever on the father of their child, "they must marry." Answering objections that this gives men free reign (sic) to engage in irresponsible sex, Murray offers a response straight out of a Dickens novel. A man who gets a woman pregnant, he observes, "has approximately the same causal responsibility" for her condition "as a slice of chocolate cake has in determining whether a woman gains weight." It is her responsibility, not the cake's, to resist temptation."[6]**

---

[6]Coontz, p. 88.

It is her responsibility if she expects to gain the rewards offered by the patriarchal system. These rewards include the raising of her standard of living by 73 percent.[7] Any diminution of these rewards weakens marriage and patriarchy (which, of course, Ms. Coontz thinks desirable). Any offering of similar rewards to women who bear children out of wedlock likewise weakens marriage and patriarchy. It is a betrayal of chaste wives, including the legal wife, or future legal wife, of the father of the illegitimate child. It makes the father less likely to marry such a legal wife, another reason why women ask, "Where are the men?"

Murray tells women who want legal claims on the father that "they must marry." But with the divorce rate at sixty percent and with more young wives than young husbands committing adultery,[8] marriage offers too little to fathers to induce them to accept the responsibilities of supporting a family. It is becoming clear to very large numbers of men that bearing the yoke and drawing the plow for an ex-wife or providing (through marriage which obligates the husband to the wife but not the wife to the husband) an opportunity for a wife to "make an amazing discovery about herself"[9] (that adultery is fun and therefore the wife's right) is not what they want from marriage and that marriage, in fact, is becoming merely an exciting way for women to be promiscuous. There is no way the father can perform his obligation of safeguarding his family and his property without society's guarantee of father custody in the event of divorce.

Ms. Coontz's proposal to make the ex-husband or ex-boyfriend pay reveals her insincerity in proposing an "alternative way of organizing parenthood."[10] She really wants wives or ex-wives to go back to being dependent on men. She just doesn't want men to take responsibility for anything except subsidizing Mom's sexual independence.

BACK TO QUEEN VICTORIA

If, as feminists wish, patriarchy is to be done away with, women must either become truly economically independent (not dependent on support money from ex-husbands or on affirmative action benefits or on welfare) or they must give up custody of children in divorce cases. If

---

[7]This is Lenore Weitzman's figure, which is dubious, but so often repeated in feminist literature that citing it is justifiable. I discuss it in my *Garbage Generation*, Chapter 8.
[8]Heyn, p. 26, citing a survey by *Playboy* made in 1982.
[9]Heyn, p. 30.
[10]The quote is from the dust wrapper of Ms. Coontz's book.

patriarchy is to be preserved, female withdrawal of loyalty to husbands, to marriage, to family, needs to be answered not only by male withdrawal of economic subsidization—the abolition of alimony and child support payments—but by a switch to father custody.

Ms. Coontz quotes feminist Katha Pollitt's rejection of the "family values crusade":

> **We'd have to bring back the whole nineteenth century: Restore the cult of virginity and the double standard, ban birth control, restrict divorce, kick women out of decent jobs, force unwed pregnant teen mothers to put their babies up for adoption on pain of social death, make out-of-wedlock children legal nonpersons. That's not going to happen.[11]**

A woman who rejects pre-marital chastity and the double standard, who claims the right to unrestricted divorce and the right to repudiate her marriage vows, to assert that legitimacy, and therefore fatherhood are meaningless—such a woman is proclaiming her independence of the patriarchal system and telling men they may not share in her reproductive life—telling them that she means to live under the female kinship system. Fine. But she is throwing away her bargaining power with men who do believe in the patriarchal system and she has no right to expect males to subsidize her sexual independence. She doesn't need a man. A husband subsidizes a wife in order that he may have a family, and women who think as Katha Pollitt thinks must be deemed unmarriageable unless men have automatic custody of the offspring procreated with them in marriage. Ms. Pollitt evidently supposes that automatic mother custody and its corollary, automatic subsidization of "her" children, are unchangeable facts of nature. She supposes that men must never play their Money Card, never demand custody of their children, never refuse to leave their homes when Mom orders them out.

Bringing back the nineteenth century would threaten women with other things that Ms. Pollitt supposes aren't going to happen—the return of the sanctity of motherhood, the Angel in the House, the feminine mystique, the role-playing, perhaps the "iron masks" detested by Ms. Friedan, in which wives "choke with impotent rage...the panicky play-acting of the old roles, with mutual contempt for our own duplicity and the ones we dupe...the bitterness, the rage underneath the ruffles, which

---

[11]Coontz, *The Way We Really Are*, p. 95.

we used to take out on ourselves and our kids and finally on the men in bed...."[12]

No self-respecting feminist would go back to that sort of role-playing, so Katha Pollitt thinks. But that sort of role-playing was what formerly got mothers custody of the kids—"wearing masks," says Ms. Friedan, "so that they wouldn't lose custody of their children."[13] That was what enabled judges to affect concern for what they really ignored, the best interests of the children who (it was convenient to say) needed the Angel in the House, even though that mother-headed house was eight times more likely to make them delinquent, five times more likely to drive them to suicide, and so on. When mothers give up that sort of role-playing they give up their spurious claim to moral superiority, signified by their pretended acceptance of the double standard and greater sexual and parental responsibility; they give up the pretense that their white wedding-gown betokened virginity. They abandoned their pledge to bear only legitimate children and their pledge that their children will have fathers to provide them with greater benefits than single mothers can provide. Giving up these pretenses and the benefits contingent on them, Ms. Pollitt may suppose, is "not going to happen" either, but they have already been forfeited as society has entered the era of the female kinship system by rejecting sexual regulation. It remains only for men to realize what has already happened and to stop subsidizing women's withdrawal from the male kinship system—and dragging "their" children with them.

Women's marriage vows and their acceptance of what Katha Pollitt rejects as things "not going to happen" were formerly the quid pro quo which motivated fathers to be providers for families. Now following the actual or threatened withdrawal of these things men are supposed to behave as though nothing had changed, as though they still had stable families.

Feminist Brett Harvey makes the following claim for women's right to total independence:

A group of feminists came together in New York in April, 1981 to talk about what wasn't being talked about: abortion rights as the key to women's sexual freedom....Women's autonomy must include the right to express ourselves as sexual beings....[W]omen cannot control our own destinies unless we can

---

[12]Betty Friedan, *It Changed My Life*, p. 232.
[13]*It Changed My Life*, p. 317.

control our own reproductive function. **At the heart of the New Right's attack on abortion rights was a traditional definition of women as childbearers— victims of nature—rather than as autonomous human beings with the fundamental right to define our own sexuality...[with] the guarantee of total sexual freedom and autonomy for women. The notions that underlie "free abortion on demand"—that women are not slaves to their reproductive systems; that women have the right to choose when, how and with whom they wish to be sexual—these ideas, the bedrock of radical feminism, are still not truly accepted. As long as women who choose not to have children, or to live alone or with other women, or to have a variety of sexual partners—as long as such women are stigmatized as "selfish" or "narcissistic," or "perverted," no woman is really free.**[14]

Ms. Harvey's program seems to exclude men from meaningful participation in reproduction, but "total sexual freedom and autonomy for women" must include a woman's right to enter a stable and enforceable contract to *share* her reproductive life with a man. It also includes, in Ms. Harvey's thinking, the right to walk out of this contract with the children in her custody. Which is it to be? She flaunts "the first law of matriarchy: women control our own bodies. Such a woman is not marriageable. No man must suppose himself obligated to subsidize her or to allow her custody of his children. Her program, "the bedrock of radical feminism," is incompatible with civilized society. If she chooses not to have children, fine. If she chooses to live alone or with other women, fine. If she chooses to have a variety of sexual partners, fine. But society must condemn her if she makes her *children* "victims of nature" by trapping them in the female kinship system, and men must condemn and oppose a legal system which permits her to do so—and compels fathers to subsidize them.

Ms. Harvey rebels against the patriarchal system which allows men to share in reproduction. But such sharing does not deny women "the right to choose when, how and with whom they wish to be sexual"; it asks them to make this choice, but to make the choice meaningful and permanent, something that men and children can depend on. Ms. Harvey wishes to make the choice over and over again, promiscuously, irresponsibly, "freely and joyously."

Her choice denies freedom and joy to the victims of her sexual disloyalty, the cuckolded or divorced husband and the children

---

[14]Brett Harvey, "No More Nice Girls," in *Pleasure and Dangers*, ed. C . Vance (Boston: Routledge and Kegan Paul,1984), pp. 205, 209.

shepherded into the female kinship system. The wife's sexual loyalty is her primary contribution to marriage, as the husband's paycheck is his. Feminists rejoice that women's growing economic independence has reduced the value of the husband's paycheck to the point where wives can afford to withdraw their sexual loyalty ("control our own reproductive freedom")—thereby making marriage meaningless to the husband and placing the children at risk.

Worse than meaningless, for the husband is not only deprived of his children, his property and the role on which he hoped to build his life, but he must actually pay to have these losses inflicted upon himself—otherwise his wife might be unable to afford the divorce, otherwise the judge might hesitate to give the mother custody of the children. The father's role is destroyed by the society which was supposed to create it, since "fatherhood is a social invention."

Very large numbers of men—ex-husbands who have lost everything in the divorce court, sons of ex-husbands who see how their fathers have been displaced and made roleless, bachelors confronting a sixty percent divorce rate and the near certainly of anti-male discrimination from judges—are bewildered and angered by this betrayal of the family by the legal system. These males, whom society ought to encourage to become providers for families, are afraid of marriage, afraid that feminist propagandists may be right in saying the nuclear family is obsolete.

It is obsolete if women are allowed to be promiscuous or to retain custody of children rendered fatherless by their repudiation of their marriage vows and to collect subsidization from males they have married or had a one-night stand with. It is obsolete if marriage is entered into "in contemplation of divorce," as a temporary suspension of promiscuity following which the wife is privileged to call it off, return to promiscuity, and still claim custody of the children. Such a wife has not given her husband a family, she has loaned him one, allowed him to fall in love with his children and then taken them away from him. The ex-husband thus defrauded is under no obligation to the ex-wife. His obligation to his children is to rescue them from the female kinship system where the law places them, and this obligation is thwarted by his financing of their mother's legal kidnapping of them. His support money is what is making the nuclear family obsolete by promoting "alternative families"— matrilines—promoting the "emerging white underclass," the female kinship system and its pathology. The law is destroying his family and compelling him to renounce his role of family protector and to help in this destruction.

The psychic mechanisms essential to accomplishing this destruction are the guilt-trip, the Mutilated Beggar Argument, the instilling in the father of the notion that he is doing the right thing for his kids by abandoning them to the female kinship system: "They are my children," he is supposed to be thinking, "and I love them and I can't abandon them." In fact he is abandoning them. He needs to have his consciousness raised so that he can see this. This consciousness-raising is the responsibility of the fathers' rights movement. If enough fathers could be made to see that the financing of women's liberation is inflicting on society the most damaging of all transformations short of total destruction—the alteration of the kinship system—they could put a stop to it and restore sexual law-and-order and the male role as head of the family, custody of the children of divorce and the abolition of alimony and child support payments and an end to the "illegitimacy revolution" which increased the number of fatherless children from 5.3 percent in 1960 to 30.1 percent in 1992 while reducing the birth rate by one-third.[15] It would replace mothers' reliance on divorce and government assisted matriarchy with patriarchal marriage and the family.

According to Gerald Heard:

As the mammal is the fetalization of the reptile and retains some of the generalized features the reptile lost when it specialized out from the amphibian; as the primates neotenically retain fetal freedoms that the rest of the mammals have lost; as man remains an infant longer than the ape and, to his infancy, adds another span of uncommitted freedom, his specific childhood; so this principle of paidomorphy is now seen to be the power of human evolution and the capacity and promise of its further advance.

It is in childhood that fatherlessness does its greatest damage. This is why 63 percent of youth suicides are from fatherless homes, why 90 percent of all homeless and runaway children are from fatherless homes, and so forth (see pages 12ff.).

Applied to specific human history, [Heard continues] this insight makes comprehensible the vast acceleration of the growth of consciousness since the rise of man. For as man has no instincts he holds together and advances

---

[15]David Hartman, *The Family in America*, July, 1997.

through social heredity. Hence, the human advance has been and must always be through the reciprocity of the two parallel lines of man's physical heredity and his social heredity. The social heredity is the die that stamps its pattern of developing behavior on the matrix of the human brain. While the physical parents beget, bear, and rear increasingly impressionable, teachable young, the begetters of the social heredity have to keep themselves young and open so that they may creatively accept new data and incorporate the new evidence into those new comprehensive conceptions that can feed the fresh, open minds of each generation.[16]

"Among nature peoples," says homosexual Arthur Evans, "sex is part of the public religion and education of the tribes....Its purpose is its own pleasure."[17] That is why they are "nature peoples"—uncivilized. The great discovery of patriarchy was that sex could be put to work to create civilization by allowing men to be sociological fathers. Ms. Harvey thinks, with "nature peoples" and Arthur Evans, that sex ought to be wholly recreational and irresponsible, and supposes (if she thinks that far ahead) that the children resulting from it, if they are not aborted, must be subsidized not by sociological fathers but by ex-husbands, discarded boyfriends or agencies of a feminist welfare state. Only thus can women be "autonomous human beings with the fundamental right to define our own sexuality." The program implies a denial of freedom to male sex partners, who must submit to both exile from meaningful reproduction and to subsidizing women's promiscuity.

Fatherhood *used* to be a social creation. But lawmakers and judges have allowed themselves to be bullied by feminists into imagining that the props needed by fathers are oppressive to women and should be done away with, thus leaving men without the role security formerly provided by the legal system. This is the feminist "progress" which Riane Eisler and Katha Pollitt celebrate. This is also why almost one-fifth of men between ages 39 and 43 are bachelors, why forty percent of the young men studied by Judith Wallerstein are "drifting, out of school, unemployed."[18]

Ms. Eisler writes of "the attempt by a growing number of women to gain sexual independence: the power to freely choose how and with whom to mate and whether or not to have children...the attempt by more and more women to reclaim the right to sexual pleasure and finally leave

---

[16]Heard, *The Five Ages of Man*, p. 285.
[17]Arthur Evans, *Witchcraft and the Gay Counterculture* (Boston: Fag Rag Books, 1978), p. 130.
[18]Hewlett, *When the Bough Breaks*, p. 141.

behind the notion (supported by both religious and secular dogmas) that women who are sexually active are 'bad women' or 'sluts'"[19] There have always been such women ("women you screw"), but men cannot hope to have families with them. Their abandoning the role of loyal wives necessitates men's withdrawing their subsidization of them. Ms. Eisler supposes men will continue to give them their children, their name, their property, their homes, and their future income. The increasing numbers of "sluts" makes father custody increasingly necessary. The recovery of men's motivation to be reliable providers without a guarantee of father custody is something else which is not going to happen.

---

[19]Eisler, *Sacred Pleasure*, p. 196.

XI) EXOGAMY

Exogamy, men "marrying out" of their kinship group, is a peculiar feature of the anthropology of primitive peoples. According to historian Will Durant,

> **Exogamy, too, was compulsory; that is to say, a man was expected to secure his wife form another clan than his own. Whether this custom arose because the primitive mind suspected the evil effects of close inbreeding,[1] or because such intergroup marriages created or cemented useful political alliances, promoted social organization, and lessened the danger of war, or because the capture of a wife from another tribe had become a fashionable mark of male maturity, or because familiarity breeds contempt and distance lends enchantment to the view—we do not know. In any case the restriction was well-nigh universal in early society; and though it was successfully violated by the Pharaohs, the Ptolemies and the Incas, who all favored the marriage of brother and sister, it survived into Roman and modern law and consciously or unconsciously moulds our behavior to this day.[2]**

Lord Raglan has cited a number of theories which purport to explain this peculiar taboo against marrying members of one's own family—or one's own clan, for in primitive matriarchal society the family *is* the clan:

> **Because such marriages are sterile (Pope Gregory I); Because the children of such marriages are weak in mind or body (Robert Burton, L. H. Morgan, Sir E. B. Tylor); Because there is an instinct which forbids such marriages (St. Augustine, Professors Hobhouse and Lowie, Dr. Westermarck); Because such marriages are unnatural (Plato, Novatian, Amyraut, Dr. Havelock Ellis); Because such marriages would tend to take place between persons of disproportionate age (Socrates, Montesquieu, Huth); As a relic of a once universal practice of marriage by capture (J. F. MacLennan, Herbert Spencer, Lord Avebury, Mr. H. G. Wells); Because relationship would become confused (Theodore Beza); Because respect for a father precludes marriage with his wife (Philo, Agathias, and Statius); Because marriages within the family would be without love (Luther); Because such marriages would lead to excessive love within the family (Aristotle, St. Chrysostom); Because such marriages led, or would lead, to family jars of various kinds (Bishop Jeremy Taylor, J. J.**

---

[1] Despite folklore to this effect, there are no evil consequences of close inbreeding. See Lord Raglan, *Jocasta's Crime* (London: Watts and Company, 1940), "Chapter 2: "Is Inbreeding Harmful?"
[2] Will Durant, *Our Oriental Heritage* (New York: Simon and Schuster, 1935), p. 41.

Atkinson, Professor Malinowski, Mr. Briffault, Mrs. Seligman); From a growing regard for the domestic proprieties (Dr. Marett); In order to promote chastity by compelling people to seek mates at a distance (Thomas Aquinas); As a penance for a primeval parricide (Freud); Because such marriages became a royal prerogative (Professor Elliot Smith); For magical, religious, or superstitious reasons (Sir J. G. Frazer, Professor Durkheim, A. E. Crawley, Dr. Raymond Firth.)[3]

The list, says Raglan, shows "at a glance the number and variety of the theories which have been advanced—how theologian has differed from theologian, philosopher from philosopher, and scientist from scientist. It should convince anyone who, having got so far, still believes that there is some simple and obvious solution, that this is not the case."

Raglan's own view is "that incest was originally nothing but a breach of the law of exogamy, that exogamy was adopted for purely magical reasons."[4]

All these contradictory explanations are proposed by men. Let's look at the problem from the woman's point of view, the person formerly in control of the arena of reproduction, but now threatened with displacement by patriarchy. Did not the black woman on the Donahue Show who said women want the right to have children without having husbands state the essence of exogamy?

When Charmaine tells her boyfriend, to get his ass out of her house she is defending the female kinship system. Males can be permitted to function as boyfriends as long as they behave themselves, but they mustn't aspire to be fathers and heads of households. Mom must remain in charge of the reproductive unit. This is woman's power base and they don't mean to give it up.

Charmaine doesn't want a man to have papers on her, which would inhibit her sexual freedom. So she kicks him out, thus creating exogamy and remaining in control of her own sexuality—"the first law of matriarchy."

She wants what most feminists want, to get back to the Stone Age arrangement, what Ms. Coontz calls (trying to make it sound up to date) "the emergence of alternative ways of organizing parenthood and

---

[3] Lord Raglan, *Jocasta's Crime*, pp. 64f.
[4] P. 57.

marriage." She doesn't want patriarchy, "to reestablish the supremacy of the male breadwinner model or to define masculine and feminine roles in any monolithic way."[5]

When Sharon Crain Bakos says "I got divorced because I didn't like being second and being a wife meant being second,"[6] she is defending the female kinship system. When she says "The clearest memory of my wedding day is what was going on in my head as I walked down the aisle in my white satin dress with the floor-length lace mantilla billowing around me: 'No. No way is this going to be forever, for the rest of my life. No.'"[7] She is defending the female kinship system. Women's right to be promiscuous. The first law of matriarchy.

When John Hodge says "The traditional Western family, with its authoritarian male role and its authoritarian adult rule, is the major training ground which initially conditions us to accept group oppression as the natural order"—he too is defending the female kinship system.[8]

Exogamy means men "marrying out," attaching themselves to women of other clans where the females have permanent status but the males are little more than visitors. It guarantees women's sexual independence. As Ms. Harvey says, "total sexual freedom and autonomy for women...to have the right to choose when, how, and with whom to be sexual."

In the Annex of the present book I have collected quotations, mostly from feminists, to show that this female hatred of patriarchy, this insistence on the right to reject sexual regulation lies at the heart of the feminist/sexual revolution. They hate the family. Ms. Heyn expected "to interview women deeply divided about their decision to have extramarital sex," but found this "not to be so." The women came to talk to her "not to discuss divided hearts or new meanings of forever but the recovery of their sexuality and the dramatic physical, psychological, and emotional ramifications of that recovery."[9] The recovery of their *promiscuity*.

Ms. Heyn would never dream of saying this:

---

[5] *The Way We Really Are*, p. 77.
[6] Susan Crain Bakos, *This Wasn't Supposed to Happen* (New York: Continuum, 1985), p. 2.
[7] *Ibid.*, p. 20.
[8] Quoted in bell hooks, *Feminist Theory: From Margin to Center* (Boston: South End Press, 1984), p.36.
[9] *The Erotic Silence of the American Wife*, pp. 283f.

Monogamy was dead, and few of those who promise sexual exclusivity were capable of keeping their promise—

But she does say this:

I began to think that perhaps I was not hearing any of these sad tales because monogamy was simply dead, and that, for whatever reasons, few of those who promised sexual exclusivity were capable of keeping their promise."

This coyly places the essential idea in subordinate clauses, obfuscates it, makes it sound harmless. But it is still there: Monogamy is dead—and with it the family and fatherhood—the whole patriarchal stick. Ms. Heyn's adulteresses have "recovered their sexuality" and emancipated themselves from patriarchal regulation. Of one of these "recovered" women Ms. Heyn says:

The one thing Anne has sacrificed...is her claim to goodness. She is permanently out of the running for the title of Perfect Wife. But what a trade: In exchange for the title, she has gained—or regained—the voice to speak about her pleasure.[10]

What a trade indeed. She has repudiated the Legitimacy Principle upon which patriarchy is based and asserted her loyalty to the Promiscuity Principle upon which matriarchy is based, her right to do whatever she wishes sexually regardless of her marriage contract. She may not realize it, but along with this she has repudiated her claim to custody of her children.

When Betty Friedan became an economically independent best-selling author, she felt "the women's movement began to give me the strength that it has given all of you. She followed Jeanne Cambrai's advice: "Get rid of HIM!" I said, "I don't care, I have to do something about my own life."[11] She went to Mexico, divorced her husband and took his children from him, creating an exogamous family and poor Carl Friedan was helpless to do a thing about it.

Briffault's Law. It was when men acquired wealth which they could offer to prospective wives that they became a meaningful part of the reproductive unit. "The original husband," says Michael Maggi,[12] was an

---

[10]Page 302.
[11]*It Changed My Life*, p. 324.
[12]In a cover letter promoting Evelyn Reed's *Woman's Evolution*.

incidental nocturnal visitor—and women did the proposing. But even this form of marriage arose only after a million years of clan life in which all men and women were 'brothers' and 'sisters,' and the term 'father' was unknown."

"A study of the sciences of biology and anthropology," says feminist Evelyn Reed, "discloses that sex competition among females does not exist either in nature or in primitive society. It is exclusively the product of class society and was unknown before class society came into existence, which means for almost a million years of human evolution."[13] It was exclusively the product of a society in which men could offer a benefit to women sufficient to induce them to share their reproductive lives, a society which would guarantee to the men that their status within the family was secure—or rather that there *was* a family rather than a female-headed reproductive unit. Only when men acquired wealth and status did women consider them worth competing for, only then did they recognize they could derive a benefit from association with them. It is man's wealth—and his secure possession of it—which ensures women's sexual loyalty and the stability of the two-parent family.

Exogamy preserves female sexual independence, female unchastity, "a woman's sacred right to control her own body." This is what Ms. Heyn's adulteresses yearn for, what Charmaine wants, what feminists demand.

THE MALE KINSHIP SYSTEM: A WRAP-UP

Males created patriarchy by intruding themselves into the arena of reproduction, an epoch-making innovation, comparable to the creation of motherhood itself, an innovation justified solely by its success. Wherever the two kinship systems can be compared the male system wins hands down—the matriarchal Indians could not compete with the patriarchal Europeans who took their land away and bottled them up on reservations; the matriarchal ghettoes and barrios of South Central and East Los Angeles cannot compete with the patriarchal suburbs whose taxes pay their bills.

---

[13]Evelyn Reed, *Problems of Women's Liberation: A Marxist Approach*, 5th ed. (New York: Pathfinder Press, 1971), p. 79.

A generation ago Ramsey Clark wrote a best-selling book called *Crime in America*, in which he rattled off the usual cliches about the causes of crime. He needs to be quoted at length:

> **Most crime in America is born in environments saturated in poverty and its consequences: ignorance, illness, idleness, ugly surroundings, hopelessness. Crime incubates in places where thousands have no jobs, and those who do have have the poorest jobs; where houses are old, dirty and dangerous; where people have no rights....[T]he clear connection between crime and the harvest of poverty—ignorance, disease, slums, discrimination, segregation, despair and injustice—is manifest....Take a map of any city—your city—and mark the parts of town where health is poorest....Find the places where life expectancy is lowest—seven years less than for the city as a whole—where the death rate is highest—25 per cent above the rate for the entire city....Mental retardation occurs in some parts of your city at a rate five times higher than in the remainder....Mental and emotional illness afflicts substantial portions of the population in some parts of town, while in others it is comparatively rare and carefully treated....Now mark the parts of town where education is poorest....Find those parts of the city where the oldest schools stand, where there are no national honor society students, where classrooms are most crowded and there are no playgrounds, where the teachers' qualifications are lowest, class days shortest and dropout rates greatest, where the ratio of students to teachers is highest and books and supplies are scant....**[14]

And so on and on. "Behold your city," says Clark—"You have marked the same places every time":

> **Poverty, illness, injustice, idleness, ignorance, human misery and crime go together. That is the truth. We have known it all along. We cultivate it, breed it, nourish it. Little wonder we have so much. What is to be said of the character of a people who, having the power to end all this, permit it to continue?**

What is to be said of Ramsey Clark, the chief law enforcement officer of the country, and of *his* character, that he fails to mention the obvious cause of all this mess—*matriarchy*? What we have really known all along is that most criminals grow up in female-headed households, created either by welfare (Mom marries the state and doesn't need a husband) or by divorce with mother custody. "The power to end all this" lies not with lawmakers who subsidize matriarchy (and thus breed it) or judges who give mothers custody in their divorce courts (and thus encourage it) but with making fathers heads of families as they were in

---

[14]Clark, pp.41ff.

the mid-nineteenth century when John Stuart Mill wrote "They are by law *his* children."

Patriarchy is artificial but it works. Female rebellion against patriarchy is *natural,* an expression of Briffault's Law and an attempt by females to regain their lost female primacy. The male must *earn* his right to participate in reproduction by making himself acceptable to, and providing benefits to, the female. Civilized society must make the female's acceptance of patriarchy a reasonable choice by emphasizing its advantages to her and her offspring, its significance and its irrevocability. Hence the ritual and prolongation of courtship. Hence the concern of the families and (formerly) the groom's asking the bride's father's permission to propose to her. Hence the church wedding, with its archaic language and hallowed customs. Hence the bride's pre-marital chastity, signified by her white wedding dress. All these stress the solemnity of the occasion, its awesome responsibility, the need for the bride and the groom to know they are going through a rite of passage—passing through a door they will never pass through again. The rite is made meaningful to the groom by making it *permanent and irrevocable,* something he and his children can depend on. The groom must know that the woman is offering him a family, not lending him one which can be later taken away and used for the purpose of extracting child support money from him.

The legal system formerly stabilized patriarchy by ensuring male headship of families. Now it does the opposite. The typical judge thinks as Robert Noland does, as the Los Angeles judges cited in the second footnote of this book do, that in the event of divorce, children belong with their mother and that the father owes the mother support money. The consequence: society is returning to the female kinship system and its pathology. Why can't Ramsey Clark see it?

The feminist rebellion against patriarchy is an intelligible reaction, a defense of what has been female territory for two hundred million years. The female wants the benefits which accompany the male intrusion without its permanence, wants Dad's paycheck without Dad's interference. Many women want sexual promiscuity or easy divorce for Mom with financial responsibility for Dad, or want AFDC. She may reward him with "free and joyous love"—which makes marriage a romantic institution rather than an economic one—following which she, like Judge Noland's cattle and Mrs. Thomas Mulder, will resume her interrupted control over reproduction.

"LIFE WITH FATHER"

Fatherhood depends on human understanding of the needs of children and an incorporation of that understanding into the social structures of marriage and the family.

Feminists like Ms. Reed relish the idea that men were once mere sexual hangers-on, boyfriends, secondary creatures. "Life with Father," she says,

> **as portrayed in old-fashioned plays and motion pictures, shows an imposing gentleman who occupies the commanding position in the family, provides for its economic needs, endows it with his name, transmits his property to his sons, and expects his wife and children to cater to his needs and obey him. This roaring lion of a father is far removed from the paternal mouse who first enters history. At that point the father was last in the line of relatives—after the mothers, the sisters, and the brothers—and it took considerable time and turmoil before he moved all the way up to first place.**

She quotes W. H. R. Rivers on the lowly condition of fathers among the Seri Indians of Baja California, without choosing to notice the connection between the low condition of Seri fathers and the low condition of Seri society itself, one of the most backward known to anthropology:

> **The male members sat under a rude shelter in order of precedence, the eldest brother nearest the fire, his brothers next to him in order of age, and then, often outside the shelter and exposed to the rain, the husbands of the women of the household.**

Rather than this heavy-handed sarcasm, why not a little approval for the *civilized* father who has come so far from such lowly beginnings and brought his woman and his children along? The underlying difference between the Seri father and the civilized father is that the Seri father is marginalized by the unchastity of Seri women who won't give up their sacred right to control their own sexuality by allowing their men to have families.

Ehrenreich, Hess and Jacobs equally support the female kinship system and exogamy. They have been quoted: "We were drawn, as women have been for ages, to the possibility of celebrating our sexuality

190

without the exclusive intensity of romantic love,[15] without the inevitable disappointment of male-centered sex, and without the punitive consequences."[16] This is the love Briffault refers to with this: "Cohabitation is, as will later be shown, very transient in the lower phases of human culture, and the sexes, as a rule, associate little with one another."[17] It is the state William Tucker refers to where "boys complained their fathers had never been around to help them," where "girls solemnly proclaimed themselves capable of raising babies without men," where "each of these declarations was met by thunderous applause from the assembled teenagers."[18]

Harriet Jacobs in her *Incidents in the Life of a Slave Girl*, 1861, pleaded for her readers to view female virtue and purity differently for slave women, in light of their inability to exercise control over their own bodies.[19] Unlike Jacobs, today's liberated women don't apologize for their promiscuity, they flaunt it as a sacred right and glory in it as striking a blow for women's independence from patriarchy. A month or two before Princess Diana's death the tabloid *Star* suggested she might be pregnant and supposed this "would be a slap in the face to Charles and his whole stuffy family. This could be Diana's way of breaking the royal ties and making it clear that she's going to live her life on her own terms."[20]: "a woman's right to have a baby without having the father around is what feminism is all about."[21]

Melanesia still has the Female Kinship System. When the missionaries there convert the natives to Christianity and teach them the Lord's Prayer, they translate the first verse as "Our *uncle* who art in heaven." Fathers have no authority in Melanesia. That's matriarchy. Women prefer it. They may dislike the poverty which accompanies it— but one cannot have everything.

According to sociologist Dr. David Popenoe,

Because men are only weakly attached to the father role and because men's reproductive and parental strategies are variable, culture is central to

---

[15]This is the same "love" Ms. Friedan speaks of.
[16]*Re-Making Love*, p. 199.
[17]*The Mothers*, I, 125.
[18]*The American Spectator*, Sept., 1996.
[19]*Oxford Companion to Women's Writing in the United States* (New York: Oxford University Press, 1995), p. 428.
[20]*Star*, 29 July, 1997.
[21]Letter circulated in August, 1996.

enforcing high paternal investment. In every society the main cultural institution designed for this purpose is marriage. Father involvement with children is closely linked to the quality of the relationship between husband and wife.[22]

The success of feminism has been its undermining of this relationship, its restoration of the female's right to be unchaste.

KEEPING PATERNITY SECRET

"The whole culture," says feminist Hazel Henderson, "could shift fundamentally in less than a generation IF women simply took back their reproductive rights, endowed by biology and Nature. All that women would need to do to create a quiet revolution is to resume the old practice of keeping the paternity of their children a secret."[23] This is what women do in the ghettos, where welfare and affirmative action programs prevent men from claiming *their* reproductive rights.

The Birmingham women aimed at one of the two major feminist goals, abolishing the marriage contract's regulation of female sexuality. The other goal is maintaining the fiscal obligations of males. Feminist diddling about women standing on their own feet "without sexual privilege or excuse" is for the purpose of securing their right to be sexually de-regulated—after which they talk like this:

> **We could now face men, our brothers, in a new way...begin to look at and to speak to men not as our masters and oppressors, not as our breadwinners or husbands, but as themselves, the people we had to live with, work with, fight with, even love in new freedom, if we were to move on in the real world we had opened.**[24]

In this real world women stand on their own feet and "no longer need men to take care of us,"[25] they enjoy "one's own hard-won strength to take care of oneself,"[26] there is no alimony, which is "a sexist concept, and doesn't belong in a women's movement for equality." HOWEVER, in this real world males will still have to maintain their fiscal obligations. There will still be "maintenance, rehabilitation, severance pay—whatever you want to call it-—[which] is a necessity for many divorced women, as

---

[22]Popenoe, p. 184.
[23]*Women of Power*, fall, 1988.
[24]*It Changed My Life*, p. 257.
[25]*The Second Stage*, p. 122.
[26]*The Second Stage*, p. 269.

is child support." Men, though "not breadwinners," must still be billpayers," must still pay the "support desperately needed for...single parent families."[27] "We could...set up our own corps to collect that child support [from ex-husbands] so that women wouldn't be at the mercy of the lawyers."[28]

This is the double-barreled feminist program—matriarchy with subsidization, whether by ex-husbands, as Ms. Friedan proposes, or by government. Women are allowed to play the Motherhood Card; men are forbidden to play the Money Card. This is how the cause of feminism is served, how the family is destroyed. Feminist Riane Eisler explains the need for this:

Since the institution of the family functions as both a social model and a microcosm of the larger society, feminists have always perceived that no real change in the status of women is possible unless the patriarchal family is replaced.[29]

Not just particular families but the institution itself, for which there can be only one replacement, the female-headed matriline which *is* now replacing it and which produces children eight times more likely to become delinquent.

"The patriarchal family," continues Ms. Eisler, "is protected by a formidable alignment of religious dogma, legal sanction and economic constraints, so that while it receives support from practically every existing social mechanism, alternative family forms are considered 'abnormal' and receive no support at all."

Would it were so. The patriarchal family needs to be protected by religion, by the law, by economic structures. The patriarchal family is the linchpin which holds all these other things together. But the patriarchal family, rather than being protected by religion is being undermined by religious faddism which tells us, as Bishop Spong says, that "the shift in the power differential between the sexes has accelerated to a breakneck speed in our generation," that "Patriarchal models of

---

[27]*The Second Stage*, p. 119.
[28]*The Second Stage*, p. 328.
[29]Riane Eisler, *Dissolution* (New York: McGraw-Hill, 1977), pp. 131f.

marriage are likewise in retreat" and that "Perhaps the high divorce rate represents something positive rather than negative for human life."[30]

The law, so far from protecting the patriarchal family, is its deadliest enemy. The law's responsibility is to ensure that children have fathers, but the feminist clamor for "equal treatment" means the removal of the few remaining props which enable fathers to function. According to Andrew Payton Thomas, in the Washington D. C. ghetto, 42 percent of black men aged 18-35 are under criminal justice supervision or in jail, on probation or parole or out on bond or outstanding warrant. About 85 percent of Washington's black men are arrested at some point in their lives.[31] The trouble with these black men is that they have been deprived of a patriarchal family to grow up in and deprived of another patriarchal family to provide for. They grew up in the "alternative family forms" of which Ms. Eisler and Ms. Coontz speak, the pathological forms now taking over the larger society, and their women's sexual independence keeps them from forming new families of thieir own.

REFORMING WELFARE

Feminist educationist Valerie Polakow complains of current attempts to reform welfare:

> Not only do such proposals punish single women for their "other motherhood" status, attempt to control their sexual behavior, and reinforce traditional gender stereotypes by rewarding them with benefits if they marry, but they fail to address the critical issues that mire single mothers in poverty, reducing them to modern-day paupers, undeserving wards of the state. Hence, in the last decade of the twentieth century, the entitlements guaranteed to single mothers and their children as civil rights in all other Western democracies are not present in the United States—not yet; wealthy, powerful, technologically advanced, but dismally failing to adequately protect its most vulnerable citizens. They are reduced to grubbing for worms in the shadows of the private garden.[32]

The way to protect the women and children is to give them husbands and fathers. The proposed regulation tries to do this—

---

[30]Bishop John Shelby Spong, *Living in Sin?: A Bishop Rethinks Human Sexuality* (San Francisco: Harper and Row, 1988), p. 54.
[31]Andrew Payton Thomas, *Crime and the Sacking of America: The Roots of Chaos* (Washington: Brassey's, 1994), p. xxii.
[32]Valerie Polakow, *Lives on the Edge: Single Mothers and their Children in the Other America* (Chicago: University of Chicago Press, 1993), pp. 171f.

controlling their sexual behavior, reinforcing traditional gender stereotypes, awarding them benefits if they marry. These controls formerly worked fairly well to prevent the ills Ms. Polakow describes. They no longer do. There are too many female-headed households, too many parasitic women with messed-up children, too many demoralized ex-husbands and ex-boyfriends unable to induce their women to behave. What is needed, I am suggesting, is to put the powerful bond between the mother and her offspring to work to create and stabilize families by guaranteeing *fathers* custody. Then the social contract swings into action on the right side of things: the mother sees the father not as an oppressive regulator of her sexuality, but as providing the benefits of a family, children, a home, higher income and higher status. Society used to do this and it worked.

Neoteny is the condition of having the period of immaturity prolonged. *Paidomorphy* is the retention in the adult of infantile or juvenile characteristics, which facilitate the "growth" so much written about (and so little evidenced) in feminist literature—the growth denied to so many children by the contemporary educational system which has transformed itself into a propaganda mill for the feminist/sexual revolution and transformed millions of children into juvenile nymphets and satyrs prematurely preoccupied with sex.

The law is a crude instrument, capable of wrecking families, capable of exiling fathers and depriving children of the benefits of fetalization, neoteny, and paidomorphy, but incapable of doing anything to offset these losses other than railing at the exiled ex-husbands for "abandoning their families." According to Sylvia Ann Hewlett, "The fact that estranged [read: exiled] fathers do not contribute significantly to the costs of college is a critical problem for many youngsters."[33] Of course. The solution is for Mom and the judge not to exile the father.

Poverty is not the worst consequence for the children of fatherless households, but it is the easiest to demonstrate: "In single-mother families," says David Blankenhorn, "about 66 percent of young children lived in poverty."[34] Feminists properly emphasize the seriousness of this poverty; but still more serious is the fact that, according to David Popenoe, "Juvenile delinquency and violence are clearly generated

---

[33]*When the Bough Breaks*, p. 141.
[34]*Fatherless America*, p. 42.

disproportionately by youths in mother-only households and in other households where the father is not present."[35]

Daughters are equally at risk. According to Dr. Popenoe, "If the growing problem of teenage sexuality and early childbearing can be resolved without bringing fathers back into the lives of their daughters, that way has not yet been found."[36]

When a judge removes a child from a two-parent household headed by the father he is removing it from where it is statistically least likely to be abused and most likely to become a good citizen. When he places it in a female headed household he is placing it where it is statistically most likely to be abused and to become an educational failure and a delinquent. He may unctuously proclaim that his sole concern is the best interest of the children, but he is choosing the worst of the options at his disposal for achieving this. The judge is the primary contributor to the crime, underachievement and demoralization of the next generation.

In 1980 crime increased a shocking 17 percent. Los Angeles Police Chief Daryl Gates, flabbergasted by such an increase, declared that nothing in the economy could explain it. What did explain it was the huge increase in divorce and illegitimacy in the mid-1960s. The translation of this breakdown in patriarchal sexual arrangements into the statistic concerning crime required the maturing of the children rendered fatherless in the 1960s into the teen-and-twenty-year-olds of 1980, and the time-lag was too long for Chief Gates to see the connection. The increase in crime was preceded a generation earlier by a sexual breakdown which destroyed legions of patriarchal families. "During the 1980s the number of persons in federal and state prisons doubled," says Sylvia Ann Hewlett,[37] focusing on the male criminal, forgetting his mother, whose rejection of sexual regulation started the mess. Ms. Hewlett complains that the cost of imprisoning the criminals is "much more than we spend on Aid to Families with Dependent Children," overlooking that more AFDC money now means more prisoners a generation from now. Once again: Crime and delinquency are like hemophilia, manifested in males but carried and transmitted by females.

---

[35] *Life Without Father*, p. 62.
[36] P. 65.
[37] *When the Bough Breaks*, p. 339.

Femininity is a set of signals conveying the female's acceptance of patriarchy. This is understood by females themselves. "Throughout the period of this study [of pregnant unmarried girls]" says Rickie Solinger, what held these groups together was a shared belief that the unwed mother 'had gotten herself pregnant' in large part because she was insufficiently feminine."[38] To which Ms. Solinger adds: "If efforts were to be expended in the girls' behalf, training in femininity represented resources...well allocated." Male anti-sociality is typically violent and is punished. Female anti-sociality is typically sexual and is rewarded by subsidies from the governments' Backup System and support payments from ex-husbands. Generally, it is the female anti-sociality of one generation which underlies the male anti-sociality of the next generation, the "vector" for it being the female-headed family.

Charles Murray thinks that "mothers with small children are not an economically or socially viable unit. They suffer under enormous rates of poverty; a wide range of studies have found a higher incidence of crime, drug abuse, truancy and other problems among fatherless children."[39] If this is true (and it is), they need fathers. The connection between female-headed households and social distress is acknowledged even by some feminists. Feminist sociologist Jessie Bernard cites a study of forty-five cultures showing that there exists "a relationship between a high incidence of mother-child households...and the inflicting of pain on the child by the nurturant agent."[40] The nurturant agent is the mother.

GENDER BALANCE: TOO FEW WOMEN

Discussing the violence of the American frontier in the nineteenth century, David Courtwright points to the surplus of men: "Though the story of the triumph of law and order on the frontier is often told from the vantage of determined marshals and hanging judges, it is more properly and essentially a story of women, families, and the balancing of the population."[41]

---

[38]*Wake Up Little Susie*, p. 127.
[39]Cited by Nina Easton in *Los Angeles Times Magazine*, 21 August, 1994.
[40]Jessie Bernard, *The Future of Motherhood* (New York: Penguin Books Inc., 1974), pp. 9-10; cited in Maggie Gallagher, *Enemies of Eros* (Chicago: Bonus Books, Inc., 1989), p. 52.
[41]David Courtwright, *Violent Land: Single Men and Social Disorder from the Frontier to the Inner City* (Cambridge, MA: Harvard University Press, 1996), p. 131.

The surplus of men made the West wild but can't explain the violence of today's inner cities, where there is a surplus of women. "Should not fewer men translate into less crime?" asks Courtwright. "Yes," he answers, but "the effect of fewer men is, over time, more than canceled out by the effects of increased illegitimacy and family disruption. There may be proportionately fewer men in the ghetto, but because they are less often socialized in intact families or likely to marry and stay married they more often get into trouble."

Because they have no fathers and are unwanted as fathers themselves—because "young black urban men are far more likely than whites of comparable age to be unemployed, imprisoned, institutionalized, crippled, addicted, or otherwise bad bets as potential husbands."[42] But having made this essential point, Courtwright then does what feminists and pols do, he transfers his concern from the men to the women and blames the men. The best way of providing the protection and support for women and children is the patriarchal arrangement—giving them husbands and fathers, which, however, means their accepting sexual regulation. They prefer to be protected and supported by agencies of government. Social psychologists Marcia Guttentag and Paul Secord have argued that

> **in high-gender-ratio situations [=fewer women] most women would prize their virginity and expect to marry up, marry young, stay home, and bear large numbers of legitimate children....Low-gender-ratio situations [=fewer men] produced the opposite pattern: more premarital sex and illegitimacy; more female-headed households and female labor-force participation; later marriages for women and more divorce.[43]**

Parallel conclusions were reached by Peter Grabowsky, who examined criminal statistics from New South Wales in the mid-nineteenth century and concluded that serious crimes against persons and property were almost solely a function of the oversupply of men— other variables hardly mattered.[44] As in frontier America, social problems grew out of a skewed, largely male population. As it became more balanced, order reestablished itself.

In the ghettos, the crime rate is high not for the reason there was crime in New South Wales and the American West in the nineteenth

---

[42]Courtwright, pp. 242f.
[43]Courtwright, p. 242.
[44]Courtwright, p. 151.

century (too many men) but because the men are young and unsocialized by the civilizing effects of family living, because the government itself "marries" their women and provides for them with AFDC, Affirmative Action, and divorce-with-mother-custody—as Adrienne Rich, Ruth Rosen, Valerie Polakow and most feminists clamor for it to do. This is what George Gilder calls "welfare state feminism." Women want it. Politicians discovered that there is a "woman's vote" which can be bought by offering women Affirmative Action benefits and castigating "Deadbeat Dads" for not supplying benefits to women. The ghetto situation, says Courtwright,

has given rise to frustration, anger, and deepening poverty among black women, whose marital prospects have declined steadily since 1960.

Not only does Courtwright transfer his concern from the men to the women; his concern is for the most advantaged women, educated and economically successful ones:

The problem has been particularly acute among educated and successful black women, for whom the pickings have become increasingly slim. They have either had to do without husbands or marry down, the opposite of the pattern on the female-scarce frontier.

In the patriarchal system, men's high achievement gives them the pick of many attractive women; in the matriarchal system women's *relatively* high achievement makes men *relative* underachievers, which gives women—who ordinarily "marry up"—slim pickings. This helps explain why patriarchal Bel Air, where the most desirable men and women pair off, is more prosperous than matriarchal Watts. The payoff for the women in Watts is that they achieve the other goal of feminism, control of their sexuality: they don't need husbands, just boyfriends.

Black women unwilling to engage in premarital sex are at a huge disadvantage in an already tight market. Black men know this and can easily exploit the situation.

Black women *willing* to engage in premarital sex are the problem, and a big one; for black men, including successful black men, know that *their* problem is finding chaste wives who will give them families; they know that black women are willing to be "exploited" and regard such exploitation as part of their emancipation. Educated and successful black women are the "beneficiaries" of the campaign of feminists like Virginia Woolf who complained that families wouldn't subsidize the education of their daughters the way they subsidize the education of their sons.

ARTHUR'S EDUCATION FUND

Ms. Woolf is so emphatic on this point, which has been repeated so often by so many feminists, that it requires answering. She cites "Arthur's Education Fund" in Thackeray's *Pendennis*, the savings set aside for the education of the family's son. Her complaint is that Arthur's sister was denied an equivalent fund, so, in effect *she*, not her parents, was the benefactor of Arthur: Arthur's sister was deprived in order that Arthur might be subsidized. Her argument is that the parents are making sacrifices to support the patriarchal system and refusing to make comparable sacrifices for matriarchy. She overlooks the fact that educating Arthur enables him to support a family and provide it with the advantages of his education, whereas educating Arthur's sister enables her to avoid having a family or to have a smaller one or to divorce her husband and transfer her children (if she has any) into the female kinship system where they can enjoy the advantages cited on pages 12ff. of this book. She ignores Briffault's Law, which says the male must have a benefit to confer on the female.

Ms.Woolf refers to Mary Kingsley, an unmarried, childless, self-educated woman, who died at age 38, the niece of Charles and Henry Kingsley. Hear Ms. Woolf:

> Let us then ask someone else—it is Mary Kingsley—to speak for us. "I don't know if I ever revealed to you the fact that being allowed to learn German was all the paid-for education I ever had. Two thousand pounds was spent on my brother's, I still hope not in vain." Mary Kingsley is not speaking for herself alone; she is speaking, still, for many of the daughters of educated men. And she is not merely speaking for them; she is also pointing to a very important fact about them; she is pointing to a fact that must profoundly influence all that follows: the fact of Arthur's Education Fund. You, who have read Pendennis, will remember how the mysterious letters A.E.F. figured in the household ledgers. Ever since the thirteenth century English families have been paying money into that account. From the Pastons to the Pendennises, all educated families from the thirteenth century. It is a voracious receptacle. Where there were many sons to educate it required a great effort on the part of the family to keep it full. For your education was not merely in book-

learning; games educated your body; friends taught you more than books or games. Talk with them broadened your outlook and enriched your mind.

Ms. Woolf misses the point upon which everything depends—the importance, but artificiality, of fatherhood. Arthur's education helps him to be a better father, makes him a better husband by making him a better provider. What would the fund have done for Arthur's sister besides make her independent of a family, of a husband and his income, like the successful heroines she mentions on page 14—Jane Austen, Charlotte Bronte and George Eliot, like the ghetto matriarchs so beloved of feminists, like Ms. Woolf herself, who was childless, like Mary Kingsley, unmarried and childless. Arthur's Fund enables him to have a family which will perpetuate his parents' family. Money spent on Arthur's sister would have made it less likely for her to have a family, five times more likely to divorce.

In the holidays you travelled; acquired a taste for art; a knowledge of foreign politics; and then, before you could earn your own living, your father made you an allowance upon which it was possible for you to live while you learnt the profession which now entitles you to add the letters K. C. to your name. All this came out of Arthur's Education Fund. And to this your sisters, as Mary Kingsley indicates, made their contribution.[45]

She really believes that Arthur's sister is paying for Arthur's education and ought not to—because it perpetuates the evils of patriarchy. Better that she should enjoy the blessings of matriarchy by receiving *conferred* benefits at Arthur's expense. Arthur's parents understand the artificial nature of patriarchy and the need for Arthur to be educated so he can support a family, to be a *father* rather than an ex-husband or an ex-boyfriend of an ex-girlfriend, who doesn't need him once he has been married and divorced and deprived of his children and cast onto the trash heap.

What does Arthur's sister contribute to Arthur's education? Nothing—zilch. The contents of Arthur's Education Fund are placed there by Arthur's father and mother, who understand as well as Arthur that the money will stabilize Arthur's family and hence society, along with the patrimony, the education, the values embedded in that education, and the patriarchal system itself. These are benefits which Arthur's sister will have conferred upon her by some contemporary of

---

[45]Virginia Woolf, *Three Guineas* (Harcourt, 1938), pp. 4-5.

Arthur, who will hope that in exchange for conferring upon *her* these benefits, *she* will consent to share her reproductive life with him (rather than divorcing him), thus perpetuating *his* family, *his* surname, *his* education, *his* system of motivation— and patriarchy and civilization.

By magnifying the benefits which might be conferred by transferring money from Arthur's Education Fund to Arthur's sister, Ms. Woolf minimizes the greater benefits Arthur's sister might confer on her future husband by marrying him and sharing her reproductive life with him.

Such benefits depend on something fragile, the marriage contract. In attacking Arthur's Education Fund, Ms. Woolf is attacking patriarchy, doing the same thing that today's sixty percent divorce rate does— permitting her to withdraw the benefits of her husband's "inheritance" from him—and mess up his life and the lives of his children, who will suffer the disadvantages listed on pages 12ff. Such income-redistribution liberates women's sexuality—which is the real idea. As Anne Koedt says (quoted on page 20) "Women could now be sexual, fully orgasmic beings not only outside of marriage but apart from men," who will become superfluous, like husbands in the Seri matriarchy.

Ms. Woolf believes that "we [females] have already contributed to the cause of culture and intellectual liberty more than any other class in the community."[46] The money is paid not by the sister but by the parents, who know that subsidizing Arthur's education will enable him to offer his wife the benefits of Briffault's Law, and that subsidizing Arthur's sister would not enable her to offer a husband what he wants, a family. Subsidizing Arthur's sister would enable her to avoid marriage or childbearing or have fewer children and have an enormously higher divorce rate—and deprive her children of their father. Subsidizing Arthur's sister would enable her to join the "respectable majority" of women who report premarital sexual experience or the proportion of married women reporting active sex lives "on the side," who (in the mid-eighties) numbered close to half.[47]

There is no "symmetry" between subsidizing Arthur and subsidizing Arthur's sister. The sister's role is guaranteed by her biology, the "biological fact," which Freud called her destiny. Arthur's role is not

---

[46]P. 86.

[47]*Re-Making Love*, page 2.

guaranteed by his biology. If Arthur doesn't get the subsidy he becomes just another male drifter—because *the male role is a social creation,* depending on social heredity and therefore having to be renewed every generation. Transferring Arthur's fund to Arthur's sister might enable her to be as successful as Arthur (but probably wouldn't, since she can always fall back on her biology, and therefore she lacks Arthur's motivation) but would deprive her of the likelihood of being a successful wife, make her more divorce-prone, and hence less marriageable, since she would have less bargaining power—be more threatening to a husband.

Funds like Arthur's represent painful sacrifices which Ms. Woolf seems to think ought to be made twice as great—so that Arthur's wife might be able to divorce him and take his kids from him—as millions of today's wives are doing.

Having an education makes Arthur more attractive to women. Having an education makes Arthur's sister less attractive to men— anyway to men who want families—unless there is an assurance of father custody. The result of subsidizing daughters rather than sons is matriarchy, because the daughters won't need husbands and the men who might have been husbands become superfluous and demoralized— which produces the ghettoizing of society. Hypergamy (women marry up, men marry down) creates stable families. Hypergamy motivates women to be chaste. The problem of educated and successful black women, who have few high-achieving men to marry up to, is that their *relatively* high achievement makes their marriages unstable, their marriage rate low, their birthrate low, their divorce rate (for those who marry) high. Their men suffer from the absence of the civilizing effects of family life because women don't need them economically and are willing to reduce them to the status of studs. Briffault's Law. As the promiscuity chic actress says: "Having children is part of my life plan; having a husband is not." She has economic independence and she has the Big Mo (momentum) of the feminist movement (and now Government) behind her. She thinks of herself as a pioneer and heroine of the New Age. She doesn't care that the New Age matriarchy shares its essential principle with Stone Age matriarchy: males are marginal.

Those who *do* marry know that when divorce time comes around they can depend on the judge to think children belong with their mother; so the father must be deprived of his bargaining power—he must not be permitted to offer the mother any benefit in exchange for her sexual loyalty. She can withdraw her loyalty and help herself to the benefit without his permission, since motherhood is sacred and since the judge's sole concern (so he says) is the welfare of the children who will (of course) remain in her custody.

Briffault's Law states the principle of hypergamy, which will never change; it's simply the way things are. It results from women's higher ascribed status based on their reproductive centrality and the reproductive marginality of males.

The problem is female promiscuity, uninhibited because of the male's inability to offer the female a benefit sufficient to induce her to behave herself. She knows, and he knows, that she can deprive him of his children and his role and his stake in society at her pleasure. Courtwright says the man can "exploit the situation" for free sex. The man's problem is not getting free sex but having a family, which means finding a chaste woman. If chaste black women are a minority (as they are) and if they want real families, they have a huge *advantage* with men who also want families. They have this desirable market all to themselves. But they suppose that they don't need men. Female economic independence and consequent sexual independence creates the mess which Courtwright ascribes to *male* opportunism.

Such sexual opportunism increases illegitimacy, and illegitimacy feeds the problems of poverty, unemployment, and violence that gave rise to the shortage of marriageable men.

These successful black women who would like to get married but cannot, are paying the price for being liberated from "Victorian prudery and hypocrisy."

XII) THE SOCIAL CONTRACT

A man wants a woman to marry him and he says to her, "If you will marry me, I will guarantee you that you will be the mother of your children." He is offering her nothing, since it is impossible that a woman should not be the mother of her own children.

A woman wants a man to marry her and she says to him, "If you will marry me, I will guarantee you that you will be the father of my children." She is talking sense. She is offering him a family. A family is made possible by a woman's agreement to share her reproductive life. The man's reciprocal offer is to be a provider for her and for their children. Feminists (and politicians who seek the feminist vote) want a social system in which the woman's offer to the man is revocable but the man's to the woman is irrevocable. Only thus can women be liberated from "the great scourge" of marriage and still remain subsidized—and still retain custody of "their" children.

Male chastity has no importance comparable to female chastity. The female body is the vehicle by which the race is reproduced. The wife's primary contribution to the marriage is her consent to share her reproductive life. She must be rewarded for this commitment and must not be rewarded for refusing it by unchastity or revoking it by divorce. The husband's primary contribution to the marriage is to supply this reward—to be a provider. If the woman is economically independent and needs no male provider, only automatic father custody can make her a good marriage prospect.

There is a growing understanding among feminists that not only will the legal system support them if they are unchaste or if they choose divorce, but that it will make itself the mechanism for attacking and overthrowing the whole patriarchal system and its sexual constitution by releasing women from their marriage vows—establishing Ms. Hoggett's principle that marriage no longer serves a useful purpose.

Feminist Margaret Sanger has been quoted as claiming for women the right to be unwed mothers. That means the right of women to deny men a right to be fathers and to deny to children their right to have fathers. If women are to enjoy this claimed right they will probably need to be subsidized, else they and "their" children will probably live in poverty. The legal system is brought into the act not for the purpose of ensuring that children shall be procreated within families but for the purpose of ensuring that families are unneeded, that mothers may procreate them singly, or drag them by divorce into the matriarchal system where males hold the status of boyfriends. Ms. Sanger's claim amounts to a claimed right of women to ghettoize society.

British feminist Joan Brown has this to say about why there are so many one-parent households:

> This growth has to be seen in the context of changes in social attitudes across the wider society. We live in an age when (according to the British Social Attitudes Survey for 1983) over 90 percent of those aged between 18 and 34 do not consider pre-marital sex to be particularly wrong, and when divorce and cohabitation are increasing and are being seen as acceptable at all levels of society. We may want to seek ways to counter these developments at an individual level, but [it] is not easy to see how we can turn back the clock to a less permissive age—short of a massive religious revival or draconian laws which attempt to control private behaviour between adults.[1]

Ms. Brown makes the same appeal as Judge Noland—to the naturalness of the female kinship system. Its sexual promiscuity is the heart of this naturalness. Everyone sees that sex is natural and is fun, that this is the way cattle and dogs and cats live, that people dislike being yoked together forever, that it is more natural to live together and have sex for limited periods of time and to split up when the cohabiting gets tiresome.

The naturalness of the female kinship system is its attraction. Many women accept it and men are grateful for the free sex. Amanda, one of Ms. Heyn's adulteresses, puts it this way:

> Love and marriage—I can no longer accept the hold on me that an old system has. I've grown past the myth of it all. I'm willing to stay married and to face what both of us have to face during our lifetimes. And I'm willing to not be married, if that is the case! I'm not willing to live with an outmoded belief system that is stultifying to both partners.[2]

---

[1]Joan Brown, "The Focus on Single Mothers," in Charles Murray, *The Emerging British Underclass* (London: IEA Health and Welfare Unit, 1990), p. 47.
[2]Heyn, pp. 220f.

She imagines that her matriarchal ideas represent advanced thinking: "You don't die or anything from affairs," she says. "You just grow....I'd rather grow than stay safe. And sometimes growth means doing something you don't understand. Years later, when your psyche is able to process it, you say, '*Now* I see what that was all about. Now I see why I did that."

Any action, however idiotic, can be justified by the plea that at some future time it might appear to have been "growth." Amanda, would "rather examine what the feelings really are that are so ferocious and primitive, where they come from, and how our attitudes about them are locked into this good-evil system. An affair is not evil."

The ferocity and primitiveness of the feelings make them forbidden, therefore attractive, therefore "growth." She wants to "examine" her feelings for the purpose of emancipating herself from patriarchal restraints. She believes in the Promiscuity Principle, wants to do what she feels like and to refuse to submit to a contract of marriage. Besides she *is* safe: few judges will deprive a mother of her children or of support money and she and her husband both know it. The naturalness of all this, its ferocity and primitiveness, seem to her reasons to go for it. Too bad that the law encourages it:

> **We haven't been taught that a lifetime of sexual exclusivity is anything but totally natural. Does anybody get that we're now talking fifty, sixty years of marriage? Look, it isn't natural to have sex with one person for half a century—that's longer than the average person's life span two hundred years ago. And if it were natural, why are so many people not able to stay faithful for a lifetime? Or a decade? Why don't we face it? Why don't we at least examine other possibilities? Why am I so bad for noticing this?[3]**

No question, matriarchy and promiscuity are natural. But if society wants family stability it should influence spouses' choice by rewarding faithfulness and punishing unfaithfulness. Wives' increasing economic independence makes them less vulnerable to economic punishment and more sexually free but it makes children and fathers more vulnerable by de-valuing the father's money card. This increases the need for a different sanction, the denial of custody.

---

[3]Heyn, p. 221.

"Examine other possibilities"? There is only one, matriarchal promiscuity. Begin by examining the ghettos and Indian reservations where matriarchy flourishes along with violence, illegitimacy and poverty. Begin by examining a husband's motives for supporting a wife.

Amanda twists the word "natural" three times to show the unnaturalness of a fifty or sixty year marriage commitment. The whole patriarchal system is artificial. It is designed to benefit the children and it does. Statistically, it benefits the husband and the wife as well, especially the wife who, as the marriage lengthens, loses her youth and beauty while the man's economic power increases. After the children are grown, it is the woman who has most to gain from stabilizing marriage.

There is nothing "natural" about a man continuing to subsidize a wife who has affairs with other men, but if he discards her on the grounds that his resentment of her promiscuity is as natural as her promiscuity itself, many women would denounce him and most judges would side with her and award her custody and support money. Such judges would imagine themselves to be rescuers of poor, poor women— but they would be creating more and more of them.

She says she is "unwilling to live in an outmoded belief system that is stultifying to both partners." She cares nothing that this belief system benefits children who depend on patriarchal stability and who are devastated by the breakdown of the system which she wants to break down. This indifference alone should disqualify women like Amanda from gaining custody of children.

Is there anything "natural" about a free ride during which a wife has her standard of living raised 73 percent by a husband from whom she deems herself entitled to withdraw her sexual loyalty? Anything "natural" about her claim to continued subsidization after she has withdrawn this loyalty by adultery or divorce? Her only pretext is her continuing custody of the children whom Heyn and her adulteresses never mention. What is unnatural is for an ex-husband to subsidize an ex-wife, especially an adulterous one,[4] who performs no reciprocal services and whose rationale for demanding them is what this adulteress objects to—marriage being a lifetime commitment.

---

[4] Judges quite regularly give custody to adulterous mothers on the ground that "children belong with their mother."

The inconvenient fact will not go away: the sexual permissiveness of the female kinship system generates much of the pathology of society. It sacrifices long-term satisfactions based on family stability and social continuity to short-term recreational satisfactions. It sees sex as something in the present rather than something spanning a lifetime and beyond, connecting men, women and children, and grandchildren to the larger society and to civilization.

Joan Brown thinks that only a massive religious revival or draconian laws could change society back to patriarchy. The change now going on—from patriarchy to matriarchy—itself depends on draconian laws aimed at ex-husbands and less draconian laws aimed at taxpayers. It requires, moreover, the consensus of society that it is right for ex-husbands to subsidize the destruction of their families and the placing of their children in female headed households.

If the man fathers the child with a woman who binds herself by a contract of marriage he is obligated to provide for her and for their children, and the law is obligated to compel him to do so, which it does—or tries to do. The present wreckage of the family is mostly caused by the *woman's* choosing not to keep her contract and by the law's assurance to her that she need not or that there need not be a contract at all. If the man fathers the child with a woman who insists upon and exercises her right to control her own reproduction, then the law's intrusion for the purpose of coercing the man violates the man's right to possess his own earnings. The law's position is that the woman who binds herself by marriage vows is not really binding herself, only pretending to. The contract is binding only on the man. This is what Lord Lane means when he says the law is unconcerned with justice.

LORD LANE'S UNCONCERN FOR JUSTICE

Lord Lane has been quoted: "The law does not seem to be about justice—it seems that the needs of children have to come first."[5] This is a refusal to implement equal justice under law; it undermines the marriage contract. The needs of children are usually best met by allowing them to grow up in two-parent families. When Lane speaks of the needs of children he means the needs of children after most of the damage

---

[5]Cited in John Campion and Pamela Leeson, *Facing Reality: The Case for the Reconstruction of Legal Marriage* (London: Family Law Action Group, March, 1994), p. 35.

resulting from family breakdown has already been inflicted upon them by the judge's placing them in female headed households. Only then—after ignoring "equal justice," after disregarding the validity of the marriage contract, after refusing to see that the greatest need of the children is to live in two-parent homes, only after having placed them where they have an eight times greater likelihood of becoming delinquents—*then* he becomes concerned for the damage inflicted on them and decides this damage is so great that it requires scrapping the very concept of justice itself.

The law's program for making men "responsible" requires men to think as lawmakers do—that they are obligated to subsidize the destruction of their families. Men do a disservice to themselves, their children and society by acknowledging this factitious obligation. Lawmakers and judges who mindlessly try to impose it on men are undermining the basis of civilized society by insisting that marriage is meaningless.

"We should," says Ms. Hoggett, "be considering whether the legal institution of marriage continues to serve any useful purpose." It has come to serve little purpose because real—patriarchal—marriage, which integrates males into reproduction as equal partners, has now been melded into the matriarchal system in which the male is merely a hanger-on, useful as a fairy godfather for Mom but otherwise disposable. Once wives become privileged to expel their husbands, marriage ceases to be the "legal institution" Ms. Hoggett refers to and reverts to being a merely biological arrangement like the breeding of cattle.

It needs to be repeated: When the law declares that it is not concerned with justice and will not enforce the marriage contract then the woman is liberated from her marriage vows and society becomes matriarchal.

What can men do about it? Play their Money Card. How else can the social contract and marriage be made meaningful? It is only, in Ms. Hoggett's words, the adoption of "principles for the protection of children and dependent *spouses*" and making them "equally applicable to the unmarried" which has eroded "the distinction between marriage and non-married cohabitation." The legal issue is this: Is a non-spouse a spouse? If so, then marriage is meaningless and society operates under the female kinship system where the wife tells the husband "to take his blanket and leave."[6] If not, the judge who destroys the marriage must not merely pretend concern for the best interests of the children, but must act as though he had such concern—by placing them in their father's custody.

The judge perpetuates the man's obligations because he simply cannot conceive of any other way for the woman and the children to be provided for. There is no other way—unless he does what he is paid to do, unless he enforces the marriage contract or administers equal justice under law, unless he acts as though marriage means something. If, as usual, it is the mother's choice to back out of the marriage, this does not entitle her to deprive the children of their father and deprive the father of his children and his paycheck. Neither does the father's choice to back out of his marriage entitle him to abandon his children to the female kinship system.

Former Prime Minister Mrs. Thatcher and the feminists want to pretend that there is no real difference between the male and female kinship systems, between marriage and shacking-up. The difference is total:

Under the male kinship system the woman offers to share her reproductive life with a man and the man offers *in exchange* to provide for her and for their children.

Under the female kinship system the woman claims the right to be sexually promiscuous.

What makes the present switchover to the female kinship system appear to work is the collusion of the wife and the judge in the pretense that her withdrawal of sexual loyalty entitles her to the same economic support as is provided in the male kinship system *in exchange* for the woman's sexual loyalty and her bearing of the man's children.

The woman's withdrawal of sexual loyalty entitles her to nothing. The present crisis in the family, the social pathology resulting from the failure to resolve this crisis, derive from the law's attempt to make the female kinship system do what only the male kinship system can do. The law no longer enables children to grow up in two-parent families,

---

[6] Seneca woman, quoted by 19th century feminist Elizabeth Cady Stanton in *off our backs*, August/September, 1998.

enables fathers to *have* families, gives fathers the motivation so conspicuously absent in men in the female kinship system.

The male kinship system is a success, the female kinship system a failure. The contrast between them is concealed by the pretense that the female kinship system creates the same male obligations and loyalties as the male kinship system and that the female kinship system breaks down only because of male disloyalty to it—as Mrs. Thatcher says, "men fathered a child *and then absconded.*" Mrs. Thatcher would not pretend to be appalled by this if she had not bullied her conscience into believing what she knows to be untrue. The overwhelming majority of the men she is blaming do not abscond *from families*, do not violate their marriage contracts, do not betray the male kinship system, do not abandon their children. They are either unwed partners of promiscuous females who refuse to procreate within marriage or they have been expelled by their wives and by the legal system which, as Lord Lane truly says, is not concerned with justice. Even feminists, who complain about everything else, don't accuse fathers of failing to support their *families*. The law is justified in compelling men to fulfill the terms of their marriage contracts, but it has no justification for holding them to a contract which has been annulled by the divorce court or one which never existed. Men's refusal to finance the female kinship system is *necessary* if patriarchy is to be restored. In particular, men's paying ex-wives who destroy their families by divorce needs to be recognized for what it is, the Mutilated Beggar principle—the use of impoverished children to finance a mother-headed begging ring.

Does the truth matter? Is there no difference between a man who abandons his wife and children, leaves his home and violates his marriage contract and a man whose wife abandons her marriage contract and withdraws the sexual loyalty pledged under that contract and (with the help of the legal system whose responsibility it is to support the *male* kinship system) expels the man and prevents him from doing anything to protect himself and save his children from falling into the female kinship system?

The male kinship system harnesses male motivation, male energy, male aggression to provide for families by channeling reproduction through marriage, thus using sex as a motivator of males and the wealth created by males as a motivator of females. The female kinship system has no purpose; it is simply what happens when the male kinship system breaks down or is destroyed by the legal system, as is now happening.

The double standard benefits women by giving them bargaining power: the woman offers a man a family, something sufficient to motivate a man to a lifetime of disciplined labor. This is patriarchy. A woman who rejects the double standard cannot offer a man a family, not a stable one.

A wife's promise of a family must have society's backup. If the woman is privileged to liberate herself from the patriarchal system by saying, "I've changed my mind. I don't love you any longer. I'm getting a divorce. My lawyer assures me I will get custody of the children. I'll need the house and I'll expect decent support payments"—then the patriarchal system breaks down and society reverts to the female kinship system and its pathology. This is what is now taking place.

Today's society will not guarantee the woman's sexual loyalty, the validity of her marriage vows, the family stability made possible by that pledged loyalty. It will not guarantee men's right to have families or children's right to have fathers. What society will guarantee is the woman's right to be liberated from her marriage vows and to live like Judge Noland's cattle. It will guarantee in addition that the suffering inflicted on children by father-deprivation shall be mitigated by the enslaving of the father. The liberation of women requires (among other things) that men shall have no security of their property. The security of men's property can be guaranteed only by father custody of children.

SHACKING-UP

Abigail van Buren gets a letter from a woman shacking up with a man:[7]

DEAR ABBY: Ted and I have been living together for several years. We are both divorced. Our children are grown and have successful careers.

We live in my house, and he gives me a generous check each month toward household expenses....

---

[7]*Los Angeles Times*, 9 Feb, 1995.

Ted is dead-set against marriage. We never discuss the future, and if I try to, he changes the subject. He is very secretive about his financial situation, but I have told him everything about mine.

I'm perfectly willing to sign a prenuptial agreement, but this makes no difference to Ted.

I know he loves me and doesn't want to lose me. I love him, too, but I'm increasingly resentful of his attitude that I should be content with things as they are.

I work very hard at our relationship and to make our lives comfortable.

Am I wrong to want the ultimate commitment? Or should I be content with what I have.

I'd like your honest opinion.

WANTS A FUTURE

Abby's reply:

A man who lives with a woman for several years, changes the subject when she tries to discuss the future and refuses to compromise is a very poor candidate for marriage.

Unless he is prepared to do a 180-degree turnaround, you're nesting with the wrong rooster.

This man is a poor candidate for marriage because the law has made marriage meaningless—or threatening—for men. She wants "the ultimate commitment" to *what*? They are both divorced, so they had both made the ultimate commitment to a previous spouse. The consequence is that they are living in "her house." One must suppose this is the house made possible by the labor of her ex-husband, so her prior commitment turned a nice profit at the man's expense. Ted had a similar "ultimate commitment" from his ex-spouse, which, one might suppose, resulted in his forfeiting a similar home made possible by *his* labor. It seems that she wants an ultimate commitment which might this time, as before, result in major benefits for the woman at the man's expense—and, perhaps benefits for her children at the expense of his children.

She cannot understand his reluctance because she has never been taken to the cleaners in the divorce court; but he has been and that is why he changes the subject when she begins talking about marriage. She tells him everything about her finances because she is under no threat (and may have little to reveal). He is secretive because he is under the same threat he faced from his ex-wife. He is dead-set against marriage because, like all divorced men, he knows the state will not enforce the marriage contract but will annul it at the wife's request and replace it with non-contractual obligations on the ex-husband. It is this irresponsibility of the legal system, which now works to this woman's disadvantage. She is willing to sign a prenuptial agreement and he is not. For the reason that the law treats a prenuptial agreement the way it treats the marriage contract, as a mere piece of paper—in order to benefit the woman.

The law treats the woman as a moral minor incapable of making a binding and enforceable contract. Ted's behavior is the logical result.

There would be no such problems if the judge ended the divorce proceedings with this: "This marriage is dissolved and you are both released from your marriage vows." This would end the use of divorce as a means of enslaving ex-husbands. "Unfortunately" it would also end the use of divorce as a means of undermining the benefits marriage confers on husbands and wives and children and society. It would end the use of divorce as a means of strengthening the female kinship system. The necessary corollary would be the automatic father custody of children, which would enable fathers to confer on wives the benefits of Briffault's Law.

XIII) NO FAULT DIVORCE

Prior to 1970, the law usually justified its wrecking of families on the grounds either of adultery or of "extreme cruelty." The sexual revolution has now made adultery a right for women ("a woman's sacred right to control her own body"); extreme cruelty was usually understood to be a legal fiction meaning no more than that one of the spouses, usually the wife, wanted out. The pretense that the husband was an extremely cruel man was in most cases sufficiently absurd that it embarrassed even judges and lawyers and it was felt necessary to "reform" divorce by perpetuating the same destruction of families under a new terminology. This is called No Fault divorce. There were label switchings. Divorce was renamed Dissolution of Marriage. The Plaintiff was renamed the Petitioner. The Defendant was renamed the Respondent. Alimony was renamed Spousal Support (the ex-wife was no longer a spouse, but calling her one "justifies" taking the man's money). The real core of the change is that it was no longer necessary to "prove" extreme cruelty to inflict upon the husband a more severe penalty than is imposed on most low-income black male felons.

The logical corollary to "no fault" would be "no punishment." But how could a judge not punish the husband in order to benefit the wife who has thrown herself on his mercy? The judge knows that mothers and children are dependent creatures and now she has only him to help her and her children whom (of course) he is expected to place in her custody, since this is what all other judges do. Besides, placing children with fathers would destroy the female kinship system, restore the male kinship system, get rid of ghettos and end the feminist/sexual revolution. The judge is as essential to that revolution as is the Welfare System. Women and children, after all, can't be allowed to starve. The judge (after destroying the family) has to do his duty.

What happens in the divorce court is that Mom makes herself and "her" kids Mutilated Beggars with the judge cast in the role of almsgiver—though the judge chouses the alms from the father. He hardly has a choice: he must deprive the husband of his children, his property, the good family car (though if there are still payments to be made on it he will allow him to keep the coupon book), his furniture and appliances, his household pets and the home made possible by his labor—because the husband is male, because this is what the other judges do, and because the husband is guilty of no fault. The arrangement is one which (together with the Welfare System) restores the female kinship system of Judge Noland's cattle.

At the conclusion of Offenbach's comic opera *La Perichole* there occurs a delightful scene in which the Viceroy proclaims a general amnesty, releases all the prisoners, and allows them to return home. It is discovered, however, that there is an aged marquis who was imprisoned by mistake twelve years previously, and since he never committed a crime, he has done nothing for which he can be forgiven. He is accordingly sent back to prison.

Very funny. That's what's known in show business as a joke. Only *this* joke is not in an operetta. American justice really does deprive American fathers of their children, their homes, their role and their income because they are guilty of no fault. There is no other way for judges to destroy patriarchal families and replace them with ghetto-style matrilines.

Let's say that again. There is no way that the patriarchal family can be destroyed except by punishing men for being guilty of no fault.

No Fault is not, as many allege, some wicked scheme to defraud wives of the security which marriage formerly gave them. It is simply an acknowledgment of the weakness of character of judges. They need some pretext for destroying the father's family and there is no other way than to accuse him of No Fault.

Maggie Gallagher claims that No Fault divorce outlaws marriage:

> **When Mary agreed to live in the same house with Jim and accept his financial support and offer her own paid and unpaid labor to the household, to sleep in the same bed and bear his children, she did so because she thought she was married. Had Jim asked her to do these things for him without getting married, she would have slapped his face. Mary knew what marriage meant...**

> **But the state of California later informed her that she was not allowed to make or to accept lifetime commitments. No-fault divorce gave judges, at the request of one half of a couple, the right to decide when a marriage had irretrievably broken down. They decided by and large that wanderlust would**

be a state-protected emotion, while loyalty was on its own. In a cruel display
of raw judicial power, the state of California made Mary a single woman again,
without protecting her interests and without requiring her consent....[1]

It was not a cruel display of raw judicial power. It was simply an
attempt to conceal judicial weakness of character. Ms. Gallagher
supposes the wife is victimized. For every Mary who is made single
without her consent, there are three Jims who are made single and who
lose their kids and their homes. The judge tries to do what he can to
protect Mary's interests by ignoring Jim's, stripping him of everything he
can. What's a poor judge supposed to do? Keep his oath of office?
Administer equal justice under law? Enforce contracts? Preserve
families? Who's kidding? This isn't the age of Queen Victoria. It's the
twentieth century, almost the twenty-first. There's been a feminist
revolution. Society is returning to the female kinship system, ceasing to
be a patriarchy and becoming a matriarchy. Women have won the right
to control their own bodies—"the first law of matriarchy." And, since
they and their children are dependent creatures, how can they control
their own bodies without also controlling the paychecks of their ex-
husbands?

Here is the judge's predicament—created by the weakness of
character of all the other judges who have been discriminating against
fathers for over a hundred years. They have so spoiled American wives
that the wives suppose themselves entitled to the benefits of the
patriarchal system without performing services to earn them. In the
typical case, where the wife sues for divorce, the judge is confronted by a
more-or-less helpless female who has forsaken dependence on her
husband and made herself dependent on *him*. Depriving her of custody
of the children would leave her with no bargaining power whatever. The
husband would have it all—kids, home, income, status. Surely no judge
could be so unchivalrous, so cruel, to a poor woman, a mother, as to give
the father custody of her children and cast her alone into the cold world.

Yes, he could. That is the only way to save the family and the
patriarchal system. That is the way patriarchy works. God says "He
shall rule over thee"—not the judge who fancies himself to be God, to be
empowered to *prevent* husbands from ruling over wives. The judge may
say "I don't want to play God," but that, like "Equal Justice Under Law,"
inscribed over the Supreme Court Building, is to be construed by the

---

[1] *The Abolition of Marriage*, p.144.

rule-of-contrary. Playing God is what he is doing, by denying equal justice to fathers and making mothers heads of families. The consequences are described on pages 12ff. of this book.

If the wife refuses to be ruled, fine; then she consigns herself to the female kinship system—but she must not take her children with her, must not contribute to the ghettoizing of society.

Ms. Gallagher continues:

> **By the early eighties the revolution was all but complete: eighteen states plus the District of Columbia had eliminated fault grounds for divorce altogether, almost all the rest added no-fault as an option for a divorcing spouse....**
>
> **No-fault divorce was supposed to permit a couple to get a divorce by mutual consent. What no-fault divorce actually did is create unilateral divorce. During the seventies, Americans gained the right to divorce-on-demand and in the process lost the right to marry. And this is the remarkable thing: no one noticed.... [T]his new social institution...more closely resembles taking a concubine than taking a spouse.[2]**

They decided that female sexual disloyalty was a state-protected emotion while the male was on his own—and was obligated to subsidize the female sexual disloyalty. Jim thought marriage was a contract and thought that it was the responsibility of the legal system to enforce contracts. That's what judges get paid for—but, with the most important contract, that's what they refuse to do, which is the main reason why society is returning to sexual irresponsibility and matriarchy. "The law does not seem to be about justice." Not only the male's best interests but the children's best interests can be ignored as long as the judge professes his *concern* for them.

Judges aren't displaying their power; they are trying to conceal their cowardice. When legislators switched to "No-Fault" in the 1970s, judges merely continued to do what they had always done. "No-fault" had always been the judicial practice; only the pretense of fault existed. What they did in the 1970s was to drop the pretense. They went on trying to disguise their weakness and dishonesty (pretending that fault existed when they knew it seldom did) acknowledging that they had never intended to enforce the contract of marriage.

---

[2]Maggie Gallagher, *Enemies of Eros: How the Sexual Revolution Is Killing Family, Marriage, and Sex and What We Can Do About It* (Chicago: Bonus Books, Inc., 1989), pp. 192f.

"The State of California informed her that she was not allowed to make or to accept lifetime commitments." She was allowed to make the commitment—but then to get out of it. But her pretense of making such a commitment was what entitled her to Jim's reciprocal commitment. Once men began to realize what was going on, this undermined women's bargaining power with them. It was a rotten thing to do to women, as Ms. Gallagher says. But as a compensation for its refusal to do what it gets paid for, the legal system did an equally rotten thing to men—insisting that Jim would have to continue to support Mary following her withdrawal of her sexual loyalty. The rationalization which accompanied this was that Jim wasn't subsidizing Mary but subsidizing his own kids—and what kind of a father would abandon his own kids, his own Flesh and Blood?

The law's concern that bad (sexually disloyal) women shall not be punished has a price tag for good (sexually loyal) women: they lose much of their bargaining power too. Since the reward for being a good woman is reduced, more are drawn into the lifestyle of bad women. Men's inducement to be loyal to their marriages—or to get married at all—is similarly impaired.[3] Society drifts back into the female kinship system when, as feminist Marilyn French says, "marriage was informal, casual"[4]—when men were not fathers but boyfriends, when their girlfriends married the government's Backup System. This is how ghettos are created. Men will have to change this. The astonishing rise in Clinton's popularity following the Lewinsky scandal represents the power of the matriarchal opposition (the feminist vote) and shows what we are up against. Bachofen warned us.

---

[3]Recall the statistics cited on page 30: about the decline in marriages.
[4]Marilyn French, *Beyond Power* (New York: Summit Books, 1986), p. 38.

XIV) DOMINATION VS. PARTNERSHIP

Ms. Riane Eisler proposes to get rid of "domination," which she supposes is bad, and replace it with "partnership," which she supposes is good. Male *dominance* (not domination) is universal. The term refers, says Professor Steven Goldberg, "to the *feeling* acknowledged by the emotions of both men and women that the woman's will is somehow subordinate to the male's and that general authority in dyadic and familial relationships, in whatever terms a particular society defines authority, ultimately resides in the male."[1] Complaining about male dominance, like complaining about women getting fewer Nobel Prizes or about women's athletic teams getting less subsidization, provides feminists with imaginary grievances and lucrative lawsuits. Ms. Eisler hopes to "succeed in completing the cultural shift from a dominator to a partnership social organization, [when] we will see a real sexual revolution—one in which sex will no longer be associated with domination and submission but with the full expression of our powerful human yearning for connection and for erotic pleasure."[2] The "real sexual revolution" means that society will become, as in the days of the prehistoric hypnocracies or surviving stone age societies, a vast promiscuous sex cult, a lifestyle which the patriarchal revolution was created to get rid of by creating the individual family based on economic relations. "Individual marriage," as J. J. Bachofen said in 1861,"has its foundation in economic relations."[3]

"Once having acquired...private property," says feminist Dr. Gerda Lerner

men sought to secure it to themselves and their heirs; they did this by instituting the monogamous family. By controlling women's sexuality through the requirement of prenuptial chastity and by the establishing of the

---

[1]*The Inevitability of Patriarchy*, (New York: William Morrow, 1973), p. 33. Women prefer dominant men. A woman is far more likely to complain of her man's weakness than of his dominance. "[O]f all wives," says Goldberg, "wives in wife-dominant marriages (marriages in which wives have the power advantages) are the least satisfied with their marriages" (p. 37).
[2]Riane Eisler, *Sacred Pleasure: Sex, Myth and the Politics of the Body* (HarperSanFrancisco, 1996), p. 199.
[3]Briffault, *The Mothers*, II, 1.

double standard in marriage, men assured themselves of the legitimacy of their offspring and thus secured their property interest.[4]

Thus could men, as Aristotle said, "leave behind them an image of themselves," enabling them to feel, as women feel, "these are my children." This is why married men earn nearly twice as much as single men, why they and their children are better citizens. "The native country under matriarchy," said Bachofen, "will know only brother and sisters, and this will last until an exclusively patriarchal era will have superseded it, dissolving the unity of the mass and supplanting all with the smaller units of the family."[5] The smaller unit is the more productive one, because its male head is motivated by long-term sexual goals. However, the smaller unit must ensure the father his role in the new creation, the family. This can be threatening to Mom if she prefers the sexual promiscuity of the female kinship system to the economic and status advantages and the social stability of the male kinship system. Then, if Mom can marry the government and sponge on "welfare state feminism"[6] she has the option of telling tell her boyfriend to get out. She will not have to live the kind of life mothers live under the patriarchal system. She will no longer feel, as feminist Evelyn Reed puts it, "dispossessed from [her] former place in society at large...[and] robbed not only of [her] economic independence but also of [her] former sexual freedom."[7] This is the economic independence and sexual freedom enjoyed by ghetto matriarchs and squaws on Indian reservations. Then they can say, with the First Wives Club, "You don't own me! You don't own me!" But if they own their children the kids will suffer the disadvantages noted on pages 12ff.

"As ancient Greece, became 'civilized,'" writes homosexual Arthur Evans,

and fell under the influence of patriarchal institutions, the worship of Pan was denounced and repressed. The new order couldn't handle the religion's open sexuality, transvestism, feminism and emotionalism.[8]

---

[4]*Creation of Patriarchy*, pp. 22f.
[5]J. Bachofen, *Mother Right* in V. F. Calverton, *The Making of Man* (New York: Modern Library, 1931), p.162. This switchover takes society from the "classificatory kinship system" to the "descriptive kinship system." See page 117.
[6]George Gilder's term.
[7]Evelyn Reed, *Woman's Evolution* (New York: Pathfinder press, 1975), p. 24.
[8]Arthur Evans, *Witchcraft and the Gay Counterculture* (Boston: Fag Rag Press, 1978), p. 26.

He cites Euripides' *Bacchae* as a protest against this new patriarchal order which tries to bury or discipline man's elemental Id forces. "The moral of the play is clear: the new order is repressing aspects of human behavior that are sacred to the god of ecstasy. The price of this repression will be a madness that tears the new order itself apart."

Translation: The price of the patriarchal program for regulating sex and putting it to work will be a feminist/sexual/homosexual revolution which will tear patriarchy apart. Dionysus, who presides over the action of *The Bacchae* as the God of Ecstasy, "is an expression of the sensual joys of life unrestrained by the state and untrammeled by the patriarchal family."

In the apt words of one commentator, his religion is "an expression of the aimless joy of life."[9]

Society will either encourage males to be providers for families or it will not. Making them providers for ex-families doesn't work and ought not to work. The chaos described on pages 12ff. is mostly the result of the legal system's attempts to make it work—and thereby to undermine the family. Politicians and judges hunger for feminist approval—so it promises men families but then takes away half of them. This used to be a matter of injustice to limited numbers of men but has now become a matter of changing the kinship system, a vast upheaval.

Bachofen warned us. There was violence in the fifth millennium B. C. when the old matriarchal system began to be replaced by the new patriarchal system. The older—peaceful—system is thus described by Ms. Eisler:

Symbolized by the feminine chalice or source of life, the generative, nurturing, and creative powers of nature—not the powers to destroy—were, as we have seen, given highest value. At the same time, the function of priestesses and priests seems to have been not to serve and give religious sanction to a brutal male elite but to benefit all the people in the community in the same way that the heads of the clans administered the communally owned and worked lands.[10]

---

[9]C. Kerenyi, *Dionysos: Archetypical Image of Indestructible Life*, trans. Ralph Manheim. (London: Routledge and Kegan Paul, 1976), p. 170.
[10]*The Chalice and the Blade*, p. 43.

Such were the happy days under the matriarchy where people worshiped a loving and caring Goddess and everybody got along fine. Descent was traced through the female, things were generative, nurturing, creative, peaceful. BUT THEN....

At this pivotal branching, the cultural evolution of societies that worshiped the life-generating and nurturing powers of the universe—in our time still symbolized by the ancient chalice or grail—was interrupted.... [T]hen came the great change—a change so great, indeed, that nothing else in all we know of human cultural evolution is comparable in magnitude. [11]

Then came the patriarchs, the Kurgans, or Indo-Europeans, who worshiped bad male gods and imposed a dominator society on the peaceful Goddess worshipers. The Kurgans were brutal, destroying, bloodthirsty, warlike, harsh, punitive, insensitive, violent—and the world has never been right since:

Under the partnership arrangement "women were sexually, economically, and politically free agents,"[12] not bound by "the morality enforcing women's sexual slavery to men [which] was imposed to meet the economic requirements of a rigidly male-dominant system that property be transmitted from father to son and that the benefits from women's and children's labor accrue to the male....[T]hese laws regulating women's virginity were designed to protect what were essentially economic transactions between men."[13]

Ms. Eisler empties the whole thesaurus of hate on the new patriarchy:

a system leading to chronic wars, social injustice, and ecological imbalance...male dominant, violent, and hierarchic...the shift in emphasis from technologies that sustain and enhance life to technologies symbolized by the Blade: technologies designed to destroy and dominate...a common preoccupation with conquering, killing, and dominating...to conquer, pillage and loot...dominance, destruction and oppression...manly pride and unthinking cruelty...male violence and destructive power...a brutal male elite...male dominance, male violence, and a generally hierarchic and authoritarian social structure...ever more effective technologies of destruction—

---

[11] *The Chalice and the Blade*, pp. xvii, 43.
[12] p. 100.
[13] Pp. 100, 97.

and so on and on and on.

The Bible is the fountainhead of this patriarchy. "To the extent that it reflects a dominator society," she says,

"biblical morality is at best stunted. At worst, it is a pseudomorality in which the will of God is a device for covering up cruelty and barbarity....Killing and enslaving one's fellow human beings and destroying and appropriating their property is, in our Bible, frequently condoned. Killing in war is in fact divinely sanctioned, as is plundering for booty, raping women and children, and razing entire cities...warfare, authoritarian role, and the subjugation of women become integral parts of the new dominator morality and society...Indo-European rule was imposed through the chaos of massive physical destruction and cultural disruption....a system that has kept us mired in barbarity and oppression...through the savagery and horror of their holy Crusades, their witch-hunts, their Inquisition, their book burnings and people burnings, they spread not love but the old androcratic staples of repression, devastation, and death."

Ms. Eisler definitely dislikes patriarchy.

Feminist historian Nawal El-Saadawi describes how things were in Arabia in better days under the mother-right, when women controlled their own sexuality:

Before Islam a woman could practise polyandry and marry more than one man. When she became pregnant she would send for all her husbands....Gathering them around her, she would name the man she wished to be the father of her child, and the man could not refuse....

According to feminist Rosalind Miles, who quotes El Saadawi, "When a Bedouin woman wanted to divorce one of her spare husbands, she simply turned her tent around to signal that her door was no longer open to him."[14]

Understandably, men found this matriarchal power unpleasant. These times later came to called "the days of ignorance." With women exercising such power there could be no stable male role, no stable family. Ms. Miles complains that under patriarchy "women became subjected to the tyranny of sexual monopoly."[15] This is code language for women giving up sexual promiscuity.

---

[14]*Women's History of the World*, p. 66.
[15]P. 48.

> The earliest families consisted of females and their children, since all tribal hunting societies were centered on and organized through the mother. The young males either left or were driven out, while the females stayed close to their mothers and the original homesite, attaching their males to them. In the woman-centered family, males were casual and peripheral, while both nucleus and any networks developing from it remained female. These arrangements continue to operate in a number of still-existing Stone Age tribes worldwide, the so-called "living fossils."[16]

America is becoming such a living fossil, with "families" centered around and organized through the mother, with males "casual and peripheral," with women having "the right to divorce, custody of children and financial maintenance."[17]

"Where was man in the primal drama of the worship of the Great Mother?" asks Ms. Miles.

> He was the expendable consort, the sacrificial king, the disposable drone. Woman was everything; he was nothing. It was too much. Man had to have some meaning in the vast and expanding universe of human consciousness. But as the struggle for understanding moved into its next phase, the only meaning seemed to lie through the wholesale reversal of the existing formula of belief. Male pride rose to take up the challenge of female power; and launching the sex war that was to divide sex and societies for millennia to come, man sought to assert his manhood through the death and destruction of all that had made women the Great Mother, Goddess, warrior, lover and queen.[18]

Since the feminist revolution, now that "the day of the kept woman is over," man is once again expected to resume his role of the expendable consort for the liberated women, to play the role of ex-husband or detachable boyfriend or taxpayer—the subsidizer of the parasitic female who is required to perform nothing in return, or (while marriage endures) very little.

Small wonder that the hypnocracies were brought to an end by male rebellion accompanied by the cataclysmic upheaval of changing the kinship system.

The millennial sex party was over. The hypnocracies, based on somnolent co-consciousness, had to give way. "We must," says Gerald

---

[16]p. 8.
[17]p. 36.
[18]p. 36.

Heard, "regard the hero as being an inevitable development of consciousness." The hero "struck out destructively against the blandishments of the mother-deity cultures"[19]:

> The critical faculty had to grow and, since the coconscious tribe had become negative to all invention and hostile to the capacity for asking questions, it had to grow because of an increasing sense of separateness. Objectivity and detachment could only arise from rejection. Spontaneous revulsion gave the position and status necessary for perspective and proportion.

This is the positive side of the "Kurgan" conquest, the Indo-European-patriarchal revolution. It was not a rampage; it was a revolution of consciousness, a psychological breakthrough. Half the world today speaks their language, Indo-European. They had something powerful going for them.

Unfortunately, Heard fails to consider the sex-war angle of the resulting "heroic revolt." It represented an expansion of consciousness, a rough, even savage one. But it was more than this, more than a violent reaction against the suffocation of "the problem that has no name." It was also a change in the kinship system, allowing the human male an equal role in reproduction.

Ms. Eisler wants to return to the Stone Age version of the feminine mystique, to

> traditions that go back to the dawn of civilization [when] the female vulva was revered as the magical portal of life, possessed of the power of both physical regeneration and spiritual illumination and transformation.[20]

Ms. Friedan wanted to do away with this "feminine mystique" but Ms. Eisler and her fellow ecofeminists want to get back to it. Sjöö and Mor begin their book *The Great Cosmic Mother* with this:

> In the beginning...was a very female sea. For two-and-a-half billion years on earth, all life-forms floated in the womb-like environment of the planetary ocean—nourished and protected by its fluid chemicals, rocked by the lunar-tidal rhythms. Charles Darwin believed the menstrual cycle originated here, organically echoing the moon-pulse of the sea. And, because this longest period of life's time on earth was dominated by marine forms reproducing

---

[19] *The Five Ages of Man*, p. 199.
[20] *Sacred Pleasure*, p. 15.

parthenogenetically, he concluded that the female principle was primordial. In the beginning, life did not gestate within the body of any creature, but within the ocean womb containing all organic life. There were no specialized sex organs; rather, a generalized female existence reproduced itself within the female body of the sea.[21]

This is the Feminine Mystique with a vengeance. It was against this basing of woman's role on her reproductive biology that Ms. Friedan protested. Simone de Beauvoir likewise complained about women being confined to reproduction and to "immanence." Sjöö and Mor can't get enough of it. They suggest that the following experiment performed in the 1970s may be "a breakthrough"—or rather a return to better days:

In some very interesting clinical experiments conducted between 1975 and 1979, a variety of female, male, and adolescent psychotherapy patients who received the subliminal message Mommy and I are one flashed on a tachistoscope screen were much more successful—and permanently successful—at losing weight, stopping drinking and smoking, and overcoming emotional problems to improve reading skills, than were patients receiving neutral or no subliminal messages [T]hese studies show that successful overcoming of problems—i.e., mature development—does not come from severing the early infantile sense of unity with the Mother, but from reestablishing it.

"Mommy," not "mother." The return is to infantilism and co-consciousness. Most societies have rites-of-passage to usher people into adulthood and get them to accept responsibilities. Here is a reverse-rite-of-passage, back to infantilism.[22] "In ancient matriarchal society," say Sjöö and Mor, "man stood always in the relation of son to the mother."[23] That's the way Mommy likes it.

THE MEANING OF SEX

Ehrenreich, Hess and Jacobs think that early writers on sex like Barbara Seaman and Shere Hite

realized that for women to insist on pleasure was to assert power, and hence to give an altogether new meaning to sex—as an affirmation of female will and

---

[21]*The Great Cosmic Mother*, p. 2.
[22]Drug addicts commonly tattoo the word MOM on their bodies and inject their needle into the "O" of the word.
[23]P. 352.

an assertion of female power. The old meaning, which in one form or another was always submission to male power, could be inverted.[24]

This is the feminist "Pleasure Principle": *Seek pleasure*—especially if you are a woman. Women hold in their hands the ultimate power of life and death—EROS.[25] It is now in woman's power to give an altogether new meaning to sex, the assertion of female power and the rejection of male power. The male usurpation of power over reproduction, only a few thousand years old, can be resisted. This is the message of feminism, the freeing of woman to pursue pleasure. To hell with men. To hell with children. To hell with the million fetuses slaughtered on the abortion tables every year. This is the message of the worship of Dionysus which drove the women of Greece to abandon their homes and their work and roam about in the mountains, swinging thyrsi and torches in the dance, seizing an animal or even a child, tearing it apart and devouring the pieces.[26] This is the message of the Birmingham ladies. Let's repeat their demand:

the right to define our sexuality [as] the over-riding demand of the woman's movement, preceding all other demands. Men's sexual domination of women, which prevented the emergence of women's self-defined sexuality, was now being formally accepted as the pivot of woman's oppression.[27]

Look at what this Pleasure Principle did for those poor waifs from broken families, Monica Lewinsky and Bill Clinton—for Princess Diana or Duchess Fergie, or for tens of millions of others caught up in the feminist cause of emancipating women from patriarchal control and seeking pleasure in the Female Kinship System—which has given us our ghettos and Indian reservations and the Republic of Haiti and the Stone Age societies described in Briffault's Chapter 13.[28]

Against this we place the patriarchal principle: putting sex to work by confining it within families and focusing not on women's pleasure (or men's) but on the welfare of children. Against women's wild hunger for the freedom of the hills of Thrace and Macedonia, for the raw flesh of

---

[24]Ehrenreich, Hess and Jacobs, *Re-Making Love*, p. 195.
[25]Cf. Supra, p. 128.
[26]*Supra*, p. 35.
[27]*Supra*, p. 102.
[28]Below, p. 229.

animals or children, for the exhilaration of swinging thyrsi[29] and torches in the dance—against their envy of the sexual freedom of ghetto matriarchs and Indian squaws, we must set "the joy and care of children"—and the principle that these children must not be separated from the father whose surname they bear and whose patrimony they inherit. Let Mom swing her thyrsus and her torch alone in the hills or at her consciousness-raising group to protest her subjection to patriarchy. Let Dad have the kids who carry his name, and the home paid for with his labor, and the paycheck he earns.

"At least I was true to myself," says Fergie, Duchess of York—meaning true to the Pleasure Principle, true to the Female Kinship System, the natural reproductive arrangements shared by cats and dogs and Judge Noland's cattle. Being true to herself was not, however, required by her marriage vow. The Archbishop didn't ask Fergie to be true to herself, but to be true to her husband and to forsake all others—to be true to the *Male* Kinship System, which ensures that her children will have a father to give them a place in the higher-status patriarchal stratum of society, to give them and her their best chance of escaping the lower-status matriarchal stratum and its problems, indicated on pages 12ff. of this book.

Feminism and the legal system have made it easier for women to be true to themselves, to abolish the double standard, to become economically self-sufficient, to escape the Male Kinship System and its regulation, to attain "equality" with males. But this freeing of women has imposed impossible burdens on men, the weak link in human reproduction, men whose marginality necessitates the "oppression" of women and explains women's rebellion against it. Let's illustrate with a few quotes:

"Premarital sex," says Robert Scheer, "is the norm in American life."[30]

"Percentages of high school students who reported ever having sexual intercourse range from 38% in ninth grade to 60.9% in 12th grade."[31]

---

[29]A *thyrsus*, plural *thyrsi,* is "a staff surmounted by a pine cone, or by a bunch of vine or ivy leaves with grapes or berries. It is an attribute of Bacchus [or Dionysus], and of the satyrs and others engaging in Bacchic rites." (Webster's New International, second ed.)
[30]*Los Angeles Times*, 4 March, 1997.
[31]*Los Angeles Times*, 18 Sept., 1998.

"California law forbids sexual intercourse with anyone under 18 except a spouse...."[32]

Dr. Joycelyn Elders tells us that "almost 82% of our teens who become pregnant did not intend to do so."[33]

"Almost 8 of 10 teen pregnancies now occur outside marriage."[34]

"Sex," says Betty Friedan, "is distorted by women's economic dependence."[35]

"All the old prohibitions and taboos would have to give way to the needs of the sexually liberated woman," say Ehrenreich, Hess and Jacobs.[36]

According to the *Cosmopolitan* survey made in 1980, 41% of women had extramarital affairs, up from 8% in 1948.[37]

"Women who lived common-law before their first marriage have a 33% greater risk of divorce than...women who do not cohabit before their first marriage," according to the *Family in America.*[38]

According to NBC Nightly News, 16 July, 1992, the proportion of American adults who were single skyrocketed from 21% in 1970 to 41% in 1992.

"Forty-three percent of all American girls will become pregnant before the age of twenty."[39]

And so on. The number of such quotations could be multiplied without limit. They add up to this: the American girl is sufficiently unchaste that the American boy cannot depend upon having a family with her. The Male Kinship System is intended to *give reassurance to the poor male that he is not inferior.* Patriarchal marriage exists to reassure the man that if he marries he can have a family. Society formerly said to men: If you want a family, if you want a meaningful reproductive role in which you will be provider for your family and socializer of your children,

---

[32]*Los Angeles Times*, 15 Sept., 1996.
[33]*Los Angeles Times*, 9 April, 1997.
[34]*Los Angeles Times*, 2 May, 1997.
[35]*The Second Stage*, revised ed., p. 359.
[36]*Re-Making* Love, p. 70.
[37]Faludi, *Backlash*, p. 404.
[38]April, 1996.
[39]*Los Angeles Times*, 23 Nov., 1990.

able (with the assistance of your loyal wife) to integrate them into a stable and civilized society, get an education, earn money, acquire stabilizing assets—a home, a pension, an annuity, a stock portfolio—and support the patriarchy which makes civilization possible. Society today says to women: If you want to escape from sexual law-and-order and your marriage vows, if you want to be liberated to return to the Female Kinship System, if you want to exclude men from any meaningful reproductive role while keeping them as studs—get educated, represent yourself as a victim, and demand compensation for your sufferings. The judge will understand.

Telling women they have a right to be promiscuous undercuts the male role and deprives males of the reassurance they need. The poor male is confronted with a sixty percent divorce rate and virtual assurance that the law will side with his wife against him, deprive him of his children and property and future income. Why should he take on such fearful odds? He shouldn't, and increasingly he doesn't. This is why there are so many bachelors, so many demoralized men. This is why so many women ask where the men are, and turn to the government for help in the form of Affirmative Action, welfare and other conferred benefits. This explains "the coming white underclass" and its demoralization. It explains the demoralization of young males, who see what happens to their fathers.

Princess Diana divorced Prince Charles and hired a lawyer who asked her "Do you know how much your husband is worth? Well, you are entitled to half of it."[40]

[This half] included half the value of Highgrove, the Glouscestershire home Prince Charles had bought from the Macmillan family fifteen years previously, which is estimated to be worth three million pounds, as well as a sizeable slice of the 4 million pound annual income from the Duchy of Cornwall, the estates vested in every Prince of Wales since 1337. As for the 130,000 rolling acres of Duchy-owned farmland and buildings spread across twenty-three counties—including the famous Oval cricket ground in Kennington, south London—well, that could be a useful negotiating counter if the princess wanted to be difficult. During clandestine meetings in offbeat Thai and Chinese restaurants in the autumn of 1993, the princess and her lawyer were discussing multimillion settlement figures—15 million pounds would be a reasonable sum.

---

[40]Andrew Morton, *Diana: Her New Life* .(New York: Simon and Schuster, 1994), p. 22.

What services did Diana perform to earn this princely sum? She gave her sexual loyalty to Charles—the loyalty which she withdrew by divorce. She bore him two sons to be heirs to the British throne won by William the Conqueror in the eleventh century and now being shaken to its foundations by her notion that it is an archaic survival deserving to be done away with, and by the law's incompetence to see that her now-withdrawn loyalty was the only contribution for which she is being rewarded.

Fergie, Duchess of York, withdrew the same loyalty from Andrew:

> There were endless conversations between the princess and duchess as they mulled over their options. The advice from the assorted ranks of astrologers, mystics, clairvoyants and tarot-card readers was a faulty thread in the weft and weave of their unhappy lives, strongly disapproved of by the Queen. One day Fergie might telephone Diana to warn her that her astrologer forecast an accident involving a royal car. Predictions by their mediums forecast variously that Prince Andrew would become king or indicated that the Queen Mother's life was in danger....These predictions added an aura of unreality to the musings of two women already living in the bizarre looking-glass world of royal life. It is hardly surprising that on the day the Duchess of York decided to leave the royal family, she consulted the Greek mystic, Madame Vasso, for advice, rather than a royal courtier.

Life in the female kinship system has no purpose. It exists to amuse these idle and bored ladies, whose real function is to enable their men to have families—while *they* suffer, like Betty Friedan, from "the problem that has no name" and diddle with the carving up of what is left of the British Empire. Such carving-up cannot be an ongoing thing, however. British taxpayers can hardly be supposed to relish having 15 million pounds handed out whenever there is a divorce with mother custody.

XV) RE-DEFINING THE FAMILY

Patriarchy was more successful a third of a century ago, before feminism's attempt to restore the matriarchal family and its accompanying illegitimacy, drug addiction, demoralization and the rest. Washington, D.C., the murder capital of the world[1], illustrates how the change came about. A century ago, in 1899, according to Professor Walter Williams,

> **the black students of Paul Lawrence Dunbar High School scored higher than any of the white schools in the District of Columbia. From 1870 to 1955, most Dunbar graduates went to college, including schools like Oberlin, Harvard, Amherst, Williams and Wesleyan. Washington was home to a broad, upwardly mobile middle class.[2]**

No more. Unfortunately Williams doesn't see that the real problem is matriarchy; he imagines it to be matriarchy's ally, liberalism. However, he accurately states the manifestations of the problem, citing an article in *Policy Review* by Philip Murphy:

> **Washington has the highest per-capita murder and violent crime rates, the highest percentage of residents on public assistance, the highest-paid school board, the lowest SAT scores, the most single-parent families[3] and the most lawyers per capita.**

"Neighborhoods, once bustling and serene," continues Williams,

> **are now economic wastelands where law-abiding residents live in daily terror. People are fleeing Washington in droves...not white flight but black flight to the suburbs. During the second half of the 1980s alone, over 157,000, or one-fifth of Washington's population moved. This exodus disproportionately consisted of black households earning between $30,000 and $50,000 a year.[4] Today Washington's population is 578,000, down from a peak of 800,000.**

---

[1] Marion Barry, former mayor, re-elected after serving prison sentence for a drug conviction, reassures us that Washington is as safe as Topeka, Kansas.
[2] *Human Events*, 21 July, 1995.
[3] Emphasis added.
[4] Read: father-headed families—D.A.

The problem is not racism. The mayor, the chief of police, the superintendent of schools and most city councilmen are black. But it is not liberalism either, though liberalism is contributory. The villain is matriarchy. There are many cities with liberal administrations but in Washington and Detroit and other high-crime areas the problem looming over all others is the enormous numbers of female headed households.

In Washington most of these households are generated by the welfare system. In the larger society most are generated by divorce. Ms. Friedan's own experience illustrates. In *The Feminine Mystique*, she tells women they "must unequivocally say 'no' to the housewife role," then quickly adds: "This does not mean, of course, that she must divorce her husband." But divorce is what she thinks of, and divorcing her husband is what she did. She dedicated *The Feminine Mystique* to her husband and her children. When the book made her a best selling author who could afford to divorce the old boy, she did so and removed his name from the dedication page. In 1974 she wrote:

I got divorced five years ago. I should have gotten divorced ten years ago.

That would have been in 1964, the year after the publication of *The Feminine Mystique*, which placed her in the group with the highest divorce rate, educated, economically independent women. Economics made the difference. "The basis of women's empowerment," she wrote in 1995, "is economic. That's what's in danger now."[5]

Her 1974 piece continues:

It would have been better for my children, probably better for my former husband, certainly better for me. To show how far we've come in this short time, let me tell you that ten and nine and eight and seven and six years ago, I was warned by my publisher, editor, agent, and my dear husband that I would be ruined, I would be destroyed, if I got divorced—that my whole credibility, my ability to write in the future about women who had gone through the experience—who I could dare to ask the things that you can't ask a lawyer or trust the lawyer to tell you the truth about. And then somehow the women's movement began to give me the strength that it has given all of you. And I said, I don't care, I have to do something about my own life.[6]

---

[5]*Newsweek*, 4 September, 1995.
[6]*It Changed My Life* (New York: Random House, 1976), p. 324.

This shows "how far we've come in this short time." The acceptance of a massive divorce rate is the measure of progress. "The strength that it has given all of you" was made possible, of course, by the assurance that Dad would be the one to leave following divorce and that Betty's economic independence would prevent him from playing his Money Card after she took his children from him and withdrew the trifling services which she referred to when she said "Society asks so little of women."[7]

Most Dads must finance Mom's switchover from patriarchy to matriarchy and if Dad doesn't come up with the money he will be stigmatized as a deadbeat whom President Clinton promises to find and make pay.

There is a jingle which incorporates what is supposed to be the wisdom of the folk: "Higamous-hogamous, woman's monogamous; Hogamous-higamous, man is polygamous." The jingle expresses not Mom's desire for marriage but her desire for Dad's paycheck. It is men who want marriages and families, women who say with Virginia Woolf that "male domination of women is a kind of fascism," who say with Jeanne Cambrai, "Get rid of HIM," who write books with titles like *Once Is Enough, The Good Divorce* and *The Courage to Divorce*, who say with the "Declaration of Feminism" that "the end of the institution of marriage is a necessary condition for the liberation of women," who say with Betty Friedan, "'Marriage as an institution is doomed' is the feeling of many women in the movement for whom the essence of women's liberation sometimes seems to be *liberation from marriage*."[8]

Nancy Yos, reviewing volume V of *A History of Women* in *Commentary* magazine, January, 1995, has this: "[T]he tome's central theme emerges with crystal consistency: 20th-century women have strained to escape patriarchy and 'phallocentrism' and its horrible servant—motherhood—but are nowhere fully free...to achieve autonomous creativity outside the domestic setting....Women's liberation is completely bound up in the thinking of those scholars with the desire and right to work outside the home. Whatever is in aid of this end (day care, unfettered access to abortion) is objectively good, whatever hinders it is bad....And children themselves are the worst of all, bringing physical

---

[7]*The Feminine Mystique*, p. 328.
[8]*It Changed My Life*, p. 238; emphasis in original.

danger, poverty, and frustration to the progressive female class. The more children women have the less they work outside the home."

What a pity that the reproductive function of sex should be allowed to interfere with its recreational function. President Clinton, on the other hand, expresses concern about yuppies (like himself and Hillary?) not having enough children. *The Los Angeles Times* of 20 July, 1995, quotes him as follows: "We have more and more young couples where both of them are working and having careers and deferring child-bearing, and in many cases not having children at all....That is a very troubling thing for our country: The People in the best position to build strong kids, and bring up kids in a good way are deciding not to do so." Clinton, says the *Times*, "apparently learned about the declining birthrate in his voracious reading. The President suggests better child care might help encourage two-career couples to have more children."

If we want better child care we might think of returning to the lifestyle of the fifties, when women based their lives on being good wives and mothers.

"Child development experts," says the *Los Angeles Times*,[9] "say, most day care ranges from mediocre to miserable":

In a 1995 study, academic researchers judging the quality of day care in four states, including California, classified 86% of those they visited as less than "good," with about three-quarters ranking in the mediocre category and 12% providing "less than minimal" care. Among those serving the youngest children, about 40% landed in the bottom category because of safety problems, poor sanitation practices, unresponsive caregivers and an absence of toys and other stimulating materials.

Painful as it may be to face—and many will not—working parents may be exposing their children to possible injury, illness, stunted intellectual growth and emotional and social impairment.

According to Maggie Gallagher, "A national study by the University of Colorado found that only 8 percent of day-care centers serving infants and toddlers offer high-quality care; in 40 percent of centers, the care is

---

[9] 16 April, 1998.

so bad that it endangers young children's psychological and cognitive development."[10]

Better child care might draw more wives into the labor market and still further lower their birthrate. The President's voracious reading evidently didn't include Nickles and Ashcraft's *The Coming Matriarchy*, where he could have learned that women who work "prefer smaller families....In fact fewer have children."[11] This is one reason why they want to work.[12] Work offers them the lure of economic independence, consequently sexual independence, meeting males and having innocent flirtations and adulteries on the job.[13] Dad's paycheck becomes less meaningful, especially when they know they are assured custody of the kids with support money, maybe welfare money to help them stand on their own feet without sexual favor or excuse. Then they can talk like Betty Friedan about giving their love "freely and joyously" rather than as "joyless dues for economic support,"[14]—as required by their patriarchal marriage vows, which everyone (=all feminists) now agree are obsolete, designed to enslave them, keep them barefoot and pregnant, breeders in an overpopulated world.

Women are following Ms. Friedan's advice to say no to the housewife role. They want careers and adulteries and fun. But it was their former acceptance of the housewife role which gave them custody of children in divorce cases. This is why judges could keep saying for a hundred years, "Children belong with their mother"—and expel the father when Mom wanted out of her marriage. Now Mom is saying, with Betty Friedan *"women have outgrown the housewife role."*[15]. She means it. She likes the below-replacement-level birthrate. She hates getting up with the baby at night. She wants to turn her maternal functions over to the day care workers. She wants a career where she can experiment with the Commandments and cuckold her husband and breed illegitimate kids, and play soldier and fireman and policeman, just like men. She wants freedom.

---

[10]*National Review*, 26 January, 1998.
[11]p. 42.
[12]*"Women have outgrown the housewife role"—The Feminine Mystique*, p. 308; emphasis in original.
[13]See Ann Landers' comment, page 270.
[14]*The Second Stage*, p. 322. "The perfect equation of marriage with romantic love, or rather with the expression of romantic love," says Maggie Gallagher, "often sounds idealistic, but it is actually profoundly self-protective. It makes not only the goodness of a marriage but its very existence dependent on its emotional satisfactions." (*The Abolition of Marriage* (Washington, D. C.: Regnery Publishing Inc, 1996), p. 220)
[15]*Feminine Mystique*, p. 308; emphasis in the original.

This is why fathers must take custody of the kids—or one reason why. The American mother has become an increasingly unfit parent—and, not incidentally, an increasingly unfit wife, as her anti-patriarchal warfare proves.

There's a new order of things now, thanks to feminism. Mom can now be true to herself. Being true to oneself follows the practice of third world peoples such as the American Indians admired by Ms. Boulding and Ms. Stephanie Coontz, who writes as follows:

> **When Jesuit missionaries from France first encountered the Montagnais-Naskapi Indians of North America in the sixteenth century,[16] they were...horrified by the childrearing methods and the egalitarian relations between husband and wife. The Jesuits set out to introduce "civilized" family norms to the New World. They tried to persuade Naskapi men to impose stricter sexual monogamy on the women of the group....[17]**

Very sensible of the Jesuits, since without female chastity there can be no family, no patriarchy, no civilization. Unchaste women may be happy, like Ms. Boulding's squaws, but their men will be underachievers. This is why the Naskapi's contribution to history is less than the contribution of the Europeans who took over their land.

> **At one point [continues Ms. Coontz], having been rebuffed on several occasions, the missionary obviously thought he had found an unanswerable argument for his side. If you do not impose tighter controls on women, he explained to one Naskapi man, you will never know for sure which of the children your wife bears actually belong to you. The man's reply was telling: "Thou hast no sense," said the Naskapi. "You French people love only your own children; but we love all the children of our tribe."**

> **That may be the best single childrearing tip Americans have ever been offered. Unless we learn to care for "all the children of the tribe," then no family, whatever its form, can be secure.**

This is what feminist sociology professor Stephanie Coontz is teaching her students: Learn from the Naskapi; you don't want a family of your own, children of your own—you can love *all* the kids, just as you can love all the women and all the women can love all the men.

---

[16]Actually seventeenth century—D.A.
[17]Coontz, p. 231.

Everyone will be one happy family. Only it will be the feminist version of "family."

Everybody loving everybody fails to explain the backwardness of the Naskapi, who can't get organized into patriarchal families capable of exploiting male aggression to do the work of society. The Naskapi men don't know what it is to be fathers and their children don't know what it is to have fathers.

Let's apply what Ms. Coontz says to a specific case, that of Callie Johnson and Rebecca Chittum, who were switched in the hospital at birth, Callie being shunted into the female kinship system because she had no father, Rebecca being lucked into the patriarchal system and endowed with a biologically unrelated father—fortunate she. Paula Johnson, Callie's Mom, accepted the First Law of Matriarchy, that she controlled her own reproduction, but forgot who the father was, and Judge F. W. Somerville refused to make her ex-boyfriend pay child support, since DNA tests proved he was not the father. Poor Callie accordingly has bastardy imposed upon her, and her biological parents are powerless to do a thing about it. If these people lived in Naskapi territory it wouldn't matter, since they can be loved by "everybody." But in the male kinship system "everybody" is victimized—both the children and all three parents.[18]

The Naskapi's way of thinking is shared by a lot of people, including Sandra Feldman, President of the American Federation of Teachers. Ms. Feldman recalls a science fiction story she read as a teenager in which children were randomly redistributed by a lottery held every four years. Ms. Feldman doesn't really suggest a childswap system but thinks it might have some good consequences:

And one thing the lottery did was to make the whole society very conscientious about how things were arranged for kids.[19]

The lottery would be run by bureaucrats who care more for kids than parents do.

In a very real sense everyone's child was—or could be—yours.

---

[18]Details from *Los Angeles Times*, 22 Sept., 1998.
[19]"Where We Stand: A commentary on public education and other critical issues: *The Childswap Society*," *Los Angeles Times* 4 Jan., 1998.

Just like the Naskapi, where everyone loves everyone else's children rather than just their own.

As a result, children growing up under this system got everything they needed to thrive....

There would be no child abuse; "The luck of the draw," as Ms. Feldman calls it, would see that all kids have good parents—unlike today when things such as the following are taken for granted:

We might not want to admit it, but don't we take for granted that some kids are going to have much better lives than others?

Most kids have better lives if they have fathers. What Ms. Feldman calls "this country's national shame [of] a child poverty rate of 25 percent" is mostly the result of fatherlessness.

We take it for granted...that the children whom the lottery of birth has made the most needy will get the least.

It is the purpose of patriarchy to ensure that birth is not a lottery, that every father and every mother shall regard the procreation of offspring as their most deliberate responsibility. Ms. Feldman sees no need for such concern, since parents can be replaced by bureaucracies:

We'd start with political figures and their children and grandchildren, with governors and mayors and other leaders. What do you suppose would happen when they saw that their children would have the same chance as the sons and daughters of poor people—no more and no less? What would happen to our schools and healthcare system—and our shameful national indifference to children who are not ours?

I bet we'd quickly find a way to set things straight and make sure all children had an equal chance to thrive.

We would insist that children have fathers and that fathers could not be exiled at the whim of mothers. We would do this by ensuring fathers custody of their children in cases of divorce. We would insist on female chastity, which would decrease the shameful 25 percent poverty rate among children. What is shameful *really* is the indifference to the family instability and the neglect of the Legitimacy Principle which allows so many children to be fatherless and impoverished and delinquent and the other ills mentioned on pages 12ff. of this book. What is shameful is the indifference to the growth of matriarchy, not to be compensated for by allowing government to intrude into families and displace fathers.

The value of the real—patriarchal—family is made clear by George Gilder:

> **The virtues of this arrangement go beyond the effective harnessing of male sexual and economic energies to the creation of family units. By concentrating rewards and penalties, the conjugal household set a pattern of incentives that applied for a lifetime. Benefits of special effort or initiative were not diffused among a large number of relatives as in the extended family; and the effects of sloth or failure would not be mitigated by the success of the larger unit. In general, the man stood alone for the rest of his life. Such responsibility transformed large numbers of preindustrial men, living in "a moving present," into relatively long-term planners, preparing for an extended future.[20]**

Men, says Gilder, "diminished their horizontal economic ties to relatives in their own and previous generations [=cared less for all the children of the tribe, less for making sure *all* children had an equal chance to thrive] and oriented themselves toward their children [=their own children] and the future." But having said this, Gilder gets the central idea all wrong by imagining that civilization is a female creation imposed by women on men:

> **In terms of male and female relations, the industrial revolution...was probably dependent upon a draconian imposition on males of the long-term rhythms and perspectives of female sexuality.**

It was dependent on men's persuading or compelling women to accept it. Either the male must be able to supply the female with the benefit stipulated in Briffault's Law or he must create a society where "He shall rule over thee." The Annex of this book and the Birmingham ladies (page 80) and Dalma Heyn and Barbara Ehrenreich, Elizabeth Hess and Gloria Jacobs—and the sixty percent divorce rate—should make this clear. Increasing numbers of women are saying they're more interested in sexual emancipation than in family stability—or in having a family at all. They have been burdened overmuch with socialization about the "long-term rhythms and perspectives of female sexuality." "For women," Ehrenreich, Hess and Jacobs rejoice, "sexual equality with men has

---

[20]George Gilder, *Sexual Suicide* (New York: Quadrangle/The New York Times Book Co., 1973), p. 86.

become a concrete possibility."[21] This means equality in promiscuity and irresponsibility, the imagined male lifestyle. They want to get rid of the onus (but not the image) of being more responsible than men. The image is important because it is what gives them custody of the kids and accompanying economic and status advantages. When feminists talk, as they do interminably, about women being denied sexual equality with men, they mean the right to be equally irresponsible, equally able to treat sex as recreation. The thrust of patriarchy is the opposite—not allowing women to be sexually irresponsible but getting men to be trustworthy so that children can have two parents. The divorce court judge is a good feminist: he exiles the father from his home and then tries to compensate for what he has done *to the wife* by telling the *husband* he must subsidize his own expulsion with support payments. Both judicial actions undermine male responsibility, undermine the family, undermine men's willingness to create families. The divorce court judge is the weak link in the patriarchal system. His pusillanimity, easily detectable and recognized by women as an exploitable resource, is the chief reason why the marriage contract has become meaningless.

Gilder continues:

The men relinquished their sexual freedom and repressed the spontaneous compulsiveness of masculinity in order to play their role as key providers for their wives and children. Their energies were released to a great extent by greatly enlarging the importance...of their role in wedlock. They were made to feel that their identities as males were dependent not chiefly on religious rituals, or gang depredations, or hunting parties, or warfare, but on work, initiative, love and responsibility for a wife and children.[22]

Gilder fails to see that this depends on female chastity, and per corollary on the male's ability to induce the female to be chaste by giving her a sufficient benefit—*and by being able to withhold the benefit*. It depends on society's support of father headship of families. If the woman can throw him out when she is tired of him she will be tempted to go it alone, divorce him, destroy his role, ruin his motivation, and mess up his kids. "For women," says Rosalind Miles, "marital bliss has always been a relatively rare event. The difference now is that there is a way out....The liberation of the divorce laws has changed [things]."[23] Now

---

[21]Ehrenreich et al., *Re-Making Love*, p. 9.
[22]*Sexual Suicide*, p.86.
[23]*London Sunday Telegraph*, 7 Dec., 1997.

the woman can liberate herself by destroying the male's role and the judge will still try to extort the benefit of Briffault's Law from the man.

The matriarchal ghetto shows the way things are going. Leon Dash tells how it is in Washington D.C.:

Jail meant a forced withdrawal from heroin for Patty, so I didn't know what to expect when we sat down to talk in her cell. She'd been in jail for a month, the longest period she had been without drugs since she was sixteen. But she seemed to be bearing up well. She had gained weight and looked nothing like the emaciated woman I had seen on that mattress.

I know Patty is Rosa Lee's favorite among the eight children, and I mention to her that Bobby had told me that she is the best at manipulating their mother. Patty agrees and laughs.

"I can manipulate her like she do me," she adds. "I'm just like her. Anything my mother did, I did it. The way she walks, I can walk. The way she talks, I can talk. I just wanted to be like my mother all my life."

Very different from the "young, white and miserable" middle-class girls who *don't* want to live the kind of life their mothers led.

Patty has had even less education than her brothers, having gone no farther than the fourth grade. She dropped out at age fourteen when she was pregnant with her son, Junior.

The teenage father of her son had wanted to marry her, but Patty wasn't interested in having a husband. A husband would tie her down, put demands on her. But giving birth to a baby changed her status in her eyes. "Ever since I had a little baby, I was a grown woman," she brags. Two pregnancies with two different men followed Junior's birth. She aborted both because she did not want any more children. One was enough for her to say she was an adult.[24]

Free and easy sex is what holds the female kinship system together, what motivates females to be independent and autonomous, what de-motivates males from committing themselves to long-term achievement:

---

[24]Leon Dash, *Rosa Lee: A Mother and her Family* (Basic Books, 1996), p. 179.

I was not prepared for her candor: Within the first hour she told me that a thirteen-year-old male relative had raped her when she was eight. He threatened to hurt her if she told anyone. The assaults continued and the relationship eventually became consensual. It ended when Patty was twenty-two.

I later confirmed her account with the relative, who agreed to discuss it as long as he was not identified. He denied threatening Patty and defended his behavior, saying Patty would often climb into the bed he shared with two other male relatives. When I pointed out the age difference between the two of them, he grudgingly acknowledged, "Yeah, I guess you could say it was rape. I hadn't really looked at it like that."...

The first rape happened in January 1966, while Rosa Lee was incarcerated in the Jessup, Maryland, prison. When Rosa Lee was released in July, Patty tried to tell her about it, but she didn't know how. Looking back, Patty says she believes her mother should have known something was wrong, should have wondered why the teenage boy was hanging around her so much. "I feel like she could have done something to stop it."[25]

Her mother (or her father[26]) could have taught Patty to be chaste, but that would be making her conform to the patriarchal rules, to capitulate to the "dominator system," to accept the hated double standard.

THE PARTNERSHIP SYSTEM

The Goddess religion of the "partnership system," like that of ancient Canaan, was a sexually irresponsible matriarchy, practicing degraded and obscene worship thus described by Professor R. K. Harrison: "One of its most prominent features was the lewd, depraved, orgiastic character of its cultic practices." According to Professor W. F. Albright the goddess religion was "orgiastic nature worship, [with] sensuous nudity and gross mythology."[27] William Robertson Smith describes Canaanite worship on the high places as "horrible orgies of unrestrained sensuality."[28] Ms. Eisler doesn't care to mention such things going on in her partnership society. She cannot see how patriarchy seeks to regulate this Id-energy and put it to work to create

---

[25]P. 180.
[26]He "didn't have much of a role in her life; when he died in the mid-1970s, Patty didn't even consider attending his funeral."
[27]Quoted in Merlin Stone's *When God Was a Woman* (New York; Dial Press, 1976), pp. xviiif.
[28]W. Robertson Smith, *The Old Testament in the Jewish Church*, p. 350.

civilization. Civilization, face it, is built on frustration and repression. Freud tells us this:

> Since a man does not have unlimited quantities of psychical energy at his disposal, he has to accomplish his tasks by making an expedient distribution of his libido. What he employs for cultural aims he to a great extent withdraws from women and sexual life.

This, one supposes, partly explains the war against patriarchy and the war of the sexes, for Freud continues:

> His constant association with men, and his dependence on his relations with them, even estrange him from his duties as a husband and father. Thus the woman finds herself forced into the background by the claims of civilization and she adopts a hostile attitude towards it.

> The tendency on the part of civilization to restrict sexual life is no less clear than its other tendency to expand the cultural unit.[29]

Freud's message is the polar opposite of that of Ms. Eisler, who hopes her book *Sacred Pleasure* "can be a useful tool for the many women and men today struggling to finally free ourselves from a basically antipleasure and antilove system":

> I am also convinced that the still-ongoing modern sexual revolution, with all its upheavals of accepted norms, offers us an unprecedented opportunity not only for a much more satisfying sexuality but for fundamental personal and social change....Now we have the opportunity to move to a second phase, to a real sexual revolution.[30]

Jacquetta Hawkes gives this picture of the Cretan matriarchy, so admired by Ms. Eisler:

> Cretan men and women were everywhere accustomed to seeing a splendid goddess queening it over a small and suppliant male god, and this concept must surely have expressed some attitude present in the human society that accepted it."[31]

Ms. Eisler, after quoting this, comments:

---

[29]Sigmund Freud, *Civilization and Its Discontents* (New York: W. W. Norton, 2d ed., 1931; reprinted 1962), pp.50f.
[30]*Sacred Pleasure*, p. 12.
[31]Quoted in Stone, p. 48.

[Hawkes] continued by pointing out that the self-confidence of women and their secure place in society was perhaps made evident by another characteristic. "This is the fearless and natural emphasis on sexual life that ran through all religious expression and was made obvious in the provocative dress of both sexes and their easy mingling—a spirit best understood through its opposite: the total veiling and seclusion of Moslem women under a faith which even denied them a soul."

"From the Paleolithic twenty-five thousand years ago, to the Bronze Age civilization of Minoan Crete only thirty-five centuries ago," says Ms. Eisler, "sex was a religious rite and sexuality and spirituality were inextricably intertwined."[32]

Society, that is, was one vast sex cult:

[T]he creative sexual power incarnated in the body of woman was for them one of the great miracles of nature. [T]o allude to these rites as just obscene prehistoric fertility cults, as some scholars have done, is to place a later, and very limited interpretation on them. And so also is to equate them with modern sexual orgies. For rather than being forbidden, dissolute, and immoral, these rites would have been socially sanctioned. And instead of being private indulgences, they would have been for the public good—and even beyond that, for an important religious purpose, including what we today would call the attainment of higher consciousness through a sense of oneness with the divine.[33]

This is what was wrong with this hypnocratic, matriarchal coconscious state: the whole society was dominated by the sex cult, like a gay bath house in West Hollywood. Such societies are made up of the "nature peoples" celebrated by homosexual Arthur Evans:

All the evidence indicates that nature people fucked for pleasure. Their purpose was to celebrate sex. Their orgies were acts of sexual worship to the power of sex they felt in themselves and in nature around them. Their religious feasts were characteristically joyous: dancing, feasting, fucking together. The Indians who have been observed in the Americas; the myths that have survived in Europe; the artifacts that exist from all over the world— all attest to the pleasure of what the celebrants were doing....Hence it is a misrepresentation for industrialized academics to call such celebrations "fertility rites," as they usually do. The orgies were not clumsy attempts to

---

[32]*Sacred Pleasure*, p. 422.
[33]*Sacred Pleasure*, p. 60, 58.

increase the gross national product by people who had a very rude understanding of economic laws.[34]

Ms. Eisler is thinking of returning to this sort of thing when she speaks of "today's search for a new spirituality and a new sexuality [which] are integral parts of the strong contemporary movement to shift to a society that orients primarily to partnership rather than domination—and with this, to healthier, more satisfying, and more sustainable ways of structuring our relations with one another and with nature"[35].

When she complains that "dominator societies" have "built into their basic social structure a number of devices that distort and repress sexuality," including the "Western dictum that sex is dirty and evil," she means that Western societies try to regulate sex by using shame and guilt, the most effective and humane regulators of behavior. "Nature people," says Evans, have "a collective tribal *feeling* of the power of sex throbbing through the whole of nature; their experience of sex was so open, public, communal and intense that they felt it reverberate through the whole cosmos....Non-industrialized societies were not in the least embarrassed to practice all sorts of sex acts in public because the notion of sexual obscenity, like the procreative ideal of sex, is a modern Christian/industrial view."

But this view is necessary to create the wealth of industrial society by confining sex to families and allowing children to have fathers. This is the patriarchal revolution which transformed the world, putting sex to work by giving fathers families and requiring mothers to be chaste wives. These changes are obviously complementary: if mothers are unchaste, fathers cannot have families. Prior to the patriarchal revolution woman was the dominant parent and empowered to tell the father to get out, empowered to turn her tent around to signal that she was bored with him.

Merlin Stone cites Charles Seltman on matriarchy in ancient Crete, where it had been a way of life:

---

[34]Evans, *Witchcraft*, p. 109.
[35]*Sacred Pleasure*, p. 9.

[Seltman] discussed the sexual freedom of women, matrilineal descent and the role of the "king," pointing out the high status of women in and around the land in which the Goddess appears to have been the very core of existence.

"Among the Mediterraneans," wrote Seltman,

"as a general rule society was built around the woman, even on the highest levels where descent was in the female line. A man became king or chieftain only by a formal marriage and his daughter, not his son, succeeded so the next chieftain was the youth who married his daughter...Until the northerners arrived, religion and custom were dominated by the female principle."[36]

Stone cites Gustave Glotz's *The Aegean Civilization* on woman's control of the Cretan religious system:

The priestesses long presided over religious practices. Woman was the natural intermediary with divinities, the greatest of whom was woman deified. Hosts of objects represent the priestesses at their duties...the participation of men in the cult was, like the association of a god with a goddess, a late development. Their part in the religious ceremonies was always a subordinate one, even when the king became the high priest of the bull. As if to extenuate their encroachment and to baffle the evil spirits to whose power this act had exposed them, they assumed for divine services the priestly costume of women...while private worship was performed in front of small idols, in public worship the part of the goddess was played by a woman. It is the high priestess who takes her place on the seat of the goddess, sits at the foot of the sacred tree or stands on the mountain peak to receive worship and offerings from her acolytes and from the faithful.[37]

Feminists like to ask men, "How would you feel if your priest, your boss, your doctor, your stockbroker—all the important people in your life—were women?" Ms. Eisler points to the time when all the important people were women, who ruled not by brutal force, as Ms. Eisler would have us believe men rule, but by the imposition of a sex cult—one of whose features was the killing of the "king" referred to above, page 97.

Such is the fate of the male under matriarchy, the "partnership" society which Ms. Eisler wants to return to.

Ms. Hawkes cites Moslem society as the opposite of such matriarchies. Moslem men seclude and strictly regulate their women because they know that without regulation these women will behave like

---

[36] *When God Was a Woman*, p. 47.
[37] P. 48.

Cretan women or as American women are coming to behave—"beyond whoredom."[38] Moslem men justifiably fear this would be the death of patriarchy and the end of a meaningful male role.

Feminist Naomi Wolf visits Israel and has an experience with the Orthodox uncle of her friend Ofra:

> I went back to Israel that summer....We had all grown real, if tentative, breasts. I made friends with another American girl, Ofra, who was visiting her Orthodox relatives. When I went to get her one afternoon to hang out, I wore my dress. Her uncle intercepted me. He looked to me like Mr. Brocklehurst in Jane Eyre: a terrifying pillar of black. "You can't visit Ofra," he said in Hebrew. "Don't try to see her again. We don't approve of you. You are dressed like a whore." I was stricken mute, partly by the shock of being reflected in his disapprobation—no one had thought of me as a bad influence until then—but also by something in his cold eyes and voice that I had never heard before. He feared me; me, a little girl. He was shaming me because he was afraid of me. What I had considered something to be proud of—my emerging sexuality—was something to be ashamed of. In the Haight, I had absorbed the idea that God liked sexuality; through Ofra's uncle I saw the possibility, which I had never considered up to that point, that God hated it—and in particular, that God localized it in women.... What I offered was an affront.[39]

In the Haight she absorbed the idea that all sexuality, regulated and unregulated, is one and the same, and also the idea that unregulated sexuality is a lot more fun—which is perhaps why San Francisco, which "prides itself on dismantling sexual mores," is "everybody's favorite city."[40]

An Orthodox Jew would know that, because of the biological marginality of the male, the feminist campaign to blur the distinction between regulated and unregulated sex, between good and bad women, threatens the patriarchal system. He would know that matriarchy can undermine patriarchy by subverting the double standard. He would know that Biblical history provides a long series of lessons concerning the battle between the female and the male kinship systems which took place in Old Testament times—and is still going on. He will know, that, as William Robertson Smith says, in Jewish law:

[38]Naomi Wolf, *Promiscuities*, p. 111: "[I]n the eyes of Muslim men...I was a representative of dissolute America, the country of women who are beyond whoredom."
[39]P. 47.
[40]*Promiscuities*, pp. 108, 225.

> a vast number of statutes are directed against the immoralities of Canaanite nature-worship, which as we know from the prophets and the Books of Kings, had deeply tainted the service of Jehovah.

This Canaanite nature-worship is the theological projection of the "partnership society" which Ms. Eisler wants to return to.

> Not a few details, which to the modern eye seem trivial or irrational, disclose to the student of Semitic antiquity an energetic protest against the moral grossness of Canaanite heathenism. These precepts give the law a certain air of ritual formalism, but the formalism lies only on the surface, and there is a moral idea below.... Thus in Deut. xxii 5 women are forbidden to wear men's garments and men women's garments. This is not a mere rule of conventional propriety, but is directed against those simulated changes of sex which occur in Canaanite and Syrian heathenism. We learn from Servius that sacrifice was done to the bearded Astarte of Cyprus by men dressed as women and women dressed as men; and the Galli, with their female dress and ornaments, are one of the most disgusting features of the Syrian and Phoenician sanctuaries.[41]

Ancient history? *Penthouse* magazine of December, 1996 tells of Episcopal clergy dressed in imitation of Marilyn Monroe and Madonna performing orgies before the altar of Saint Gabriel's church in Brooklyn, and a marriage ceremony with a Brazilian boy, complete with cocaine, liquor, whipping and humiliation, buggery, declarations of love and respect before God, exchange of rings. The priests dressed as women, one in black church robes with only panties beneath, one dressed as a nun carrying a statue of the Blessed Virgin. Music by Cyndi Lauper, porn films. Two priests asked the Brazilian boys to defecate on them.

It's the same rebellion of the Id against regulation as Servius ascribes to the Syrian and Canaanite priests. These things don't change. The forbiddenness of it constitutes most of the attraction. The sexual rituals take place in *sacred places;* the priests wear *church vestments;* cross-dressing and defecating on one another is *forbidden* and hence attractive.

This foolishness signifies a rage to get rid of sexual regulation, the same message conveyed by Ehrenreich, Hess, Jacobs, Dalma Heyn—and the 60 percent divorce rate. Nothing but father custody can re-impose sexual regulation upon women who say they are unwilling to surrender the range of possibilities opened up by a sexual revolution. The

---

[41]William Robertson Smith, *The Old Testament in the Jewish Church*, 2d ed. (London: Adam and Charles Black, 1892), pp. 365f.

millennial history of the war between the two kinship systems has again and again ended by a regression into the hypnocracy and sexual anarchy of matriarchy. Merlin Stone describes the process:

> **The female religion, especially after the earlier invasions, appears to have assimilated the male deities into the older worship and the Goddess survived as the popular religion of the people for thousands of years after the initial invasions.**[42]

This was thousands of years before Judaism came into existence. Free sex and stupefied coconsciousness were the gifts of the old religion and for thousands of years they were enough. Gerald Heard calls this the "protohistory when man lived in a cultured society compacted largely by coconscious suggestion: a suggestion hypnotically so powerful that I have called this form of government a hypnocracy."[43]

"The Great Mother of the Gods," writes Arthur Evans, was worshiped with sacred orgies" and "many ancient cultures...worshipped horned gods in addition":

> **Behind all these gods was a common ancestor that went back to the stone age. In pre-Christian times he appeared under many different names. In the Greco-Roman world he was Dionysus, Bacchus, or Pan...**

> **He usually had the horns of a goat or a bull and was worshipped with rites that included sexual orgies, animal masquerades, and transvestism....Among the ancient Greeks, as with the Celts, the horned god was associated with homosexuality....As ancient Greece became "civilized" and fell under the influence of patriarchal institutions, the worship of Pan was denounced and repressed. The new order couldn't handle the religion's open sexuality, transvestism, feminism and emotionalism.**[44]

Of course it did handle them—by imposing patriarchal law-and-order upon them and putting their Id-energies to work for socialized, rather than anti-social, purposes. It is this regulation of sexuality which makes patriarchy possible.

"[A] woman," says Ms. Eisler,

---

[42]Stone, *When God Was a Woman*, p. 68.
[43]Gerald Heard, *The Five Ages of Man*, p. 20.
[44]Evans, *Witchcraft*, p. 26.

who behaves as a sexually and economically free person is a threat to the entire social and economic fabric of a rigidly male-dominated society. Such behavior cannot be countenanced lest the entire social and economic system fall apart.[45]

A woman who behaves as a sexually and economically free person may function in patriarchal society, but she will be judged unfit for marriage. The essence of marriage is the woman's acceptance of a man's right to share in her reproductive life—i.e., she voluntarily gives up her "freedom": this is her primary contribution to her marriage. Free women, especially if they flaunt their freedom, do threaten the system, as can now be seen when their numbers have become so great as to deprive very large numbers of men of fatherhood, to inflict crushing first generation welfare costs and even more crushing second generation crime/delinquency/drug/gang costs. These women have escaped the "dominator society" and are "sexually free" but few of them are economically free, for most find themselves and their victimized offspring in the culture of feminized poverty.

Ms. Eisler frames the choice between a partnership model in which everyone is free and a dominator model in which one person or group regulates the other person or group. The real choice is between two dominator systems, one of which regulates the woman by a voluntary contract of marriage, the other of which reduces the ex-husband, ex-boyfriend or taxpayer to servitude in order that the woman may be "sexually and economically free."

In a "partnership society" it's OK for a woman to deprive her child of a father by deciding there need be no marriage partnership, even though she contracted to create one. Such "partnerships" are thought of by feminists like Ms. Eisler and Ms. Marilyn French as "informal, casual" ones.[46] They are of little value to males, since they perpetuate the male's biological marginality.

---

[45]p. 97.
[46]Ms French's words, *Beyond Power*, p. 38.

XVI) ALIMONY AND CHILD SUPPORT

Feminist Lynette Triere will be quoted on page 260 as saying women leaving marriages have counted on alimony and child support as income and have hinged their future plans on it: "This money is certainly a reasonable and fair thing to expect.... Women used to expect alimony as a reward for years of faithfully taking care of the duties and responsibilities of family and home. Divorced women were entitled to a just compensation in the form of monthly support payments."[1]

But she *was* rewarded for her sexual loyalty, for accepting the double standard and for bearing legitimate children for her husband, for giving him a family, for performing her maternal and housekeeping functions. Her reward was lavish—according to Lenore Weitzman's celebrated statistic, a 73 percent higher standard of living.

Now, says Ms. Triere, "things have changed." Now women may repudiate the double standard and their sexual loyalty and still be compensated for having accepted it in the past—*may withdraw their sexual loyalty and be compensated for doing so:*

It was recognized that the woman's work was in the home, and once that came to an end she deserved recognition for it in terms of money. Whether it worked or not in practice, the notion was that women could rely on an unending financial connection with her husband. Granting alimony was akin to a kind of lifetime pension for women.

Imagine an employee quitting her job and demanding to be paid for doing so. A wife *can* rely on an unending financial connection with her husband; one of the purposes of marriage is to provide this support. But the man is no longer a husband following divorce, following the withdrawal of the wife's loyalty and services. "A kind of lifetime pension for women" is what *marriage* offers women. To transfer this obligation from a husband to an ex-husband is to undermine marriage. Why is the woman entitled to a pension? For bearing the man's children and giving him a family? These are not things which she is giving him, as she promised to do when she took her marriage vows. These are things she

---

[1]Lynette Triere, *Learning to Leave*, p. 154.

is taking away from him when she divorces him. She would have been entitled to a lifetime pension for maintaining rather than undermining his connection with his children and for preserving his family. This is the idea of marriage—why it is a lifetime contract. Ms. Triere wants the woman to be able to exploit her status as a Mutilated Beggar—a self-imposed status if, as usual, the wife initiates the divorce. Her Mutilated Beggar status is made more plausible because she is allowed to make Mutilated Beggars of her children as well and because she is permitted to appeal not to the husband, from whom she withdraws her loyalty, but to the judge, who suffers nothing from this divorce.

The preposterousness of this whole shakedown—of the wife demanding to be paid for reneging on her marriage vows—would be revealed by automatic father custody. Then she would no longer "hinge a whole set of future plans on the money she thinks she will be receiving." She will no longer be able to bribe herself with her ex-husband's money.

"The idea of...compensatory payment," says feminist law professor Mary Ann Glendon in discussing alimony, "is to remedy 'so far as possible' the disparity which the termination of marriage may create in the respective living conditions of the spouses."[2] This deprives the husband of both his role and his bargaining power. If wives suppose that divorce entitles them to such "compensatory payment" they have a motive to divorce. It is one purpose of *marriage* to remove the disparity between the husband's and wife's income. The husband's ability to remove this disparity is what gives him his role and motivates him to be a provider and a high achiever—and motivates the woman to marry him. By having divorce perform the same function, Ms. Glendon would undermine marriage and the male motivation which creates the disparity in the first place. The woman wants the man because he is the means of removing this disparity. The disparity attracts the woman to the man. The man's role is to create this disparity and use it for the benefit of his wife and children. Ms. Glendon is telling the woman that all that was required of her was to go through the marriage ceremony, after which the legal system will see to it that the disparity will not reappear.

The termination of the marriage *should* create a disparity. The man and the woman are no longer spouses. It would be well if women suffered more from divorce, for this would mean they gain more from

---

[2]Mary Ann Glendon, *The Transformation of Family Law* (Chicago: University of Chicago Press, 1989), p. 210.

marriage—the benefits of Briffault's Law. Why should there not be a
disparity? Why should the woman live under approximately equal
conditions, since she performs no services for the man who is expected to
perform services for her? Her only claim on him is that the judge gives
her custody of the couple's children to be used as hostages. This is the
death of marriage and patriarchy. This is how children are deprived of
fathers, how society is becoming ghettoized.

Compensatory payment, like *spousal support, maintenance,
rehabilitation, severance pay*, is a synonym for alimony, as is "child
support" itself—a means of compelling the man to subsidize the woman
while permitting the woman to withdraw her services. This deprivation of
the man's bargaining power and motivation reduces him to the position
of the Naskapi, helps ease patriarchy into matriarchy. It reduces his
motivation to marry. It deprives the woman of her own bargaining
power, since she is offering less when she pledges to share her
reproductive life and since her offer implies the threat of canceling her
pledge and replacing it with a crippling penalty.

If there were no "disparity" in the incomes of the husband and the
wife, the wife's only reason for marriage would be "love," which
evaporates following divorce (if not sooner) and is replaced by her
grasping for the man's money.

"European explorers," says Ms. Coontz, "were scandalized to find
that Indian women had 'the command of their own bodies and may
dispose of their persons as they think fit.'"[3] The Indian women, in other
words, rejected stable marriage. Stable marriage would have enabled
marginal males like the Naskapis to be heads of families—and Naskapi
women, like Ms. Boulding's squaws, like ghetto matriarchs, like
Charmaine, like increasing numbers of American wives, would prefer to
keep their men marginalized.

Divorce counselor Lynette Triere tells her clients that they must not
feel guilty about walking out of their marriages. "Feeling guilty will not
mean that your kids will be better fed, clothed, or adjusted."[4]

It will mean precisely that if the guilt *prevents* divorce and the
placing of the kids in the female kinship system where they will be

---

3Coontz, *The Way We Never Were*, p. 125.
[4]Lynette Triere, *Learning to Leave: A Woman's Guide* (New York: Warner Books, 1982), p. 75.

deprived of most of Dad's paycheck and will be 5 times more likely to commit suicide, 32 times more likely to run away, and the other problems listed on pages 12ff.

What Ms. Triere means is that if her female clients disregard their guilt and get divorced anyway, if they are not deterred from inflicting these injuries on their children, the guilt will have been "wasted," so why feel guilty? The reasoning is very feminine.

"If your marriage is intolerable," says Ms. Triere, "*and* you are not happy with it, don't feel guilty about following your natural *survival* needs—they point the way toward a healthy existence."[5]

"Intolerable" is feminine hyperbole designed to remove the guilt. The real meaning is "if you are not happy with it." If you dislike the sexual regulation that marriage requires of you. If you feel that "I don't care, I have to do something about my own life....I want out." If you feel that "women, despite initial pain and income loss, tend almost immediately to feel that they benefit from divorce [and are] happier and [have] more self-respect than they had in their marriages."[6] If you are divorce-prone, like most of the women responsible for the sixty percent divorce rate, go ahead. "Intolerable" is a permissible prevarication for helping a good cause.

This truth is flaunted by feminist Jessie Bernard who places on the cover of her book *The Future of Marriage* these parallels:

HIS	HERS
Traditionally, Men consider marriage a trap for Themselves and a Prize for their wives.	Traditionally, all women want to marry, and most want to become mothers.
Statistically, Marriage is good for men physically, socially, and psychologically.	Statistically, childless marriages are happier; and marriage, literally, makes thousands of women sick.

Ms. Bernard's table states two of the theses of this book: patriarchy is an artificial system and women don't like it. They prefer the female

[5]*Ibid.*; emphasis added.
[6]Stephanie Coontz, *The Way We Never Were* (HarperCollins, 1992), p. 224.

kinship system. All the more, then, that women should be made to see the *advantages* the male kinship system offers them and stop trying to gain these advantages through divorce. The way to make them see these advantages is to make father custody automatic. Ms. Bernard is in agreement with the great psychologist who wrote the Garden of Eden story, the Charter, as feminists truly complain, of the patriarchal system which today's feminists vow to overthrow. "It is not good for man to be alone" (Genesis 2:18) and "He shall rule over thee" (Genesis 3:16). Men need marriage, and (apart from its economic and status advantages) women don't. The family is a patriarchal/male creation, benefiting men and regulating (and benefiting) women. This is why women are divorce-prone, why Mrs. Pankhurst called marriage "the great scourge," why Margaret Sanger called it "the most degrading influence in the social order," why Betty Friedan says (in italics, yet) *"Women have outgrown the housewife role."* Let's say rather, women hate the patriarchal system and want to claim the privilege of promiscuity (=demand the female kinship system) as a "sacred right." They want to get back to the female kinship system which gives Ms. Boulding's squaws their peace of mind and quiet sureness. "[W]e are really changing society," says Ms. Friedan. "We have *begun to change society in reality.*" She demands "the right, the inalienable human right to control our own bodies,"[7] a "federal statute recognizing the right of every women to control her own reproductive life,"[8] which means a federal statute denying men any reproductive rights under the marriage contract—a return to matriarchy.

These feminists hate marriage, hate "the family of western nostalgia," and the "aberration" of the nineteen fifties when "never had so many people, anywhere, been so well off." They hate Ozzie-and-Harriet, and the Cleavers and Donna Reed and the feminine mystique and all the artificial gimmicks men use to keep women in their place. They want to live without sexual regulation like Indian squaws and the ghetto matriarchs who "produce responsible, assertive *daughters"*[9] in addition to the roleless sons who clog the criminal justice system. They're getting what they want. They "have come too far to surrender the range of possibilities opened up by a sexual revolution."

"Childless marriages are happier," says Ms. Bernard. So economically independent women have a low birth rate and destroy more

---

[7] *It Changed My Life*, p. 153.
[8] *It Changed My Life*, p. 102.
[9] *Mother Daughter Revolution*, p. 130; emphasis added.

fetuses on the abortion tables every year. Moms clamor to place the survivors in child care centers, or "daytime orphanages" where most care "ranges from mediocre to miserable." "Marriages, literally, make thousands of women sick," Bernard says. This is because marriage is part of the system for imposing sexual law-and-order and they don't want law-and-order. So—most divorces are initiated by wives.

Women, says Ms. Bernard, "have been socialized to buy protection at the cost of independence" but they must now be given "new patterns of socializing girls...preparing them for autonomy":[10]

They will have to be prepared to become autonomous women, not economically dependent; women whose economic dependence does not weight every alternative in favor of remaining in a marriage, regardless.

The husband's control over his paycheck stabilizes marriage, which patriarchy thinks is good but which Ms. Bernard thinks is bad. The wife's economic *dependence* is the principal benefit offered by the husband to the wife.

The subject here is...the woman's extra load of economic dependency added to the emotional dependency that has to be lightened. A union between a man and a woman in which, when it breaks down, one loses not only the mate but also the very means of subsistence is not a fair relationship.

It's not a relationship at all when it breaks down; but if society wants children to grow up in two-parent households, it should adopt policies which *do* weigh in favor of remaining in a marriage. Ms. Bernard says that a good thing, like a bill-paying husband, when it is taken away is no longer a good thing, and that this is "unfair." Therefore there ought to be compensation—for the woman. It is unfair to women that men should subsidize them in marriage. Therefore they ought to subsidize them in divorce. This will not deprive the wife (or of course "her" children) of "the very means of subsistence." This will, as feminist Mary Ann Glendon says, "compensate, so far as possible, for the disparity which the disruption of the marriage creates in the conditions of their respective lives."[11] Thus women will not need to follow a lifestyle which degrades them by buying "protection at the cost of independence," which leads "men to surrender seats and open doors." Better they should be

---

[10]Jessie Bernard, *The Future of Marriage* (New York: World Publishing Company, 1972), p. 321.
[11]Mary Ann Glendon, *Abortion and Divorce in Western Law* (Cambridge, MA: Harvard Univ. Press, 1987), p.84.

required instead to surrender alimony and child support money, which makes women independent of them.

Ms. Triere's telling her female readers they are entitled to claim that their marriage is *intolerable* and that getting divorced is a matter of *survival*, which is to say is part of the machinery for making them independent and for changing society back to matriarchy. This change must be accomplished with a minimum of pain to women. Let *him* suffer. Tell yourself the kids won't suffer. You know that they will—that keeping Dad and Dad's paycheck in the family means the kids are better fed and clothed and adjusted—but don't think about it. Don't believe the statistics (pages 12ff.) about what happens to fatherless children; they'll make you feel guilty too. "For once," says Ms. Triere, "*put yourself first.*" The judge will understand.

Once you are free of him, you don't have to feel guilty about taking his money: the more he pays the better. He expects it. Speaking of spousal and child support, Ms. Triere has this:

> **Women leaving marriages have traditionally counted on these two sources as a means of income. Often a woman will hinge a whole set of future plans on the money she thinks she will be receiving. For some, it is a matter of survival. This money is certainly a reasonable and fair thing to expect. And if a woman can depend on, for example, $160 a month for each child and another $300 in spousal support, it creates a base from which to work. The courts often make such awards.[12]**

It's not a matter of survival. It's an inducement to divorce. If Mom couldn't depend on the money, she would have a motive to work things out—the base from which to work would be her marriage, not her divorce; her husband, not her lawyer.

> **Women used to expect alimony as a reward for years of faithfully taking care of the duties and responsibilities of family and home. Divorced women were entitled to a just compensation in the form of monthly support payments. It was recognized that the woman's work was in the home, and once that came to an end she deserved recognition for it in terms of money.[13]**

---

[12]P. 154.
[13]Triere, p. 154

Once she no longer performs her services, she deserves to be paid for performing them. That's what the lady says. Women expect to be paid for quitting their jobs, rather than for performing them.

Whether it worked or not in practice, the notion was that a woman could rely on an unending financial connection with her husband. Granting alimony was akin to a kind of lifetime pension for women.[14]

The woman *gets* an unending financial connection with her husband. Ms. Triere's argument requires calling him a "husband" after his status as husband has been annulled by the divorce court. She ceases to perform services for him because she is no longer his wife; just a *woman*, but he is held responsible to perform services for her because he is said (falsely) to be a *husband*. Feminists call this standing on her own feet "without sexual favor or excuse."[15] This tormented logic commends itself to the woman, and also to the judge because he supposes that the children must be provided for and the children are in the custody of the mother. But why should they be in the custody of the mother? Because without the children, the mother would have no bargaining power. Why should the mother have the bargaining power to wreck her family and deprive the children of their father and of much of the father's income? Because the female kinship system is normative—shared by dogs, cats and cattle (who, however, don't have husbands). So the father's real function is to step in to the female kinship system to prepare for the divorce and then to step out again—and leave his paycheck behind—and his children and property and hopes and plans—everything for which he got married, everything on which he planned his life. It's rough on the father, but better than being rough on Mom and the kids. Again, What's a poor judge to do?

Good question. Deserves an answer. The poor judge should keep his oath of office and administer equal justice under law and enforce contracts, especially the marriage contract upon which everything else depends. The poor judge should understand that he is part of the male kinship system, not the female kinship system.

A lifetime pension, says Ms. Triere. Why is she entitled to a pension? Hardly for having performed the modest domestic chores upon which Ms. Friedan poured her ridicule in *The Feminine Mystique*. "It was

---

[14]*Ibid.*
[15]Betty Friedan, *The Feminine Mystique* (New York: Norton, 1963), p. 346.

not that too much was asked of them but too little."[16] She has already been paid for these services by her husband's raising her standard of living 73 percent during the marriage.[17] If she deserves a pension it must be because she has borne her husband's children and given him a family, her major contributions to the marriage. It was because of her marriage contract to give him children and a family that the man married her. But in the usual case, *she* divorces *him*—because women are more divorce-prone, because "she has to do something about her life," because "she wants out," because "she won't take it any longer," because "most women are happier and have more self-respect after their divorce," because of Briffault's Law which says that when her male no longer gives her any benefit—or has already given it to her or can be depended upon to continue giving it anyhow—their association ends. Mostly, because the judge agrees with the woman that she is entitled to take the Old Boy to the cleaners and because the Old Boy has come to expect it.

So the man discovers she never gave him a family at all, only promised him one. She waved a fraudulent contract at him and he bought it and now he finds it's too late to do anything about it because the judge agrees with her that she need not keep her marriage vows— that the contract is a mere piece of paper.

So she is not giving him children and a family, she is taking them away from him—depriving him of most of what gives his life meaning. And for this she imagines herself entitled to a lifelong pension from the man she victimizes. Good God, it out-chutzpahs chutzpah!

According to the director of child support enforcement in Dade County, Florida,

Most men simply do not pay support until they are forced into it....If they don't pay for electricity, it's cut off...if they don't make car payments, the car is taken away...but if they don't make child support payments, nothing happens.[18]

Nothing should happen. For paying his electric bill he gets electricity. For making his car payment, he gets a car. For making support payments he gets nothing but a reminder that his marriage

[16]*Ibid.*, pp. 328, 252.
[17]The 73 percent figure is discussed in Chapter 8 of my *Garbage Generation*.
[18]*Miami Herald*, 24 March, 1980; cited in Triere, p. 157.

contract was fraudulent, that the courts have destroyed his family and are trying to make him pay the costs of the destruction.

But surely a father will not let his own children starve? The kids *really are* Mutilated Beggars, dependent on him. His wife would not have divorced him if she hadn't been confident that he would keep paying: "This money," we are assured by Ms. Triere, "is certainly a reasonable and fair thing to expect."

It is this appeal to male decency which allows the ongoing destruction of families, a destruction which will continue until fathers understand that they must demand custody of their children and must play their Money Card to get it. There is no other way to save the kids from the hemorrhaging of families into the female kinship system. There is no other way—so Briffault's Law assures us—that they can confer a secure benefit to their wives which will endure as long as marriage and which will terminate with divorce—a benefit which will strengthen marriage and discourage divorce as it did in the mid-nineteenth century. Briffault's Law applies to all animals, not just to humans. Female cats and dogs don't want male cats and dogs around except when they're in heat, "capable of free and joyous love."[19] What makes stable human marriage possible is the ability of the husband to confer, and keep conferring, a benefit—his paycheck—on the wife. If the judge, rather than the husband, has the power to confer this paycheck, there is too great a chance the wife will go running to the judge with the plea that her marriage is "intolerable" and divorce a matter of "survival." This why we have a sixty percent divorce rate.[20]

Feminist lawyer Mary Ann Glendon has been quoted: compensatory payment is to remedy the disparity in the living conditions of the non-spouses (called "spouses"):

> **It depends on the establishment of the fact of a disparity between the situations of the [ex-]spouses, and its aim is to enable both of them to live under approximately equivalent material conditions.**[21]

The purpose of marriage is to benefit women and children by giving them husbands and fathers—and by giving the husbands and fathers a

---

[19] *Feminine Mystique*, p. 117.

[20] See page 16 for evidence of the 60% divorce rate.

[21] Mary Ann Glendon, *The Transformation of Family Law* (University of Chicago Press, 1989), p. 210; the ex- is added by DA.

role which makes them more stable and productive citizens. The idea of compensatory payment is to let wives know that once they marry they are privileged to withdraw their services, to *deprive* the husband/father of his role and still "live under approximately equivalent material conditions."

If the ex-husband can be forced to supply the equivalent material conditions, he is fulfilling his purpose (as Mom sees it) and Mom can let him go. Once again: "Escaping control of the patriarchy," says feminist Linda Wagner-Martin, "has long been a central theme in writing by contemporary women."[22]

If (the usual case) the ex-husband earns more money why is he not entitled to spend what he earns, just as the ex-wife is entitled to spend what she earns? She probably married him because of the disparity. If she can divorce him and not lose the disparity why should she not? He can offer her no benefit because the law privileges her to take it from him without his offering it.

Marriage then becomes meaningless for the man: once the ceremony is gone through, the judge will see to it that the ex-wife and "her" children are provided for by the ex-husband. This makes divorce the great benefactor of wives, taking over the economic functions of marriage. Perfectly logical and proper from the wife's point of view. The great benefactor, that is to say, of *disloyal* wives who are bored with their husbands or who can say with Marcia Clark that they no longer find them intellectually stimulating, or say with Ms. Friedan, "I don't care....I want out," or say with Adrienne Rich that she seeks to enjoy "a delicious and sinful rhythm." Boredom is enough reason for divorce and is so recognized by the law, a recognition which properly dispenses with, among other things, any need even to create a provocation:

Some women, under stress and impatient, will *create* an incident. Initiating a fight is most common. At times, it may even mean prodding him to violence, or it may take the form of the woman having an affair with another man and doing it so blatantly as to be easily discovered.[23]

---

[22]Linda Wagner-Martin, *Telling Women's Lives: The New Biography* (New Brunswick, N.J.: Rutgers University Press, 1994), p. 23.
[23]Triere, p. 45; emphasis in original. President Clinton tells men they must never, ever raise their hand against a woman, which tells women they may be as provocative as they wish. It's for a good cause—changing the kinship system back to matriarchy.

Here's an example, from Britain. According to the London *Daily Mail* of 28 August, 1997:

Wronged Husband Ordered From Home

A husband who pushed his wife against a door after she confessed to an affair with one of his close friends yesterday lost his fight to remain in their home.

Despite expressing sympathy for his plight and accepting [that] it was his estranged wife who "created the situation," two appeal judges refused to overturn an earlier ruling ordering him out of the house.

The deputy headmaster, who had no history of violence and vowed never to hurt his wife again, has less than a fortnight to leave the family home in the Portsmouth area.

Judges at the Civil Court of Appeal in London gave him until noon on September 6 to leave so his wife and their three children, aged nine, seven, and five, can return from the women's refuge where they have been staying. The couple, both in their 30s, had been happily married for 13 years when the wife confessed to an affair with a family friend in June this year.

The London *Daily Telegraph* quotes the wife as saying "I believe it is the right decision. It is unacceptable for an individual to be living in a four-bedroom house while his three children are homeless."[24]

And the judges agree with her. She is the one who commits adultery and this privileges her to throw her husband out of his home and take his children from him. "You don't own me—I own you, and your children, and your home, and your future income."

The newspapers don't even mention the obviously right solution: letting the adulterous wife leave, letting the victimized man have custody of his children, letting him continue living in his home. If the wife had been faced with automatic father custody rather than automatic mother custody, there would have been little likelihood of adultery, little likelihood of divorce, and no likelihood of the man being wiped out and seeing his children transferred to the female kinship system. How obvious.

---

[24]*Daily Telegraph*, 29 August, 1997.

CHILD SUPPORT AGAIN

Feminists insist that the sexes must now be regarded as equal. Ms. Glendon quotes Julliot de la Morandiere:

[I]t is no longer the man alone who earns the living for the family; the wife generally has an education equivalent to that of the husband, and she has equal political rights. The notion of a head of the family is contrary to good sense and contrary to reality.[25]

According to this view, the father ought not to be head of the intact two-parent family; but, come divorce, the mother becomes undoubted head of the new father-absent "family." This is "good sense" and "reality." This is also the female kinship system. A major purpose of divorce is to allow the wife to use her education and her political rights to create a fatherless family, the basis of the female kinship system. If fathers have no educational superiority they are unnecessary. Get rid of them. It's good sense and it's a manifestation of a deep-seated female instinct, the "enormous potential counterforce" represented by the quotations in the Annex to this book. Many women dislike patriarchy. They know it to be an artificial system imposed upon them by men.

Come divorce time, Mom gets custody of the children, and since the judge's sole concern is the welfare of these children (so he says) he is obligated to award Mom whatever he can give her of the husband's resources which will give her the equality she is entitled to.

There is the further consideration that the ex-husband was only a minority of one in his family. A mother and two children constitute three-quarters of the family and ought to have three-quarters of the income. If the husband's larger income is owing to his superior education, his superior occupational skills and experience, his superior status, his customer good will and so forth, these things must be understood as "assets of the marriage" and it is unfair for the father to walk away with them.

The real unfairness lies in the wife depriving the children of these assets by divorce and in the judge penalizing the husband for possessing them. The judge supposes that destroying the man's family justifies him also in taking his assets away—these assets constituting much of what

---

[25]Glendon, p. 90.

makes him a useful citizen. Now his usefulness and his wealth are to be used to pay for the destruction of his family.

In compensation for this destruction the wife and the judge offer the children the benefits of the matriarchal system indicated on pages 12ff. of this book. And of course the wife secures control over her own body, the primary goal of feminism.

The divorce of Monica Lewinsky's mother was made acceptable to her by monthly alimony of $6,000 and child support of $5,000, but poor Monica was devastated, and driven into the arms of psychiatrists. According to the *Los Angeles Times* of 1 Feb., 1998, "After her parents' divorce, Monica's self-confidence and ebullient personality faded." She had affairs, sought father figures, became a White House "clutch," had her affair with the President. All so that her Mom could enjoy the benefits of the female kinship system (plus the subsidies of the male kinship system.) Clinton himself grew up without a father. Such sexually shaky people often can't make dependable commitments; they seek out others like themselves, they turn to the courts and to government for father-surrogates.

In seventeenth century tribal America the Indian female kinship system (the "partnership way") was thus described by Father Sagard Theodat:

The young men have licence to addict themselves to evil as soon as they are capable of doing so. Even fathers and mothers commonly act as pimps to their daughters. At night the young women and girls run from one hut to another, and the young men do the same and take their pleasure where they like, without, however, using any violence, for they rely entirely upon the will of the woman. The husband does the same with regard to his nearest female neighbour, and the wife with regard to her nearest male neighbour; nor does any jealousy appear amongst them on that account, and they incur no shame or dishonour.[26]

Champlain wrote of the Canadian tribes using almost exactly the same words:

The young women go at night from one hut to another, and the young men do the same, taking their pleasure as they will.[27]

---

[26]Robert Briffault, *The Mothers* (New York: Macmillan, 1927) II, 33.
[27]*Ibid.*

What does this have to do with alimony and child support payments? Under such conditions family life is impossible. Everything will conform to the matriarchal pattern, in which men are mere boyfriends. For example, among the Ahts, or Nutkas, of Vancouver, if a partnership is dissolved, "the property reverts to the woman's sole use, and is a dowry for her next matrimonial experiment." There is little property, however, because the males have no motivation for accumulating any, since "[t]he children remain with the mother."[28]

That is why the Ahts, or Nutkas, are incapable of becoming civilized. "Even at the present day," says Briffault, "the surviving American Indian communities that keep to themselves in the Indian Reserves have not essentially modified their native customs."[29] The women like it that way. This is the secret of their "quiet sureness," envied by Dr. Boulding, which is more-or-less the "greater morality" of Ms. Heyn's adulteress. The men, glad to get free and irresponsible sex, conform—at first—to their wishes. "Many men, at first," writes Erin Pizzey, former feminist, "responded with cries of delight. Blinded by lust and the lure of relationships without any responsibility, many men fully concurred with the women's movement." But then:

> Slowly, as women moved into positions of power, men began to feel the iron fist of the women's movement on their backs....Today, millions of men look back at the devastation this movement created in their lives....A generation of young men in their early twenties is now adrift in a sea of misandry....No wonder they turn to mental illness, suicide and drugs....What we have left, thanks to this evil movement, is a vast number of lone women trying to keep what is left of family life going.[30]

The men, of course, have no say, nothing to offer the women to induce them to be chaste. The pattern is depicted in the following letter from Servant Ministries describing co-ed dormitory life at the University of Michigan:

> On most Saturday and Sunday mornings, students search from floor to floor to find a bathroom they can use....Most of the bathrooms are just plain unusable. The floors are covered with vomit and stale beer, toilets have been stopped up, cans and bottles litter the sinks....Pornography is everywhere. Not just inside the dorm rooms but on the outsides of doors.... disgusting, degrading

---

[28]Briffault, I, 271.
[29]II, 35.
[30]Erin Pizzey, "Why I Feel Sorry for Women," *Male View*, Apr/June, 1998.

photos. And it's not just male students who display pornography. Many women now decorate their walls and doors with pictures of naked men....Fornication is central to dormitory living. Nearly all university students fornicate—about 85 percent according to most statistics....If you've been inside a big secular universities—or smaller colleges—you know this is true, not just at the University of Michigan but all over the country.

On 1 March, 1997, NBC Nightly News ran a story on drinking-and-sex parties at the University of Michigan. The pattern was for the young men and women to get stone drunk and then have meaningless sex with partners they do not even bother to greet on campus the following day. The performance was strictly mechanical, for the release of sexual tension, following which they returned to their academic pursuits.

The saddest thing about the NBC story was the weakness, drabness and boredom reflected in the faces of these young people. There is, one must suppose, little romance on the campus of the University of Michigan. Free at last.

This is matriarchy, the pre-family, Stone Age, tribal system. This is what Ms. Eisler calls, the "healthier, less dysfunctional, less hurtful way of structuring sexual (and more generally, human) relations."[31] It is the same pattern portrayed in the following description of Indian life by A. F. Currier:

There are few of the tribes, yet uncivilized, in which women are compelled by custom and sentiment to be virtuous. From testimony of most of my correspondents, whose information is gained by personal contact with Indians, it is apparent that as little restraint is imposed upon their sexual appetites by both men and women as upon the passional appetites in general.[32]

This is the lifestyle held up by Ms. Coontz and Ms. Boulding as a model for Americans. This is the lifestyle of which Singapore's Prime Minister Goh has said, "America's and Britain's social troubles—a growing underclass which is violence-prone, uneducated, drug-taking, sexually promiscuous—are the direct result of their family unit becoming nonfunctional."[33]

---

[31]*Sacred Pleasure*, p. 2.
[32]Briffault, II, 35f.
[33]Cited in *The Free American*, October, 1994. Tiny Singapore, population 3 million, and with no natural resources other than its fine harbor, is the ninth-richest country on earth and has the world's best schools, far superior to those of Germany and Japan (*Los Angeles Times*, 23 February, 1997).

In this matriarchal arrangement, loss of the economic advantages obtainable through submitting to patriarchal discipline is deemed less important than sexual freedom. American women would like to believe that there is no connection between the economic advantages and sexual regulation. They would like to believe that the divorce court judge can give them benefits comparable to those a loyal husband could give them.

Ms. Coontz has been quoted on women's divorce proneness. Here is her fuller statement:

> **But women, despite initial pain and income loss, tend almost immediately to feel that they benefit from divorce. A 1982 survey found that even a year after a divorce, a majority of women said they were happier and had more self-respect than they had in their marriages. The proportion rises with every passing year. Researchers at the University of North Carolina report that women are more likely to have a drinking problem prior to a divorce or separation than after it, and that divorce reduces the risk of alcohol dependence among women who were problem drinkers before.[34]**

All they need to get to this happy state is a judge willing to give them custody of the kids. Ann Landers tells how most female divorcees were glad to get out of their marriages:

> **DEAR READERS: Recently I asked this question: "Looking back, do you regret having moved so rapidly to be divorced, and do you now feel that had you waited, the marriage might have been salvaged?"**
>
> **I asked for a "yes" or "no" answer on a postcard, but thousands of readers felt compelled to write long letters. I'm glad they did. I learned a lot.**
>
> **To my surprise, out of nearly 30,000 responses, almost 23,000 came from women. Nearly three times as many readers said they were glad they divorced, and most of them said they wished they had done it sooner.[35]**

This survey would naturally be responded to by women trying to justify their actions—but it still confirms Briffault's Law.

Dalma Heyn favors adultery as a means of undermining the patriarchal system. "Successful adultery," she says—"and by that I mean an affair that enriches a woman's life regardless of its outcome, is

---

[34]Stephanie Coontz, *The Way We Never Were*, p. 224. Cf. *Reader's Companion to Women's History*, p. 25: "The heaviest drinking rates tend to be among women who are divorced, separated or never married."
[35]*Los Angeles Times*, 22 February, 1993.

an oxymoron—the two words so antithetical, the notion so heretical, it sounds inconceivable."[36] But Heyn's view is that "adultery is, in fact, a revolutionary way for women to rise above the conventional." Her book is a program for helping women to do this. Successful adultery is no oxymoron to the feminist who sees female sexual disloyalty as the weapon of choice against patriarchy, whether this disloyalty takes the form of divorce or adultery.

Ms. Heyn wants to get back to matriarchy and sexual promiscuity and the female kinship system of the Nutkas and the Montagnais-Naskapi—to the follies which sociologists like Ms. Boulding and Ms. Coontz are teaching their students, and Ms. Heyn is peddling to housewives.

The women I talked to, says Ms. Heyn, were experiencing grief over their missing sexual selves—their lost promiscuity, their sacred right to control their own sexuality.

The loss they talked about was not a potential loss, not a threat of a severed emotional attachment, but a fact; not an inchoate fear about a future loss, but an insistent echo of a past one—aching, aching throughout the terrain of their bodies like phantom limbs. They were not anxious about a connection that might soon end, but mourning a capacity for pleasure that had already ended. Where it ended—where they had lost their sexuality—was not in marriage per se, but in goodness.

Marriage itself was OK as long as one could commit adultery. What was intolerable was sexual loyalty to one man. If only they could harvest the economic and status rewards of patriarchy without sharing their reproductive life with one man they would achieve their happiness and patriarchy would be undermined, perhaps overthrown.

Why *not* marry in contemplation of divorce—why not go along with the pretense of forming a family for awhile and then rely on the good judge to earn his salary by giving Mom a divorce and custody of the kids, and compelling the man to continue subsidizing her? Why not? Ms. Heyn answers:

---

[36]Heyn, p. 10.

> **Marriage was merely the occasion for capitulation to this goodness, and the vehicle for supporting and sustaining it (later, motherhood only adds fuel).**[37]

Therefore, obviously, marriage must go, but only marriage which means anything, marriage regarded as a contract which the legal system is bound to enforce.

Feminists write of "the marriage-divorce system as it is emerging in American culture."[38] This can only mean that divorce is the sequel and fruition of marriage and is expected to perform the functions formerly performed by marriage, of subsidizing mothers and children. This expectation will end when men realize that means the death of patriarchy, the male role and the family.

> **However frightened these women were about staying in relationships in which they had stifled their sexuality [writes Ms. Heyn—meaning relationships in which they accepted sexual regulation and kept their marriage vows] they also feared attempting to reclaim it. That would leave them with nothing, they feared, but the total loss of relationship and self....Here is where each woman faced not a depressing choice, but a paralyzing one: She could continue to become the "female impersonator" Gloria Steinem has said we are all trained to be, or she could attempt to reclaim her sexuality and follow the passionate, doomed heroine of the romantic novel straight to her fate under a train.**[39]

To not be a "female impersonator" is to be true to oneself and ignore one's marriage vows, which are, anyway, only part of the doomed patriarchal system.

I have quoted Ms. Heyn's agreement with Hawthorne's *The Scarlet Letter* (above page 106)–that her heroine Hester's mission

> **would be to reveal "the new truth that could establish men's and women's relations on a surer ground of mutual happiness": She alone could bring in a new age of love and compassion, an understanding and a harmony between men and women, and the scarlet A on her breast was "the symbol of her calling."**[40]

Would this "understanding and harmony" include an understanding by men of what Ms. Heyn demonstrates in her book—

---

[37]Heyn, pp. 119-120.
[38]Ellen Lewin, *Lesbian Mothers* (Ithaca: Cornell University Press, 1993), p. 167.
[39]P. 120.
[40]Heyn, p. 122.

272

women's hatred of sexual regulation, of patriarchy, of being sexually loyal to one man in marriage? Of woman's acceptance of the fact that the human species has evolved to the stage where a *family* with two parents is necessary if children are to be properly procreated, cared for and socialized? An understanding that the matriarchal system where the mother was everything and the father next to nothing was suitable for lower mammals and for the Naskapi, but unsuitable for civilized human beings? That women's drift into this matriarchal system and the legal system's abetting this drift is responsible for the contemporary social chaos and illegitimacy?

One of Ms. Heyn's adulteresses talks this way about a "greater morality" such as Hawthorne spoke of:

Those words I'd scoffed at, words like "growth" and "experience" came to me in a rush: I suddenly felt my own life was a human-potential movement and this was the only way to develop my human potential and I'd be throwing away what I knew was right for me if I didn't pursue it. I'd be a woman with no life in her, a silly, scared wimp. All my "Grab the Moment" impulses; all my "Don't Let Opportunity Pass You By" feelings came up and squashed my puny little "Don't Because You're a Married Woman" prohibitions, which suddenly felt about as compelling as my "Don't Eat Sugar" vows. I was surprised by my own vehemence, and about the stupidity I was able to ascribe to my own prohibitions. It wasn't as if morality didn't exist; it was as if a greater morality, one I hadn't yet been aware of, had finally made itself visible to me. This must be how people rationalize murder, I thought. They tell themselves: It Is Good. God wants it that way. Do it.

And so I decided, since I wasn't even on the fence about this, that I wouldn't dredge up some fatuous rationale to try to justify it or dissuade myself. I'd go with it, and deal with the rest later."[41]

A greater morality. Growth. A mission. God wants it. This is the way feminists see their right to control their sexuality, to disregard their marriage vows—*and it is the way the law sees it*—which is why society is reverting to matriarchy. The law doesn't have the vaguest notion what it is doing when it replaces father-headed families with mother-headed ones. Far too many women yearn for the life of the Indian squaw, for the life of the ghetto matriarch, admired by Debold, Wilson and Malave,[42] and

---

[41]Heyn, p.38.
[42]*Mother Daughter Revolution*, p. 130: "Within parts of the African-American community, mothers who might be considered authoritarian also produce responsible, assertive daughters."

by Richmond-Abbott[43] and most feminists—for the life of the adulteresses endorsed and abetted by Ms. Heyn.

Ms. Heyn does a service to patriarchy by revealing that this sort of shallowness is what motivates her adulteresses and drives them to undermine their families. These women—and there is no reason for supposing they are atypical except in being better educated and more intelligent—are moral minors with no intention of keeping their marriage contracts. They have the judges on their side, and the judges don't understand how patriarchy works, that its functioning requires two-parent families headed by fathers.

It is natural that women should hate patriarchy and the regulation it imposes on them, natural that they should see marriage and family as unnatural and promiscuity and easy divorce as natural. Look, once again, at the hostility to patriarchy of the Birmingham women on page 80. It is only by women's acceptance of sexual regulation that men can be brought into equal sharing in reproduction. How are women to be persuaded to allow husbands this reproductive sharing? The husband must be able to offer the wife a family, a home, his status and his paycheck. Automatic father custody of the children enables him to do this. Automatic mother custody, as now, enables the judge to wreck his family. Father custody is the civilized way to go, establishing male authority in the family. God does not tell Eve "He shall reason with thee." Hatred of patriarchy is not to be overcome by reason.

Female unchastity threatens the kinship system—has already undermined it. The Church of England, according to Paul Johnson,[44] thinks "living in sin" is so common that it is scarcely sinful. Abigail van Buren tells us every other month that there is no such thing as an "illegitimate" child. A correspondent writes her:

> **Our son and his girlfriend (both in their 20s) aren't married. And when they first announced she was pregnant we weren't elated, but we accepted the situation.**
>
> **Your answer was terrific: "There are no illegitimate children—all children are 'legitimate' in God's eyes." I could never say the word illegitimate or even consider it. I see only a beautiful, healthy, bright child who, with his parents'**

---

[43]Marie Richmond-Abbott, *Masculine and Feminine: Sex Roles Over the Life Cycle* (Menlo Park, CA: Addison-Wesley, 1983)
[44]*London Daily Mail*, 17 June, 1995.

and God's help, will be an asset to this world....Keep up the good work. We're not here to judge; God handles that!

To which Abby replies:

Your letter was an upper. The world would be far less complicated if more people thought as you do. I admire your attitude and agree with your philosophy.[45]

Abby and her correspondent don't realize they are proposing to solve our most pressing problem by changing the kinship system, by rejecting patriarchy and embracing matriarchy because patriarchy stigmatizes and humiliates illegitimate children and their mothers for the purpose of enforcing female chastity and normalizing the patriarchal family. By getting rid of the stigma, by refusing to use shame to regulate sexual behavior, Abby and the feminists would have us believe society can reduce human suffering.

Is it so? There is no stigma for illegitimate ghetto mothers or ghetto children who bear their mothers' surnames and who may not even know their fathers' surnames. But they suffer. Are the children of the ghetto happier than the children of patrician families who trace their ancestry through male kinship back to ancient roots? The difference lies in the benefits conferred by fathers.

Los Angeles Times columnist Robert Scheer, illegitimate and angry at the society which stigmatizes him for being so, rejoices that "'Born-free' children, as I prefer to call them, are now far more common because parents are freer."[46]

Also more common are crime,[47] drug addiction, educational failure, gangs, second generation illegitimacy, teenage suicide, and other accompaniments of father absence. Scheer continues:

Movie stars have made out-of-wedlock kids more acceptable, and single parents can get jobs to support their children.

---

[45]*Los Angeles Times*, 14 April, 1995.
[46]*Playboy*, January, 1992, p. 55.
[47]Demographic corrections must be made. Most crime is committed by young males and the aging of the population has reduced the number of these; but the *proportion* of young males who commit crimes continues to mount.

Promiscuity chic actresses have helped to de-regulate the sexuality of women and girls. Single mothers get jobs to support their latchkey children. They neglect them and clamor for "free" child care in order to be independent of the fathers, and in order to leave them without their own care for much of the day. (Mother custody originally became the rule because Mom *didn't* absent herself from the home.) Anti-patriarchal social policies such as Affirmative Action, quotas and comparable worth have made it easier for single mothers to support fatherless households and therefore to create them. For every single mother who gets a job to support her children there is a roleless male looking for trouble.

Scheer rejoices that he is now a role model, like the glamorous movie actresses. But such admired role models are increasing the number of imitators who are increasing the number of fatherless children who will be overrepresented in socially pathological groups. These children will suffer less stigma but they will suffer more of other disadvantages. And there will be more sufferers. Society will suffer.

A report produced by a consortium of federal agencies in 1997 decried the trend of increased numbers of births to unmarried women. The report called this one of the significant "changes in American society" that is directly linked to the prevalence of child poverty.[48]

The same report "touted the increase in food availability for low-income children, saying this development not only reduces the reliance of families on emergency feeding programs, but also on "scavenging or stealing." Let's say it reduces the reliance of "families" on fathers and thus promotes the "trend of increased numbers of births to unmarried women."

Today, after three decades of feminism's sexual revolution, as female promiscuity and sexual disloyalty have left marriage and the family in ruins and practically abolished sexual law-and-order, we can judge the sincerity of the original promise to liberate men from their provider role and their obligation to subsidize parasitic wives and ex-wives. The creation of millions of fatherless families and the consequent feminization and infantilizing of poverty, both resulting from the success of feminism, is perceived by feminists as necessitating the re-riveting of

---

[48]*Los Angeles Times*, 3 July, 1997.

276

the provider role on divorced men, with each and every reciprocal service of the wife removed. Slavery.[49]

ENFORCING CHILD SUPPORT AGAIN

Researchers Irwin Garfinkel and Donald Ollerich estimate child support might equal 17 percent of the noncustodial parent's gross income (a much larger figure than his net income) for one child, 25 percent for two, 29 percent for three, 31 percent for four and 33 percent for five or more children. "Those estimates," say Garfinkel and Ollerich, "indicated that the poverty gap—the difference between the incomes of poor families headed by single mothers and the amount of money they would need to move above the poverty level—would be reduced by 27 percent." Such an exaction would be great for Mom, less great for Dad, who might be ruined financially and psychologically. What is he to expect in return for such crippling? Nothing except forced labor, loss of his children, loss of his role, and reduced marriageability. Implementing the Garfinkel/Ollerich policy would escalate the divorce rate and shrink the marriage rate.

"Eight out of ten teen-agers who have kids," says Kathy Kristof, "end up poor for the rest of their lives." According to William P. O'Hare, coordinator of Kids Count at the Annie E. Casey Foundation in Baltimore, "the negative consequences of having a child when you are 15 or 16 years old seem so clear that it is hard to imagine why anyone would do it....But the homes that many of these girls live in are so crummy that having a child and getting [welfare] is a way of getting out— an escape."[50] Most of the homes are crummy because they are fatherless.

The pattern of joyous and guiltless breeding is the central idea of matriarchy. It is an attractive idea—the sort of thing spoken of by this girl in a maternity home: "We had one wonderful week together—it was worth every bit of what I'm going through now."[51] (Perhaps also what her child will go through?) The sort of thing that made Margaret Mead's *Coming of Age in Samoa* popular in the 1920s, the idea that what was

---

[49]Feminist Lenore Weitzman's puerile attempt to show that ex-husbands enjoy a 42 percent rise in their standard of living is analyzed in Chapter 8 of my *Garbage Generation*.
[50]*Los Angeles Times*, 28 August, 1994.
[51]Rickie Solinger, *Wake Up Little Susie: Single Pregnancy and Race Before Roe v. Wade* (New York: Routledge, 1992), p. 141.

needed to achieve sexual sanity was to get rid of Victorian puritanism, hypocrisy and patriarchal sexual regulation.[52]

Let's consider an example. Lydia Nayo was an unwed welfare mother at age 16. Also a good example of a type much praised in feminist literature, the black matriarch—but one who rises above welfare dependency and becomes, no less, an associate professor of law at Loyola Law School, and in consequence a role model who gets invitations to speak at ghetto schools where the girls are considering the plunge into unwed motherhood and the matriarchal lifestyle. She tells the girls about how unwed motherhood didn't stop her. She got pregnant at age 15 and bore a daughter:

> I once was, in the language of social science, an economically disadvantaged, single teen mother. Statistically, I should not be a law-school professor, nor should my daughter be an only child or a college graduate. These facts are vital elements of my discussion, because the risk exists that some members of the audience are or will become single teen parents.[53]

She can help the girls by showing that the matriarchal lifestyle need not prevent "success"—if you don't go "all the way" by continuing to breed illegitimate kids and increasing your welfare dependency. This is to say, the War Against Patriarchy can be a success—if you accept patriarchy and its values, as Ms. Nayo finally does.

> I tell them about my origins and my early parenthood, not merely as a cautionary tale, but also as an offering of hope. It is as important to me to include unplanned parenthood in my presentation as it is to point out how I got into college, what my grades were like or the route I took from law student to law professor. It is part of my objective of presenting possibility to these students: You can have a life after early, unexpected parenthood.... [W]hat seems like a mistake can become an opportunity.

The guidance counselor suggested that she withdraw from her college-preparatory course, enroll in a vocational school, learn a trade and maybe find a husband for herself and a father for her child: "I ignored her and graduated with my class; my mother brought my daughter to the ceremony." To find a husband/father would have been the path of failure—accepting the patriarchal lifestyle. She rejects

---

[52]Derek Freeman, *Margaret Mead and the Heretic: The Making and Unmaking of an Anthropological Myth* (Penguin Books, 1996) has shown how Mead was the victim of a joke perpetrated by Samoan girls.
[53]*Los Angeles Times*, 25 May, 1994.

marriage for herself because it would make her dependent on a man. She rejoices in her daughter's independence—she won't need a husband either—though Ms. Nayo's account ends happily with a reference to the daughter's coming wedding, traditionally signaling success in the patriarchal script.

Since, as Ms. Nayo's case proves, you can have an elitist career after early, unexpected motherhood, you not only don't need a man, you don't need the bargaining power in the patriarchal sexual arena which chastity formerly gave women by allowing them to offer a man a family based on a stable marriage.

There are women you screw and women you marry. Since the triumph of feminism, there are more to screw and fewer to marry. To insist that children be legitimate would offend Scheer and Abby and Murphy Brown and legions of promiscuous women. More and more men are having to content themselves with what feminism is willing to allow them, a marginal role perhaps as stud, perhaps as stepfather, perhaps even as traditional father—though with tenure at Mom's pleasure—a sixty percent chance of divorce and loss of children—and then support payments.

Ms. Nayo speaks of "unexpected parenthood." The wisdom of feminism says "Don't worry about it." The wisdom of patriarchy says that parenthood ought to be the most deliberate and responsible choice of your life.

In a later piece written for the *Times*, Ms. Nayo tells of being a poor pregnant 15-year-old:

I was a book-smart ugly duckling. When an older guy with a glamorous-sounding job expressed an interest in me, I was grateful. From my current vantage point of maturity and higher self-esteem this seems so little to commend a suitor. While I never collected a cash grant, I could not have gotten from his abandonment and disavowal of his child to my current life without food stamps and Medicaid, without reduced-cost school lunches for my daughter.[54]

So maybe she *did* need a man, a taxpayer, to pay for her food stamps, Medicaid and the rest. She complains of the father's

---

[54]12 April, 1995.

"abandonment and disavowal" of his child. His problem was that he had no claim to the child, no way of making a meaningful commitment to it, or to her. He gave her a little flattery and "I was grateful." He didn't offer her much. But she didn't offer him much—a one-night stand, evidently. If she had had "higher self-esteem"—if she had been chaste, if she had accepted the patriarchal system when she was 15—she would have had no reason to complain of abandonment. What could he have offered her besides flattery? His chance of having a stable family with a female he knew to be unchaste was insufficient to motivate a reasonable man to make a lifetime commitment justifying bringing new life into the world. She wouldn't offer him this and so she, and society, couldn't expect commitment from him. Society refuses to offer him a meaningful role as a father, so society must subsidize the illegitimate child of an unchaste girl. The assurance of father custody would have given them both reason to marry—or to remain chaste—and would have probably made both of them responsible parents.

Her piece is written to show that the welfare system ought not to be reformed by denying money to "penniless teen mothers":

The minds that conceived a provision denying AFDC to teen mothers have forgotten exactly how young 16 is. Sixteen is young enough to have a limited idea about how pregnancy occurs.

That is why she should have been taught chastity. The flattery she got from her boyfriend "seems so little to commend a suitor." It was; but he was not even a suitor: her unchastity kept him from being one and he knew it. This is the predicament of millions of black males, and now increasingly of white males.[55] Ms. Nayo, naturally, has no compassion for him; as she sees it, *he* brought troubles on *her*. Politicians, in pursuit of the women's vote, will agree with her: they too can't see the marginality of the male role in matriarchy, the need for female chastity if the ghettos—and now the larger society—are to escape from the female kinship system.

Ms. Nayo's pitch is made to girls: "You can have a life after early, unexpected parenthood....What seems like a mistake can become an

---

[55]Her child is really the victim of Marian Wright Edelman's advice to girls: "Always carry a condom when you go on a date." This will signal to the boyfriend that sex with her is not to be taken seriously.

opportunity"—though the welfare system must not deny assistance to penniless 16-year-old mothers.

What do the boys think of this? Many of them think that the welfare system which pays girls for being single mothers has displaced them from their provider role.

Suppose a mother cashed in the family's life insurance policy and used the money to buy lottery tickets. Foolish. Yet there are cases where such foolishness had a happy ending, with (say) the lottery winnings financing the children's college education. The foolishness would then seem wisdom to someone who wanted a justification for playing the lottery.

Ms. Nayo's case has the same logic. Teenage illegitimacy is a disaster in most cases—for the mother, the child, and for society (maybe even for the marginalized father). But Ms. Nayo is overwhelmed with requests for speaking engagements. She beat the odds which consign most teenage mothers and their kids to lives of poverty, underachievement, demoralization, if not delinquency. But Ms. Nayo is a role model because girls want to believe that irresponsible teen-age sexuality is OK—and because they hate patriarchal discipline. They like to hear about the *good* consequences of illegitimacy, divorce and fatherless households.

Three and a half decades ago, in *The Feminine Mystique*, Betty Friedan wrote of sexually precocious teenage girls that "One cannot help wondering (especially when some of these girls get pregnant as high school sophomores and *marry* at 15 or 16) if they have not been educated for their sexual function too soon, while their other abilities go unrecognized."[56] Ms. Friedan told them they ought to become self-actualizers, lady Einsteins and lady Edisons. At least these girls and their kids were saved for the patriarchal system by marriage. At least the teenage mothers Ms. Friedan complained of gave their children fathers, which is more than Ms. Nayo did. Ms. Friedan told them they should have a higher ambition than marriage and having babies—because "*women have outgrown the housewife role*":[57]

---

[56]P. 116; emphasis added.
[57]*Feminine Mystique*, p. 308; Ms. Friedan's emphasis.

The comfortable concentration camp that American women have walked into, or have been talked into by others is just such a reality, a frame of reference that denies woman's adult human identity. By adjusting to it, a woman stunts her intelligence to become childlike, turns away from individual identity to become an anonymous biological robot in a docile mass. She becomes less than human, preyed upon by outside pressures and herself preying upon her husband and children.

Ms. Friedan supposes these girls ought to have had a higher ambition; but three and a half decades of feminism have shown that the danger is having a lower ambition. She complains that

In the very years in which higher education has become a necessity for almost everyone who wants a real [read: elitist] function in our exploding society, *the proportion of women among college students has declined year by year.*[58]

This was 1963. Today there are more women in college than men. They don't do much breeding, since they have been emancipated from the feminine mystique and family living and the housewife role. The breeding is done disproportionately by high school dropouts who turn to their maternal functions as the principal source of meaning in their lives—like the young married women who four decades ago accepted the feminine mystique. The difference is that four decades ago the mothers were married and educated, sometimes affluent—the envy of other women all over the world, whereas today the mothers are unmarried, uneducated, impoverished and increasingly recognized as the source of social pathology.

For every one of the "girls having babies" who has been drawn away from marriage by the triumph of feminism there is an unattached, probably underachieving and possibly disruptive male wondering what society wants him to do, and there are probably some underachieving, possibly messed-up kids. Mom and the kids are economic liabilities to society, dependent to a greater or lesser degree on society's Backup System. The feminist campaign against motherhood has succeeded only with educated women who ought to be mothers. Its campaign against fatherhood has weakened male commitment to marriage and family living and produced millions of men who realize that feminism and the anti-male bias of the legal system have made fatherhood problematic.

---

[58]*Feminine Mystique*, p. 162; emphasis in original.

"Sixteen," says Ms. Nayo, "is possibly insecure enough to believe a boy or man who professes to have the thorny area of contraceptives under control or who says that he will stand by you if anything happens." A girl of sixteen should instead believe her patriarchal father who will be asked on her wedding day, "Who gives this woman?" and who will reply, "I do," signifying "I brought her up to believe in patriarchal values, including premarital chastity, and I am now turning her over to a husband who will love, honor and protect her within the same patriarchal system—which will maximize her chances for happiness and a stable family—and maximize the chances for happiness of her husband, her children and her grandchildren and will help stabilize society by reinforcing patriarchy, the best friend women ever had."

The contrary feminist view of this ceremony is expressed by a correspondent to Ann Landers:

DEAR ANN: You deserve a thump on the head for calling that bride spoiled, immature and hostile because she chose not to have her father walk her down the aisle.

We've come a long way, baby, from the days when we were "given away" at our marriage ceremonies. Today, many enlightened women are choosing to exercise their right to begin marriage as full partners, not as Daddy's Little Parcel to be handed over to another male.

That bride's parents did not approve of her living with the groom before marriage. Too bad. That young woman is an adult. Her parents should be jumping for joy that she opted for the legal ceremony. Instead, they are "hurt and insulted" over their daughter's decision to walk down the aisle alone. It's their daughter's wedding, isn't it? She has chosen not to be "given away," which is an archaic and brainless concept at best. It seems her parents can't handle it. Well, that's tough. Someone should welcome them to the 20th century.

—S. B., Chico, Calif.[59]

S. B. thinks "It's her daughter's wedding, isn't it?" Not entirely. It's also the groom's wedding, and because of the male's biological marginality he needs assurance that when he undertakes to become a provider for his wife and their children he can *have* a family. The

---

[59]*Los Angeles Times*, 14 July, 1996.

symbolism of the patriarchal ceremony is that the father has socialized his daughter to accept her role as a wife who will guarantee her husband this family. The symbolism is that the woman, whose status was formerly provided by the father within the male kinship system will now have her status provided by the husband within the male kinship system.

Feminist Bishop Spong thinks "the ultimate symbol of female degradation in marriage has persisted, in the form of the officiating minister's question, "Who gives this woman to be married to this man?":

Normally the father of the bride, who had marched his daughter down the aisle, responded, "I do," and so one man gave the woman away to another man. One does not give away what one does not own. By implication the bride was the father's property and as such she could be given...to another man. As sensitivities have risen, this embarrassing liturgical anachronism has been changed a little. The father may now say, "Her mother and I do," or the parents might say together, "We do."[60]

It is a minor objection to this that the bride is just as much "property" if she has two owners rather than one. The real point of the daughter being given by the father is that she is not to be abandoned to the lower-status female kinship system and she is not to be treated like de-classed women within the male kinship system, those whom Spong refers to as "prostitutes, servants, lower-class women, and women of oppressed racial minorities [who] were formerly used as sexual objects by socially prominent young men."[61]

The question is, "Who has hitherto assured this woman a place within the male kinship system and paid her bills and is now giving her to a man who will assure her *and her children* a place in the male kinship system and will pay her bills?"

What is truly degrading is the pretense that this bill-paying is not voluntarily assumed by the groom as a quid pro quo for his bride bearing his children and giving him a family—that the bride has now, after she has gone through the marriage ceremony, a right to remove her children from the male kinship system by divorce and place them in the female kinship system and continue to have her bills paid by the deprived ex-husband because she is female and therefore entitled to a free ride.

---

[60]Bishop John Spong, *Living In Sin?* (San Francisco: Harper and Row, 1988), p. 57.
[61]Spong, p.48.

The symbolism of the bride's walking down the aisle by herself is that she is rejecting the male kinship system and refusing to guarantee her husband a family. If the groom gets the message, he realizes that his commitment to provide for his bride and their future children has a shaky quid pro quo. The corollary of her implied claim never to give up control over her own reproduction should be his claim to the secure possession of his paycheck and the custody of his children.

Feminist Naomi Wolf, in her *Promiscuities*, has a chapter titled "The Technically White Dress," in which she attacks the traditional custom of treating brides as property handed "by one man to another...chattel to be bartered...a shallow symbol from an outmoded ritual system."[62] Feminists choose to interpret the father's giving away the bride as male degradation of women. Why may it not be interpreted as the bride's way of emphasizing the magnitude of the gift she is awarding her husband, her assurance to him that he will have a stable family and will not face a 60 percent divorce rate. Thus does the bride *give* her troth, rather than merely *pledging* it like the groom (see p. 37). The bride offers the greater gift, without which a family is impossible. But the father of the bride and the groom must safeguard the gift—save it from the female kinship system and preserve it for the male kinship system or it loses much of its value. If she refuses to have her father "give her away" she is signaling that her gift is of lesser value, that she is less committed to the marriage, more desirous of claiming a right to control her own reproduction—more divorce-prone, more threatening to her husband, who must protect himself and his children and his property from divorce and matriarchy by insisting on father-custody.

"Even though, as a feminist, I had 'deconstructed' the institution of marriage," Ms. Wolf says,

> **and knew perfectly well that a white wedding derives from traditions that value women's virginity as a form of currency and that transfer the woman herself as property from one man to another, still I returned again and again to the visions of white.**

But then this:

> **Few of us want the bad old days of enforced virginity to return. But there is a terrible spiritual and emotional hunger among many women, including myself,**

---

[62]P. 221f.

for social behavior and ritual that respect and even worship female sexuality and reproductive power.[63]

She doesn't want chastity to give women power, but it does. Unchastity forfeits women's power, cheapening it, making woman's "troth" worthless, making both her and her man lesser things. The purpose of this "social behavior and ritual" is to "respect or worship female sexuality or reproductive power," to signal that this sexuality is power to be shared with a man, permitting him to be a father. This signaling is worse than meaningless—it is frightening—if the woman retracts her vows and deprives the man of his children and reduces him to servitude. It is the law, and the church, once and properly the guardians of the family and of good women, which now permits and encourages her to do this—to abandon the ranks of good women and join the ranks of bad women and drag her children with her.

Bishop Spong rejects the oath of obedience formerly required of the bride when she was presumed to be a good women:

Obedience is a quality appropriate to the master-slave or the parent-child or even the master-pet relationship. It certainly is not appropriate to a mutual or peer relationship. Indeed, only a society that believes women to be inferior to men would require of the woman an oath of obedience to her husband.[64]

The male is marginal. If a father-cat comes around, the mother-cat chases him out. The black matriarch says "I don't need that man." But she does need a man, even if only a taxpayer, even if only economically.

The true agenda of marriage at its inception [says Spong] was by far more economic than it was moral. The women would produce the heirs to the man's wealth and property. Among the upper classes, who really made the rules, the virgin status of one's bride and the faithfulness of the married women were the only guarantees a man had that his heir would be legitimate and therefore the one to whom he could pass on his fortune. As one wag suggested, the essential difference between knowledge and faith is that in childbirth the woman knows the baby is hers, while the man only has faith.[65]

This is why the woman is (or formerly was) required to obey. This serves the double purpose of assuring the father of the legitimacy of his

---

[63]P. 223.
[64]Spong, p. 56.
[65]Spong, p. 48.

offspring and of assuring the mother of her bargaining power with him— she is really giving him a family.

The only way faith could be changed into indisputable knowledge for the man was through strong moral prohibitions on female extramarital sex and the organization of society to prevent a wife from having any opportunity to be indiscreet. Religious, cultural, political, and economic institutions provided those prohibitions.

This is the most important reason these institutions—including Bishop Spong's own church—exist. In particular, the economic basis of marriage needs to be emphasized if the institution is to be re-stabilized. When the wife says, "John, I don't love you; I'm getting a divorce," John must be able to say "I will take custody of the children and I will need my paycheck and my home to properly provide for them."

Wives are far more divorce-prone than husbands; working wives five times more prone than housewives, educated and economically independent wives so divorce-prone that they ought to be considered unmarriageable. Women's increasing education and increasing economic independence and consequent sexual independence are powerful reasons why fathers must demand custody of children. How fortunate the legitimate heir would be to have a chaste mother who would give his father the guarantees which the Bishop speaks so lightly of; how fortunate he would be to have a patriarchal father who insisted on them; how fortunate he would be to live in a society whose family policies, churches, legal system and mores stabilized this gender arrangement and thus guaranteed the heir's legitimacy and his *patri*mony, his economic advantages, his greater likelihood of superior socialization and education and achievement. Would that all children might receive these advantages. That would, of course, require the re-stabilizing of the patriarchal system which Bishop Spong wants to get rid of.

For years before this legitimate heir was born his future father had been educating and disciplining himself in preparation for responsible fatherhood in order that he might later confer upon his legitimate heir the economic and status advantages Bishop Spong sneers at. Such discipline presupposes powerful motivation on the father's part, motivation which can only be based on the prospect of having a stable family, on the assurance that his work and achievement will really benefit his children, on the assurance that society will compensate him for his biological marginality by providing him with the artificial social supports and importance which patriarchy gives to fatherhood—which today's feminists are seeking to remove on the ground that they are discriminatory against women. Instead of this needed social support today's father finds himself confronted with a sixty percent probability of divorce and the wreckage of his family and his hopes, reduced to an object of plunder to be cut up and picked over by an ex-wife resentful of his greater motivation, seeking to compensate for her lesser motivation by weakening his, desirous that his achievements and the "assets of his marriage" shall be seen as discriminatory against women, shall be seen by his children as deriving from her effort (and her lawyer's) rather than his. He will see his wife's disloyalty reinforced by a pusillanimous judge eager to curry favor with her by chivalrous posturing—by bestowing the husband's earnings upon her.

This destruction of male motivation is the greatest offence of the judge. Patriarchy puts sex to work; the judge, by rewarding female sexual disloyalty, impairs its working. Male motivation is why "white males (or the shrinking numbers of them who still have stable marriages) have all the stuff," and why fewer black males do. The destruction of male motivation is why Princeton economist William Baumol was proved wrong when he said in the mid-1960s that "In our economy, by and large, the future can be left to take care of itself." The good times of the "special decades [when] the economy grew at an unprecedented rate and economists began to assume that rapid growth would roll into the future"[66] were the times when families were stable, before Betty Friedan persuaded women they had outgrown the housewife role, the times of the feminine mystique. Baumol would have been proved right if the patriarchal good times had been permitted to roll, but the wealth created during those special decades was plundered to finance such follies as the Great Society and its Affirmative Action programs, the Apollo Moon Mission, the Vietnam War, the feminization of the service academies and the inanities of the feminist revolution and Lyndon Johnson's other programs.

Back in "those special decades" the big problems weren't the destruction of the family, the thirty percent illegitimacy rate, the sixty percent divorce rate, the sexual anarchy, the yearly birth of 375,000 drug

---

[66]Quoting Sylvia Ann Hewlett, *When the Bough Breaks* (New York: HarperCollins, 1991), p. 199. The Baumol quote is from the same page. Ms. Hewlett's subtitle "The Cost of Neglecting Our Children" might better have been, "The Cost of Neglecting Male Motivation and of Destroying Patriarchy."

damaged babies, the Central Park "wildings," the gang wars, the feminization of poverty, the forty percent of young men "drifting, out of school, unemployed."[67] The big problem was said to be women suffering from *acedia*, "the problem that has no name." American women were said to suffer from being incarcerated in a "comfortable concentration camp"—a posh suburban home. This was a spiritual distress which surfaced because American housewives had had their *other* problems solved by their husbands and by the patriarchal system. Today these other problems have returned with a vengeance and led not to the solving but to the burying of the problem that has no name, which is no longer even mentioned in feminist literature (have you noticed?).[68]

Bishop Spong says that the agenda of marriage was more economic than moral, and it is economic in the sense that much of the advantage conferred by the father on his heirs and on his wife is wealth; but there can be few more moral undertakings—based on disinterested love—than that of the future father who accepts the discipline of the schoolroom and the workplace in order that he may benefit children who do not yet exist and who cannot be expected, once they do come into existence, to ever pay him back in economic form a fraction of what he gives them.

It used to be accepted that children would pass the gifts of the parents on to *their* children. But few children can think that far ahead today. For today's fathers such a moral undertaking has become barely compatible with a sixty percent divorce rate and the anti-father bias of judges. Perhaps a father ought *not* to encourage his son to follow in his footsteps, to educate himself, to acquire an occupational skill, to marry, to buy a home, to create a family. The costs are too great, the probability of losing it all too devastating, the female kinship system too entrenched. The son's prospective bride will not like this advice, with her biological clock ticking, but she must pay the price for the liberation of the Sisterhood, mostly childless.

The liberal politician will say the child benefiting from patriarchal arrangements has done nothing to merit them, whereas a fatherless child has done nothing to deserve his predicament, his greater risk of mistreatment, neglect, poverty and delinquency. From these perfectly true premises the politician draws the fallacious conclusion that society should tax the responsible patriarchal father for the benefit of the

---

[67]Hewlett, p. 141.
[68]I discuss *acedia* in the fourth chapter of my *Garbage Generation*.

irresponsible mother (and her children). Feminist Carolyn Shaw Bell actually proposes taxing all men to subsidize all women. Similarly feminist Martha Sawyer proposes the subsidization of women by "the most advantaged class in society, white males." This would ghettoize society by removing the motivation which *makes* white males the most advantaged class in society and reducing them to the status of black males whose role-deprivation has demoralized them to where it would be ridiculous to tax them for the purpose Ms. Sawyer has in mind—making women parasitic.

Bishop Spong attacks the double standard on the ground that it oppresses women and separates the "good" from the "bad," those belonging to "the dominant strand of the social order" who were expected to be chaste, and "prostitutes, servants, lower-class women and women of oppressed racial minorities" who were not.[69] Which group of women is advantaged, the sexually promiscuous ones or the chaste ones who "save themselves for marriage"? Which group would Bishop Spong wish his daughters to belong to? The sexual regulation accepted by the chaste ones is not oppressive but advantageous to them since it gives them bargaining power with men who must depend on their loyalty if they are to have stable families.

Male chastity is no doubt also important, but less so, for a man's promiscuity does not affect the biological integrity of his own family, the security of the family's property and the motivation of its breadwinner.

Feminists would like to remove the moral basis of marriage entirely without removing the economic benefits to women. All the more, then, should men emphasize the economic benefits and insist on removing these economic benefits when women withdraw their loyalty from the family and the system. The divorce court which rewards women for divorcing their husbands is the deadly enemy of the family and the system. It is also the enemy of women and children, as the anguished complaints of women living in the Custody Trap show. The abolishing of alimony and child support awards would show women that their true friend is patriarchy, which gives them husbands, not the judge who takes them away.

---

[69]Spong, pp. 43, 48.

Robert Scheer returns to the subject of illegitimacy in a piece in the *Los Angeles Times* on 26 September, 1995, entitled "All Children Deserve a Chance." It is based on the Mutilated Beggar Argument, the plea that children, whose procreation took place before they existed and was beyond their control, and who therefore have nothing to do with their own illegitimacy, ought not to suffer for the sexual irresponsibility of their parents. Of course not. But how better to ensure their proper and responsible procreation and socializing than by appealing to the love and social responsibility of those who are obligated to love them most, these parents themselves? Scheer supposes that by taking this responsibility away from the parents he is doing the offspring a favor.

Affirmative action was originally conceived as a means to benefit black men. According to the *Los Angeles Times* of 30 October, 1996, "White women are 16 times more likely to benefit from affirmative action than black men." Affirmative action serves to liberate white women from patriarchal marriage by giving them economic independence which increases their divorce proneness by a factor of five. In other words, it enables more white women to castrate white men, as black men have been castrated by black women.[1] The "benefit" it confers on black men is to inform employers that they can fill two quotas by giving employment and promotion preference to black women, thus still further displacing black men from their proper role as providers for families. "Black women's wages have risen dramatically relative to those of black men....Black women now make slightly more than black men." [1](Maggie Gallagher, *The Abolition of Marriage*, pp. 189, 285)

"God desires that man shall have the dignity of causality," said Pascal. What one does or fails to do really matters. If a mother neglects her baby it will die. If she denies it a father it will be disadvantaged. Our legal system swarms with judges and bureaucrats eager to help women to disadvantage their offspring in order that *they*, the judges and bureaucrats, may receive pats on the head from feminists.

The problem of male reproductive marginality means that women must accept the obligation of chastity or have it imposed on them by wearing of veils and chadors or some similar disagreeable system of male coercion—or else men must insist on custody of their children as a protection against female sexual disloyalty whether by adultery or divorce. This can best be enforced by men's control of their paychecks.

Half a century ago the locker room wisdom was that if you knocked up a girl you had to marry her. The girl expected it, the families expected it and the boy would have been deemed a rat for getting a girl into trouble and then deserting her and his child. So they married, the child's legitimacy and the girl's status within the patriarchal system were assured, and a family was formed. It wasn't as desirable as a church wedding planned long ahead but it was an OK outcome. One supposes that a great many families were formed in this way and that they functioned well enough.

This outcome resulted from the operation of shame. The girl would have been ashamed to bear an illegitimate child, the boy would have been ashamed to desert her. Both would want to protect their child from the shame of being a bastard.

Enter Murphy Brown and Robert Scheer and promiscuity-chic movie actresses to tell us that shame is cruel, that the child ought not to be stigmatized for something happening before he was created, that there is no such thing as an illegitimate child. But there are illegitimate children and they are disadvantaged—largely because their parents were unregulated by shame. If the mother believes with Murphy Brown that there is nothing wrong with procreating her child out of wedlock then the mother's shamelessness makes the father equally shameless—he is exonerated from shame and can shrug his experience off as just another one-night stand. He can move on to other women. He feels that his girlfriend doesn't want marriage, and therefore he cannot hope to have a family with her. This is how matriarchy is generated. Scheer would have us believe all this benefits the illegitimate kid who is saved from stigma. He is not, however, saved from matriarchy, which is an all-around bad deal for women and children—and for men. All are denied the civilizing influences of family life and the patriarchal system.

This refusal to employ shame has led to an enormous increase in the number of illegitimate children, to male withdrawal from participation in marriage, to male marginalization, male demoralization, male underachievement. The *purpose* of this is to promote female promiscuity, the root cause of matriarchy.

"Entitled to the same opportunities," says Scheer. He implies that the opportunities are supplied by government agencies rather than by fathers. If government is handing out rights, why not the right to have a father, who is capable of supplying opportunities that government bureaucracies can't? Scheer cites Alexander Hamilton, Erasmus and other distinguished people as examples of illegitimate children who made a mark in the world. Of course many fatherless children turn out well, but this is irrelevant to social policy: Social policy which provides children with fathers is good policy. He cites Pope John Paul II that "each and every child is a gift from God," a sentiment, says Scheer, "endorsed by virtually every major religious leader." The sentiment is fine, but has nothing to do with the problem that a fatherless child is disadvantaged. This is why its mother turns to social programs like welfare and Affirmative Action to offset its disadvantage—at the expense of the patriarchal sector of society. If matriarchy becomes normative and is given benefits at the expense of patriarchal taxpayers, these taxpayers are discriminated against, victimized by taxation and by Affirmative Action, an attack on Caucasian males for the benefit of "minorities and women."

No doubt the Pope is right that every child is a gift from God. But is he a gift for Mom alone, or is the father to receive the gift too—and recompense it by supplying the little creature with the advantages fathers are capable of bestowing—giving it a place in patriarchal society where it will be better off? Or is Mom to be privileged, as a reward for her unchastity, to help herself to the absent father's income or to the largesse of taxpayers? Either way Mom and "her" child are parasitic upon the patriarchal sector. Either way males are deprived of fatherhood and marginalized. Scheer thinks, as Ms. Nayo thinks, that denying welfare to "penniless teen mothers" is cruel and that "minds that conceived a provision denying AFDC to teen mothers have forgotten how young 16 is." Too young perhaps to be bringing fatherless children into the world and demanding that society prevent them from being disadvantaged. These girls need to be taught the importance of chastity because they are so young, so incompetent to be parents, especially single parents. Is it not Joycelyn Elders and Marian Wright Edelman and "Murphy Brown" and the Planned Parenthood people who want to give them condoms, and is it not feminist teachers who tell girls they have the right to "control" their own sexuality, meaning the right to be promiscuous—is it not these people who have forgotten how young 16 is?

The greatest disadvantage blacks (and now increasingly whites) suffer from is fatherlessness. Affirmative action enables more women to deprive more children of fathers and more fathers of children. "The main reason for increased marital breakup was the abandonment of the marriage by women who had newfound economic independence." (Blumstein and Schwartz, *American Couples,* quoted in Gallagher, p. 287)

VILLAINOUS MALE SEDUCERS

Few illegitimate mothers are victims of villainous male seducers. "It is not true," says Leontine Young,

> **that women become pregnant out of wedlock mainly through irresponsibility or ignorance. Some do, of course, but in the great majority of cases the action is purposeful, often unconsciously so, and has its origin in the woman's family background. The unmarried mother wants a baby, specifically an out of wedlock baby, without a husband.[70]**

Scheer and Nayo want no show of resentment from the people who must pay the costs, lest the poor kid be unfairly humiliated for something he was never responsible for. Of course he wasn't. He is the victim of Mom and, increasingly, of a feminist and permissive society, now submerging into matriarchy.

Scheer speaks of a time

> **when we were a despised subcategory of the population with severely limited legal rights particularly as to inheritance. But that is no longer the case, even in England. At 31%, their rate of out-of-wedlock births is actually higher than in this country. England finally had the good sense in 1987 to pass the Family Law Reform Act, which formally ended the distinction between legitimate and illegitimate children.**

Formally ended it, he says. The dear, good lawyers and lawmakers, always friends of women and children, have passed a law that there is no difference. But there is a difference. It is really an advantage for a child to have a father. A child with no father is as much disadvantaged as ever.

The benefits conferred on promiscuous women are made closer to those conferred on loyal wives, thus reducing the significance of marriage and decreasing the reward to wives for their loyalty. Marriage is penalized in order that fornication may be rewarded. It is the purpose of

---

[70]Leontine Young, *Out of Wedlock* (New York: McGraw-Hill, 1954). The quotation is from the dust wrapper.

marriage to provide for wives and legitimate children; this purpose is undermined when fathers are made to be providers for ex-girlfriends and illegitimate children. Ms. Hoggett's view that marriage is meaningless is vindicated, matriarchy made normative.

Emancipation from patriarchy is, as feminist Ellen Willis says, "real progress for women, open[ing] up the possibility of a livelihood independent of fathers and husbands...enabl[ing] women to fight for basic perquisites of citizenship and ultimately to make the far more radical demand for control over their sexual and reproductive lives."[71] This really is the feminist program—to make men superfluous. Ms. Willis seems not to realize how this "progress," this livelihood independent of fathers and husbands, this control over their sexual and reproductive lives forfeits women's claim to support money.

A man who marries expresses his intention to be a father and take responsibility for his children. Abolishing the distinction between legitimacy and illegitimacy, between marriage and cohabitation, between "good" (sexually loyal) and "bad" (promiscuous) women, prevents him from doing this, puts legitimate children on a par with illegitimate ones and restores the matriarchal system.

The political purpose [continues Scheer] not the virtue, is clear. At a time when the welfare system is to be eliminated without any serious thought as to what will replace it, it is politically expedient to dismiss the children supported by that program as expendable. Once labeled as illegitimate, they can be dismissed as counterproductive from birth. If we think of them as throwaway children, then undermining their life support system does not suggest a societal loss.

The political purpose of what *Scheer* proposes is to further the War Against Patriarchy and promote matriarchy by using the children as Mutilated Beggars. The way to discourage illegitimacy is to appeal to the love and responsibility of the parents, especially the mother, who victimizes the child, and often the man as well by excluding him from the "joy and care of children." Scheer and the feminists would be willing to make all children fatherless at Mom's option.

---

[71]*Los Angeles Times*, 12 January, 1997.

XVII) FREE LIKE BLACKS

"It may well be believed," wrote William Graham Sumner a century ago, "that the change from the mother family to the father family is the greatest and most revolutionary in the history of civilization."[1] The reverse change is now taking place, the restoring of the mother-family by the feminist revolution. The change from matriarchy to patriarchy was a prerequisite for the creation of civilization as we know it. The reverse change, which is ghettoizing society, is viewed by feminists as progress and they do not mean to give it up: "Women have come too far to surrender the range of possibilities opened up by a sexual revolution."[2]

> Although black illegitimacy is close to 80 percent, there are still many stable "Ozzie-and-Harriet" black families whose members dine at a regular hour and enjoy stimulating conversation at the dinner table. They go on vacations together, visit museums together, go to the beach together. The daughter takes piano lessons, the son has a telescope. They have shelves filled with good books, subscriptions to interesting magazines, and so forth. The children go to college and enter the mainstream of American life. These families are headed by fathers.

Male demoralization and underachievement are the conspicuous features of the female kinship system, underlying which is the refusal of females to accept patriarchal regulation. Let me repeat: Like crime, like hemophilia, male demoralization is manifested in males but it is carried and transmitted by females. The Mother Daughter Revolution which created the ghettos is now attacking the larger society.

"A majority of girls," according to a survey by the American University Association of University Women, "are confident and assertive in the lower grades, [but] by the time they reach high school fewer than a third feel really good about themselves."

---

[1] *Folkways*, p. 355.
[2] *Ms.*, July 1986.

They encounter "the wall," the need to accept patriarchal socialization and behave like ladies, as boys must behave like gentlemen. The mother daughter revolution is a rebellion against this. Psychologist Dr. Joyce Brothers' has quoted Janie Ward page 132 as saying that one factor enabling black girls to resist "the wall" might be that black girls are surrounded by strong women they admire."

Also, Ward said, many black parents teach their youngsters that there's nothing wrong with them, only the way the world treats them.[3]

Ms. Ward calls the mothers "parents" and calls the daughters "youngsters." Why the attempt at gender neutrality? To disguise that sons receive a very different treatment, that sons are not surrounded by strong men they admire, that the socialization of daughters to feel good about themselves has a price for the sons, who feel less good about themselves, who feel marginalized, as their fathers have been marginalized in order that their mothers and sisters may feel good about themselves. This difference, inconspicuous, seemingly minor, lies at the heart of the female kinship system and the failure of the ghettos to advance into patriarchy. In the ghettos the Mother Daughter Revolution is complete. The strong black women admired by their daughters (and by white feminists including Dr. Brothers) have succeeded in making the ghetto what it is by reducing their men to the status of studs who, when their women tire of them, can be told to get lost.

Most strong black women think, "I don't need that man." This is the psychological basis of matriarchy, made possible by "welfare state feminism," women's marriage to the government's welfare and Affirmative Action bureaucracies and by routine mother custody in divorce. It amounts to society's withdrawal of the props required by the artificial male role. Black females enjoy their feeling of superiority and don't intend to give it up. *Black* women, especially, have "come too far to surrender the range of possibilities opened by a sexual revolution."

Today white females are using the assistance of divorce court judges—and increasingly also welfare and Affirmative Action—to impose matriarchy on the larger society, to change the kinship system, to get rid of father headship of the family and make the mother head of the reproductive unit (which feminists want to continue calling "the family"

---

[3]*Los Angeles Times*, 17 April, 1997.

for the purpose of disguising what's going on). It gives women a sense of power, of control; it places Mom in the driver's seat, makes her feel free, like Ms. Heyn's adulteresses. It manifests the "enormous potential counterforce" which has been roiling in women's souls since "the world historical defeat of the female sex,"[4] by men's creation of patriarchy five or six thousand years ago. Ghetto women have returned their society to the Stone Age pattern where "marriage was informal, casual." White women are now doing the same by creating a reproductive unit which excludes the male.

The strong black women grew up as strong black girls. They are confident and assertive in the lower grades, and they continue to be confident and assertive—no dip in self-esteem and self-assurance because, unlike white girls, they refuse to accept the patriarchal socialization which makes families possible, which gives males a meaningful role in reproduction and allows children to have fathers. Patricia Pearson describes the girls in one ghetto high school:

> **Black girls in [this] community consider themselves to be tough; there's no feminine currency in being frail, because, in large part, black women hold the community together. They can't look to men for protection: the men aren't around.[5]**

Here's the way the girls talk:

> **"Who you tellin'? Who you tellin'? You gonna beat me up with your umbrella?" one girl shouts. "Ain't nobody gonna do shit to me." For a moment it looks as if the confrontation will escalate, as if one of the girls will produce her "boxcutter," a razor-sharp knife that's the preferred weapon of New York City girls at this moment, good for slashing wincing cuts into one another's cheeks.[6]**

Unladylike. But she will grow to be a strong matriarch, will be admired by her daughters and by feminists, a free woman, not hobbled with the patriarchal socialization that lowers the self-esteem of white girls by trying to make them ladies who bottle up their rage. No such repression for these future matriarchs.

---

[4] Elgels's famous phrase in *The Origin of the Family*.
[5] Patricia Pearson, *When She Was Bad: Violent Women and the Myth of Innocence* (New York: Viking, 1997), p. 28.
[6] Pearson, p. 27.

The girls' refusal to accept patriarchal socialization and act like ladies means most boys will refuse to accept the complementary socialization to act like gentlemen. They will refuse to submit to the discipline of the classroom and the workplace which would enable them to fulfill the role of family provider, the role which most of their females don't want them to have anyway. This refusal to accept sex role socialization is what creates ghettos by creating the Siamese twins of female sexual promiscuity and male violence.

The males are powerless to do much about this as long as mother custody is automatic, as long as society grants wives the privilege of throwing their husbands out, as long as women can say, with Betty Friedan, "I don't care. I have to do something about my own life." "Something" meant divorcing her husband, depriving him of his children and bringing them up in a matriarchal household.

With an illegitimacy rate of thirty percent and a divorce rate of sixty percent and automatic mother custody, it won't take long to bring about the feminist goal of making most "families" mother-headed, of changing the kinship system.

Research by E. D. R., a polling firm dealing with women's issues, shows that daughters now think more highly of their mothers than they have in the past.[7] The corollary is that sons think less highly of their fathers—if they have fathers. "Over the last twenty years or so," says Rosalind Miles,

> **women have had their own contracts to reconsider and redraw, and suddenly all the old deals are off. A decade or two of feminism has not only changed the world for women, it has produced a crisis of response for the thinking man. How in this brave new post-patriarchal world is he to "be a man" when all the time-dishonored scripts, prerogatives and perks have been abolished or swept away?**

> **Inevitably the current crisis of male identity, sexuality and violence is accompanied worldwide by an epidemic of divorce. Contrary to the widespread notion of marriages mutually breaking down, the vast majority of petitions for divorce are brought by wives.[8]**

---

[7]Judy Mann, *The Difference*, p. 273.
[8]Rosalind Miles, *Love, Sex. Death and the Making of the Male* (N.Y.: Summit Books, 1991), p. 23.

The chief contract which women have "reconsidered and redrawn" is the contract of marriage, which gives men their father-role and provider-role and allows children to grow up in two-parent families. Now, says Ms. Miles, "all the old deals are off." They are if men are willing to continue allowing it to happen—allowing women to wreck the institution of the family—and having men pay for the wrecking. That this is what too many women want is shown by the Annex to this book.

The ex-husband is expected to "be a man" by continuing to subsidize his former wife with support money. Suppose the ex-husband woke up to the reality—that in three cases out of four they were paying their wives to divorce them and to drag their children into the matriarchal system where they will be at eight-fold greater risk of delinquency. Suppose that they refused to make the payments and insisted on taking custody of their children themselves. This would solve the crisis of male identity and re-stabilize the family.

Then there would be a realization by women that stable marriage in the patriarchal system conferred on them enormous advantages—that divorce would not earn but forfeit child custody, would not earn them but cost them support money. There would be a realization by men that heterosexual marriage was sexually the right way to go, better than the *Playboy* lifestyle, better than shacking up. There would be a realization by both women and men that the weakness of character of divorce court judges who deny fathers equal justice is no longer an exploitable resource for women, that marriage vows mean what they say, that the family is primarily concerned with the proper procreation and socialization of children; and that ensuring this proper procreation and socialization is the most important function of society.

"The chief difference between the viewpoints of black and white women," according to a student cited by Janet Harris,

is that black women "have not been dominated by black males." The black woman is the dominant figure in the home. She finds it easier to make a living, for she can always be a domestic, although her earnings are lower than white females and black males. "Black men are put down by white society," the student continued. "It's up to black women now to give them their manhood."[9]

---

[9] *A Single Standard*, (N.Y.: McGraw-Hill, 1971), p. 130.

Black men will have a long wait. A news broadcast of 3 January, 1999 lauded the "success" of a government program for getting welfare recipients off welfare and into jobs. The welfare recipients were black single mothers, whose fatherless children will henceforth get along with reduced services from their sole parent, Mom—another victory for the female kinship system, which marries Mom to the state. Stephanie Coontz has been quoted that "African American women have made the largest income gains relative to men of any ethnic group, producing new options for women both inside and outside of marriage."[10] In other words, African American men have suffered the greatest income loss relative to women of any ethnic group, denying options to men both inside and outside of marriage. Giving black men their manhood would mean giving them headship of families and the authority to make their wives behave themselves. It's not going to happen—not as long as mothers get automatic custody of children in the divorce court or get welfare by breeding fatherless children. Under the expanding—or exploding—matriarchy, women's independence, especially sexual independence, is increasing all the time. "Women's support for motherhood out of wedlock," says Susan Faludi,

> rose dramatically in the 80s. The 1987 Woman's View Survey found that 87 percent of single women believed it was perfectly acceptable for women to bear and raise children without getting married—up 14 percent from just four years earlier. Nearly 40 percent of the women in the 1990 Virginia Slims poll said that in making a decision about whether to have an abortion, the men involved should not even be consulted.[11]

No matter whether the men are married to the women or not, the women are privileged to marginalize them.

Men might come to realize that they ought not to pay for this marginalizing, that they ought instead to save their children from the matriarchal monkey-trap by demanding custody of them. The present drift into matriarchy requires the *consent* of males, and males must refuse that consent.

In the other camp, white females are waking up to what black females have known for two generations, that patriarchy is an artificial system, that it requires *their* consent if males are to participate as equals

---

[10]Stephanie Coontz, *The Way We Never Were* (HarperCollins, 1992), p. 254.
[11]*Backlash*, p. 404.

in reproduction, that they can wreck it if they refuse—or are permitted to refuse—this consent. The Feminist Revolution and the Mother Daughter Revolution are convincing them that they need no longer submit to patriarchal arrangements, that they can marginalize males as their black sisters have done. This is what is now happening. All that is required is that the marriage contract be made meaningless.

The problem resolves itself into this: How can females be induced to give their consent to patriarchy? How can they be made to see its benefits—to themselves and their children as well as to men? Nothing but automatic father custody will accomplish this.

American women, says Phyllis Schlafly truly, are "the most fortunate class of people on the face of the earth."[12] But the majority don't realize it. They want more—especially the right to be promiscuous. They don't realize that this demand for promiscuity is throwing it all away.

They will not, however, lightly consent to the loss of their children. If the mother-child tie is placed on the side of family stability, rather than being used as the lever for wrecking it, the family will be stabilized.

Since the Divorce Revolution women have acquired the idea that they can be supported by claiming tax money or child support money—and that then they can reduce their "relational" association with men to recreation only. The one relation they need to bother about, so they think, is that with their children, which can be reduced by child care services, preferably free.

The evidence given on pages 12ff. shows that the ongoing change in the kinship system is too expensive, the problems mothers are inflicting on their children and men and society are intolerable. This would be obvious if it were not for the time-lag, the generation-long span between the sexual breakdown and its consequences.

Ms. Pearson cites Colin Wilson's view that "It seems unlikely that female crime will ever become a serious social problem. The reason is obvious: woman's basic instinct is for a home and security, and it is unlikely she'll do anything to jeopardize that security." She won't jeopardize her own security. But the problem is intergenerational. How

---

[12]*Phyllis Schlafly Report*, January, 1997.

about the security of her children and grandchildren growing up in a matriarchy—especially the boys deprived of fathers and made to see how society devalues the male role? According to *The Liberator*,[13] "between 1970 and 1996 the number of divorced persons has more than quadrupled, from 4.3 million to18.3 million, while the number of never married adults has more than doubled from 21.4 million to 44.4 million." This is the world we are sending our children into.

> **Men [says Pearson] may flamboyantly display force to promote and defend status in the public realm, but women as surely need their own aggressive strategies to defend, maintain, and control their intimate relations, not just to "defend their cubs," which is the sentimental view, but to defend their aspirations, their identity, and their place on the stage.**

This "aggressive strategy" typically takes the form of divorce or adultery, both expressions of women's hatred of patriarchal regulation, both means of furthering the feminist revolution, both means of exiling men from families and making them Naked Nomads, loners, underachievers.

It is usually women who feel that divorce benefits them. Small wonder, since it is women who are rewarded not only by support payments and welfare backup but also by the gratification of revenge against the patriarchal regulation which confines their "intimate relations" and makes them accept second class status. The revenge may be directed not only against husbands and "the system" but also sometimes against their own offspring. Ms. Pearson has this:

> **Psychologist Shari Thurer has suggested that a woman's resentment of her status as a second-class citizen related to high infanticide rates among Greek aristocrats. Historian Ann Jones describes widespread infanticide in colonial America as a "revolutionary" act in a "patriarchal society," committed by women who resented being punished for sex.[14]**

There is much resentment. Girls resent the loss of autonomy required to make ladies of them. Grown women often feel it is better to live in poverty and be free—as long as they can use this imposed poverty to make Mutilated Beggars of their children and excite pity by exhibiting their sufferings.

---

[13]July/August, 1998.
[14]Pearson, p. 78.

Betty Friedan's complaint in the sixties was that society asked so little of women. It asks far more of men, as men's seven year shorter life expectancy proves. The pretense made in the 60s was that feminism would "liberate men too" from being breadwinning drudges and payers of alimony: "Man is not the enemy," said Ms. Friedan, "but the fellow victim of the bind of half-equality we are in now.... I see so clearly and hear from the mouths of men how they also are sensing that they are going to be freed to greater self-fulfillment as human beings as we women are released from the binds that now constrain us from full development of our own human potential."[15]

Bullfeathers, Betty. A generation and a half has rolled by and we have now become the society you wished for—with messed-up females breeding illegitimate and messed-up children living in feminized poverty. And unsocialized males wondering bewilderedly what their role is supposed to be now that marriage confronts them with a sixty percent probability of divorce—with the same support obligations which you promised to liberate them from—still the exploited breadwinners but without the satisfactions of family living that made male labor meaningful in their grandfathers' day.

EISLER'S GOOD MATRIARCHIES AGAIN

Feminist Riane Eisler looks back to the ancient cultures of Crete, the Indus Valley and "Old Europe" with their "feminine spirit" as showing the path we ought to follow. "Feminine," she thinks, is good— "generative," "nurturing," "creative," associated with "peace," "prosperity," "peace and harmony," "feminine values such as peace and creativity," "compassion," "responsibility," "caring," "love."

"Masculine" or "male" is bad—"idealizing armed might, cruelty, and violence-based power," "brutal," "destroying," "harsh," "punitive," "insensitive," "violent and hierarchical," "cruel," "unjust," associated with "violence," "domination," "murder," "pillage," "rape," "enormous physical destruction," "barbarity and destruction," "dominance," "inequality," "conquest," "insensate, destructive technology," "brute force and threat," "conquering, killing and dominating."

---

[15] *It Changed My Life*, p. 212.

304

Ms. Eisler focuses on female maternal functions in this Neolithic society. It was woman-centered. "[I]f the central religious image was a woman giving birth and not, as in our time, a man dying on a cross, it would not be unreasonable to infer that life and the love of life—rather than death and the fear of death—were dominant in society as well as art." "[T]he Goddess appears to have been originally worshiped in all ancient agricultural societies. We find evidence of the deification of the female—who in her biological character gives birth and nourishment just as the earth does...."[16]

The glorification of woman giving birth is the epitome of the feminine mystique, which Betty Friedan wrote her book to get rid of. Now Ms. Eisler would make it the central image of society once again— though the woman must not be sexually regulated, which would mean male domination. What Ms. Friedan and Ms. Eisler have in common is a hatred of, and a determination to reject the sexual law-and-order required if fathers are to have a meaningful reproductive role, if children are to have two parents.

The two-parent family was, as has been indicated, the pattern in America during "the best years," 1945-1965, the years of the feminine mystique, the years which feminists would like to dismiss as "an aberration." "Throughout most of human history," writes feminist Shari Thurer,

> **mothers have devoted more time to other duties than to child care and have delegated aspects of child rearing to others, except for a brief period after the Second World War. Fleeting as it was, this period was ossified in a number of TV sitcoms (a new rage in the 1950s), like "The Adventures of Ozzie & Harriet," and "Leave it to Beaver," so that even now we think of those midcentury family arrangements as good and right, and the way things were since time immemorial. But the 1950s was a decade unique in American history, and the breadwinner-housewife form of family was short-lived. As for the decade itself, it was never the familial paradise it was cracked up to be, even in white, middle-class suburbia, where outward domestic cheer often masked a good deal of quiet desperation, especially among women."[17]**

Ms. Thurer's pitch is that of Stephanie Coontz also. Her book *The Way We Never Were* is thus reviewed by Constance Casey:

---

[16]Riane Eisler, *The Chalice and the Blade* (San Francisco: Harper and Row, 1987), p. 20.
[17]Shari Thurer, *The Myths of Motherhood: How Culture Reinvents the Good Mother* (New York: Penguin Books, 1995), p. xix.

Coontz's take on the Golden Age of the family—Ward and June, Ozzie and Harriet—is not brand new, but worth restating. "The apparently stable families of the 1950s were the result of an economic boom—the gross national product grew by nearly 250% and per capita income by 35%. Most important, there was steady employment for the Ward Cleavers of America.[18]

The causal relationship was the reverse—the economic boom of the 1950s and the 250% growth in the GNP were the result of the stable families of the time and the high male motivation they produced. The hated feminine mystique was women's principal contribution to that prosperity. It meant wearing a mask and playing a role, but *it kept men playing their role as husbands, fathers and providers.* It was artificial, but so is everything about civilization. It worked. It kept women behaving—kept them from being as "natural" as they are in the ghettos. It gave children fathers. The "problem that has no name" of which Ms. Friedan complained was the result of women having had most of their other problems solved by the patriarchal system and being confronted with the problem at the apex of the "hierarchy of needs," the spiritual problem of finding enlarged meaning in life. Betty Friedan, an unspiritual lady, imagined the vacuum might be filled by an elitist career, an economic solution. It hasn't worked out. Most liberated women are more miserable than ever. They have a below-replacement birthrate and a sixty percent divorce rate. Men are roleless, children confused.

Women's desperation, their "rage" (Betty Friedan's favorite word in describing it) is at the heart of the sex war: the rage can only be removed by freeing women from regulation—which means by denying men meaningful fatherhood and destroying the family.

"A want of fixity in the marriage tie," says W. Robertson Smith, "will favour a rule of female kinship."[19] A want of fixity in the marriage tie provides the mechanism for establishing fatherless families. A want of fixity in the marriage tie promotes crime, delinquency, illegitimacy, educational failure, demoralization, sexual confusion, poverty and most of the other bad characteristics of the Garbage Generation. A want of fixity in the marriage tie is what Ramsey Clark is pointing to when he says of the criminal class he writes about in *Crime in America* that three-quarters come from broken homes. A want of fixity in the marriage tie

---

[18]*Los Angeles Times*, 23 October, 1992.
[19]W. Robertson Smith, *Kinship and Marriage in Early Arabia* (London: A. and C. Black, 1903), p. 78.

has created a demand for an enormously expensive, ineffectual, indeed counterproductive, Backup System—welfare, crime control, delinquency control, drug programs—a System which further weakens the marriage tie. A want of fixity in the marriage tie is the most striking feature of the most disastrous of all experiments in social engineering, the American ghetto. A want of fixity in the marriage tie has created a brittle upper class of liberated elitist career women who figure prominently as exemplars in the agitprop of feminism—and a larger underclass of female losers caught in the Custody Trap and the feminization of poverty, an underclass whose role in the feminist program is to be pitiable examples whose miseries can be pointed to as proving the need for further enlarging the Backup System, which will in turn further weaken the fixity of the marriage tie.

There is a simple solution to the problem created by the want of fixity in the marriage tie, a problem which has been growing since the late nineteenth century when judges began to switch from automatic father custody to mother custody. Father custody must be made once again mandatory. A hundred years of anti-male discrimination proves that if judges have any discretion they will abuse it to give women what they want, which is to escape from the "great scourge" of marriage, and regain control of their own sexuality

In "the best years" American GIs came home from the war yearning not at all to impose a ruler-ruled, master-subject "dominator society" on women, but yearning (in the words of a popular song of the day) to "settle down and never more roam and make the San Fernando Valley my home," to get married and have a family and children and a home. They were the best fathers, Margaret Mead tells us, that any civilized society had ever known. Their yearning created the most prosperous era in history, when families were stable, when "never had so many people, anywhere, been so well off."

Then came feminism, the female rebellion against sexual law-and-order, women's "declaration of sexual independence,"[20] now culminating in the near abandoning of the marriage contract—the program for a return to the female kinship system.

---

[20]Ehrenreich, Hess and Jacobs, *Re-Making Love*, p. 70.

This is seen in mirror-image by Ms. Eisler who reveals her wish to get back to Stone Age matriarchy when she says, "the worship of the Goddess was central to all aspects of human life...[when].feminine figures and symbols occupied the central place."[21] Masculine symbols typically either occupied peripheral positions or were arranged around the female figures and symbols. This is the feminine mystique: "the life-giving and sustaining powers of the world [were] in female rather than male form."

Ms. Eisler sees this feminine paradise as having been destroyed by the intrusion of patriarchy, during the centuries following 4000 B. C.— "the great change," she calls it—"a change so great, indeed, that nothing else in all we know of human cultural evolution is comparable in magnitude."

"FROM REVERENCE TO RAPE"

There was another—albeit brief—feminine paradise during "the best years," the postwar years of family values, the patriarchal years of 1945-65, when "never had so many people, anywhere, been so well off," when there were likewise feminine figures and symbols everywhere. Women were placed on pedestals. These years created the Baby Boom and doubled the American industrial plant in two decades—accomplishments of an "essentially peaceful character,"[22] and of a *patriarchal* character. The disruptive feminism which followed, and reacted against this patriarchal prosperity, terminated the Baby Boom, exchanging it for a below-replacement level birthrate, thirty percent illegitimate, and with a sixty percent divorce rate—and millions of fatherless children. The feminist revolution convinced women that family values are *not* central to all aspects of life for women, but that women can establish their sexual autonomy by male-style achievement in the world of work. The result has been swarms of females taking over male jobs—and expecting Affirmative Action benefits and special favors for their sex, lest they be discriminated against, lest they be supposed to need husbands. Result: income redistribution on a massive scale, male rolelessness and demoralization on a massive scale—and female unchastity on a massive scale, entrenched and now presumed to be a right—"the sexual revolution has transformed not only our behavior, but our deepest

---

[21]Eisler, *The Chalice and the Blade*, pp. 14, 15.
[22]Eisler, *The Chalice and the Blade*, p. 13.

understanding of sex and its meaning in our lives," to quote the dust wrapper of *Re-Making Love.*

What Ms. Eisler says about "partnership" promoting peace and stability is true—confirmed by the statistics concerning crime and marriage. Prisons are filled with single men unable to create partnerships with women. Subsidized housing tracts are filled with single women (and their fatherless children) unable to create stable partnerships with men. While the single males are committing their crimes and serving their prison sentences, the single women with whom they fail to form partnerships, are breeding the next generation of troublemakers. Ms. Wolf says of promiscuous females,

> **It is no wonder that even today fourteen-year-old girls, who notice, let alone act upon, their desire, have the heart-racing sense that they are doing something obscurely, but surely, dangerous....[A] modern woman wakes up after a night of being erotically "out of control," feeling sure, on some primal level, that something punitive is bound to happen to her—and that if it doesn't it should.**

She feels, with Dr. Mary Jane Sherfey, that she, like all females, are potential nymphomaniacs ("out of control") and that society must make them submit to patriarchal regulation. But rejecting this regulation, as Dalma Heyn's adulteresses witness, as Bill Clinton and Monica Lewinsky witness, is part of the fun, forbidden, exciting. A French writer, describes his adulterous heroine driving in a taxi to meet her lover and passing a sign reading DANGEROUS CORNER. She hugs herself in ecstatic excitement, knowing that she is not only about to have sex with her lover, but that it is dangerous, *forbidden,* and that she is therefore winning a skirmish in the War Against Patriarchy and its hated regulation of her. Good!

"Something obscurely but surely, dangerous," Ms. Wolf says. Dangerous because it undermines the male role, the validity of the marriage contract, the legitimacy of children, the proper socialization of the young, the motivation of work, and the security of property. It threatens society with a return of the female kinship system ("the progress women have made in our society"), something which Ms. Wolf seeks to trivialize, thus removing shame as a regulator of female sexuality.

The feminist revolution has achieved the first stage of its goal: An adulterous woman can now claim the *right* to be promiscuous, to reject sexual loyalty to her husband and thereby deprive him of assurance of having a family and depriving her children of their right to have a father. No small matter to men and children.

THE CRETAN MATRIARCHY AGAIN

In the days of Cretan matriarchy, writes Ms. Eisler, "the worship of nature pervaded everything."[23] "Personal ambition seems to have been unknown; nowhere do we find the name of an author attached to a work of art nor a record of the deeds of a ruler."[24] "Of particular interest is that long after Crete enters the Bronze Age, at the same time that the Goddess, as the giver and provider of all life in nature, is still venerated as the supreme embodiment of the mysteries of this world, women continue to maintain their prominent position in Cretan society."[25]

Cretan society was unknown to the philosopher Giambatista Vico but he saw the "Heroic Age" as being preceded by other prehistoric hypnocratic cultures. Vico's finding is thus described by Gerald Heard:

> **Vico, the seventeenth- and eighteenth-century Neapolitan historian (1688-1744) had perceived, with extraordinary insight aided by studies of epic literature and hints from the Sumerian fragments embedded in the Hebrew Pentateuch, that beside and behind the saga and epic ages lay another epoch that was as different from barbarism as barbarism was alien to civilization. Vico's insight, however, had to wait until this century to become convincing....Now, such discoveries as those made by Arthur Evans of the Minoan culture (which was millennially previous to and far more lasting than its successor, the Hellenic, classical Greece) together with those made about the Sumerian and Indus cultures and the Shang Dynasty in China have made historians realize that there was a protohistory, when man lived in a cultured society compacted largely by coconscious suggestion....[26]**

The hypnotic power of such coconsciousness leads Heard to call it a "hypnocracy."[27] Not all of them are civilized:

---

[23]Eisler, *The Chalice and the Blade*, p. 34.
[24]Nicolas Platon, *Crete* (Geneva: Hagel Publishers, 1966, cited in Eisler *loc. cit.*
[25]Eisler, p. 38.
[26]Gerald Heard, *The Five Ages of Man* (New York: Julian Press, 1963), p. 20.
[27]See supra, p.252.

> **In Central Australia, and later in Papua, tribes were found living a balanced life which, though at the price of the inhibition of experiment and adventure, avoided the self-willed violence of the epic barbarian.**

They avoided going "out of control."

> **Here, there can be no doubt, there was not only another type of culture, there was another quality of consciousness. Beside the unreflective, boastful violence of the barbarian and the critical constructiveness of the civilized man there was also at least (and back of them both, it is reasonable to surmise) a third type of mind that was precritical but creative, preindividual but considerate.**[28]

Preindividual. "Nowhere do we find the name of an author attached to a work of art nor the record of the deeds of a ruler," says Ms. Eisler. This millennially long hypnocracy was broken by the irruption of the "hero," the self-assertive man. "We must," says Heard,

> **regard the hero as being an inevitable development of consciousness. The critical faculty had to grow, and, since the coconscious tribe had become negative to all invention and hostile to the capacity for asking questions, it had to grow because of an increasing sense of separateness. [T]he heroic epoch is such an inevitable reaction to the rigidifying of the coconscious tradition that we find it (together with its characteristic, the saga-epic literature) in all the giant cultures. It was so emphatic, so aggressive that until this century there was no general recognition, among historians, of the preheroic, priest-kingly, coconscious, or hypnocratic culture that lay behind it, from which the hero was ejected and which the hero in turn destroyed.**[29]

As pointed out previously, Heard fails to connect this impingement of the heroic revolt on the coconscious civilizations which preceded it with *the sex-war, which created patriarchy.* Women were comfortable and enjoyed higher status than men in the hypnocracy. It was the lower status male who was motivated to rebel against it, to demand a place in the sun, to end "the deification of the female."[30]

William Graham Sumner has been quoted on the momentous change from the mother family to the father family: "the greatest and most revolutionary in the history of civilization."[31] Let me repeat: The reverse change is now taking place, the restoring of the mother-family by

---

[28]Heard, p. 21.
[29]Heard, pp. 213
[30]*Chalice and the Blade*, p. 21.
[31]*Folkways*, p. 355.

the feminist revolution. The change from matriarchy to patriarchy was a prerequisite for the creation of civilization as we know it. The regression now taking place, which is ghettoizing society, constitutes feminist "progress." They do not mean to give it up.

Women are pulled on the one hand by the wish for home and security and relationships, especially to their children, and on the other hand by the First Law of Matriarchy, "a woman's sacred right to control her own body"—a woman's yearning for the sexual freedom of the matriarchal system. They would like to have both. Patriarchy tells them they can have only one: they must choose between civilized patriarchy and promiscuous matriarchy, between allowing men to share their reproductive life and excluding them. Society must motivate her to choose patriarchy by linking the matriarchal alternative to the loss of her children.

XVIII) VIOLENT LAND

Single men are dangerous. This is made clear by David Courtwright's *Violent Land*, a book reviewed by *The Family in America* as follows:

> Whether in the saloons of 19th century cowtowns like Abilene or Dodge City or in the ghettos of modern metropolises like Chicago or Los Angeles, young men living outside of marital and familial restraints have wreaked havoc....Courtwright argues that the gunfights and brawls in frontier America reflected a "temporary breakdown in the familial mechanisms of controlling young men," a breakdown remedied when women, wedlock and family life caught up with and civilized the rootless men on the frontier.

It was pointed out in Chapter XI that the wildness of the Western frontier was owing to too many men and not enough women and that the wildness of the ghetto was owing to too many women and not enough men. Courtwright shows that "too many women" makes for illegitimacy and family disruption. The men of the ghetto are "less often socialized in intact families or likely to marry and stay married." What is needed is a balance of numbers with men as providers for families. This minimizes male violence and what needs to be seen as its major cause, female absence or female sexual irresponsibility. There is no way to reconcile this goal with Ellen Willis's goal for women: "a livelihood independent of fathers and husbands...and ultimately...the far more radical demand for control over their sexual and reproductive lives."

This is Briffault's Law. *The Family in America* continues:

> On the wild frontier, as in the ghetto, Courtwright finds, "the total amount of violence and disorder in society is negatively related to the percentage of males in intact families of origin or procreation." But the number of males living outside of intact families has exploded since the 1960s, a decade Courtwright views as "the hinge of modern American history." On this hinge, America swung away from a social era defined by marriage and family life into a new era of "divorce, illegitimacy, sex and violence." Marriage rates tumbled, and the long-term historical "decline of the family as the basic social unit" accelerated sharply, as "more and more of its socializing and punishing functions devolved upon the professions, private enterprise and the state, the parent of last resort."

313

The era of "divorce, illegitimacy, sex and violence" is the era of the feminist revolution.

As family life has decayed in modern America, "hyperghettos" have multiplied: in these hyperghettos "two-thirds or more of the families [are] headed by single mothers and three-quarters of all births [are] illegitimate." Predictably, the young men in these hyperghettos, "growing up without a father, and growing into anomic lives with no regular family life of their own...[are] a good deal more than twice as likely [as men in intact [families] to become involved in shoot-outs or run afoul of the law."

Enlarging the criminal justice system is not the answer:

[T]he voice of family-instilled conscience is always more cost-effective than that of a police officer." Courtwright concedes that we may "reasonably doubt" whether contemporary American leaders know how to pull our crime-ridden hyperghettos out of "the riptide of history." "What we should not doubt," he concludes, "is the social utility of the family, the institution best suited to shape, control, and sublimate the energies of young men."

This means patriarchally regulated sex, the opposite of the feminist goal of sexual promiscuity or "reproductive freedom." Concerning such freedom, we have the following from Gloria Steinem:

[T]here can never be reproductive freedom, or informed human policy toward new birth technologies, without national policy and support that makes childbearing choices real for all women.[1]

"All women" means married or unmarried, sexually responsible or sexually irresponsible. Ms. Steinem seems to be calling for the abolition of the entire patriarchal sexual constitution, including marriage (other than for providing women with ex-husbands), the Legitimacy Principle and any significant male control over reproduction. This is the condition of the ghetto—mother-right and promiscuity, promoted by "national policy" and with "national support."

"[I]ndependent women," says Ms. Steinem, "undermine the patriarchal family, deprive the world of its biggest source of unpaid labor, and transform the masculine/ feminine paradigm on which much of the world's polarized thinking depends." She wants to undermine the family, which she calls "the patriarchal family." One means of defending the

---

[1]*Ms.*, July/August, 1987.

314

family would be to insist that these women be *given* the independence she speaks of, by depriving them of alimony, child support money, affirmative action benefits, comparable worth benefits, quota benefits, and other conferred—unearned—benefits that keep them from being independent. She speaks of "unpaid labor." She means wives are unpaid prior to divorce, prior to their withdrawal of the $25,000 worth of services they provide to their husbands (Ms. Steinem's own estimate, made some years ago; it would be more today). When divorce makes them "independent," however, they discover that their standard of living has fallen by 73 percent (feminist Dr. Lenore Weitzman's estimate), and the standard of living of the husband deprived of her services skyrockets by 42 percent (Dr. Weitzman's estimate). So, far from being unpaid, the wife's services were paid by a 73 percent higher standard of living, provided by a husband who has not so much benefited from her $25,000 worth of services as he has sacrificed 42 percent of his own standard of living to give her 73 percent.

Ms. Steinem attributes women's dependence and underachievement to the "definition of masculinity that depends on violence, aggression, and superiority to women." This describes not patriarchal masculinity but matriarchal masculinity, that of the ghetto, of the single males studied by Courtwright, of roleless males unsocialized by family living. These constitute the male half of the underclass which produces most of the crime/gang/drug culture—while the female half enjoys the "reproductive freedom" Ms. Steinem covets for them and breeds the next generation's underclass.

Many modern women say they want to be independent, but they don't at all mind being dependent after divorce, after they have sexually de-regulated themselves, after they have withdrawn the reciprocal services which formerly justified their dependence and gave men a meaningful role.

Men need to be needed, they need families who depend on them. This is what Margaret Mead calls the "nurturing behavior of the male, who among human beings everywhere helps provide food for women and children" (see page 164).

Women's sexual liberation deprives men of this role. The exile of men from "marital and familial restraints" made the West wild and creates today's ghettos. But the demand for this liberation is the core of

315

the feminist revolution. Betty Friedan's "Bill of Rights for Women" insists on federal legislation "recognizing the right of every *woman* to control her own reproductive life"[2]—the right of women to exclude men from sharing in reproduction—other than subsidizing it. Ms. Friedan speaks of breaking through sex discrimination and creating "the new social institutions that are needed to free women, not from childbearing, or love or sex or even marriage, but from the intolerable agony and burden those become when women are chained to them."[3] This chaining—stable marriage—allows men a meaningful role in reproduction and guarantees children that they shall have two parents and guarantees society the sexual and social stability which accompanies two-parent families and properly socialized children. Wives must not be "chained." Charmaine (see p. 4) and Ms. Friedan both see the naturalness of the female kinship system and the burdensomeness of the male kinship system. Both suppose, however, that the male kinship system must be partially retained for the purpose of subsidizing the female kinship system through welfare and support payments.

In Sweden, the feminist paradise, Ms. Friedan talks to an editor who picks up his baby girl and says "proudly that she relates to him more than to the wife...and in the Volvo factory, even the P. R. man with a crew cut says the same thing":

> **I couldn't believe it! I asked, how do you explain this? How does everybody have these attitudes? And they said, education. Eight years ago, they decided that they were going to have absolute equality, and the only way you can have this is to challenge the sex-role idea.[4]**

Absolute equality, he says. The girl may relate more to the father than to the mother, but if there is a divorce the mother will be given custody of her. Mom will be relieved of her chains and Dad will have to put them on and continue to subsidize Mom because calves never follow bulls and because the Swedes don't mean what they say about "absolute equality" any more than Ms. Friedan does, any more than Judge Noland does when he talks about "equal justice under law." Nobody intends to "challenge the sex-role idea" where it matters. Judges know that fathers are more responsible and will continue to submit to the mother-custody-

---

[2]Betty Friedan, *It Changed My Life* (New York: Random House, 1976), p. 102; emphasis added.
[3]*It Changed My Life*, p. 144.
[4]*It Changed My Life*, p. 118.

extortion-system, as ex-wives would almost never do—but this knowledge fails to lead to father custody, since "children belong with their mother."

A man who wants a family must find a woman who will promise him her sexual loyalty and he must live in a society which will guarantee this loyalty by assuring him that he cannot be deprived of his children at her pleasure—that she cannot play her Motherhood Card while he is prevented from playing his Money Card. The stability of society requires that males shall be induced to accept responsibility for the support of two-parent families and the socializing of children within them. But in the feminist scenario, where women are "unchained," the marriage contract gives men no reproductive rights and when the contract is annulled the law rivets chains on *him.*

Ms. Friedan thinks that only economically independent career-elitist ladies are capable of experiencing free and joyous "love" (see the quote from *The Feminine Mystique* given on page 69). But what Ms. Friedan calls love bears much resemblance to the Promiscuity Principle and her emphasis on the importance of such love means that when it is no longer experienced, stable and long-term family commitments, however desirable for men and children and for society, become an unnecessary burden ("chains") for wives. What Ms. Friedan really is insisting on is the sanctity of recreational sex, "freely and joyously given." Ms. Heyn and her adulteresses would agree.

"Sickening her for love," says Ms. Friedan. Giving wives the privilege of marrying for love gives them also the privilege of divorcing at pleasure and at the husband's expense.

"Her destiny depended on charming men," says Ms. Friedan (see page 45 supra). How undignified, she thinks, for women to put on a hypocritical show of charm in order to "earn" the economic and status advantages conferred by men. Why cannot women earn their own economic security and status and thereby be enabled to love freely and joyously and promiscuously? It is their lack of freedom to do this which creates their festering resentment. This is what preoccupies Ms. Friedan so much with "rage": the "*rage* and bitterness...discharged in blind reactive hatred against men...the *rage* women have so long taken out on themselves, on their own bodies, and covertly on their husbands and children...the *rage*, the impotence that makes women so understandably angry,   *rage*...translate our *rage* into action...that energy so long buried

317

as impotent *rage* in women...mistaking the *rage* caused by the conditions that oppress us for a sexual *rage*...Frankly, I don't think we will be able to work out these problems in our own individual lives until we make basic changes in society... transform society in ways more radical and more life-enhancing than any other...free ourselves and men from obsolete sex roles that imprison us both, the hostility between the sexes will continue to inflame the violence of our nation."?[5]

This was written when there was a great deal less violence than now. The "basic changes in society" are nothing new—a reversion to the female kinship system, with the reproductive unit headed by the mother—with conferred benefits supplied by absent males or taxpayers. "Fifty women in the Senate"[6] but not fifty percent of women on the curbsides of Skid Row or in the cells of prisons, and not fifty percent of military casualties or industrial accidents.

(Why is it less dignified for women to charm men than to bully them?)

Benazir Bhutto, feminist former Prime Minister of Pakistan, speaks of setting half the population free—de-regulating women—by "transforming social habits and attitudes":

Ultimately, empowerment is attained through economic independence. As long as women are dependent on men, they will face discrimination in one form or another.... Before we can bring about the political and social emancipation of women, we will first have to ensure that they can stand on their own feet.[7]

Ms. Bhutto thinks that men ought *not* to learn what Ms. Mead says they must learn, to be providers for "some female and her young." The only realistic way of doing what Mead says is to make the male part of the reproductive unit a *sociological* as well as a biological father, one who cannot be deprived of his offspring.

Ms. Bhutto wants women to be economically independent, to stand on their own feet. This is matriarchy. Matriarchy denies that marriage is an economic institution in which women and children are dependent on men.

---

[5] *It Changed My Life*, pp. xiv, 144, 153, 157, 162, 188, 191.
[6] *It Changed My Life*, p. 153.
[7] *Los Angeles Times*, 1 September, 1995.

Feminists like to talk about marriage as a romantic institution held together by women's bestowal of their love upon their lucky men[8]–an institution, however, in which women are privileged to withdraw their love when they no longer feel like bestowing it—when they get bored with the Old Boy and resent being "chained" to him. Ms. Bhutto tells us "We will all have to cooperate" to attain "the final emergence of women." That will be a world in which women (and of course "their" children) don't need men as providers, a world filled with roleless men. But as the ghettos show, roleless men don't create peace and prosperity. The only thing to do with most men—if we want them to be high achievers, to accept discipline, to be law-abiding, to accumulate stabilizing assets, to socialize their children properly and transmit patriarchal values to them—is to make them heads of families.

---

[8]"What surprises are in store for men," exclaims Ms. Friedan, "and for us, as we give up some of that manipulating control of the family we once used to keep them emotional babies...." *Second Stage*, p. 122.

XIX) HYPERGAMY

A cinder girl may hope to marry Prince Charming, but a chimney sweep cannot hope to marry Princess Charming. Many doctors marry nurses, but no women doctor marries a male nurse. Acquiring education, wealth and status make a man a desirable husband, but place a woman where there are fewer men to "marry up" to and make her more divorce-prone.

Hypergamy, or "women marrying up," does not discriminate against women; it acknowledges women's higher ascribed status, something which men must equal by work and achievement. It is this male work and achievement which creates the wealth and stability of society. A girl not socialized to acknowledge the universal fact of hypergamy will be disadvantaged—and will disadvantage her man, her children and society.

Patriarchy employs sex as a motivator of male achievement. It says to boys: "If you will accept discipline, if you will make money, if you will acquire a reputation for integrity, for loyalty to your employer, if you will acquire high status, then you will be able to marry an attractive woman."

There is no way in which society can organize itself to use sex as a motivator of female achievement. What would happen to a society which tells girls, "If you will accept the discipline of the classroom and the workplace and do the other things we urge boys to do, then you will qualify yourself to marry—what? A fast-talking gigolo? A muscular surfer? A drug-addicted rock musician? A Swedish crooner like Joan Collins's former husband? Go to! Even if society could persuade females to believe such foolishness, it would self-destruct in doing so, for it would deprive men of the motivation to achieve. Will such discipline make females attractive to high-achieving, high status men? Not likely. A man and a woman will both know that the man has nothing to offer the woman that she cannot provide for herself. Briffault's Law.

PATRIARCHY'S GREAT GIFT: STABLE MARRIAGE

A nubile young woman fulfills her dream of marrying a powerful and high-achieving man and bestowing her love freely and joyously on

320

him. Each is accounted a winner if the marriage is stable. Society is a winner. The man works for the benefit of his wife and children, and the wealth he creates circulates through the productive and creative portions of the economy, not through the parasitic portions such as the legal profession, the government's bureaucracies and its lotteries, its Backup System of welfare and treatment programs, the enforcers of child support payments, process-servers, promoters of feminist agitprop, affirmative action intermeddlers who intrude themselves into and weaken the market economy. This is how patriarchy puts sex to work, by making marriage stable, creating wealth rather than transferring it from its creators to parasites.

It may seem unfair to powerful and high-achieving women that the female in this scenario exploits her youth and nubility rather than her achievements, that she counts success in terms of being a wife and mother and having a stable marriage to a successful man. The powerful and high-achieving woman might suppose that her own achievements entitle her to be admired and pursued by men, as high achieving men are admired and pursued by women. It doesn't work that way. President Kennedy and President Clinton found themselves surrounded by willing females; Madeleine Albright and Janet Reno would get nowhere with their male underlings by making passes at them. Hypergamy prevents such gender-switches. If Betty Friedan, Adrienne Rich, and Marcia Clark imagined that being successful movers and shakers would make them attractive to men and allow them to become sexual predators like Kennedy and Clinton, they found out otherwise. Powerful women are not attractive to men. This is why women are lesser achievers than men. It's the reverse side of Briffault's Law. "The eternal feminine draws us on," said Goethe—us men—but only when men supply women with benefits. If marriage is stable, the benefits enrich society as well.

Women are attracted to wealthy and high-status men; but men are not attracted to wealthy and high-status women. Women want to marry men who are older, taller, more muscular, richer, better educated, and have higher status than themselves. When they do, their friends tell them they have made a good match. A woman who chooses to marry a man younger, shorter, less muscular, poorer, less educated and with lower status—or even one of two of these things—will be judged to have married beneath herself. A low-status man who pursues a wealthy, high status woman will be deemed a gigolo or be nominated for membership in the Dennis Thatcher Society, named for the husband of the former

Prime Minister. Many executives marry their secretaries but no female executive marries a male underling. Catherine the Great did not consider marrying one of her studs. Hypergamy is simply the way things are—a way of acknowledging women's higher ascribed status and of motivating men to *achieve* status by their own effort. Goethe said that we admire a girl for what she is and admire a boy for what he promises to become. It is well that things are this way, benefiting women and children—and men and society. But it requires that society shall stabilize marriage. It works by giving men a meaningful role, unlike the matriarchal alternative which establishes itself by depriving men of their role (telling women they too can be firepersons). Hypergamy serves society's interest—or rather say patriarchal society makes its arrangements conform to the principle of hypergamy: the highest achieving men get the most attractive women. This is how patriarchy puts sex to work. It explains why men earn more money; it explains why affirmative action is anti-social; it explains why high achieving women are not especially attractive to men.[1]

Dr. Watson in Conan Doyle's *Sign of the Four* is dismayed at the thought that the woman he loves might be an heiress. At the end of the story, when it is revealed that the Agra treasure she was to inherit has been scattered on the bottom of the Thames, he exclaims "Thank God!"

"Why do you say that?" she asked.

"Because you are within my reach again," I said taking her hand. She did not withdraw it. "Because I love you, Mary, as truly as ever a man loved a woman. Because this treasure, these riches, sealed my lips. Now that they are gone I can tell you I love you. That is why I said 'Thank God.'"

"Then I say 'Thank God' too," she whispered."

Ms. Friedan's interpretation would be: Now she has lost the Agra treasure and is compelled to go back to using feminine wiles and tricks which amount to selling her (feigned) affection in exchange for the economic benefits a man can confer upon her. The idea that a woman's assuming economic dependence on a man is a gift to *him*, the gift of a meaningful reproductive role and a stable family, would not occur to Ms. Friedan. She imagines that a woman's "free and joyous" gift of a one-

---

[1]For a fuller discussion of hypergamy, see Chapter 9 of my *Garbage Generation*.

night stand, or of an unstable or temporary marriage, is something greater than a gift of sexual loyalty. Ms. Friedan and her feminist sisters and her promiscuous friends and Ms. Heyn's adulteresses have the idea that sex ought to be recreational and that adultery is a human right. Allowing feminist troublemakers and lawyers into the act prevents women from offering this gift of a stable marriage—which is, of course, risky. Unlike "the good divorce," which offers safety but seldom delivers it. Dr. Watson and the rest of patriarchal men (and properly socialized women) have the idea that sex ought to be primarily reproductive, that women, like men, ought to accept the "work ethic"—not only because reproductive law-and-order is essential to a stable and prosperous society, but because it is really sexier, it gives meaning to human sexuality—for meaning exists in the primary sex organ, the brain. It might not be *free*, but it is more likely to be joyous because it gives the man a role and gives the woman the benefits of Briffault's Law—and gives children the benefits of the two-parent family, which is the whole idea. The idea is not to "put yourself first" (in Ms. Triere's words) but to give children their best chance to escape matriarchy and live under patriarchy.

Ms. Friedan, writing before feminism had made adultery chic, defended female economic (therefore sexual) independence on romantic grounds, that it permitted the flourishing of "love." Only economic independence, she tells us, can enable a woman to leave a loveless marriage—a loveless marriage being a marriage which a woman desires to leave. Ms. Friedan quotes "Liz": "It makes such a difference once you make enough money, that you're not dependent. You can choose to be dependent, emotionally, if you want to be. But you don't have to be. If I got married to him again, I'd be afraid I'd fall into the old ways."[2] Once you make enough money, you become divorce-prone, which is great for Mom, but, as pages 12ff. show, less great for the kids.

It makes such a difference for the man too. The man's money was what held his marriage together—gave him his provider-role. Economic independence was what enables her to divorce him. Obvious. She wanted sexual liberation; she got it—and she moved society a notch closer to matriarchy. Briffault's Law.

---

[2]*Second Stage*, p. 117.

We read in Briffault that "the North American Indians, and the Illinois in particular...laughed at the unheard-of notion of any marriage being otherwise than temporary."[3] Only economic *dependence* can assure the woman's not leaving the marriage, a conclusion confirmed by the high divorce rate of economically independent women. Briffault's Law. The fact needs to be insisted upon. The fact explains why fathers must be given custody in divorce. If, as now, mothers have assurance of custody and the privilege of enslaving fathers, the whole patriarchal system collapses because of the deprivation of male motivation.

This is central to social stability and it is commonly misunderstood. Thus George Gilder tells us that "greater sexual control and discretion— more informed and deliberate powers—are displayed by women in all societies known to anthropology. Indeed, this intelligent and controlled female sexuality is what makes human communities possible."

This difference between the sexes gives the woman the superior position in most sexual encounters. The man may push and posture, but the woman must decide. He is driven; she must set the terms and conditions, goals and destinations of the journey. Her faculty of greater natural restraint and selectivity makes the woman the sexual judge and executive, finally appraising the offerings of men, favoring one and rejecting another, and telling them what they must do to be saved or chosen. Managing the sexual nature of a healthy society, women impose the disciplines, make the choices and summon the male efforts that support it.[4]

Very edifying. Ehrenreich, Hess and Jacobs, however, have a different idea:

Nor do we expect women's sexuality to be simply passive and decorative in its public manifestations. Even in the staid and married suburbs, women flock into male strip joints, provide a market for the new, "couple-oriented" pornographic videotapes, and organize Tupperware-style "home parties" where the offerings are sexual paraphernalia rather than plastic containers. And in media fiction, we no longer find the images of women divided between teasing virgins and sexless matrons: Whether on the prime-time soaps or in the latest teen film, women are likely to be portrayed as sexually assertive, if not downright predatory.[5]

---

[3]Briffault, *The Mothers*, II, 93.
[4]*Men and Marriage*, p. 13.
[5]*Re-Making Love*, p. 3.

If the woman is economically independent she doesn't need the man and they both know it. According to Shere Hite, "Ninety-three percent of single, never-married women say they love the freedom of being on their own":

> **"It's great to be responsible for no one but yourself. I love being able to flirt with anyone I please, not being tied down, having an apartment exactly the way I want it, not having to answer to anyone....I like being single—I like to check out the merchandise....I love being single—but not alone. That's probably why I have two men instead of one. The thing I like best about being single is there are no commitments. I come and go as I please."[6]**

"The woman must decide," says Gilder. The trouble is that the woman doesn't want to decide. She wants to play it safe, to pretend to decide but to keep "the good divorce" in hand, never to risk everything on the big throw. The woman wants the man to take that risk, even to pay her lawyer to help wreck his family, to deprive him of his property, and to attack his character. The feminist revolt has made women's "greater natural control and discretion" spurious. This control came from "the wall"; it was something they formerly learnt from the socialization which made ladies of them. Today's feminist movement rejects this patriarchal socialization. Such rejection has this corollary: It is fathers rather than mothers who must now take responsibility for maintaining the two-parent reproductive unit. This is the real success of feminism.

Things are different under matriarchy. There unsocialized women, women who "don't want to live the kind of life their mothers lived," have no need to exercise "greater sexual control and discretion," as Gilder would discover from reading Chapter 13 of Briffault's *The Mothers*, from which the following is extracted. (No apologies for the length of this. The Gilders and the judges need to know what women are really like when they lack patriarchal socialization. These savage women and girls have achieved the primary goal of feminism, control over their own sexuality.)

> **Among the tribes of the Gran Chaco the great majority of children were destroyed. The Abipones never brought up more than two children in a family; all others were killed to save trouble. The Lengua and Mbaya women do not usually bring up more than one child, namely the one which they believe will be their last. The Guaycurus and the Lules not only killed all their pre-nuptial children, but a woman brought up only the children which she**

---

[6] *Los Angeles Times Magazine, 18 October, 1987.*

might have after she was thirty. Children born in wedlock are thus disposed of in primitive societies at least as commonly as those born out of it....When, as among the Masai and other northern Bantu, and the 'areoi' society of the Friendly Islands, abortion or infanticide is regarded as obligatory in the case of extra-nuptial children, the object of the rule is that no restriction should be placed on the promiscuous character of the sexual relations by the establishment of any bonds of parenthood. "The Aleutian women are, properly speaking, not so much women as animal females; all notion of shame or modesty is unknown to them."..."An Aleutian who I questioned on the subject," he [Count Langsdorff] adds, "answered me with perfect indifference that his nation in this respect followed the example of sea-dogs and sea-otters."...Father Morice says that the description given by Father Demers is only too fully justified, and cites his report that the Dene "know of no moral restraint; promiscuity seems to enjoy an uncontroverted right. They outdo animals in the infamy of their conduct." Father Morice refers also to the account of McLean, who states that "the lewdness of the women cannot possibly be carried to a greater excess. They are addicted to the most abominable practices, abandoning themselves in early youth to the free indulgence of their passions. They never marry until satiated with indulgence." ...[S]exual intercourse before puberty with strangers is regarded by the Dene as absolutely imperative. They believe that menstruation cannot make its appearance without such pre-nuptial intercourse, and when missions were established amongst them nothing astonished them more than the discovery of the fact that a virgin could menstruate....Even at the present day the surviving American Indian communities that keep to themselves in the Indian Reserves have not essentially modified their native customs. Dr. Currier, who has very carefully collected reports from medical men, concludes that "there are few of the tribes, yet uncivilized, in which women are compelled by custom and sentiment to be virtuous."[7]...The Dume Pygmies...have no idea of morality whatsoever, the young men and girls indulging in promiscuous intercourse with one another....The Igorots of Luzon place their daughters in the "olag" at a very tender age; there they have complete freedom to receive the visits of boys and young men. Even married men at times visit the girls' "olags." Boys generally visit several of these girls' houses where they spend the night with various young girls. The girls themselves solicit boys and men. One way in which they do this is by stealing a man's pipe, his cap, and even his breeches. He is then obliged to come at night and recover his property....There is among the Igorots [Dr. Jenks says] no conception of modesty. "There is no such thing as virtue, in our sense of the word, among the young people after puberty."..."There is not much to be said about their morals," says one of the more recent explorers, "for, I am sorry to say, they have none." They "do not understand what feminine virtue signifies, says Mr. Willshire. The Australian aborigines...are marked by

---

[7]These are the Indian squaws whom Ms. Boulding holds up as exemplars for American middle-class women to emulate. The non-virtuousness of these women explains much about the poverty and squalor of Indian reservations and the "inner serenity and quiet sureness" of these women. They will not submit to patriarchal regulation.

"absolute incapacity to form an even rudimentary notion of chastity." To them, says another writer, the virtue of chastity is "not even comprehensible as an object or motive of conduct." "Of chastity," says Mr. Jukes speaking of the natives of northern Queensland, "they have no idea." "Chastity or fidelity," says Mr. Taplin, "are quite unknown to them." "Chastity is quite unknown amongst them" says Mr. Beveridge, "and it is a hopeless task endeavouring to make them understand the value of the virtue."..."The natives," says Dr. Eylmann, "know no restraint in the satisfaction of their sexual passions." "One of the darkest features in the aboriginal character," says Mr. Parker, "is its gross sensuality. I cannot portray the appalling details of the dark picture." Mr. Parker was well acquainted with most of the tribes of New South Wales and Victoria; "I find but little difference in the habits and customs of the people," he reports: "I see everywhere the same gross and beastly sensuality." "No one but he who has occasion to mix frequently with the natives," says another witness to the sexual depravity of the aborigines, "can form a correct opinion on the subject."...The female children, reports a missionary in evidence supplied to the Colonial Office, are "cradled in prostitution, as it were, and fostered in licentiousness." Australian women "exhibit the worst type of unchastity. They crawl on hands and knees through the long grass to cohabit with other blacks who have no right to their companionship." The Australian females, says Dr. Eylmann, appear, many of them, to be absolute nymphomaniacs. It is difficult to restrain young girls even in the mission schools; the teachers themselves are not immune from their direct solicitations. It has been found impossible to conduct mixed classes of aboriginal children, even of the tenderest age.

This is matriarchy in savage societies, societies where women and girls are free to bestow their love freely and joyously. In civilized societies, things are more discreet, as Dalma Heyn's adulteresses attest, but nevertheless "the day of the kept woman is over," and "women's struggle against the assertion of male entitlement to their bodies is not so different," in Ms. Eisler's opinion, "from the struggle against the assertion for freedom that led to the establishment of the United States of America by what were once British colonies...the right to self-determination."[8] "Wherever," says Briffault, "individual women enjoy, in a *cultured* society, a position of power, they avail themselves of their independence to exercise a sexual liberty."[9] I have quoted Sjöö and Mor: "The first law of matriarchy is that women control our own bodies."[10] Gilder doesn't know these secrets; he imagines the ladies of his acquaintance, who receive the benefits spoken of in Briffault's Law would behave themselves and accept the patriarchal system in the absence of

[8]Riane Eisler, *Sacred Pleasure*, p. 352.
[9]Briffault, abridged by G. Ratray Taylor, p. 386; emphasis added.
[10]*The Great Cosmic Mother*, p. 200.

the benefits. "The female responsibility for civilization cannot be granted or assigned to men," Gilder says.[11] In fact, this responsibility is created and partly delegated by men, and accepted by women because of its accompanying benefits.

PATRIARCHY'S BENEFITS TO WOMEN

Feminist Riane Eisler complains that "in patriarchal societies the issue is not what women do or do not do, but the fact that it is women who do it":

> **In the patriarchal scale of values, it is a woman's time and efforts which are not respected. Consequently whatever women do, be it housekeeping, bank-telling, typing, or child-rearing, is never highly rewarded, economically or socially.**

> **It is for this reason that no existing American divorce law provides payment to a woman for raising her children, and that child-support awards, like welfare payments, deal only with the expenses needed by a woman to feed, clothe, and house her children, but not with any compensation for her services. It explains why whole professions decline in status and pay as soon as women are admitted in sizable numbers, and why the massive movement of women into the general labor market has not and will not equalize the situation.[12]**

Ms. Eisler's "explanation" is no more than a tautology: women's services are undervalued because they are undervalued. The explanation of the explanation is that men have more aggression than women and that society organizes itself to reward greater male aggression when it is properly socialized, lest, as in the ghettos, it become anti-social. When patriarchy does utilize this aggression everyone benefits, including women and children.

Debold, Wilson and Malave make this benefit into a grievance:

> **The invention of motherhood as we know it, safely nestled in the nuclear family, ensured the increased consumption of goods necessary to a growing economy.[13]**

---

[11]*Men and Marriage*, p. 13.
[12]Riane Eisler, *Dissolution*, pp. 180f.
[13]*Mother Daughter Revolution*, p. 248.

It ensured the wife the privilege of spending three-quarters of her husband's paycheck. It allowed this greater consumption, of which women were the beneficiaries. Debold, Wilson and Malave wish to represent this consumption as some kind of victimization of women, poor things. Fact is, it has made American women living in nuclear families the envy of the rest of the world's women. Feminist Jessie Bernard calls their spending of Dad's paycheck "women's extra burden of economic dependence."[14] Isn't that precious?

The feminist revolution and the Mother Daughter Revolution and the anthropological evidence offered by Briffault show that women left to themselves do *not* manifest "the intelligent and controlled female sexuality that makes civilized human communities possible." Patriarchally socialized women want the benefits of patriarchy enough to make patriarchal civilization possible. Men must be able to *confer* these benefits on them and to *deny* benefits to them when they withdraw their loyalty from the patriarchal system.

A BOY IS LISTENING

Boys are listening when the feminist teacher tells girls "You want to have a career so that you won't have to depend on a man." That feminist teacher aims a deadly blow at the boys' motivation; a boy recognizes himself as that superfluous man who will have no meaningful role in the life of a successful woman, a woman who "doesn't want to live the kind of life her mother led," who doesn't want to be "chained" to a stable marriage contract, to pregnancy and parturition and diaper-changing and getting up at night with the baby.

The feminist revolution tells girls they don't have to put up with these things, that marriage vows aren't binding on the woman, that if they break them they are still entitled to custody of their children and a third of their ex-husband's paycheck. This is what women's liberation is all about.

---

[14]Jessie Bernard, *The Future of Marriage* (New York: Bantam, 1972), p. 322.

XX) GANGBANGING AND ILLEGITIMACY

Father Gregory Boyle, former director of Dolores Mission in the Los Angeles barrio, laments that "The week before Christmas, I had to bury the 40th young person killed by what is still a plague in my Eastside community. I've grown weary of saying that gangbanging is the urban poor's version of teen-age suicide....Poor, unemployed youth are hard-pressed to conjure up images of themselves as productive and purposeful adults sometime in their future."[1]

Father Boyle also describes the girls' problem—which is not gangbanging but sexual promiscuity:

> **The 15-year-old girl, bounding ecstatically into my office with the news of her pregnancy, explains, "I just want to have a kid before I die." She says this not because she's been diagnosed as having a terminal illness, but because she lives in my community—a place of early death and where the young lack the imagination to see something better.**

Father Boyle is a little lacking in imagination himself, for he supposes that the familiar litany about poverty, racism and discrimination points to the real problem. He fails to see the causal connection between the boy who gets himself killed and the girl who pretends to be "ecstatic" over becoming pregnant "before I die." The behavior of each is routine in a matriarchy where neither males nor females can hope for stable families—because females insist on controlling their own sexuality rather than sharing it with husbands, and because the resulting male amotivation makes males poor marriage material. The community he describes is one where social arrangements do *not* chain women so that men can depend on having families with them. The girl supposes that turning to sexual promiscuity is an affirmation of life, in contrast to the boys' choice of death. But her words "before I die" show that her ecstasy is a pretense and that her offspring will recycle the same matriarchal pattern of female promiscuity resulting in male violence. Without stable families there is reduced hope for both boys and girls. The girl brings a fatherless child into the world because she inhabits a matriarchy where females control their own sexuality and

---

[1]*Los Angeles Times, 6 January, 1995.*

can deny males families. "One does not move freely and joyously ahead," says Ms. Friedan, "if one is always torn by conflicts and guilts, nor if one feels like a freak in a man's world, if one is always walking a tightrope between being a good wife and mother and fulfilling one's commitment to society...."[2] Fact is, society's primary demand of women is that they accept the responsibility of being good wives and mothers, that they perform their maternal functions—the most important functions of society—with competence. Ms. Friedan wants to minimize the importance of these functions while maximizing the far less important goal of becoming an elitist career woman, which she supposes means "fulfilling one's commitment to society"—and in probable consequence becoming a poorer wife and mother, certainly more divorce-prone.

"Men," says Dr. Popenoe, "need cultural pressure to stay engaged with their children, and that cultural pressure has long been called marriage....Currently marriage is an institution that is quietly fading away....[A] man's chances of staying with the mother are considerably lower when he is not formally married. We should increase social, cultural, and economic supports to help couples stay married."[3] He should have added "*legal* support." A man's assurance that he will have custody of his children will make the mother's chances of staying with the father higher—and will make his chances of staying with the mother higher, for he will not wish to place himself in the situation of today's single mothers.

"I would warn you," says Ms. Friedan,

that those societies where women are most removed from the full action of the mainstream are those where sex is considered dirty and where violence breeds.

By "women" Ms. Friedan means middle-class, educated white women, by "full action of the mainstream" she means elitist careers where women are economically independent and, not incidentally, free to follow a liberated matriarchal lifestyle and engage in adulterous adventures—to "do bad and feel good." For lower-class inner city black women who are two generations in advance of their white sisters down the slippery slope into matriarchy, this lifestyle has developed into a

---

[2]*It Changed My Life*, p. 70.
[3]David Popenoe, *Life Without Father: Compelling New Evidence that Fatherhood and Marriage Are Indispensable for the Good of Children and Society* (New York: Martin Kessler Books,1996), p. 198.

virtually complete rejection of the patriarchal family, to an illegitimacy rate verging towards 80 percent and a male demoralization and amotivation which traps one-third of young black males in the criminal justice system. It does not serve the purposes of Ms. Friedan's propaganda to say what she knows as well as the rest of us, that it is here in the matriarchy that *real* violence breeds. "Where stable family life has been the norm for men and boys," says David Courtwright, "violence and disorder have diminished. That was one important reason why, during the mid-twentieth century marriage boom [=the era of the feminine mystique, when women were "most removed from the full action of the mainstream"], violent death rates showed a sustained decline."[4]

Ms. Friedan continues:

If we confront the real conditions that oppress men now as well as women and translate our rage into action, then and only then will sex really be liberated to be an active joy and a receiving joy for women and for men, when we are both really free to be all we can be.[5]

Everyone who reads the newspapers knows that the high crime areas are those where females *are* sexually de-regulated, "liberated," "unchained," and where men are denied a family role. "The rage women have so long taken out on themselves, on their own bodies, and covertly on their husbands and children, is exploding now," says Ms. Friedan.[6] Men prefer this rage to be bottled up rather than "exploding now." Automatic mother custody provides a major motive for the explosions of divorce and adultery, by which feminists de-regulate themselves. The "rage" they affect to justify this de-regulation is mostly spurious—which is why, as I explain on page 216 "extreme cruelty" (the legal fiction which embarrassed even judges and lawyers) had to be replaced by No Fault. Nothing would do more to prevent the explosion than automatic father custody. Nothing would do more to make divorce court judges behave themselves than letting them know they are not paid salaries to facilitate the explosion of women's rage in divorce actions which displace fathers.

Women, like men, must accept regulation if children are to have fathers and grow up in two-parent homes. Father custody is the most humane way of imposing this regulation, far more humane than

---

[4]David Courtwright, *Violent Land* (Cambridge, MA: Harvard University Press, 1996), p. 280.
[5]*It Changed My Life*, p. 144.
[6]*Ibid.*

gynaecia, harems, chadors, clitoridectomies, foot-binding, suttee. Father custody would make wives see the benefits they receive, those required by Briffault's Law—a family, children, a home, the father's paycheck, the higher status conferred by patriarchy. Mother custody with equal division of the property—the "assets of the marriage after there is no marriage"—is the big temptation which the legal system dangles before the wife—since "children belong with their mother." It is this sanctity of motherhood which transforms "marriage in contemplation of divorce" into solid cash.

The real sanctity of motherhood, and of wifehood, and of family, was understood by Queen Victoria's prime minister, Benjamin Disraeli: "The nation is represented by a family, the royal family; and if that family is educated with a sense of responsibility and a sense of public duty, it is difficult to exaggerate the salutary effect they may exercise over the nation."

The feminist revolution emphasizes two things: (1) male reproductive marginality; (2) women's reluctance to de-marginalize the male by allowing him to share in reproduction. It fails to emphasize the need for the legal system to enforce the marriage contract. This betrayal of marriage and the family by the legal system is what has permitted the feminist revolution and the consequences noted on pages 12ff.

The solution is obvious: father custody. "It is [Princess Diana's] greatest concern," wrote her biographer Andrew Morton, "that her children will be taken away from her.[7] If Diana had really known this would happen all would have been well. She would have known that it was Charles who gave her children, her royal status, her wealth, her admired situation in British society as one of the most glamorous women in the world. He did not make her "irrational, unreasonable and hysterical...her behavior ...endangering the future of her marriage, the country and the monarchy itself."[8]

With automatic mother custody, the "enormous potential, and *natural*, counterforce" against regulation came into play. Chaucer's Wyf of Bath told us that what women want most is mastery over their husbands. Ehrenreich, Hess and Jacobs tell us "The clitorally aware

---

[7] Morton, *Diana: Her New Life* (New York: Simon and Schuster, 1994), p.10.
[8] Morton, p. 162.

woman is sexually voracious to the point of being a threat to the social order."[9] This is partly because

much of [her] private dissatisfaction centered on marital sex, which fell short of being a glowing payoff for a life of submersion in domestic detail. At the same time, new opportunities were opening up for women. As jobs for women proliferated, young single women crowded into the major cities, and began to enlarge the gap between girlhood and marriage, filling it with careers, romances, and—what was distinctly new—casual sexual adventures.

Female promiscuity before marriage, female adultery within marriage[10] and the appalling divorce rate, mostly female initiated, all work to destroy families and undermine men's desire for them and for legitimate children. The "distinctly new...casual sexual adventures" made possible by female economic emancipation are what make father custody especially needed today. The only means of restoring what marriage has to offer males is for society to guarantee men custody of their children regardless of female sexual irresponsibility. "The more decisively sex can be uncoupled from reproduction, through abortion and contraception," say Ehrenreich, Hess and Jacobs, "the more chance women have to approach it lightly and as equal claimants of pleasure....[S]ex has been overly burdened with oppressive 'meanings,' and especially for women."[11]

Uncoupling sex from reproduction is an aim incompatible with civilized society, which must make reproduction its most serious business, and must support the two-parent family by supporting the father's role. Women who wish to uncouple sex from reproduction—to be promiscuous—must be prevented from claiming custody of children procreated within marriage.

A woman's claimed right to control her own sexuality has two corollaries: the man's right to control his own paycheck and his obligation not to let it be used for alimony and child support payments to subsidize the placing of his children in the female kinship system. The primary purpose of marriage and of patriarchal society is to allow children to have fathers. They can have mothers—and the mess described on pages 12ff.–without patriarchy. The primary purpose of the

---

[9]*Re-Making Love*, p. 70.
[10]*Ibid.*, p. 165: "Among *Playboy*'s readers, young married wives were 'fooling around' more than their husbands."
[11]Pp. 196, 9.

feminist revolution is to deprive children of fathers (though not of their paychecks), thus releasing women from sexual regulation.

The main means for bringing about this result, simplicity itself, is indicated by Ms. Heyn. "The original immutable marriage contract," she says, "a commitment to permanence, has shifted to a commitment to the quality of the relationship—a mutable phenomenon if there ever was one—so if one partner or other decides the quality has diminished sufficiently, all the court has to do is simply agree and the marriage is over."[12] And Mom walks away with the kids. So the marriage contract is no contract at all.

A University of Chicago study concludes that "marriage in the U.S. is a "weakened and declining institution" because "women are getting less and less out of it."[13] The opposite is true of divorce, because women are getting more and more out of it—or expecting to, an expectation encouraged by judges and politicians ("We will find you. We will make you pay.") The way to make marriage deliver more is to have divorce deliver less.

Feminist Marilyn French repeats the feminist party line when she says "[W]omen choosing to raise their children alone is not a social problem unless it is accompanied by severe poverty,"[14] but the facts disprove her. Divorce and single motherhood are unhealthful for children. "Marriage," says Nicholas Eberstadt of the Harvard Center for Population and Development Studies, "is a far more powerful predictor of infant mortality than money: If the mother is unmarried, the risk of death to her infant more than doubled....Despite the well-established link between education and infant health, *a baby born to a college educated unwed mother is far more likely to die than a baby born to married high school dropouts.*[15] Similarly with the other problems mentioned on pages 12ff.

Lesbian feminist Laura Benkov says of her fellow lesbian feminist Adrienne Rich that she "saw the institution of motherhood as inextricably bound to the institution of heterosexuality and the oppression of women":

---

[12]Heyn, p. 53.
[13]Heyn, p. 52.
[14]*War Against Women*, p. 142.
[15]Maggie Gallagher, *The Abolition of Marriage*, p. 42; emphasis in original.

She pointedly questioned the nature of motherhood in our society. What ideas about mothering do women bring to the experience of raising children? How do these ideas affect family relationships? Where do these ideas come from? And most important of all, What other possible ways of constructing motherhood are available? Describing time spent alone with her three young sons, she wrote:

[W]e fell into what I felt to be a delicious and sinful rhythm. It was a spell of unusually hot, clear weather, and we ate nearly all our meals outdoors, hand to mouth; we lived half naked, stayed up to watch bats and stars and fireflies, read and told stories, slept late. I watched their slender, little-boys' bodies grow brown, we washed in water warm from the garden hose lying in the sun, we lived like castaways on some island of mothers and children. At night they fell asleep without a murmur and I stayed up reading and writing as when a student, till the early morning hours. I remember thinking: This is what living with children could be—without school hours, fixed routines, naps, the conflict of being both mother and wife with no room for being simply myself....We were conspirators, outlaws from the institution of motherhood; I felt enormously in charge of my life.[16]

The passage shows how many women feel about the patriarchal system. She got rid of her husband; she has economic independence; she is de-regulated. And she likes it that way. So do many women. Feminist Kate Chopin describes the sadness and exhilaration of a woman who hears that her husband has died in a railroad wreck: "She will miss him, but loves her freedom more."[17] This is the matriarchal pattern, that of Ms. Boulding's Indian squaw, that of the ghetto matriarch. Ms. Rich had divorced her husband, deprived him of his children and the poor man, driven to despair, killed himself. She was liberated; he was dead, a small price, we are to suppose, for Ms. Rich's freedom to be "enormously in charge of my life" and having custody of her three sons, who, however, will not wish to live the kind of life their father led, as Marcia Clark's sons and tens of millions of other sons living in female headed households will not wish to live the kid of life their fathers led—just as Ms. Coontz's and Ms. Breines's and Ms. Debold's and Ms. Wilson's and Ms. Malave's girls did not wish to lead the kind of life their mothers led. Females, clearly, are chafed by patriarchal marriage; males have hitherto had to depend on it if they want to have families, but they are coming to realize, as Adrienne Rich's husband and Marcia Clark's husband came to realize, that they can no longer depend on it: if their wives choose to drag

---

[16]Adrienne Rich, *Of Woman Born: Motherhood as Experience and Institution* (New York: Norton, 1976), p. 195; cited in Benkov, p. 22.
[17]In her "Story of an Hour."

them into the divorce court the judge will deprive them of their children and the role on which they hoped to build their lives.

Ms. Benkov's comment on Rich's thinking is this:

As an "outlaw from the institution of motherhood," Rich discovered the pleasure of being in charge of her own life and the joy of being able to be herself along with her children, who also were able to be themselves. Noting these feelings as extraordinary, she thought about how her usual experience of mothering made her feel less in control of her life. She recognized that this loss of control was not a necessary corollary of motherhood but rather a direct consequence of particular societal expectations of mothers—expectations quintessentially linked to women's oppression....When a mother extricates herself from the experience of oppression and begins to value her capacity to act from a strong sense of herself, both she and her children can thrive.[18]

This is code language for getting rid of the father and returning to the female kinship system, where Mom runs things and Dad is a boyfriend or an exile—or in this case a cadaver. Ms. Rich extricates herself from "the experience of oppression" and "both she and her children can thrive." Much of the thriving of the single mother is done in the "feminization of poverty"[19] and "her children" are eight times more likely to become delinquents. The one-third of fatherless ghetto males who do their thriving in prison, jail, on probation or parole are being joined by increasing numbers of fatherless whites, "the growing white underclass."

How the fatherless male children of the matriarchal ghettos will thrive when they grow up is indicated by the following from the *Los Angeles Times* for 5 October, 1995:

Nearly one in three African American men in their 20s is in jail, prison, on probation or parole—a sharp increase over the approximately 25% of five years ago, a study concluded Wednesday....African American women in their 20s showed the greatest jump of all demographic groups under criminal justice supervision—up 78% from 1989 to 1994....What has changed in recent years is the age composition of those males engaged in violent crime, particularly with a substantial and disturbing increase in the murder rate of young black men since the mid-1980s.

---

[18]Benkov, p. 22; emphasis added.
[19]Ms. Rich thinks the burdens laid down by fathers should be picked up by taxpayers: "Both major parties have displayed a crude affinity for the interests of corporate power while deserting the majority of the people, especially the most vulnerable." ("Why I refused the National Medal for the Arts," *Los Angeles Times*, 3 August, 1997)

This is the way things drift when Mom is "enormously in charge of her life" and "extricated from oppression," sexually de-regulated, or "unchained." The crucial lack is male motivation. Formerly this motivation was created by women's acceptance of sexual law-and-order—including the "feminine mystique," the most important feature of the feminine mystique being the female chastity which made families possible. Women's rejection of sexual regulation is destroying it. Women's former acceptance of patriarchy gave men a role, gave them families, and society thrived. Ms. Benkov would like us to suppose that women and children thrive in the female kinship system, but the ghettos, the areas of feminized poverty, are the least thriving parts of society.

It was the great discovery of Ms. Friedan that women hated this thriving patriarchal society. Also girls, as signified by Ms. Breines's title, *Young, White and Miserable*, where young females talk like this:

[I]t was clear to me...I did not want my life to be anything like my mother's life!...None of us wanted to do any of the things our mothers did—nor anything the way they did it—during the postwar years.[20]

They didn't want to live as their mothers did during the era of the Feminine Mystique. They wanted to live like the black girls whose lifestyle elicits the admiration of Debold, Wilson and Malave:

[W]ithin segments of the African-American community, mothers are granted respect and authority that, by and large, non-African-American mothers are not.[21]

This confuses authority and power. A wife may have unlimited power over her husband and be able to get him to do anything she wishes, yet have no authority—and if she tries to exercise authority she loses her power. Black men are denied authority in order that black women may be promiscuous. This is why the ghettos are "hostile and dangerous"—the danger coming from other blacks. Debold, Wilson and Malave would like to reduce white society to the same matriarchal pattern so that white women can enjoy the same liberation as these admired black women. This is the "revolution" of their title.

---

[20]Breines, p. 78. The title of Ms. Breines' book *Young, White and Miserable* suggests the alternative title *Young, Black and Happy*—but white girls wouldn't want to live in the ghetto, any more than boys would.
[21]*Mother Daughter Revolution*, pp. 14, 131.

White mothers have the power to spend three-quarters of their husbands' paychecks, in part because they acknowledge male authority. The black mothers have both authority and power—but they spend a smaller paycheck. The white mothers give up authority to gain power and they spend three-quarters of a larger paycheck.

To say that "women compete against each other" is to say men have bargaining power, something to offer women, this being their income and status, things which lift a society out of matriarchy and civilize it. Such men are worth competing for, just as attractive and chaste women are worth competing for. When such men and women find each other they create stable families and well-behaved, high-achieving children. It ought to be the object of social policy to get such people together to create such children. Debold, Wilson and Malave don't want women to compete with each other, but a society in which women think men aren't worth competing for would be a society in which men are low achievers or anti-social, like many men in the ghettos, whose women Debold, Wilson and Malave wish white girls to imitate. It would be a society in which most women would be worth competing for only on the shallowest basis, for their desirability as partners in short-term, unmeaningful relationships.

The patriarchal culture they wish to undermine is condemned as "sexist." It is sex-centered in the sense that it puts sex to work for the most worthwhile and long-term goals, those related to the family, the future and the overall good of society. Also the past, for in such societies ancestors are revered. Where there is no such regard for the past there will be little regard for the future or concern for those united by family ties.

Feminist sociologist Stephanie Coontz was quoted on page 173 as complaining that the double standard increases the number of prostitutes. The double standard is part of the patriarchal idea, a means of motivating males to support families, of elevating the status of chaste women deemed to be suitable wives, and lowering the status of unchaste women, those for whom Ms. Coontz is concerned. Feminists would like to obliterate the distinction between good and bad women. Women who have premarital sex have an eighty percent higher divorce rate. Formerly they would have been condemned as bad women and unsuitable marriage material. Now the feminist revolution considers such condemnation to be "sexist." Thus a correspondent to Ann Landers:

DEAR ANN: I read those 12 guidelines to help sons choose a mate, and I think some of them are clearly sexist. No. 3, for example, says to leave her alone if "she has sex with you on the first date." Well, if she had sex, so did he.

The same goes for the one that says to leave her alone if "she can get her pantyhose off in less than five seconds. It means she has had lots of practice." If the man has had enough experience to set a time limit, he, too, has had "too much experience."...

I have no beef with the man's warning signals, but why didn't you point out that some of these red flags also reflected poorly on men? It is considered perfectly OK for men to have one-night stands, get drunk and want sex on the first date, but women who do this are called tramps. It's time men were held to the same standard.

Ann Landers' reply is naive—"Thanks for nailing those male chauvinist attitudes." The man's primary contribution to marriage is his paycheck, the woman's is her sexual loyalty. If what she offers is accompanied by the threat of an eighty percent greater divorce rate, and if the legal system automatically gives her custody of his children he is a ruddy fool not to consider the woman poor marriage material. And telling women their unchastity makes them no less attractive as potential wives is no favor to women (or men). The good new life as seen by Ann Landers is that previously described by Ehrenreich, Hess and Jacobs, where young single women crowd into the cities in search of sexual adventures.

FATHERS AND BOYFRIENDS

Patriarchy separates the "good" women, who delay sex, from the bad ones, the madonnas from the whores, the women who are willing to give men families from the women who are willing to give them one-night stands. Men and women who think that our divorce rate and illegitimacy rate are unconscionably high ought to see that these rates are the result of the sexual revolution which tries to obliterate the distinction between good and bad women, between legitimate and illegitimate children, between fathers and boyfriends—and the result of the legal system's perverse promotion of the female kinship system, of which bad women are the principal "beneficiaries."

Ms. Friedan speaks of women's "inalienable" right to control their own bodies—regardless of a marriage contract. The meaningfulness and

340

enforceability of that contract are essential to the patriarchal system and since the law has now come around to the feminist view and refuses to enforce it, fathers must remove discretion from the legal system and take custody of their own children. The legal system will not support the family and accordingly it is necessary to remove all discretion from it and make father custody automatic and mandatory. The present situation is too threatening to men—and children and good women. Men once trusted women's commitment to the contract and the legal system's commitment to enforce it. Neither commitment is now taken seriously. Ms. Friedan speaks for millions of women when she says woman's right to disregard it is "inalienable." Judge Noland speaks for most judges when he says human reproduction ought to be modeled on that of cattle. It is no wonder so many men are afraid of marriage, afraid of judges willing to do the bidding of disloyal wives—judges whose weakness encourages wives to *be* disloyal.

The maintenance of the distinction between good and bad women (and men) is essential to the patriarchal system, to maintaining family stability and the procreation of legitimate children. The *breakdown* of this distinction is essential to the feminist program. Feminists wish to trivialize this breakdown. Ms. Coontz says: "Much of the modern sexual revolution consists *merely* of a decline in the double standard, with girls adopting sexual behaviors that were pioneered much earlier by boys."[22] "Pioneered" suggests progress—that the girls are catching up to a good thing already enjoyed by the boys. Ms. Coontz, however, realizes the magnitude of the sexual revolution:

> **Much of the new family topography is permanent. It is the result of a major realignment of subterranean forces, much like plate tectonics and continental drift. Women will never again spend the bulk of their lives at home. Sex and reproduction are no longer part of the same land mass, and no amount of pushing and shoving can force them into a single continent again.**[23]

Sex and reproduction are no longer part of the same land mass for liberated women, for squaws on Indian reservations, for ghetto matriarchs like Rosa Lee, for women who don't need men—for women living in the female kinship system. But suppose men woke up to the realization that for them, since they need the male kinship system which exploits male aggression and creates male motivation—for them sex and

---

[22] *The Way We Never Were*, p. 185; emphasis added.
[23] p. 204.

reproduction must be part of the same land mass because sex and reproduction and work and creativity and responsibility and family life are all interconnected and the loss of their children is the loss of everything. Men must, if they are not to lose everything, be assured of the custody of their children and must refuse to share their paychecks with women who discard the double standard which enables men to participate as equals in reproduction.

"New family patterns," says Ms. Coontz, "are the result of pluralism, increased tolerance, and the growth of informed choice."[24] These bad things are thus explained by Ann Landers: "Many more women are in the workplace. They have more visibility, more mobility, more temptations and greater economic independence....Is the trend toward infidelity going to change? I don't see how. Cheating on spouses is now an equal-opportunity sport."[25]

Equal opportunity but unequal damage, since the woman's sexual loyalty to the man is of greater importance to him than is his sexual loyalty to her. Her sexual loyalty is her primary contribution to marriage, comparable only to her husband's economic loyalty. This breaking down of patriarchy seems natural to women because it *is* natural, because patriarchy itself is artificial, dependent on the stability of fatherhood. Men and children must have the patriarchal family—and men must not be jollied into subsidizing its deadly enemy, the female-headed matriline, with AFDC and child support money.

"Black girls," says feminist Marie Richmond-Abbott,

who are less eager to marry, show higher self-esteem, more independence, and much less fear of success than do white girls....The woman may be reluctant to be tied to a man she feels is not worth the restrictions. He may be reluctant to take on the role of provider, particularly if he feels that he will not be able to fulfill it well.[26]

They have high unemployment because they lack the motivation provided by families. The "strong family connections" of black girls described by Debold, Wilson and Malave are not family ties at all, but matriarchal ties. Few of these girls have fathers. The "fewer resources"

---

[24]p. 185.
[25]*Los Angeles Times*, 15 Dec., 1991.
[26]Marie Richmond-Abbott, *Masculine and Feminine: Sex Roles Over the Life Cycle* (Menlo Park, CA: 1983), pp. 173, 285.

and the loss of "economic security" are the price they pay for living in the matriarchy and being able to avoid collision with "the wall" of patriarchy—being able to escape patriarchal socialization.

Debold, Wilson and Malave quote Beverly Jean Smith, an African-American educator: "When I read the psychological research about mother-daughter relationships, mostly what strikes me is daughters' pain, anger, hate, rejection, fear and struggle to find self....This way of speaking about the mother-daughter relationship runs counter to my experience."

In fact, Smith tells us, what research there is suggests stronger connections between African-American mothers and daughters: "A decisive 94.5 percent expressed respect for their mothers in terms of strength, honesty, ability to overcome difficulties and ability to survive."[27]

This female solidarity explains why so many of them live in ghettos:

At the edge of adolescence every girl collides with the wall of the culture. But this wall is not simply made of the power relations between women and men. There are other bricks in the wall: racism, classism, homophobia, and bias against persons with disabilities.

"Earning all the stuff" enables men to have families. Girls don't need to earn all the stuff, as boys must if they are to find wives. It is earned, not a gift. Patriarchy, let it be said again, is the system which creates a civilized male role, enabling males to claim their status in families by their achievement. Hence Arthur's Education Fund, which enables Arthur to support a wife and children. This is why men earn more than women: they must and they know it. They know that ghettos result from men's not earning more than women—and women not needing men.[28] Briffault's Law. Women earning as much as men would wreck the patriarchal system by making males superfluous and roleless.

According to William Murchison,

Between 1983 and 1993 births to unwed mothers soared by more than 70%. This means that 6.3 million children under 18 lived last year with a never-married parent. The truly astounding thing, perhaps, is to look back three decades to 1960. How many children lived that year with a never-married

---

[27] *Mother Daughter Revolution*, p. 56.
[28] I discuss this further in the 9th chapter of my *Garbage Generation*.

parent?   Just 243,000.   Since that time, we have undergone social revolution.[29]

According to the *Los Angeles Times*, "Nearly 500,000 teen-agers have babies annually—the highest adolescent birthrate in the developed world." About 90 percent of the federal welfare payouts go to fatherless families "most often started with unwed teenage childbearing."[30]

Many will turn to drugs to forget their problems. According to the *Times*, "African Americans and Latinos were found to constitute nearly 90% of offenders sentenced to state prison for drug possession."

Children have to put up with father-deprivation in order that their Moms may be free to "thrive." Boys must accept matriarchy and a high probability of rolelessness. Girls may like their freedom from sexual regulation but they too are trapped in the role of impoverished single motherhood, where they wonder where the men are.

Judith Wallerstein's study has been cited, showing that only half of the male students she followed completed college, and that forty percent of the young men were drifting—on a downward educational course, out of school, unemployed. When so many of them have seen their fathers expelled from the homes they bought for their families, when they themselves face a sixty percent chance of divorce and the loss of their children and their role, they wonder why they should work as hard as their fathers and grandfathers did in the years after the war. Feminists now say "the ultra-domesticity of the 1950s was a historical aberration,"[31] ultra-domesticity meaning that women accepted sexual regulation and the housewife role. It was the judge's conviction that she (and not her husband) was fitted by nature for this role which gave her custody of the children. But many women—those for whom Betty Friedan wrote *The Feminine Mystique*—knew this domesticity to be an assigned role, unnatural, a "mask," and hated it.

Of course feminists were right that the domesticity of the fifties was artificial. They have proved this by proving what is natural—the matriarchal lifestyle of the ghettos, the barrios, the Indian reservations, the Stone Age, the barnyard, the rain forest. This matriarchy is the natural pattern of human—and all animal—society when there are no

---

[29]*Los Angeles Times*, 14 February, 1995.
[30]*Ibid.*
[31] Ellen Willis, *Los Angeles Times*, 12 January, 1997.

artificial props for patriarchy. Automatic mother custody has enabled
women to destroy the prosperity of millions of males by destroying the
motivation which produced it. This motivation can be restored by
automatic father custody and this motivation will restore the economy of
which William Baumol said in those better days, "In our economy, by
and large, the future can be left to take care of itself."[32]

If you ask a man why he works at his job, he will bring out his
wallet and show you pictures of his family. Males have lost confidence
that a society with a sixty percent divorce rate wants them to be heads of
families rather than providers for ex-families. This is what they hear
when President Clinton tells ex-husbands "We will find you. We will
make you pay." It is what men hear when California ex-Governor Wilson
says, "If you abandon your responsibility to your child...you forfeit the
freedoms and opportunities that come with being a responsible
citizen....We cannot and will not tolerate parents who walk away from
their children."[33] He means men who have been *deprived* of their
children. This is like stabbing a man in the back and accusing him of
carrying a concealed weapon.

The troubles of fatherless boys have led to government programs to
provide them with role models or *mentors* to replace their missing
fathers. Governor Wilson dedicated $15 million for this purpose and
hoped to expand the number of mentors from 70,000 to at least a
million. "Mentoring programs," says the *Los Angeles Times*,

> **are based on the premise that many youth turn to the camaraderie of gangs or
> to destructive peers because they lack a role model to inspire their confidence
> and encourage responsible behavior....The biggest problem facing mentoring
> programs is finding adults willing to volunteer their time.**[34]

There are millions of *fathers* willing to volunteer their time—which
is why they got married. The Governor himself undertook to mentor a
fatherless Sacramento boy "for at least an hour a week." "I am
convinced," he says, "that unless a whole lot of us step forward...a lot of
very decent kids are going to wind up making very tragic mistakes that
hurt themselves and the people who love them and hurt society in a
variety of ways. I think that an awful lot of kids are hungry for the kind

---

[32]Quoted in Sylvia Ann Hewlett, *When the Bough Breaks: The Cost of Neglecting Our Children*
(HarperCollins, 1991), p. 199.
[33]*Los Angeles Times*, 29 September, 1995.
[34]*Los Angeles Times*, 28 April, 1997.

of affection and the kind of attention that they don't get and frequently can't get."

They find it difficult to get it from fathers thrown out of their homes. Governor Wilson imagined that an hour of his mentoring time once a week could replace a real father in a boy's life. Why not instead guarantee the father's role within the family by an assurance that if he undertakes to be a provider for his family he cannot be expelled from it?

Once again: men can end this foolishness by raising their consciousness. If men realized that they were primarily responsible to be *fathers* to their children, not sugar daddies to Mom, not willing handmaidens and servitors to the stupid judges who are wrecking over half of society's families. The judges assume that fathers will accept the injustice they are handed more readily than mothers would, which is why they give mothers custody and victimize the fathers. (I'm repeating, but this needs repeating.) Suppose the fathers saw through this fakery and didn't feel themselves obligated to "go ahead and pay anyway—they're my kids and I love them." Frederic Hayward has the right slant on this:

> **[It] sounds like a kidnapper's demand: "I want money. It's not ransom, because I don't intend to return your child. But still, I'm running low on cash, so start sending me one-third of every pay check from now on." My hunch is that most parents would reply: "You have some nerve asking me to subsidize your torture of me. If you can't afford my child, return it." A father who refuses this extortion, however, is just another Deadbeat Dad....**

> **Imagine your child is kidnapped and you receive a ransom demand. You call the police, but they put you in jail for failing to pay the ransom. Their only concern, they tell you, is that the kidnapper not go on welfare. And insisting that what the child needs most from you is not your love, attention or a relationship but simply money, they cynically tell you that they're looking out for your child's "best interests." How do you feel?[35]**

Blaming the victim. There is virtual unanimity of support for the folly of wrecking families by expelling fathers and then holding them responsible for their own victimization.

"Reno Stepping Up Pursuit of Child-Support Delinquents," says a *Los Angeles Times* headline:

---

[35]*Los Angeles Times*, 7 August, 1985; *Everyman; A Men's Journal*, Sept/Oct, 1997.

Even her severest critics agree on this: More than any other U.S. attorney general in history, Janet Reno has gone to bat for children.[36]

Ms. Reno's program for helping children is more mindlessness—making it easier to deprive them of fathers, making divorce more attractive to mothers, making marriage less attractive to men, encouraging judges to continue discriminating against males as they have been doing for over a century:

Under a recent Reno directive, the Justice Department is stepping up the pursuit and punishment of deadbeat parents who fail to make court-ordered child-support payments after moving across state lines. The move is intended to put sharp teeth into a 1992 law that made the practice a federal crime for the first time.

Prior to the Civil War this was known as a Fugitive Slave Law, punishing slaves who tried to escape from their obligation to perform forced labor for the benefit of another person. Ms. Reno's attempt to enforce slavery is thought to be justified by the following untruth, previously noted:

Reno, the first woman to serve as attorney general, hopes the accelerated enforcement will have a genuine impact on a national problem of staggering proportions. More than half of all court-ordered child support currently goes unpaid, and the accumulated IOUs total an estimated $34 billion.

Susan Faludi complains that ex-husbands are so selfish they don't even want to support their ex-wives. Her argument is the same as Reno's:

The real source of divorced women's woes can be found not in the fine print of divorce legislation but in the behavior of ex-husbands and judges. Between 1978 and 1985, the average amount of child support that divorced men paid fell nearly 25 percent. Divorced men are more likely to meet their car payments than their child support obligations—even though, for two-thirds of them, the amount owed their children is less than their auto loan bill.

As of 1985, only half of the 8.8 million single mothers who were supposed to be receiving child support payments from their ex-husbands actually received any money at all, and only half of that half were actually getting the full amount. In 1988, the federal Officer of Child Support Enforcement was

---

[36]*Los Angeles Times*, 28 December, 1994.

collecting only $5 billion of the $25 billion a year fathers owed in child support.[37]

Ms. Faludi's figures are faked, but apart from the fakery why should an ex-husband pay *anything* to an ex-wife? What services does she perform for him that entitle her to share his income? The support money he is alleged to owe her serves the bad purpose of financing the destruction of his family.

Donna Shalala makes her contribution to the promotion of matriarchy by doubling Ms. Faludi's spurious figure of $25 billion to $50 billion, ten times the true amount. (Lying is OK for a good cause.) According to Stuart Miller, cited on page 151 above, senior legislative analyst for the American Fathers Coalition in Washington, "there was about 10.9 billion in court-ordered child support owed by all Americans, and of that, a little more than $6 billion was paid. That leaves $4.9 billion in unpaid child support for 1992—far short of the $50 billion Ms. Shalala hopes to raise."[38] A better estimate is that half of court-ordered child support is paid in full and another quarter is paid in part. The wildly different estimates are significant; they show how muddled the existing system is, how little anybody knows about what's going on or how little concern there is for the truth, how much concern for saying whatever will promote the feminist program.

Suppose President Clinton could make good on his threat to Deadbeat Dads: "We will find you. We will make you pay." Can it be doubted that child support awards would skyrocket, that divorce would become yet more attractive to women, marriage yet less attractive to men? "Divorce almost always guarantees a woman severe financial hardship," says the *National NOW Times* of Feb/Mar 1989. It is well that it does; it would be better if it guaranteed more hardship. To say that divorce hurts women is to say that marriage benefits women. It is the purpose of marriage to benefit women (and children). Hence the folly of the present system of virtually automatic mother custody and the need for replacing it with automatic father custody. The feminist/political "solution" to the poverty of single mothers is to still further penalize fathers for having undertaken the responsibilities of marriage—more discrimination against men, not only because the ex-wives want the money but also because most of them are resentful of their continued

---

[37]*Backlash*, p. 24.
38*Wall Street Journal*, 2 March, 1995.

dependence, and their resentment makes many of them vindictively rejoice at the law's punishment of their ex-husbands.

Irv Garfinkel, author of *Assuring Child Support,* and Sara McLanahan and President Clinton and virtually every judge are assisting this erosion of marriage. It is astonishing that the manifest connection between matriarchy, family destruction and violence is invisible to these people. The same obtuseness is shown in the following from Garfinkel and McLanahan's book:

Stronger child support enforcement for cases involving out-of-wedlock births is likely to eventually result, in our view, in a decrease in such births by the following reasoning. Increasing the probability that men will have to contribute to the support of children they father out of wedlock will increase their incentives to father fewer children.[39]

Increasing the probability that men will have to contribute to the support of children they father out of wedlock will increase mothers' incentives to bear more children out of wedlock and to make the children they do have fatherless, since many mothers hate patriarchy and many want "the right to have children without having a man around," since, as Betty Friedan says, "our so-called sexual liberation isn't real and isn't possible as long as...women are still trapped in mutual torments and rage by their obsolete sex roles,"[40] and since, as feminist Barbara Seaman says, they believe "the sexual morality of an *individual* is and should be a private matter, for it has no bearing on the general welfare if *she* conducts *herself* responsibly."[41] "If there is going to be a breakthrough in human sexuality," says Ms. Seaman–

and I think such a breakthrough might be in the wind—it is going to be because women will start taking charge of their own sex lives. It is going to

---

[39]P. 154.
[40]Betty Friedan, cited on the dust wrapper of Barbara Seaman's *Free and Female*. The ellipsis omits the words "men and." The full quotation is this: "I firmly believe that our so-called sexual liberation isn't real and isn't possible as long as men and women are still trapped in mutual torment and rage by their obsolete sex roles. But the antisexual reactionaries [=those who believe in the patriarchal family] who would repudiate [=regulate] *women's* [emphasis added] sexuality along with men's are antihuman and antilife. I hope soon all *women* [emphasis added] will be liberated enough to be 'free and female' in Barbara Seaman's sense—to explore and affirm honestly their own sexuality as subject, not object, and to experience a fully human sexual relationship with man."
The *reactionaries* are those who accept the patriarchal principle that sex ought to be channeled into marriage and family life.
[41]Barbara Seaman, *Free and Female: The Sex Life of the Contemporary Woman* (New York: Coward, Macann and Geoghegan, 1972), p. 207; emphasis added. Marriage is a public matter, adultery a private matter; but *responsible* adultery is OK, so Ms. Seaman seems to be saying.

occur because women will stop believing that sex is for men and that men (their fathers, their doctors, their lovers and husbands, their popes and kings and scientists) should call the shots.[42]

It is going to occur because women will stop believing that sex is for men *and children*—and believing that children need fathers. It is going to occur if men are foolish enough to suppose that if they stop calling the shots women will continue to submit to sexual law-and-order and allow men to have families and children to have fathers. It is going to occur because men imagine they ought to continue subsidizing the destruction of their families. Patriarchy, fatherhood and the stabilizing of the two-parent family are only possible when men do call the shots.

"There are women you screw and women you marry." A promiscuous woman places herself in the former category and for doing this Garfinkel and McLanahan propose to reward her with support money. Even on the absurd assumption that they could frighten 90 percent of males into being chaste, the remaining 10 percent would sire as many bastards as the 90 percent, if women are unchaste. The obvious, tried and successful way for making men sexually responsible is by allowing them to be heads of families.

"Parents are obligated by law to support their children," say Garfinkel and McLanahan:

When a parent lives with a child, this obligation is normally met through the course of everyday sharing. When a parent does not live with the child, the obligation is supposed to be discharged through child support—a transfer of income from the noncustodial to the custodial parent....Most noncustodial fathers do not pay even a reasonable amount of child support.[43]

With the exception of a minuscule number of token cases, where enforcement almost never enters the picture, "parents" is interpreted to exclude non-custodial mothers. No judge would dream of compelling an ex-wife to go to the home of an ex-husband who has won custody of her children and mop his floors and do his laundry. The ex-husband's obligations to the ex-wife ought to be identical with the ex-wife's obligations to the ex-husband, which are non-existent. They are identical to his obligations to Frederic Hayward's kidnapper who steals

---

[42] *Ibid.*, p. 49.
[43] P. 24.

his children and then hires a lawyer to drag him into court to collect support money on the ground that he is obligated to support them.

Feminist Sylvia Ann Hewlett makes the same mistake as Garfinkel and McLanahan:

> By rewarding "good" behavior and penalizing "bad" behavior, our divorce laws send a clear signal to citizens about what kind of behavior is valued and what is not, as well as nudging people in the "right" direction by creating an appropriate set of carrots and sticks.
>
> If a divorce court awards a significant amount of spousal and child support to a thirty-year-old homemaker with two preschool children, it is in effect rewarding the woman's devotion to her children and giving her permission to continue to stay home with them. It is also reinforcing heavy ongoing responsibilities on the part of an ex-husband and creating a deterrent effect (severe financial burdens may cause other husbands to think twice before divorcing). But if a divorce court denies the housewife spousal support, awards minimal child support, and tells her she must get a job to support herself and her children, then the legal system is sending out a very different signal. It is opting for day care for the children of divorce and releasing the ex-husband from most of the responsibility for the continued support of his family, thus making divorce a less onerous alternative for many husbands and fathers.[44]

Talk about a double standard! Let's put the shoe on the other foot. If a divorce court awards a significant amount of spousal support to *Dad* it is in effect rewarding the man's devotion to *his* children and giving *him* permission to stay home with them and continue to earn the salary needed to support them and himself. It is also reinforcing heavy ongoing responsibilities on the part of an ex-wife and creating a deterrent effect (severe financial burdens may cause other wives to think twice before divorcing). But if a divorce court denies the father spousal support, awards minimal child support, and tells him he must get a job to support himself and his children, then the legal system is sending out a very different signal. It is opting for day care for the children of divorce and releasing the ex-wife from most of the responsibility for the continued support of her family, thus making divorce a less onerous alternative for many wives and mothers.

---

[44]*When the Bough Breaks*, p. 144.

Ms. Hewlett affects not to know that most divorce actions are initiated by wives. If a divorce court awards a significant amount of spousal and child support to a homemaker it is rewarding the woman's defection from her husband by giving her permission to continue to stay home with "her" children. Increasing the rewards of such women will result in more divorces. Husbands are already deterred from divorce—which is one reason why most divorces are initiated by wives. Ms. Hewlett's proposal will also deter—has already deterred—men from marriage. Recall Ms. Coontz: "At age 29 nearly 40 percent of American men have not yet settled into a stable long-term job."[45] The anti-male bias of the divorce court has frightened them away from marriage. Ms. Coontz has been cited on women's proneness to divorce: "Women, despite initial pain and income loss, tend almost immediately to feel that they benefit from divorce." Ms. Hewlett would increase this benefit, thus exacerbating the already high divorce rate, which will in turn exacerbate the sufferings of the children concerning whom she writes her book—whose subtitle is "The Cost of Neglecting Our Children." Father custody will deter both wives and husbands from divorce.

The Janus survey found that "women were more likely than men to *disapprove* of the mother's taking career time off for child care":

They have heard tales of the reentry—poorer pay, lower ranked position, less or different responsibility, and less interesting work all await women who take a few years' leave of absence to devote to raising their children.[46]

Ms. Hewlett's proposals—and indeed the whole feminist program—de-motivate men from what society ought to induce them to do for their own sake, for the sake of women, children and society—becoming providers for families.

The male must be able to offer a woman a sufficient benefit to induce her to accept the sexual regulation required for family stability—he must "settle into a stable long-term job" and become a family provider. But he must also have society's guarantee that when the woman does accept sexual regulation by entering a marriage contract the contract will be enforced. The legal system is not responsible to create motherhood; it is responsible to create fatherhood and to support it. The

---

[45]*The Way We Never Were*, p. 69.
[46]Samuel and Cynthia Janus, *The Janus Report on Sexual Behavior* (New York: John Wiley and Sons, 1993), p. 211.

fathers' rights movement must make judges and lawmakers understand this. Only in this way can the male's non-biological contribution to marriage be made equivalent to the female's biological contribution. Only thus can men have stable families. Only thus can marriage be made meaningful.

We have on page 24 quoted feminist Susan Faludi's explanation of how the feminist program proposes to make marriage meaningless. She follows this with the *Cosmopolitan* quote we have had from Ehrenreich et al: "The woman we're profiling is an extraordinarily sexually free human being" whose new bedroom expressiveness constitutes a "break with the old double standard." Ms. Faludi cites *Cosmo*'s figure that they have a 41 percent adultery rate. There seems to be no comprehension of how this female sexual promiscuity, this rejection of the double standard, removes the husband's economic responsibility to the wife and along with this the grounds for mother custody. This female withdrawal of sexual loyalty to husbands and to marriage positively requires a complementary male withdrawal of subsidization of these promiscuous women and a switch to father custody. Otherwise there will be matriarchy—since "an extraordinarily sexually free human being" can not have a stable family. Fathers should be grateful to *Cosmopolitan*, to Ehrenreich, Hess and Jacobs and to Ms. Faludi for throwing this ball into their hands. What need is there of further witnesses?

Let me repeat, for it is crucial: Married men bound by a marriage contract are not "at liberty to have sex on their own terms." They pay for it. Women who suppose themselves at liberty to control their own bodies are entitled to no bargaining power at all, for they will use it, as Ms. Faludi acknowledges, to undermine patriarchy and restore matriarchy. "*Women* were at last at liberty," Faludi says—oblivious to the distinction between good and bad women, women willing to give a man a family and women who marry in contemplation of divorce and continued subsidization by an ex-husband.

It is women's loyalty to the male kinship system and to their families which entitles them to the benefits bestowed by patriarchy on *good* women. The female sexual disloyalty which Ms. Faludi celebrates is incomparably more threatening and damaging to civilized society than men's philandering. It makes the man's role in reproduction meaningless and reduces the woman's role in reproduction to what it is in the ghetto. It forfeits the woman's right to subsidization by the man not only following marriage but within marriage.

Ms. Weitzman has been quoted on page 26: "Our major form of wealth comes from investment in ourselves—our 'human capital'—and in our careers. Despite the ideology of *marriage* as a partnership in which both partners share equally in the fruits of their joint enterprise, the reality of divorce is quite different. When it comes to dividing family assets, the courts often ignore the husband's 'career assets.'"[47]

Ms. Weitzman's plea is that divorce should benefit the woman equally with marriage. For women this would be an incentive to divorce. The wife could reason, "I don't need a husband since I can exchange him for an ex-husband who can be compelled to subsidize me *since I have custody of his children.* My contribution of going through a marriage ceremony is equivalent to his contribution of getting an education and acquiring status in his field of work and raising my standard of living by 73 percent." Ms. Weitzman is really pleading that the wife's non-assets ought to be considered as assets, at least as long as she can cling to "her" children and make her demands in their name. The wife's greatest asset is having a husband; Ms. Weitzman's program for shafting ex-husbands by punitive divorce awards will deprive a very large number of women of husbands.

Ms. Weitzman wants us to suppose the ex-husband's previous earning ability was made possible by his ex-wife's previous services to him. But obviously the withdrawal of these services must cripple him, as the providing of them formerly benefited him—especially if their withdrawal is accompanied by the deprivation of his children, the chief "assets of the marriage" from his point of view. What she calls assets of the marriage are really assets of the husband, the chief inducement he had to offer his wife to marry him.

If the male has no Money Card to offer the female, or if the female doesn't think his money is worth the trouble of her submitting to sexual regulation, the male can forget about having a family.

As pointed out on page 33 men have not yet woken up to what this means to them and to their children, a return to Stone Age arrangements, to the worship of the Goddess under whom, as in Crete,

---

[47]*Ms.*, February, 1986.

"the fearless and natural emphasis on sexual life that ran through all religious expression and was made obvious in the provocative dress of both sexes and their easy mingling."[48] Homosexual Arthur Evans, tells us (no doubt correctly, since the human Id is always the same, whether in the medieval witch cult or in the hypnocracies of remote antiquity), "The old religion, was polytheistic":

> Its most important deity was a goddess who was worshipped as the great mother. Its second major deity was the horned god, associated with animals and sexuality, including homosexuality. These and other deities were worshipped in the countryside at night with feasting, dancing, animal masquerades, transvestism, sex orgies, and the use of hallucinogenic drugs. Sexual acts were at the heart of the old religion, since theirs was a worldly religion of joy and celebration.... The material substructure of the old religion was a matriarchal social system that reached back to the stone age....In later European history, witchcraft retained this characteristic hostility to institutional authority.

Evans appropriately quotes Jeffrey Russell:

> In the history of Christianity, witchcraft is an episode in the long struggle between authority and order on one side and prophecy and rebellion on the other.[49]

So is feminism, the revival (or continuation) of this rebellion against male authority. "The sexual autonomy of women in the religion of the Goddess," says Merlin Stone,

> posed a continual threat. It undermined the far-reaching goals of the men, perhaps led or influenced by Indo-European peoples, who viewed women as property and aimed at a society in which male kinship was the rule, as it had long been in the Indo-European nations. This in turn required that each woman be retained as the possession of one man, leaving no doubt as to the identity of the father of the children she might bear, especially of her sons. But male kinship lines remained impossible as long as women were allowed to function as sexually independent people, continuing to bear children whose paternity was not known or considered to be of any importance.[50]

---

[48]Jacquetta Hawkes, quoted in Merlin Stone, *When God Was a Woman*, p. 48.
[49]Evans, *Witchcraft and the Gay Counterculture*, p. 79, citing Russell, *Witchcraft in the Middle Ages* (Cornell U., Ithaca New York, 1972), p. 2.
[50]Merlin Stone, p. 189.

This focuses on the essential difference between the two kinship systems. Patriarchy decrees that *Women must not be permitted to function independently of men in reproduction."* Patriarchy requires that she must share reproduction with a man.

Is paternity of any importance? Not in the ghetto. Not among "primitives," Evans's "nature people," for whom the purpose of sex is its own pleasure:

> **Among nature peoples...sex is part of the public religion and education of the tribes. It becomes a collective celebration of the powers that hold the universe together. Its purpose is its own pleasure.**

Among nature peoples, sex is unregulated by marriage or by shame. In patriarchy, it is put to work:

> **Sexual relations [says Evans] have been reduced to productive relations. The basic unit of people-production is the monogamous heterosexual family. Sex itself is locked up in secrecy, privacy, darkness, embarrassment, and guilt. That's how the industrial system manages to keep it under control.**

It is left uncontrolled by "nature people"[51] and "Any group of people with such practices and values can never be dominated by industrial institutions." This is to say, among nature peoples sex is merely recreational, whereas among patriarchal peoples it is regulated. Among nature peoples marriage is virtually meaningless and sex is public; among patriarchal peoples marriage is a public ceremony and is stable, and sex is regulated and private.

> **That's why the first thing industrial societies do on contact with "primitives" is make them feel guilty about sex and their bodies. The historical tools for doing this have been patriarchal religions.... The whole industrial system is like one great night of the living dead where the entire populace has been reduced emotionally to the level of zombies.[52]**

Among the ancient Celts, says Evans,

> **nudity was never regarded as shameful since the nude body was respected as a source of religious power.[53]**

---

[51]See the passage from Briffault's *The Mothers*, chapter 13, page 325.
[52]*Witchcraft*, p. 130.
[53]*Witchcraft*, p. 82.

The clothed body is likewise a source of religious power; and the disciplined sexuality represented by clothing has greater power—deriving from the same "nature" as that represented by nudity and the sexual anarchy represented by nudity. Patriarchy is also "natural"—in a deeper, less obvious way, however, than matriarchy and sexual anarchy.

THE WAR BETWEEN THE KINSHIP SYSTEMS—AGAIN

There is perpetual war between the two kinship systems, a war to determine whether there shall be a two-parent family or a return to a promiscuous matriarchy in which, as Ms. Eisler says, there will be "a politics aimed at nothing less than transforming our familial and sexual relations, our economic and work relations, our intranational and international relations, our relations with nature, and even our relations with our own bodies."[54] The war has many battlefields, the most decisive one at present being the divorce court. Ms. Hewlett thinks the law ought to "reward the [divorcing] mother for her devotion to her children" with larger support awards. Why should not the law equally reward the father for *his* devotion to his children—rather than punishing him even more drastically, as Ms. Hewlett proposes?

Ms. Friedan thinks that "Society asks so little of women." Why should the triflingness of women's services be rewarded not by the husband who receives the trifles, but by the ex-husband who is deprived of them?[55] Ms. Hewlett quotes the report by a British Law Commission cited earlier:

Society has no special interest in permanently maintaining the legal shell of a marriage that has failed, and the role of the law in such cases is to manage the dissolution process with the minimum human cost.[56]

The minimum cost to Mom. As pointed out on page 33, the cost to Mom is minimized by increasing the cost to Dad and the kids and society. Civilized society must be "a man's world," since the woman's world is the ghetto or the grasslands of Africa; but the law now works to destroy the man's world by destroying the father's motivation and role,

---

[54]Eisler, *Sacred Pleasure*, p. 364.
[55]Ms. Friedan quotes one of them, *Feminine Mystique*, page 63: "By 8:30 A.M., when my youngest goes to school, my whole house is clean and neat and I am dressed for the day. I am free to play bridge, attend club meetings, or stay home and read, listen to Beethoven, and just plain loaf."
      She is also able to contemplate the sort of mischief suggested by Dalma Heyn or Barbara Seaman or a hundred other encouragers of female promiscuity.
[56]Hewlett, p. 136.

telling the mother she is entitled to chuck the marriage if she feels like it.[57]

---

[57]See the quote from the *Los Angeles Daily News*, 18 December, 1996 given on page 34.

XXI) SUMMARY

We are becoming a society with no rules regulating female sexuality, where women seek, as Ms. Friedan puts it, an "inalienable human right to control our own bodies."[1] This gets to the heart of it: Will women allow men to participate as equals in reproduction? Ms. Friedan speaks for millions of women when she invokes their right to disregard the marriage contract as infringing on this "inalienable" right. The maintenance of the distinction between good and bad women—women who will allow a husband to share in their reproductive life and those who will not—is essential to the patriarchal system, essential to maintaining family stability and the procreation of legitimate children. But the breakdown of this distinction is essential to the feminist program. Feminists wish to trivialize this breakdown, as Ms. Coontz's does ("*merely* a decline in the double standard.") The good new life as seen by Ann Landers ("Cheating on spouses is now an equal-opportunity sport") is the same as that described by Ehrenreich, Hess and Jacobs, where young single women crowd into the cities in search of sexual adventures.

Children must suffer father-deprivation in order that their Moms may be free to "thrive." Boys must accept matriarchy and a high probability of rolelessness. Girls may like their freedom from sexual regulation but they too are trapped in the role of impoverished single motherhood.

Today, after a third of a century of family breakdown, illegitimacy, delinquency, educational failure, drug addiction—of women pretending to be soldiers, firemen and policemen and demanding Affirmative Action benefits to prove that they are really competent to perform in such occupations, it is time to end the feminist charade and get back to the family.

Feminists rejoice in women's freedom to divorce while remaining subsidized. Feminist Lynette Triere has been quoted: "There is no reason

---

[1] *It Changed My Life*, p. 153.

that a *woman* should be bound for life to a mistaken choice....It is an unreasonable demand." This is feminism. Women's reproductive independence means pretty much getting rid of the two-parent family ("the way my mother lived"), reducing fatherhood to meaninglessness by a sixty percent divorce rate and a thirty percent illegitimacy rate.

In the early years of the feminist movement it was a commonplace of feminist propaganda that the destruction of the patriarchal Sexual Constitution and the abandoning of the sex role socialization upon which it is based would liberate not only women but men by getting rid of the stereotype that a woman was dependent on a man. Feminism, it was asserted, would make a woman stop "preying upon her husband"[2]—the husband driven into a seven-year earlier grave by her parasitism. "Doing it for *ourselves*," said Ms. Friedan, "is the essence of the women's movement: it keeps us honest, keeps us real, keeps us concrete."[3] They would no longer try to earn their way in the world by being doll-wives. They would stand on their own feet. This is what they said.

FATHER CUSTODY: NOTHING NEW

There were only a few thousand divorces annually in the mid-nineteenth century when divorce cost wives their children and Dad's paycheck. This family stability began eroding as later nineteenth century divorce courts, under pressure from the rising feminist movement, began awarding child custody to mothers. "Between 1870 and 1920," says James Jones, "the divorce rate rose fifteenfold, and by 1924 one marriage out of seven ended in divorce.[4]

From the viewpoint of our present sixty percent divorce rate, one out of seven sounds like Victorian stability itself; but in 1924 it was properly seen as an alarming statistic. Few, however, thought that giving mothers custody of children might be the main reason for this undermining of the family. Few thought that a return to father custody might be the solution to such family destruction.

Many reformers blamed these figures on poor sexual adjustment in marriage. The best way to save the institution of marriage, they insisted, was for couples to enjoy more and better sex at home. Sexual

---

[2] *The Feminine Mystique*, p. 308.
[3] *It Changed My Life*, p. xviii; emphasis in original.
[4] James H. Jones, *Alfred Kinsey: A Public/Private Life* (New York: W. W. Norton, 1997), p. 292.

enthusiasts like Robert Latou Dickinson abolished the controls on passion, ended restrictions on experimentation (albeit within marriage), and acknowledged the sexual equality of men and women.

It required another generation for feminists to start asking: Why sex *at home*? Why *within marriage*? Why not chuck the whole patriarchal system and emancipate women completely? Why not let women stand on their own feet without sexual favor or excuse? Why not allow women to control their own sexuality like Ms. Friedan says? The judges are on women's side. Politicians have discovered there is a woman's vote worth buying and no men's vote—not yet anyway.

This is where we are today. The implication is that now women are really free, free from patriarchal regulation. Today we have a half-library of feminist books telling women that sex away from home is more fun, less responsible, unburdened with the feminine mystique or patriarchal oppression, or the Victorian "work ethic" or the Angel in the House crap. A half century ago Theodore Van de Velde rejoiced that sex had become "the foundation of marriage"—patriarchal marriage. Today it is the foundation of women's emancipation from patriarchy and marriage. Free at last.

But men are roleless. Men are unwilling to take up the burden which must be taken up if women are to be free economically as well as sexually, the burden of subsidizing their ex-wives and ex-girlfriends and the AFDC ladies and their children. How do we persuade the men that these children are also *their* children? If we can't do this the men will be joining the "coming white underclass" Charles Murray warns us about. We will have to give up on what Margaret Mead called society's big problem, what to do with males. Nobody has ever found anything to do with males but make them heads of families—which means going back to patriarchy. Only as heads of families are they in a position to confer benefits on wives which will reconcile the wives to accepting the patriarchal system, the best friend they ever had.

Let me conclude with two quotations, the first from William Robertson Smith, quoted already:

Originally there was no kinship except in the female line, and the introduction of male kinship was a kind of social revolution which modified society to its very roots.

The second from Bronislaw Malinowski:

If once we come to the point of doing away with the individual family as the pivotal element of our society, we should be faced with a social catastrophe compared with which the political upheaval of the French Revolution and the economic changes of Bolshevism are insignificant.

ANNEX

WOMEN'S DIVORCE-PRONENESS

WOMEN'S HATRED OF PATRIARCHY AND ITS REGULATION

WOMEN'S YEARNING TO RETURN TO THE FEMALE KINSHIP SYSTEM

Robert Briffault: "Where the female can derive no benefit from association with the male, no such association takes place." (*The Mothers*, I, 191)

Barbara Ehrenreich, Elizabeth Hess and Gloria Jacobs: "Women have come too far to surrender the range of possibilities opened up by a sexual revolution." (*Ms.*, July, 1986)

Barbara Ehrenreich, Elizabeth Hess and Gloria Jacobs: "The homosexual delight in sex as a defiant expression of liberation was catching on with heterosexual women." (*Re-Making Love*, p. 97)

Susan Faludi: "A 1985 *Woman's Day* survey of sixty thousand women found that only half would marry their husbands again if they had it to do over." (*Backlash*, p. 15)

Susan Faludi: "The more women are paid, the less eager they are to marry. A 1982 study of three thousand singles found that women earning high incomes are almost twice as likely to *want* to remain unwed as women earning low incomes. 'What is going to happen to marriage and childbearing in a society where women really have equality?' Princeton demographer Charles Westoff wondered in the *Wall Street Journal* in 1986. 'The more economically independent women are, the less attractive marriage becomes.'" (*Ibid.*, p. 16)

Declaration of Feminism: "The end of the institution of marriage is a necessary condition for the liberation of women. Therefore it is

important for us to encourage women to leave their husbands...
(November, 1971)

Mary Ann Mason: "For many women the route to liberation from
domestic drudgery was liberation from the family. The only chance for
true equality with men lay outside the patriarchal family structure....In
the real world of the 70s full-time housewives were ending their careers
on the rocks of divorce in astonishing numbers." (*The Equality Trap*, p.
120)

Barbara Bergmann: "We seem to be in the process of change back
to the single-parent method." (*The Economic Emergence of Women*, p.
232)

Barbara Bergmann: "[M]any women and young girls relish their
new freedoms and opportunities. Many mothers and fathers are
delighted that their daughters will have a chance to express their talents
and will be able, if they wish, to avoid complete dependence on the good
will of a 'breadwinner.' The welfare system traps single mothers into
remaining poverty-stricken pseudo-housewives and sentences their
children to deprivation. It underwrites sexual and reproductive
irresponsibility by relieving both women and men of providing out of their
earnings for the children they create. It should be replaced with a
system under which single parents would be earners, but would have
government guarantees of child support payments out of the earnings of
the other parent, health care, and high quality child care." (*Ibid.*, pp. 4-5)

Barbara Dafoe Whitehead: "[Sociologist Jessie] Bernard argued that
marriage was good for men and bad for women. While marriage
conferred health and happiness on men, it had the opposite effect on
women. Marriage could make women sick. Compared with unmarried
women, Bernard claimed, married women were more likely to suffer from
a host of mental and physical problems, including insomnia, trembling
hands, nightmares, fainting, headaches, dizziness, phobias, and heart
palpitations. Thus the marital institution itself was pathological. 'To be
happy in a relationship which imposes so many impediments on her, as
traditional marriage does,' Bernard wrote, ' a women must be slightly ill
mentally.'"(*The Divorce Culture*, p. 51)

Barbara Dafoe Whitehead: "Too, according to the 1970s data,
women held more liberal views of marriage than men; they were more

likely to describe their marriages as 'two separate people' and to approve of divorce." (*Ibid.*, p. 52)

Barbara Dafoe Whitehead: "The study's author, sociologist Catherine Riessman, observes that 'more than half of the women in the sample, particularly those separated less than a year, actively engaged in reconstructing a self, emphasize this outcome. They say they 'got born,' have 'the freedom to be myself,' feel 'more like a free person.'" (*Ibid.*, p. 57)

Barbara Dafoe Whitehead: "Thus, the awakened woman must take the initiative to end the marriage. As a woman moves out of a relationship that has become involuntary and therefore a kind of servitude, she accomplishes her personal transformation. She opts for freedom, and in the exercise of her freedom she becomes at last, like Pinocchio, a real person." (*Ibid.*, p. 60)

Maggie Gallagher: "And for more than two decades now these [women's] magazines have idealized divorce, peddling the experts' advice to a broad, general audience. Most women's magazines have become as skittish about using the M-word as any academic journal. Though most women are married, there is no longer a single prominent, nondenominational women's magazine explicitly addressed to married women. Instead, we also find such carefully ambiguous and ambivalent terms as *couples* and *partners*, which embrace a range of relationships from last Saturday's date to a second husband and thus seem to imply they are all very similar. (*The Abolition of Marriage*, p. 208)

Robin Morgan: "I want a woman's revolution like a lover. I lust for it, I want so much this freedom, this end to struggle and fear and lies we all exhale, that I could die just with the passionate uttering of that desire." (Quoted in Mary Daly, *Beyond God the Father*, p. 1)

Susan Faludi: "[Connie Marshner's] Mother read Friedan's *Feminine Mystique* when it first came out," Marshner says, "and I remember her saying, 'You won't understand how awful married life is until you read it.' Mother was always saying to me, 'You don't want to marry and ruin your life. Be independent.'" (*Backlash*, p. 242)

Mary Jane Sherfey: "Finally, I will bring in evidence to corroborate the thesis that the suppression by cultural forces of women's inordinately high sexual drive and orgasmic capacity must have been an important prerequisite for the evolution of modern human societies and has continued, of necessity, to be a major preoccupation of practically every civilization....Many factors have been advanced to explain the rise of the patriarchal, usually polygynous, system and its concomitant ruthless subjugation of female sexuality (which necessarily subjugated her entire emotional and intellectual life). However, if the conclusions reached there are true, it is conceivable that the *forceful* suppression of women's inordinate sexual demands was a prerequisite to the dawn of every modern civilization and almost every living culture. Primitive woman's sexual drive was too strong, too susceptible to the fluctuating extremes of an impelling, aggressive erotism to withstand the disciplined requirements of a settled family's well-being and where paternity had become as important as maternity in maintaining family and property cohesion. For about half the time, women's erotic needs would be insatiably pursued; paternity could never be certain and with lactation erotism constant infant care would be out of the question.

"There are many indications from the prehistory studies in the Near East that it took perhaps 5,000 years or longer for the subjugation of women to take place. (*The Nature and Evolution of Female Sexuality*, pp. 52, 138)

Maggie Gallagher: "Marriage is one of the few contracts in which the law explicitly protects the defaulting party at the expense of his or her partner." (*The Abolition of Marriage*, p. 150)

Arlene Skolnick: "One measure of change was the gradual fading of the term 'illegitimate child.' As soon as it became acceptable for an unmarried middle-class woman to keep a child she had conceived accidentally, growing numbers of middle-class women in their 30s and 40s deliberately set out to become pregnant and bear children on their own." (*Embattled Paradise*, p. 188)

Arlene Skolnick: "[T]he pollster Lou Harris recently reported that while 87 percent of men say they would remarry their wives, only 76 percent of women say they would remarry their husbands." (*Ibid.*, p. 221)

Barbara Dafoe Whitehead: "In this advice literature, however, marriage itself becomes the focus of romantic protests. Women are cloistered in a 'cozy cocoon' of marriage, "casualties of a marital subculture that crushed their emerging identities.' The literature engages in a rhetorical shift as well, turning divorce, rather than marriage, into the symbol of a mature and accomplished identity. It is divorce, not marriage, that defines a sense of self and leads to greater maturity and self-knowledge. It is divorce, not marriage, that is stimulating and energizing and growth-enhancing. Thus, divorce becomes the defining achievement of women's lives, the great article of their freedom." (*The Divorce Culture*, p. 61)

Barbara Dafoe Whitehead: "Professionals who worked closely with children also offered a gloomier assessment of the impact of divorce on children. Judith Wallerstein and Sandra Blakeslee's study rejected the idea that the vast majority of children bounce back quickly from their parents' divorce. Five years after the divorce, more than a third of the children were experiencing moderate or severe depression. At ten years a significant number of the now-grown young men and women appeared to be troubled, drifting, and underachieving. At the fifteen-year mark, many of the thirtyish adults were struggling to establish secure love relationships of their own. In short, far from making a speedy recovery from their parents' divorce, a significant percentage of the young adults in the study were still suffering its effects. Cruelly, the experience of parental divorce damaged many young adults' ability to forge strong attachments of their own, in both their work and their family lives. The emotional difficulties associated with divorce lasted much longer and involved a higher percentage of children of divorce than the first wave of thinking claimed. (*The Divorce Culture*, pp. 98f.)

Alice Walker: "Ninety-nine and ninety-nine one hundredths percent of traditions should be done away with because women did not make them. Like marriage. Say you woke up one morning in a beautiful world and you had everything you wanted: You had your friends, you had good lovemaking. Would you really look around and say, 'What do I really need now? I guess I need to get married.'" (*Insight*, Sept., 1992)

Judy Mann: "'What is crucial,' writes the philosopher Maxine Greene,' is the recognition that women's relegation to private life is neither biologically based nor given in the nature of things.'" (*The Difference*, p. 201)

Judy Mann: "The great store of knowledge about the ancient world that science has uncovered since world War II is mounting an unprecedented assault on the most fundamental underpinnings of the male-dominated churches and the patriarchies they are upholding. Archaeologists, art historians, linguists, and anthropologists are making convincing cases for the proposition that male domination is neither a universal truth nor part of a natural order—for it was not the principle of social order in Paleolithic and Neolithic times. It is a relatively recent development in the history of humankind. The importance of these revelations cannot be overstated: It means that patriarchies are neither immutable nor inevitable. They can be challenged, changed and replaced." (*The Difference*, p. 202)

Barbara Dafoe Whitehead: "With the rise of expressive divorce, this view of divorced motherhood changed. In studies based on personal interviews, middle-class divorcing mothers report a new sense of control and 'a seeming zest and delight' in their new identities as single mothers. Even in the traditional tasks of nurturing, some mothers cite a greater sense of freedom." (*The Divorce Culture*, p. 64.)

Barbara Dafoe Whitehead: "In 1962, on the threshold of the divorce revolution, researchers asked women whether they agreed or disagreed with the statement that 'when there are children in the family parents should stay together even if they don't get along.' Opinion was roughly divided, with 51 percent of the women disagreeing. By 1977, when researchers posed the question again to the same sample of women, 80 percent disagreed. In the course of fifteen years this group of women had moved from divided opinion to an overwhelming consensus that unhappily married parents should not stay together for the children's sake." (*The Divorce Culture*, p. 82)

Mary Daly: "In dealing with the problem of cooptation, women can start with the basic principle that our own liberation, seen in its fullest implications, is primary in importance. When sexual caste is seen as the 'original sin' upon which other manifestations of oppression are modeled, it becomes eminently unreasonable to feel guilt over according it priority." (*Beyond God the Father*, p. 59)

Mary Daly: "As the women's movement begins to have its effect upon the fabric of society, transforming it from patriarchy into something that never existed before—into a diarchal situation that is radically new—it can become the greatest single challenge to the major religions of the world, Western and Eastern. Beliefs and values that have held sway for thousands of years will be questioned as never before. This revolution may well be also the greatest single hope for survival of spiritual consciousness on this planet." (*Ibid.*, p. 13)

Naomi Wolf: "One by one, the families began to come apart. In my girlfriends' houses, the most difficult thing they would face was the abdication of so many of the fathers. The boys shared equally in this pain. Every second kid in my elementary and middle school, it seemed, had a story about birthday gifts that their separated or divorcing dads had promised but which had never arrived in the mail, missing child support checks, custody visits abandoned for the sake of the dads' vacations, and the dads' new girlfriends, new wives, and new children taking all the money." (*Promiscuities*, p. 19)

Susan Faludi: "The real change was women's new ability to regulate their fertility without danger or fear—a new freedom that in turn had contributed to dramatic changes not in the abortion rate but in female sexual behavior and attitudes. Having secured first the mass availability of contraceptive devices and then the option of medically sound abortions, women were at last at liberty to have sex, like men, on their own terms. As a result, in the half century after birth control was legalized, women doubled their rates of premarital sexual activity, nearly converging with men's by the end of the 70s." (*Backlash*, p. 404)

Naomi Wolf: "But girls' experience of the absence or abdication of their fathers marked them in all these ways—and in one more. The fathers' departure led directly to the girls' often shaky sense of sexual self-esteem....To the female children on the block...there was a new kind of anxiety. How could one grow up to become, through sex, the kind of woman a dad would not want to go away from?" (*Promiscuities*, p. 19)

Michael Medved: "'Illegitimacy chic' is as much a part of the contemporary Hollywood scene as a passion for distributing condoms or saving the rain forests. As [Jessica] Lange, mother of three out-of-wedlock children, told *Glamour* magazine in 1988: 'My family doesn't think marriage is all that important.'...In a 1985 interview with the Los Angeles Herald Examiner, [Nancy] Meyers emphatically declared: 'I'm not very fond of what a lot of wives go through in their marriages. Especially when you're a mother....I'm adamant about being separate....We were very comfortable about not being married.'...*Time* magazine observed in

November 1991 that 'traditional child bearing has virtually disappeared from the airwaves.'" (*Washington Post*, 4 Oct., 1992)

Anne Wilson Schaef: "The power that these little beings—our children—have over us and the fact that they can validate our existence makes us 'hate their guts.' We love our children, but we hate what they stand for." (*Women's Reality*, p. 81)

Louis Henry Morgan: "The influence of property and the desire to transmit it to children furnished adequate motives for change to the male line." (*Ancient Society*, p. 352)

Norval D. Glenn and David Blankenhorn: "An important new book fundamentally challenges this view. In "A Generation at Risk," just published by Harvard University Press, Paul Amato of the University of Nebraska and Alan Booth of Penn State University painstakingly analyze data from a large national sample of families, seeking especially to isolate the independent effects of divorce on children from the effects of preexisting marital conflict. The results call into question the rationalizations of our high divorce rate.

"That many children are harmed by parental conflict is not in doubt, nor is the fact that some children benefit from parental separation because it lessens their exposure to conflict. But Amato and Booth estimate that at most a third of divorces involving children are so distressed that the children are likely to benefit. The remainder, about 70%, involve low-conflict marriages that apparently harm children much less than do the realities of divorce. Moreover, Amato and Booth estimate that, as the threshold of dissatisfaction at which divorce occurs becomes ever lower, an even higher proportion of future divorces will involve low-conflict situations in which divorce will be worse for children than the continuation of the marriage. This reasoning leads to a startling conclusion, especially coming from two liberal social scientists: For that majority of marriages in trouble that are not fraught with conflict, 'future generations would be well served if parents remained together until children are grown.'" (*Los Angeles Times*, 31 Dec., 1997)

Adrienne Rich: "[Dorothy Dinnerstein is] seemingly unaware of the repeated struggles of women to resist oppression (our own and that of others) and to change our condition; she ignores, specifically, the history of women who—as witches, *femmes seul*, marriage resisters, spinsters, autonomous widows, and/or lesbians—have managed on varying levels *not* to collaborate....The fact is that women in every culture and throughout history *have* undertaken the task of independent, nonheterosexual, women-connected existence, to the extent made possible by their context, often in the belief that they were the 'only ones' ever to do so. They have undertaken it even though few women have been in an economic position to resist marriage altogether, and even though attacks against unmarried women have ranged from aspersion and mockery to deliberate gynocide, including the burning and torturing of millions of widows and spinsters during the witch persecutions of the fifteenth to seventeenth centuries in Europe and the practice of suttee on widows in India." ("Compulsory Heterosexuality and Lesbian Existence" in *Feminist Frontiers,* ed. Laurel Richardson and Verta Taylor, p. 219)

Brenda Scott: "A radical feminist, [Margaret] Sanger deplored the institution of marriage, calling it 'the most degenerating influence in the social order.'" (*Children No More,* p. 82)

Judy Mann: "Christianity, patriarchy, and abuse are all wrapped up together, and together they doom girls to second-class citizenship." (*The Difference,* p. 289)

Judy Mann: "We have reached a time of history when the sticky fog of patriarchy is being dissipated, and we can begin to rediscover who we really are and the history that has brought us to this point." (*Ibid.,* p. 284)

Edward Carpenter: "What woman most needs today is a basis of independence for her life. Nor is her position likely to be improved until she is able to face man on an equality; to find, self-balanced, her natural relation to him; and to dispose of herself and her sex perfectly freely, and not as a thrall must do." (*Love's Coming of Age,* p. 68)

Katherine Anthony: "Such an opportunity came with the declaration of war in Germany, when the soldiers' wives suddenly found themselves in possession of a cash pittance from the government and so lost their heads that their behavior was considered a public scandal. Writing about these women in the *Frauenfrage,* Anna Pappritz asked, 'On whom does this situation reflect, on the women themselves or the economic subjection in which they have been kept? For many of these women, dependence is so oppressive that they feel their present independence as a veritable salvation. This legalized humiliation of the married woman is the humiliation of all women, and until the economic position of the married woman is improved the subjection of women will continue to endure.'" (*Feminism in Germany and Scandinavia*, p. 202)

Mary Daly: "Marriage is a male institution and serves male interests....Sisterhood means revolution." (*Beyond God the Father*, p. 59)

Andrew Payton Thomas: "Single parents in general are far more likely, by the mere fact of that status, to raise children who have trouble obeying the law. Seventy percent of juvenile offenders come from single-parent homes....17 percent of children raised by never-married mothers are suspended or expelled from school, 11 percent of children from divorced families draw the same sanctions." (*Crime and the Sacking of America*, p. 161)

Carol Anderson and Susan Stewart: "...the qualities of the single life that some women find extraordinarily valuable: freedom, independence, and most of all, *self-determination*." (*Flying Solo*, p. 35)

Susan Faludi: "Women also became far more independent in their decisions about when to have children, under what marital circumstances, and when to stop. In these decisions the biological father increasingly didn't have the final say—or much of a say at all. Women's support for motherhood out of wedlock rose dramatically in the '80s. The 1987 Women's View Survey found that 87 percent of single women believed it was perfectly acceptable for women to bear and raise children without getting married—up 14 percent from just four years earlier." (*Backlash*, p. 404)

Lytton Strachey [Describing Florence Nightingale's book *Suggestions for Thoughts to the Searchers After Truth Among the Artisans of England*]: "Then, suddenly, in the very midst of the ramifying generalities of her metaphysical disquisitions there is an unexpected turn, and the reader is plunged all at once into something particular, something personal, something impregnated with intense experience—a virulent invective upon the position of women in the upper ranks of society. Forgetful alike of her high argument and of the artisans, the bitter creature rails through one hundred pages of close print at the falsities of family life, the ineptitudes of marriage, the emptiness of convention in the spirit of an Ibsen or a Samuel Butler. Her fierce pen, shaking with intimate anger, depicts in biting sentences the fearful fate of an unmarried girl in a wealthy household. It is a *cri du coeur*; and then, as suddenly, she returns once more to instruct the artisans upon the nature of Omnipotent Righteousness." (*Eminent Victorians*, illustrated ed., p. 108)

Katherine Anthony: "To those women, on the other hand, who believe in the future of their sex the ultimate triumph of volitional motherhood over sex slavery, is one of the indispensable conditions of that future." *(Feminism in Germany and Scandinavia*, p. 99)

Irwin Garfinkel and Sara McLanahan: "Many people have noted that the explosion of divorce and decline in marriage that took place in the 1960s and 1970s followed quite closely the rise in labor force participation of married women with children....Several studies based on longitudinal data have found that married women who are in the labor force or who have higher earnings potential are more likely to divorce than more dependent women....

"Several researchers have shown that husbands of employed wives have lower self-esteem and are more depressed than are husbands of full-time homemakers." (*Single Mothers and Their Children*, pp. 64ff.)

Celeste Fraser Delgado: "The voluntary motherhood movement of the 1870s and 1880s insisted upon women's right to refuse sex with their husbands." (*Oxford Companion to Women's Writing in the United States*, p. 759)

Los Angeles Times: "The census counted 41 million never married adults and noted that this is nearly double the 21 million counted in 1970." (17 July, 1992)

Urie Bronfenbrenner: "American families and their children are in trouble, trouble so deep and pervasive as to threaten the future of our nation." (Quoted in Nigel Davies, *The Rampant God*, p. 277)

Los Angeles Times: "'I don't think women have to be home to teach their children family values,' said Liz Bute, a 37-year-old manager at Citibank whose five children have all spent their pre-school years in day care. 'I think we're past that.'...'It's up to society as a whole' to share the burden. That, said Bute, is part of what values are all about." (17 June, 1996)

373

Betty Friedan: "In 1956, at the peak of togetherness, the bored editors of *McCall's* ran a little article called "The Mother Who Ran Away." To their amazement, it brought the highest readership of any article they had ever run. 'It was our moment of truth,' said a former editor. 'We suddenly realized that all those women at home with their three and a half children were miserably unhappy.'" (*The Feminine Mystique*, p. 50)

Feminist Leader: "A woman's right to have a baby without having the father around is what feminism is all about." (Quoted in 1996 Defense of the Family Survey of Christian Coalition)

Los Angeles Times: "The number of American children living with single parents is up sharply, and the number of those parents who have never been married nearly equals the share who are divorced." (20 July, 1994)

Stephanie Coontz: "A national survey conducted in 1989 found that 36 percent of the single women polled had seriously considered raising a child on their own." (*The Way We Never Were*, p. 186)

Planned Parenthood: "Many people believe that sex relations are right only when they are married. Others decide to have sex outside of marriage. This is a personal choice." (Pamphlet titled "Sex Facts," quoted in Marshall and Donovan, *Blessed Are the Barren*, p. 108)

Molly Yard: "The right of women to control their reproductive lives...the right of all women to be free! We refuse to be intimidated and bullied one more day!" (Letter from NOW, October, 1989)

Adah Isaacs Menken: "I don't believe in women being married. Somehow they all sink into nonentities after this epoch in their existence." (Wallace, *The Intimate Sex Lives of Famous People*, p. 505)

Monica Sjöö and Barbara Mor: "What would it have been like if patriarchy had never happened? To get an idea, we have to comprehend the first law of matriarchy: Women control our own bodies." (*The Great Cosmic Mother*, p. 200)

Dora Black [Mrs. Bertrand Russell]: "I held that one entered into a sexual relationship for love which was given and received freely; this might last long, it could also be very brief. No other motive but such love, which must involve awareness and acceptance of the other's personality was to be tolerated." (*Autobiography*, p. 147)

Los Angeles Times: "Percentages of high school students who reported ever having sexual intercourse range from 38% in ninth grade to 60.9% in 12th grade." (18 Sept., 1998)

Zelda West Meads [of the marriage guidance agency Relate, one of Princess Diana's circle]: "One of the biggest changes over the years has been that women are not prepared to put up with bad marriages for any longer than they need to. They say to me, 'I have only one life and I don't want to be trapped in this relationship for most of it.'" (Andrew Morton, *Diana: Her New Life*, p. 24)

Elise Boulding: "One of the anomalies of the child's role in industrial society is the absurd stigma of illegitimacy for children born to unpartnered women." (*The Underside of History*, p. 787)

Susan Faludi: "Nearly 40 percent of the women in the 1990 Virginia Slims poll said that in making a decision about whether to have an abortion, the man involved should not even be consulted." (*Backlash*, p. 404)

Evelyn Reed: "New sexual mores rigidly curtailed the former freedom of women. Whether these are called sexual 'morality,' 'purity,' 'virginity,' or 'chastity,' they are imposed by men upon women, not by women upon men." (*Woman's Evolution, p. 428)*

Betty Friedan "We have to ask the questions that will open up alternative lifestyles for the future, alternatives to the kind of marriage and nuclear family structure that not only women but men want out of today." (*It Changed My Life*, p. 113)

Robert Briffault: "The homage of the troubadour poets was, without an exception, addressed to married women. That circumstance was emphasised as an essential principle of those very conventions which laboured to establish a distinction between 'refined,' 'idealised,' 'courtly,' honourable' love and gross, vulgar relations, or 'villeiny,' as the poets called it. A woman who should plead her duty of fidelity to her husband was stigmatised as behaving 'like a bourgeoise.'" (*The Mothers*, III, 475)

The Mahabharata: "Women were not formerly immured in houses and dependent upon husbands and relatives. They used to go about freely, enjoying themselves as best they pleased....They did not then adhere to their husbands faithfully;...they were not regarded as sinful, for that was the sanctioned usage of the times. Indeed, that usage, so lenient to women, hath the sanction of antiquity. The present practice, however, of women being confined to one husband for life hath been established but lately." (Quoted in Briffault, *The Mothers*, I, 346)

Irwin Garfinkel and Sara McLanahan: "Fairly good evidence indicates that girls who grow up in families headed by single women are more likely to become single parents themselves." (*Single Mothers and Their Children*, p. 167.)

Susan Crain Bakos: "Runaway moms told interviewers: It was something they had to do for themselves, to fulfill their own needs." (*This Wasn't Supposed to Happen*, p. 82)

Susan Crain Bakos: "'We wouldn't let them get away with so much,' Kara says, 'if they were not the ones who make the most money.'" (*Ibid.*, p. 127)

Kara: "When men began talking about commitment, I got out. Making a commitment meant marriage; and for women, marriage means giving a man too much power in your life. I just knew I wasn't going to do it; and I was glad we lived in a time where a women could have sex, all the sex she wanted, without getting married.

"I thought in vague terms of having a kid someday of being a single mother. I didn't give up on having kids then, just marriage." (Quoted in Susan Crain Bakos, *Ibid.*, p. 223.)

Rosalind Miles: "[I]t is evident that women at the birth of civilization generally enjoyed a far greater freedom from restraint on their 'modesty' or even chastity than at any time afterwards....Sacred, often orgiastic, dancing was a crucial element of Goddess worship, and the use of intoxicants or hallucinogens to heighten the effect was standard practice: the Goddess demanded complete abandon....To have intercourse with a stranger was the purest expression of the will of the Goddess, and carried no stigma....This unhistorical projection of anachronistic prejudice (sex is sin, and unmarried sex is prostitution) fails to take account of historical evidence support in the high status of these women." (*The Woman's History of the World*, pp. 34f.)

Rosalind Miles: "Of all the early patriarchies, though, perhaps the most surprising in its attitude to women is Islam; the gross oppressions which later evolved like veiling, seclusion, and genital mutilation (the so-called 'female circumcision') were brought about in the teeth of the far freer and more humane regime of former times. [According to feminist historian Nawal El Saadawi]:

"Before Islam a woman could practise polyandry and marry more than one man. When she became pregnant she would send for all her husbands....Gathering them around her, she would name the man she wished to be the father of her child, and the man could not refuse...." (*Ibid.*, p. 66)

Mary Daly: "What *is* the substance of the chain that has 'linked the fathers and the sons,' culminating in the Auschwitzes, the Vietnams, the corporations, the ecclesiastical and secular inquisitions, the unspeakable emptiness of the consuming and consumed creatures whose souls are lost in pursuit of built-in obsolescence? This is precisely the chain that derives its total reality from the reduction of women to nonbeing. The strength of the chain is the energy sapped out of the bodies and minds of women—the mothers and daughters whose lifeblood has been sucked away by the patriarchal system. The chain that has drained us will be broken when women draw back our own life force." (*Beyond God the Father*, p. 177)

Betty Friedan: "I was horrified to hear not one single mention of the right of woman to decide and choose in her own childbearing....Asserting the right of a woman to control her own body and reproductive process as her inalienable, human, civil right, not to be denied or abridged by the state or any man....After the Supreme Court decision maternal mortality dropped to an all-time low in the U.S., for abortion deaths dropped by nearly 600 percent." (*It Changed My Life*, p. 122 [It is impossible for anything to drop more than 100 percent—D. A.])

David Hall: "Women who lived common-law before their first marriage have a 33 percent greater risk of divorce at any time in their marriage than...women who do not cohabit before their first marriage." ("Marriage as a Pure Relationship," *Journal of Comparative Family*

Studies, xxvii (1996), 1-12; epitomized in *The Family in America: New Research*, April, 1996)

Barbara Seaman: "Yet, undeniably, for some women, intimacy breeds boredom or contempt. One girl admitted, "I can only be uninhibited in sex with people (men) I don't know very well." (*Free and Female*, p. 59)

Maggie Gallagher: "Cohabitation not only undercuts marriage, but it also produces less stable marriages. In 90 percent of cohabitations at least one of the sex partners expects the arrangement to end in marriage. Almost half will be disappointed. Axinn and Thornton found that 'cohabiting experiences significantly increase young people's acceptance of divorce." (*The Abolition of Marriage*, p. 170)

Phyllis Chesler: "Any father who puts a child and his mother through the pain of a custody battle or who attempts to separate them from each other is by definition an unfit father." *(Mothers on Trial*, p. 441)

Leontine Young: "Usually she [an unwed mother] has come from a background characterized by chronic insecurity, rejection, and serious family problems. Most of these girls come from broken homes...." (*Out of Wedlock*, p. 101)

Ira Reiss: "All the results of this study pointed to the normality of the unwed mother." (Quoted in Solinger, *Wake Up Little Susie*, p. 226)

Irving Wallace et al.: "Margaret [Sanger] was not only a proponent of birth control but also vigorously espoused 'free love' and sensual, spiritual sex. She told her first husband, William Sanger, an architect, that she must be free to make love with other men if she wished. It was for 'the cause,' she explained." (*Sex Lives of Famous People*, p. 432)

Barbara Seaman: "Several of these women said that while they loved their husbands, they wished they had the courage not to be monogamous." (*Free and Female*, p. 136)

Barbara Seaman: "Today it seems to me, a great many young women are merely swapping the old-fashioned sex-is-for-men sexual masochism of their mothers for a new type of self-punitive behavior. They are trying to copy the *worst* sexual behaviors of men, the promiscuity and exploitation. Sometimes they bed down with people who hardly attract them at all, merely to add another conquest to the 'list.' (Indeed, I know of one high school sorority where the girls are actually keeping such lists. The 'champ,' a pretty 17-year-old, has 121 entries on it.)" (*Ibid.*, p. 210)

Betty Friedan: "Only economic independence can free a woman to marry for love, not for status or financial support, or to leave a loveless, intolerable, humiliating marriage, or to eat, dress, rest, and move if she plans not to marry." (*The Feminine Mystique*, tenth anniversary ed., p. 371)

Arthur Evans: "One legacy of the older ways was the continued high status of Celtic women. They were independent and chose their sexual partners freely....This sexual openness continued well into Christian times. Around 395 AD, the Christian propagandist Jerome complained that 'the Irish race do not have individual wives and...none among them has a spouse exclusively his own, but they sport and wanton after the manner of cattle, each as it seems good to them.'" (*Witchcraft and the Gay Counterculture*, p. 18.)

Arthur Evans: "The old religion was polytheistic. Its most important deity was a goddess who was worshipped as the great mother. Its second major deity was the horned god, associated with animals and sexuality, including homosexuality. These and other deities were worshipped in the countryside at night with feasting, dancing, animal masquerades, transvestism, sex orgies, and the use of hallucinogenic drugs. Sensual acts were at the heart of the old religion, since theirs was a worldly religion of joy and celebration....Women were the chief priests and leaders of the old religion, performing the roles of prophet, midwife and healer....The material substructure of the old religion was a matriarchal social system that reached back to the stone age." (*Ibid.*, p. 79)

Douglas Smith and Roger Jarjoura: "The percentage of single-parent households with children between the ages of twelve and twenty is significantly associated with rates violent crime and burglary." (*Journal of Research in Crime and Delinquency*, Vol. 25, # 1, Feb., 1988)

Harper's Index: "Chances that an American child living with both biological parents will have to repeat a grade in school: 1 in 9. Chances that a child living with a single mother will have to repeat a grade: 1 in 4." (August, 1992)

London *Daily Telegraph* :"The fact is that the files of relevant government bodies are bulging with evidence that broken homes mean more battered children. Research has shown that it is 20 times more dangerous for a child if the natural parents cohabit rather than marry. It is 33 times more dangerous for a child to live with its natural mother and her boyfriend than with the natural parents in a marriage relationship." (28 Dec., 1996)

Brenda Scott: "Federal statistics show an incredible 25.4 % increase in violent crime by female juveniles between 1982 and 1992....In Massachusetts, for example, 15 % of female juvenile arrests were for violent crimes in 1982. By 1991, they accounted for 38 %." (*Children No More*, p. 20)

Phyllis Chesler: "The male legal ownership of children is essential to patriarchy....Freud once asked: 'What do women want?' For starters, and in no particular order: *freedom,* food, nature, shelter, leisure, freedom from violence, justice, music, *non-patriarchal family,* poetry, community, *independence....*" (*Patriarchy,* pp. 47, 13; emphasis added)

Phyllis Chesler: "We all understand that the opposition to women's right to control our own bodies maintains men's power." (*Ibid.,* p. 50)

Wini Breines: "It is worth pointing out that Alfred C. Kinsey's 1953 study of female sexuality mentions women's regrets about not having had intercourse before marriage because they believed their sex lives would have been better later." (*Young, White and Miserable,* p. 221)

Wini Breines: "I want to suggest that they [white middle-class girls of the 1950s] were drawn to black music and difference—delinquent and dark boyfriends, working-class, Beat, and bohemian lovers, jazz and rock and roll—because these were inappropriate and forbidden. Such girls longed for something more than their domesticated lives offered, 'real life' they often called it." (*Ibid.,* p. 19)

Wini Breines: "Describing her attraction to Luther, her secret black boyfriend in high school, Loretta wonders how she can explain how he has 'captured her imagination': 'Surely part of it was that he was forbidden.'...She feels comfortable and real (a word white middle-class girls say often in their characterization of what they are missing) with him and his family." (*Ibid.*, p. 83)

Wini Breines: "The expansiveness and male privilege of the Beats, their intensity, adventures, frenetic activity, interest in black culture, and rejection of conventional middle-class life attracted 1950s teenage girls, as did rock and roll stars. But they were interested not simply as girlfriends and fans, which was the simplest form their attraction could take; they were interested in them as models. They wanted to *be* them. The possibility of a break with domesticity was critical to this appeal. Despite the Beats' chauvinism, for girls their rejection of bourgeois respectability and the family was explosive." (*Ibid.*, p. 147)

Rickie Solinger: "This study aims to argue most forcefully—both implicitly and explicitly—that politicians and others in the United States have been using women's bodies and their reproductive capacity for a long time to promote political agendas hostile to female autonomy...." (*Wake Up Little Susie*, p. 19)

Leontine Young: "Some of the motives behind this powerful drive for an out-of-wedlock baby are clear. Jealousy and revenge are one. The girl's way of having this baby lets her mother know that she is at long last paying off an old score. Her frequent statement 'I have to make up to my mother for what I've done to her" falls into place here. Without realizing it, the girl admits her intention to 'show' her mother and to get even with her and at the same time reveals her appalled terror at what she has done. Like a small child, she expects her mother's wrath to annihilate her and seeks by abject appeasement to save herself.

"She also demonstrates that Mother is not the only one who can have a baby, who can fulfill the deep female urge to give life. Forced to secrecy, blindness, and subterfuge, she has nevertheless accomplished the one act that is exclusively and totally feminine, that by its nature is a declaration of independence and maturity as a woman...."(*Out of Wedlock*, p. 57)

Leontine Young: "The effect of this kind of existence upon a girl's capacity to be a good mother and upon her ability to provide a warm and happy life for her child is often disastrous. Her own frustrations and unhappiness, her uncertain community position, coupled with the emotional problems that created this problem in the first place, may result in a variety of reactions toward the child: overprotection, unconscious seduction, resentment, neglect, hatred. Whatever the specific expression, they are all crippling to the child and deeply damaging to the mother. It is not surprising that desertion is a recurrent problem in this group." (*Ibid.*, p. 155)

Margaret Mead: "[T]here is no society in the world where people have stayed married without enormous community pressure to do so." (Quoted in Wallerstein and Blakeslee, *Second Chances*, p. 297)

David Popenoe: "Juvenile delinquency and violence are clearly generated disproportionately by youths in mother-only households and in other households where the biological father is not present." (*Life Without Father*, p. 62)

David Popenoe: "The teenage population is expected to rise in the next decade by as much as 20 percent, even more for minority teenagers....This has prompted criminologist James Fox to assert: 'There is a tremendous crime wave coming in the next 10 years.' It will be fueled not by old, hardened criminals but by what Fox calls 'the young and the ruthless'—children in their early and mid-teens who are turning murderous." (*Ibid.*, p. 63)

Benazir Bhutto [former Prime Minister of Pakistan]: "Ultimately, empowerment is attained through economic independence. As long as women are dependent on men, they will face discrimination in one form or another....Before we can bring about the political and social emancipation of women, we will first have to ensure that they can stand on their own feet." (*Los Angeles Times*, 1 September, 1995)

Dalma Heyn: "They [adulteresses] feel that even though the goodness role is 'dishonest' and 'destructive to women' and had led to the stagnation, not the contentment, of their mothers—it is also still very much 'part of the marriage contract.' They would have to fight hard against its hold on them. Angry about the collusion of women in the perpetuation of this Donna Reed model, yet feeling simultaneously very much in its thrall, all the women find themselves walking a tightrope. If they succumb to total selflessness, they see themselves manipulated by a society that still requires them to be good girls. They are furious when they sense themselves giving in to this model and this demand, when they hear their own voices becoming muted, and feel their own desires giving way to the desires of others, as if the process were somehow uncontrollable and ineluctable." (*The Erotic Silence of the American Wife,* p. 149)

Dalma Heyn: "Adultery is, in fact, a revolutionary way for women to rise above the conventional—if they live to do so." (*Ibid.,* p. 10)

Brenda Scott: "There are numerous reasons kids join gangs. Part of the allure is a sense of 'glamour' teens see in a dangerous, risky lifestyle....Other reasons given for gang involvement are a desire to have friends, a need for protection, a longing for a family relationship the child doesn't have at home, and a desire to make money through theft or drug trade. For some, gang membership is a family tradition, for others, it's a way to deal with boredom....Most young people who join gangs come from homes without fathers or any significant role models to enforce discipline." (*Children No More,* pp. 73, 76)

Shere Hite: "If the mother-child family was prevalent in pre-history, and indeed is a flourishing form of family in our own societies today, this is something of which we can be proud, not terrified." (*The Hite Report on the Family,* p. 359)

Lynn Smith: "One recent study, the Who's Who Among American High School Students, surveyed thousands of high-achieving teenagers and parents and found that parents consistently underestimated their children's cheating, sexual activity, drunk driving, friends' drug activity, pregnancy and suicide worries." (*Los Angeles Times,* 26 June, 1997)

Rosalind Miles: "Child sexual abuse, according to 1988 National Society for the Prevention of Cruelty to Children figures, is rising by over 20 percent a year, and the number of all children registered as victims has more than doubled since 1984." (*Love, Sex, Death and the Making of the Male,* p. 110)

Judy Mann: "In recent years, much of the anti-feminist drumbeat has been the attempt to regulate women's reproductive freedom. What are the anti-abortionists telling an eleven-year-old girl about her right to run her own life? A whole generation of girls has grown up listening to men debate abortion: It is a debate in which men are desperately fighting to maintain control over women. The hierarchies of the Catholic and Mormon churches made common cause with the fundamentalist

Christians in a crusade to keep women in check, to protect the traditional place of males as heads of families." (*The Difference*, p. 12)

Daniel Patrick Moynihan: "By 1983 the poverty rate reached its highest level in 18 years....The principal correlate had been the change in family structure, the rise of the female-headed household." (*Family and Nation*, p. 95)

National Fatherhood Initiative: "Almost 40% of America's children will go to sleep in a house where their biological father does not live.

"The number of children living only with mothers grew from 5.1 million in 1960 to over 17 million today.

"40% of children who live in fatherless homes have not seen their father for at least a year.

"Almost 75% of children in single-parent families will experience poverty before the age of eleven, compared with 20% in two-parent families.

"Father absence is associated with higher levels of youth suicide, low intellectual and educational performance, greater mental illness, violence and drug abuse.

"Studies have shown that 60% of rapists, 75% of adolescent murderers, 70% of long-term prisoners grew up in fatherless homes.

"Single-parent family daughters are 53% more likely to be teenage mums (164% more likely outside marriage).

"The relationship of father absence to crime is *so* strong that in contrast the effects of income and race are negligible. The chief predictor of crime in a community is the percentage of father-absent households." ("State of Fatherhood," *Father Facts*, quoted in *McKenzie* October, 1997)

Riane Eisler: "[A] psychoanalyst who accepted a contract to work in Saudi Arabia (being a woman, this meant working only with women) told me how shocked she was by all the unconscious ways in which women in that society expressed this resentment toward men. She reported acts such as sexual abuse of male babies (for instance, grandmothers sucking baby boys' penises) and women egging their sons on to ever greater recklessness (reflected in the many abandoned Cadillacs and other expensive foreign cars found on Saudi Arabian roads after crashes due to driving at incredibly high speeds) [personal communication with a psychoanalyst who did not wish to have her name revealed]." (*Sacred Pleasure*, p. 447)

Cassell's Queer Companion: "There was a great growth in such relationships [romantic friendships] toward the latter half of the nineteenth century when movements among women for suffrage and employment gained impetus. This allowed some middle-class women to find, often for the first time, the economic independence to resist matrimony and devote themselves to woman-oriented relationships." (p. 216)

Cassell's Queer Companion: "SIND ES FRAUEN? (Are These Women?) 1903 novel by Aimee Duc which shows the influence of the writings of the 19th century sexologists such as Richard von Krafft-Ebing. The plot deals with women who prefer a professional fulfillment to the questionable joys of marriage. One is a doctor, others are studying for Ph. Ds. They all reject romantic love to maintain their professional freedom. They acknowledge that such wayward behavior can only mean one thing in the light of the sexological theories of the day, that they are CONGENITAL INVERTS. They adopt this label happily because of the independence it gives them, and refer to themselves as Krafft-Ebingers." (p. 234)

Rosie Jackson: "Fantasies of leaving *had* to be repressed: the consequences were—as *East Lynne* reveals in exaggerated form—just too appalling. The passion informing Ellen Price's writing and the extent of the suffering and punishment inflicted on the abdicating mother show just how urgent the message—and the need for repression—were. *East Lynne* was the effective *deterrent* women needed, echoing their own desperate containment of their equally desperate passion and desire.

"Seen in this light, *East Lynne* is an extraordinarily sado-masochistic fantasy, and one that powerfully affected the collective female response to a mother escaping from husband and children." (*Mothers Who Leave*, p. 56)

Eva Keuls: "It is clear that the Athenian man, after excluding women from all the significant aspects of public life, felt uneasy about them. As the surviving dramas show, men fantasized hysterically about women rebelling against male supremacy. They peopled their tragic and comic stages with women taking their revenge by slaughtering husbands and sons and defying the social order." (*The Reign of the Phallus*, pp. 124f.)

Victoria Woodhull: "All that is good and commendable now existing would continue to exist if all marriage laws were repealed tomorrow....I have an inalienable constitutional and natural right to love whom I may, to love as long or as short a period as I can, to change that love every day if I please!" (Quoted in Germaine Greer, *The Female Eunuch*, p. 345)

Riane Eisler: "Since the institution of the family functions as both a social model and a microcosm of the larger society, feminists have always perceived that no real change in the status of women is possible unless the patriarchal family is replaced. But it is precisely because the whole structure of patriarchy rests so heavily on the institution of the family that any challenge to it is perceived as a fundamental threat. The patriarchal family is protected by a formidable alignment of religious dogma, legal sanction, and economic constraints, so that while it receives support from practically every existing social mechanism, alternative family forms are considered 'abnormal' and receive no support at all." (*Dissolution*, pp. 139f.)

Hillary Rodham Clinton: "[T]here has been an explosion in the number of children born out of wedlock, from one in twenty in 1960 to one in four today.

"More than anyone else, children bear the brunt of such massive social transitions. The confusion and turmoil that divorce and out-of-wedlock births cause in children's lives is well documented. The results of the National Survey of Children, which followed the lives of a group of seven- to eleven-year-olds for more than a decade, and other recent studies demonstrate convincingly that while many adults claim to have benefited from divorce and single parenthood, most children have not.

"Children living with one parent or in stepfamilies are two to three times as likely to have emotional and behavioral problems as children living in two-parent families. Children of single-parent families are more likely to drop out of high school, become pregnant as teenagers, abuse drugs, behave violently, become entangled with the law. A parent's remarriage often does not seem to better the odds.

"Further, the rise in divorce and out-of-wedlock births has contributed heavily to the tragic increase in the number of American children in poverty, currently one in five." *(It Takes a Village*, pp. 313f.)

Barbara Dafoe Whitehead: "According to Wallerstein and Blakeslee's study, for example, 80 percent of divorced *women*...believed they were better off out of their marriages." *(The Divorce Culture*, p. 102; emphasis added)

Barbara Dafoe Whitehead: "Moreover, although the psychological experience of divorce is difficult and painful, it can also be transformative. At the end of the 'crazy time,' Trafford notes, comes the 'emergence of self.' Unlike the bad feelings engendered by death, prolonged illness, or chronic joblessness, the bad feelings of divorce can lead to good things. Divorce can trigger a kind of emotional counterresponse, a marshaling of inner resources to ward off the assault on the self. As the author of one popular divorce book writes, 'After being in a long-term marriage in which they tended to deny so much of themselves, divorce gives many *women* their first chance to validate their reality, to explore who they are, to cherish newfound identities, to heal old wounds, and ultimately to take care of themselves." *(Ibid.*, p. 55; emphasis added)

Betty Friedan: "To show how far we've come in this short time, let me tell you that ten and nine and eight and seven and six years ago, I was warned by my publisher, editor, agent and my dear husband that I would be ruined, I would be destroyed, if I got divorced—that my whole credibility, my ability to write in the future about women who had gone through the experience—who I could dare to ask the things that you can't ask a lawyer or trust a lawyer to tell you the truth about. And then somehow *the women's movement began to give me the strength that it has given all of you and I said, I don't care, I have to do something about my own life." (It Changed My Life*, p. 324; emphasis added)

Stephanie Coontz: "Children's initial response to divorce is often negative, although they do adjust if the parents do not continue battling afterward. But *women*, despite initial pain and income loss, tend almost immediately to feel that they benefit from divorce. A 1982 survey found that even one year after a divorce, a majority of *women* said they were happier and had more self-respect than they had in their marriages. The proportion rises with every passing year." (*The Way We Never Were*, p. 224; emphasis added)

Riane Eisler: "[Homosexuality] threatens the very foundations of a society in which men are supposed to control women and a small elite of men are supposed to control the masses of women and men....[L]esbian relations...offer women an alternative to the so-called traditional family: the male-dominated, procreation-oriented family that is the cornerstone of the dominator society. Moreover, because they promote bonding between women, they can lead to what many lesbian groups in fact are today engaged in—social and political action for fundamental structural and ideological change." (*Sacred Pleasure*, p. 352)

Haya Shalom: "Lesbianism is a way of life, is a culture, is a challenge to the patriarchy, and lesbians exist in every society; in the East as well as the West, in the North as in the South, in Israel as in Jordan, in Brazil as in Japan, in Africa as in Scandinavia, in Russia as in the U.S.A." (*off our backs*, November, 1996)

David Goodstein: "A few years ago, Vito Russo, a gay film historian, told me the nuclear family is the real enemy of gay people." (*The Advocate*, 1 May, 1980)

Soviet Comintern, 16 November, 1924: "The Revolution is impotent as long as the notion of family and of family relations continues to exist." (Quoted in Simone de Beauvoir, *The Second Sex*, p. 127)

Cassell's Queer Companion: "Lesbian feminism argues that all crime, inequality and distress are the effect of men trying to enforce their rule over women. The key way that men maintain their power as a group, lesbian feminists argue, is via the institution of heterosexuality. It is through the mechanism of heterosexuality that women are made subordinate and cowed into good behavior. Patriarchal societies ensure women enter heterosexuality by stigmatizing, devaluing and applying sanctions to all alternatives." (p. 149)

Ira Reiss: "As I have said many times, to build pluralism we must firmly root out the narrow thinking about sex that exists in all of our basic institutions: family, political, economic, religious, and educational.

We need to change our basic social institutional structure." (*An End to Shame*, p. 273

   Los Angeles Times: "A 1990 survey from the National Center for Health Statistics found an 'alarmingly high' prevalence of emotional and behavior problems among all children, with rates two to three times higher for single-parent and stepparent families than for intact families....

   "Fatherlessness is probably the single most important factor in the rising juvenile delinquency rate, [sociologist David] Popenoe said." (12 June, 1992)

   Leontine Young: "Another interesting reflection of the existent cultural pattern is the high percentage of unmarried mothers coming from homes dominated by the mother and showing the pattern of personality damage which results when this form of family relationship exists in severe and pathological degree....Under these circumstances it is to be expected that the girls from father-dominated homes would constitute a considerably smaller percentage of the total, and this is borne out in fact." (*Out of Wedlock*, pp. 118f.)

   Rene Denfeld: "According to state agency reports on child abuse women are involved in twice as many incidents as men." (*Kill the Body, the Head Will Fall*, p. 50)

   Ehrenreich, Hess and Jacobs "Sex did not have to be a microdrama of male dominance and female passivity; it was, properly understood and acted upon, an affirmation of woman's strength and independence...visible proof of woman's sexual autonomy....All the old prohibitions and taboos would have to give way to the needs of the sexually liberated woman." (*Re-Making Love*, pp. 69ff.)

   Havelock Ellis: "Alexandre Dumas, in *Les Femmes qui Tuent*, writes that a distinguished Roman Catholic priest had told him that eighty out of one hundred women who married told him afterwards that they regretted it." (*Views and Reviews*, 2d series, p. 6)

   Robert Briffault: "In all uncultured societies, where advanced retrospective claims have not become developed, and the females are not regularly betrothed or actually married before they have reached the age of puberty, girls and women who are not married are under no restrictions as to their sexual relations, and are held to be entirely free to dispose of themselves as they please in that respect.

"To that rule there does not exist any known exception." (*The Mothers*, II, 2.)

Brett Harvey: "At the heart of the New Right's attack on abortion rights was a traditional definition of women as childbearers—victims of nature—rather than autonomous human beings with the fundamental right to define our own sexuality....Still we are far away from that blank piece of paper [women's abortion law]—the guarantee of total sexual freedom and autonomy for women. The notion that women are not slaves of their reproductive systems; that women have the right to choose when, how and with whom they wish to be sexual—these ideas, the bedrock of radical feminism, are still not truly accepted. As long as women who choose not to have children, or to live alone or with other women, or to have a variety of sexual partners—as long as such women are stigmatized; as 'selfish' or 'narcissistic,' or 'perverted,' no woman is really free." ("No More Nice Girls" in *Pleasure and Danger*, ed. C. Vance, p. 205)

Carole Vance: "Feminism must, of course, continue to work for material changes that support women's autonomy, including social justice, economic equality, and reproductive choice. At the same time, feminism must speak to sexuality as a site of oppression, not only the oppression of male violence, brutality, and coercion which it has already spoken about eloquently and effectively, but also the repression of female desire that comes from ignorance, invisibility, and fear. Feminism must put forward a politics that resists deprivation and supports pleasure. It must understand pleasure as life-affirming, empowering, desirous of human connection and the future, and not fear it as destructive, enfeebling, or corrupt. Feminism must speak to sexual pleasure as a fundamental right, which cannot be put off to a better or easier time." (*Pleasure and Danger*, pp. 23f.)

Barbara Dafoe Whitehead: "Too, according to the 1970s data, women held more liberal views of marriage than men; they were more likely to describe their marriages as "two separate people" and to approve of divorce. Therefore, [Jessie] Bernard's notion of separate marital stakes and experiences captured, however distortedly, some of these attitudinal differences. But perhaps more important, her argument suggested, at

390

least implicitly, a therapeutic imperative for women: "Get better by getting out." (*The Divorce Culture*, p. 52)

Barbara Dafoe Whitehead: "The study's author, sociologist Catherine Riessman, observes that 'more than half of the women in the sample, particularly those separated less than a year, actively engaged in reconstructing a self, emphasize this outcome. They say they "got born," have "the freedom to be myself," feel "more like a free person."''' (*Ibid.*, p. 57)

Cindy Loose: "Fatherlessness repeatedly shows up in studies as a leading indicator for a plethora of societal problems: infant mortality, alcohol and drug abuse, criminality, low test scores, depression—even suicide." (*Los Angeles Times*, 15 January, 1998)

Barbara Seaman: "We now know from psychology and animal studies that there is no such thing as a maternal instinct. At least, there is more concrete evidence against it than for it. We also know from anthropology that there is no primitive culture where mothers are expected to spend as much time in exclusive company of their babies and young children as they are expected to spend in the United States....Women, then, should feel freer to select their own life-styles than many of them do. The old arguments that we-cannot-be-happy-unless-we-have-children and we-cannot-raise-normal-children-unless-we-stay-at-home-with-them are simply invalid, no more than wishful thinking on the part of males." (*Free and Female*, p. 208)

Andre Maurois: "What Sand [George Sand, French feminist] wanted was to see restored to women those civil rights of which they were deprived by marriage, and to have repealed a law which exposed the adulterous wife to degrading penalties—'a savage law the only effect of which is to make adultery a permanent feature of our society, and to increase the number of cases in which it is committed.'" (*Lelia: The Life of George Sand*, p.325)

Susan B. Anthony: "Don't you break the law every time you help a slave to Canada? Well, the law that gives the father the sole ownership of the children is just as wicked, and I'll break it just as quickly. You would die before you would deliver a slave to his master, and I will die before I will give up the child to its father." (quoted in Phyllis Chesler, *Patriarchy*, p. 38)

Betty Friedan: "The right of every woman to control her own reproductive life....The right, the inalienable right, to control our own body....To create new social institutions that are needed to free women, not from childbearing or love or sex or even marriage, but from the intolerable agony and burden those become when women are chained to them." (*It Changed My Life*, pp. 102, 153, 144)

Anne Wilson Schaef: "A mother may love her son dearly, but he is nevertheless a member of a class that has controlled and oppressed her. As a result, she cannot help but feel rage and hostility toward him." (*Women's Reality*, p. 80)

Helen Diner: "A free disposition over one's own person is an original right in a matriarchal society." (*Mothers and Amazons*, p. 31)

Evelyn Reed: "[Betty Friedan] likens the blind docility with which middle-class women accepted their fate to prisoners in Nazi concentration camps, who became unprotesting 'walking corpses' marching to their own doom:

"In a sense that is not as far-fetched as it sounds, the women who 'adjust' as housewives, who grow up wanting to be 'just a housewife,' are in as much danger as the millions who walked to their own death in the concentration camps—and the millions more who refused to believe that the concentration camps existed.

"True, the barbed wire surrounding the 'comfortable concentration camps' of Suburbia was invisible. What was visible to these victims of 'The American Dream' were the gilded trappings of the standard middle-class home. As a lifetime occupation, however, they were bogged down in domestic trivia requiring the intellectual exertions of an eight-year-old. Even then there was not enough work to occupy their full time." (*Problems of Women's Liberation*, pp. 88f.)

Betty Friedan: "It is urgent to understand how the very condition of being a housewife can create a sense of emptiness, non-existence, nothingness, in women. There are aspects of the housewife role that make it almost impossible for a woman of adult intelligence to retain a sense of human identity, the firm core of self or 'I' without which a human being, man or woman, is not truly alive. For women of ability, in America today, I am convinced there is a sense that is not as far-fetched as it sounds, the women who 'adjust' as housewives, who grow up wanting to be 'just a housewife,' are in as much danger as the millions who walked to their own death in the concentration camps....Strangely enough, the conditions which destroyed the human identity of so many prisoners were not the torture and the brutality, but conditions similar to those which destroy the identity of the American housewife." (*The Feminine Mystique*, p. 305)

Debold, Wilson and Malave: "Daughters need to be invited into an underground—not a psychological underground but an underground of resistance." (*Mother Daughter Revolution*, p. 192)

Robert Briffault: "Cohabitation is, as will later be shown, very transient in the lower phases of human culture, because the sexes, as a rule, associate little with one another." (*The Mothers*, I, 125)

Marilyn French: "The great good upheld by this book is pleasure....[T]here is nothing sacrosanct about a sexual or marriage tie. The greater stability of marriage in patrilineal groups often arises not from choice but from coercion." (*Beyond Power*, pp. 23, 58)

Mary Daly: "Androgynous integrity and transformation will require that women cease to play the role of 'complement' and struggle to stand alone as free human beings." (*Beyond God the Father*, p. 26)

Frithof Capra: "The first and perhaps most profound transition is due to the slow and reluctant but inevitable decline of patriarchy....[F]or the past three thousand years Western civilization and its precursors, as well as most other cultures, have been based on philosophical, social, and political systems 'in which men—by force, direct pressure, or through ritual, tradition, law and language, customs, etiquette, education, and the division of labor—determine what part women shall or shall not play, and in which the female is everywhere subsumed under the male' [quoting Adrienne Rich]....It is the one system which, until recently, had never in recorded history been openly challenged, and whose doctrines were so universally accepted that they seemed to be laws of nature; indeed, they were usually presented as such. Today, however, the disintegration of patriarchy is in sight. The feminist movement is one of the strongest cultural currents of our time and will have a profound effect on our further evolution." (*The Turning Point*, p. 29)

Elizabeth Nickles and Laura Ashcraft: "Women...who work prefer smaller families, and fewer children means more time to devote to personal and nondomestic interests. Our survey also showed that working women have less successful marriages....[W]orking wives are more than twice as likely as housewives to have had affairs by the time they reach their late thirties....Researchers have found that the longer a wife is employed, the more both partners think about divorce—an increase of one percentage point for each year of employment. Things get worse as she earns more money." (*The Coming Matriarchy: How Women Will Gain the Balance of Power*, pp. 42f.)

Constance Ahrons: "Today record numbers of women have options for the first time in their lives. One enormous option is to leave a marriage that does not meet their needs....It's fair that you should start divorce with a standard of living similar to that of your exspouse." (*The Good Divorce*, pp. 35, 174)

Constance Ahrons: "Even though most women's incomes had dropped sharply, they enjoyed their new control over their lives, their finances not being dependent on their partner's behavior or good will." (*Ibid.*, p. 16)

Robert Briffault: "Individual marriage has its foundation in economic relations." (*The Mothers*, II, 1)

Barbara Dafoe Whitehead: "In 1974 women disagreed by more than two to one with the statement that 'There is no reason why single women shouldn't have children and raise them if they want to'; by 1985, the last time the question was asked, slightly more women agreed than disagreed....Across the socioeconomic spectrum, from inner-city teenagers to middle-class college students, young women say that they will have a child 'on their own' if the right man doesn't come along." (*The Divorce Culture*, pp. 149f.)

Evelyn Reed: "Dispossessed from their former place in society at large, they [Stone Age women] were robbed not only of their economic independence but also of their former sexual freedom." (*Woman's Evolution*, p. 24)

Senator Daniel Moynihan: "We knew this was coming. In the early 60s we picked up the first tremors of the earthquake that was about to shake the American family. The single most powerful indicator is the ratio of our-of-wedlock births. Today it is 43%, and in some districts as high as 81%." (*Human Events*, 28 Jan., 1994)

Betty Steele: [Citing Dr. Elliott Barker, chief of the Province of Ontario's maximum security facility for the criminally insane at Penetanguishene and also president of the Canadian Society for the Prevention of Cruelty to Children] "[A]ll those extremely deprived children of the wealthy, the middle-class and the poor, 'thrown away' daily into day care.... [Dr. Barker] coined the phrase 'daytime orphanages' in describing day care centers. Children in such centers, he had found, are simply unable to form 'close, stable bonds with constantly changing and rotating caretakers, and consequently fail to develop the trust, empathy and affection that are the basic qualities of character sought in personality development.' Dr. Barker warned that 'within 15 years we can be faced with a generation of psychopaths—adults who are superficial, manipulative and unable to maintain mutually satisfactory relationships with others." (*Together Again*, pp. 201-3)

Betty Steele: "The numbers of teenage boys and girls in the courts steadily rose throughout the eighties; their roster of crimes included muggings, assault and battery, intimidation, and murder, often wanton murder. Teenage runaways—from impossible home situations, a significant number of them involving step-parents—are the prostitutes and drug addicts to be found living and dying on the streets of every large city in North America....In Canada, 10,000 teenagers are reported to be living on the streets of Toronto alone, with the police sometimes picking up prostitutes under the age of 12.

"The past decade has seen a steady climb in the suicide rate among teenagers, with children under 10 known to be escaping from a harsh, unnatural society in which the care of children has developed into our lowest priority." (*Ibid*, p. 202)

Sex Information and Education Council of the United States (SIECUS): "No form of sexual orientation or family structure is morally superior to any other." (Quoted in George Grant and Mark Horne, *Legislating Immorality*, p. 76)

Susan Faludi: "Men are also more devastated than women by the breakup—and time doesn't cure the pain or close the gap. A 1982 survey of divorced people a year after the breakup found that 60 percent of the women were happier, compared with only half the men; a majority of the women said they had more self-respect while only a minority of the men felt that way. The nation's largest study on the long-term effects of divorce found that five years after divorce, two-thirds of the women were happier with their lives; only 50 percent of the men were. By the ten-year mark, the men who said their quality of life was no better or worse had risen from one-half to two-thirds. While 80 percent of the women ten years after divorce said it was the right decision, only 50 percent of the ex-husbands agreed." (*Backlash*, p. 26)

Maggie Gallagher: "Today, the white family stands poised, eerily, almost exactly where the black family was twenty-five years ago, before its rapid descent into a post-marital world." (*The Abolition of Marriage*, p. 126)

Riane Eisler: "But history, like time, will not stand still and the historical moment for the nuclear patriarchal family, has already come and gone." (*Dissolution*, p. 135)

Los Angeles Times: "But while the divorce rate has leveled off, more children are being born outside marriage. Nothing in the figures suggests the return of the traditional family." (27 November, 1996)

Armand M. Nicholi, Jr., M.D.: "The breakdown of the family contributes significantly to the major problems confronting our society today. Research data make unmistakably clear a strong relationship between broken or disordered families and the drug epidemic, the increase in out-of-wedlock pregnancies, the rise in violent crime, and the unprecedented epidemic of suicide among children and adolescents....Two-career families compound the problem of emotional inaccessibility. And single-parent families, where the mother is burdened with providing the children with emotional support as well as economic support, are an overwhelming problem in our society." (*Looking Forward: The Next Forty Years*, ed., John Templeton, pp. 132, 134)

Armand M. Nicholi, Jr., M.D.: "Several other recent studies bear on the absence or inaccessibility of the father, and all point to the same conclusions: A father absent for long periods contributes to (a) low motivation for achievement; (b) inability to defer immediate gratification for later rewards; (c) low self-esteem; and (d) susceptibility to group influence and to juvenile delinquency. The absent father tends to have passive, dependent sons, lacking in achievement, motivation, and independence....When we consult the scientific and medical literature, we find an impressive body of data based on carefully controlled experiments that corroborate the impression that a parent's absence, whether through death, divorce, or time-demanding job, can exert a profound influence on a child's emotional health. The magnitude of this research paints an unmistakably clear picture of the adverse effects of parental absence and emotional inaccessibility. Why has our society almost totally ignored this research? Why have even the professionals tended to ignore it? The answer is the same reason society ignored for scores of years sound data on the adverse effects of cigarette smoke. The data are simply unacceptable. We just don't want to hear the facts because they demand a change in our lifestyle.

"Because families provide the foundation of our lives as individuals, as well as the vital cells of our society, we can no longer afford to ignore this research on the family." (*Ibid.*, pp. 139f.)

Susan Crain Bakos: "Sexual freedom eliminated one pressing reason for marriage—physical gratification. We no longer had to be married to have sex. That, coupled with the pill, allowed us for the first time in history to triumph over our own biology....If single, we saw no reason to marry, since we didn't yet want children. If married, we were beginning to see plenty of reasons for getting divorced. And one of the reasons was sex." (*This wasn't Supposed to Happen*, pp. 11f.)

Betty Steele: "Dr. E. Kent Hayes...told Janet Enright in an interview she reported in the *Toronto Star* that 'in the past ten years there has been a 500 percent increase in the number of middle and upper class children in North America who have been admitted to a mental institution or a prison.' Psychiatrists have heard distraught parents begging to have their children committed to mental institutions, and it is estimated that hundreds of children are now unjustifiably incarcerated simply on the evidence of these distraught parents, who are no longer able to cope, particularly with the drug problems." (*Together Again*, p. 217)

Andre Maurois: "Impatient of all masculine authority, she [George Sand] fought a battle for the emancipation of women and sought to win for them the right to dispose freely of their bodies and their hearts." (*Lelia: A Life of George Sand*, p. 13)

Gisela Schlientz: "In *Lelia*, the vague malaise of the era was sharpened into an indictment of marriage, the church, and the whole social order that left women a choice only between marital submission and prostitution. In France, the resulting storm of indignation over the heroine (and her creator), who dared to talk about her feminine needs and experiences in love, was overwhelming." ("George Sand and the German Vormarz" in *The World of George Sand*, p. 154)

Hazel Henderson: "All that women would need to do to create a quiet revolution is to resume the old practice of keeping the paternity of their children a secret." (*Woman of Power*, Fall, 1988)

Robert Scheer: "Premarital sex is the norm in American life." (*Los Angeles Times*, 4 March, 1997)

Ira Reiss: "Seeking economic independence has an impact on many parts of the female role—including the sexual. Economic autonomy reduces dependence on others and makes sexual assertiveness a much less risky procedure." (*An End to Shame, p. 88*)

Debold, Wilson and Malave: "In Dalma Heyn's exploration of women who have affairs within marriages they had not considered leaving, the women found that they got 'themselves' back by transgressing patriarchy's boundaries so completely, so desirously. Some of the women even felt that their affair was good for their children because afterwards they were more confident, more rooted in the lifeforce of desire. Eleanor says, 'I mean look: Before I had the affair, I used to detach from my children because of my own insecurity and depression, buying the teacher's verdict about people I knew better than she—siding, in effect, with the authorities. It's a small issue, maybe, but now I see that as such a gross injustice, such betrayal of the people I care about, such a betrayal of my own real feelings. It's as if something snapped into place in me and I can see now, and feel my own real feelings. As if I had manufactured feelings before—this is what a mother feels; this is what a wife feels. The affair has made me feel the feelings of the outsider, while still giving me the authority and concern of the insider. I feel like me.'" (*Mother Daughter Revolution*, pp. 185f.)

Debold, Wilson and Malave: "In Alice Walker's *Possessing the Secret of Joy*, Tashi, the heroine, finds herself in the consulting room with a white male psychiatrist. 'Negro women, said the doctor, are considered the most difficult of all people to be effectively analyzed. Do you know why?' Tashi says nothing. 'Negro women, the doctor says into my silence, can never be analyzed effectively because they can never bring themselves to blame their mothers.' The shared comradeship of mothers and daughters in the African-American community is turned into a source of sickness by experts." (*Mother Daughter Revolution*, p. 21)

Los Angeles Times: "Nearly one in four children in the United States is born outside of marriage and the divorce rate is among the world's highest. More than twice as many households are headed by divorced, separated or never-married people than those in traditional families. Mothers who are single by choice say they are only the latest branch on society's changing family tree....

"A 1990 survey from the National Center for Health Statistics found an 'alarmingly high' prevalence of emotional and behavior problems among all children, with rates two to three times higher for single-parent and stepparent families than for intact families....'Fatherlessness is probably the single most important factor in the rising juvenile delinquency rate,' [sociologist David] Popenoe said.

"The risk for girls in fatherless homes is premature sexuality and later divorce, said [Frank] Pittman, author of 'Men Without Models.' The girls 'both overvalue and distrust men so they have great difficulty with relationships with men,' he said." (12 June, 1992)

Betty Steele: "The acceptance of the single cult was also obvious in divorce becoming the norm throughout the Western world—divorce initiated by women in 75 to 90 percent of all cases (as reported in major surveys). A large percentage of these women, if they had children, would then face social and economic deprivation often accompanied by unendurable loneliness. Loneliness would become the number one psychiatric disorder throughout North America, with suicide often in its wake.

"As statistics recorded a dramatic increase in the divorce rate (500 percent in Canada between 1968 and 1983), the American Association of Suicidality, a research body based in Los Angeles, was noting a 600 percent increase in the suicide rate among the 15- to 30-year-old age group in the United States since 1963. Two-thirds of the 50,000 people who died of tranquilizer overdoses in 1984 were women, although general statistics indicate three times as many men as women commit suicide.

"While 50 percent of all marriages in North America are still being dissolved, with the resulting anguish engulfing all members of the families, particularly the children, an urgency to rethink modern attitudes to marriage and divorce in our society has been born." (*Together Again, p.* 3)

Judith Wallerstein and Sandra Blakeslee: "The children of divorce are likewise afraid but more so. It is never easy to play the queen of hearts, but the children of divorce have a dead child under the table; their entry into young adulthood is encumbered by an inescapable need to reexamine the past. What they see are the long shadows cast by their parents, who failed to maintain a loving relationship. Now that it is time to venture forth, to trust, and to make a commitment, the children of divorce find that their search for love and intimacy is ghost-ridden. In adolescence they think about these issues, but in young adulthood anxiety about them hits full force. They fear betrayal. They fear abandonment. They fear loss. They draw an inescapable conclusion: Relationships have a high likelihood of being untrustworthy; betrayal and infidelity are probable." (*Second Chances,* p. 55)

Aaron Kipnis: "According to the sociologist Annette Lawson, who recently surveyed over six hundred men and women, modern women are usually the *first* partner to develop sexual liaisons outside their marriages. They begin sexual relations with other men on the average of 4.5 years after getting married—somewhat earlier than men." (*Knights Without Armor, p.* 48)

Aaron Kipnis: "[C]ontrary to the myth of men's untrustworthiness as single parents, the majority of violent child-abuse incidents, resulting in tens of thousands of injuries and hundreds of deaths every year, are perpetrated by women. A majority of these victims are boys averaging two and a half years old." (*Ibid.,* p. 49)

Nicholas Davidson: "In a 1987 article in *Social Work*, researchers John S. Wodarski and Pamela Harris linked the increase in suicides to the proliferation of single-parent households....Study of 752 families by researchers at the New York Psychiatric Institute reported in the *Journal of the American Academy of Child and Adolescent Psychology* in 1988:

Youths attempting suicide differ little in age, income, race, religion, but are more likely in nonintact family settings." ("Life Without Father," *Policy Review*, Winter, 1990)

Betty Friedan: "Women are doing the battering, as much or more than men." (*It Changed My Life*, p. 126)

Paul G. Shane: "In general, homeless youth are more likely to come from female-headed, single-parent, or reconstituted families with many children, particularly step-siblings." ("Changing Patterns Among Homeless and Runaway Youth," *American Journal of Orthopsychiatry*, April, 1989)

Robert Rector: "Children raised in single-parent families, when compared with those in intact families, are one-third more likely to exhibit behavioral problems such as hyperactivity, antisocial behavior, and anxiety. Children deprived of a two-parent home are two to three times more likely to need psychiatric care than those in two-parent families, and as teenagers they are more likely to commit suicide. Absence of a father increases the probability that a child will use drugs and engage in criminal activity." ("Requiem for the War on Poverty," *Policy Review*, Summer, 1992)

R. F. Doyle: "More than one in three children of broken families drop out of school." (*The Rape of the Male*, p. 145)

Isidore Chein, Donald Gerard, Robert Lee and Eva Rosenfeld: "Mother dominance was a common feature of addict families. The strongest finding, though, was a close relationship of youthful addiction to 'the absence of a warm relationship with a father figure with whom the boy could identify.'" (*Family in America*, July, 1988)

Martha Farnsworth Riche: "I concluded that in many ways wives have fired husbands. The economic motivation for marriage has gone, and at that point what a spouse is confronted with is, 'What am I getting out of this?'" (*Los Angeles Times*, 21 Oct., 1992; Riche is Director of Policy Studies at the Washington-based Population Reference Bureau)

Los Angeles Times: [According to Neil Kalter, University of Michigan psychologist]: "For kids, the misery their parents may feel in an unhappy marriage is usually less significant than the changes [the children] have to go through after a divorce. They'd rather their parents keep fighting and not get divorced." Kalter also found "a higher rate of sexual activity, substance abuse and running away among adolescent girls, especially when the divorce occurred before elementary school and the father had departed. Other studies show that female children of divorced parents are more likely to have marital problems of their own, more likely to choose 'inadequate husbands' and to be pregnant at their weddings." (12 Nov., 1987)

Rex Forehand: "Children in high-conflict divorced families did the worst, considerably worse than children who remained in homes where their mother and father fought constantly." (cited in Maggie Gallagher, *Enemies of Eros*, p. 200)

Samuel Osherson: "The interviews I have had with men in their 30s and 40s convince me that the psychological or physical absence of fathers from their families is one of the great underestimated tragedies of our times." (Quoted in James Nelson, *The Intimate Connection*, p. 119)

Dan Quayle: "And for those concerned about children growing up in poverty, we should know this: Marriage is probably the best anti-poverty program of all. Among families headed by married couples today, there is a poverty rate of 5.7 percent. But 33.4 percent of families headed by a single mother are in poverty today." (Address to the Commonwealth Club of California, 1992; quoted in FACE, August, 1992)

Humboldt's Sheriff's Crime Prevention News: "Various studies of gang members suggest some of the catalysts include coming from a single-parent home without a strong authority figure, the breakdown of the family unit, a need for love, acceptance and peer support, gaining confidence and protection from other gang members." (Fall/Winter, 1992)

Los Angeles Times: "Half of all children in the state will live at some time in a single-parent household. One in four is born to an unmarried mother and more than half the black children in California are born to single mothers. Such factors tend to be accompanied by increased health, academic and social problems for youngsters." (14 February, 1989)

Los Angeles Times: "A vast majority of American teachers say that abused, neglected or sick children are serious problems in their schools and that teachers have little impact on the education process, despite publicized reforms, a report said. A growing gap between the home and school, blamed on parental disinterest in their children's education, also troubles teachers, according to the report from the Carnegie Foundation for the Advancement of Teaching. The report, 'The Condition of Teaching: A State-by-State Analysis, 1988,' was based on a national survey of 22,000 public schoolteachers. Among the highlights: 90% of teachers say lack of parental support is a problem, 89% report abused or neglected children in their classes, nearly 70% cite sick and undernourished students." (13 Dec., 1988)

Riane Eisler: "[A] woman who behaves as a sexually and economically free person is a threat to the entire social and economic fabric of a rigidly male-dominated society. Such behavior cannot be countenanced lest the entire social and economic system fall apart." (*The Chalice and the Blade*, p. 97)

Betty Friedan: "Motherhood is a bane almost by definition, or at least partly so, so long as women are forced to be mothers—and only mothers—against their will. Like a cancer cell living its life through another cell, women today are forced to live too much through their children and husbands (they are too dependent on them, and therefore are forced to take too much varied resentment, vindictiveness, inexpressible resentment and rage out on their husbands and children)." (*It Changed My Life*, p. 126)

Le Monde: "Eight out of ten minors who are drug addicts come from broken homes." (17 Oct., 1969; quoted in Daniel Patrick Moynihan, *Mankind and Nation*, p. 118)

Los Angeles Times Magazine, quoting Kay Mills: "What," I asked [Carolyn Heilbrun], "pushed her into feminism?"

"'From childhood on, I never liked the life of women set out for them,' she says. 'And against enormous odds in the 1950s, I didn't live it.' In the 1960s, she read Betty Friedan's 'The Feminine Mystique,' and 'the book certainly spoke to me'—as had Simone de Beauvoir's 'The Second Sex' a decade earlier....Then the woman's movement flowered, and Heilbrun says she discovered who she was. All those ideas about the way she had been living, the thoughts she had been thinking, even the work she had been doing, had a name: feminism. 'There was so much discovering occurring, so much strength developing, and it was glorious.... We have to a great extent stopped internalizing the [patriarchy's] idea of what women's lives should be."' (18 July, 1992)

Valerie Polakow: "Children who live with their mothers are far more likely to live in poverty: 51 percent of such children were poor in 1989, compared to only 22 percent in single-father-headed families and 10 percent in two-parent families." (*Lives on the Edge*, p. 59)

The Liberator: "A study by feminist researcher Jane Mauldon of the University of California at Berkeley found that children of divorce are at a greater risk of becoming ill than those of intact families. The illnesses continue even if the mother remarries....

"The gist of Mauldon's article was that the unfortunate condition of children of divorce is the fault of fathers rather than mothers." (September, 1990)

David Popenoe: "We and other modern societies are drifting toward a situation where the male becomes more and more superfluous....It's a trend that is very, very dangerous." (*Los Angeles Times,* 12 June, 1992)

Cosmopolitan: "The woman we're profiling is an extraordinarily sexually free human being, [whose new bedroom expressiveness constitutes a] break with the old double standard." (quoted in Faludi, *Backlash*, p. 404)

Caryl Rivers: "That was the worst of all, I thought, a life where nothing ever happened. I looked around me and saw women ironing dresses and hanging out clothes and shopping for food and playing mah-jongg on hot summer afternoons, and I knew I couldn't bear to spend my life that way, day after drab day, with nothing ever happening. The world of women seemed to me like a huge, airless prison where things didn't change. Inside it, I thought, I'd turn gray and small and shrivel up to nothing." (*Virgins*, quoted in Wini Breines, *Young, White and Miserable*, pp. 135f.)

Wini Breines: "The life plan set out for these girls was unacceptable to them. Their society's expectations and, closer to home, those of their parents, did not coincide with their own yearnings. 'I couldn't stand girls who wanted to get married and have engagement rings. I knew I was different, and I was glad,' recalls one young women who became a beatnik. Janis Joplin, who lived in Port Arthur, Texas, during the 1950s, expressed a more earthy version of these sentiments. She describes herself as 'just a plain overweight chick': 'I wanted something more than bowling alleys and drive-ins. I'd've fucked anything, taken anything, I did.'" (*Ibid.*, p. 136)

Sandra Schneiders: "The final goal of women's liberation is a human social order in which women are fully self-determining." (*Beyond Patching*, p. 15)

Sandra Schneiders: "In regard to the institutional church all women who are both Catholic and feminist desire passionately the conversion of the institution from the sin of sexism and know that this requires a full and final repudiation of patriarchy....If the real life energy of the church is diverted into the swelling torrent of feminist spirituality, the patriarchal institution will soon be a dried up river bed, an arid trace of a lifeform that refused to change and so remains as a more or less interesting crack in the surface of history." (*Ibid.*, 108)

Katherine Anthony: "Women have to demand a great many things which may not necessarily be good in themselves simply because these things are forbidden. They have also to reject many things which may not necessarily be evil in themselves simply because they are prescribed. The idea of obedience can have no moral validity for women for a long time to come." (*Feminism in Germany and Scandinavia*, p. 236)

Ira Reiss: "[W]e must make changes in our fundamental institutions if free sexual choice is to flourish for women as well as for men." (*An End to Shame*, p. 222)

Otto Kiefer: "Aristocratic women enrolled themselves as prostitutes for the sake of living a free life." (*Sexual Life in Ancient Rome*, p. 60)

Phyllis Schlafly: "[Joycelyn] Elders said on CBS's 60 Minutes that every girl should take a condom in her purse when she goes out on a date. That's tantamount to turning minor girls into sex objects by telling them that fornication is the expected social activity on a date....The supposed purpose of the Condom Clinics is to reduce teenage pregnancies, but condom distribution has miserably failed to achieve that goal. The pregnancy rate rose in ten of the eleven Arkansas counties where she installed school Condom Clinics." (*The Phyllis Schlafly Report*, Oct., 1993)

Phyllis Schlafly: "The same day, most newspapers carried pictures of Ruth Bader Ginsburg taking her seat on the Supreme Court. At her confirmation hearings, no member of the Senate Judiciary Committee scraped enough nerve to ask this radical feminist about her bizarre published writings, such as her demands that the laws against statutory rape and prostitution be repealed, that prisons be sex-integrated, that the age of sexual consent be reduced to age 12." (Ibid.)

Ann Landers: "The pressure on young people to have sex, and at an earlier age, is getting stronger and stronger. This is a different era than when you and I were growing up. The media—TV, radio, movies, magazines and, yes, newspapers—are much more explicit. Some of the language startles me, and I'm pretty hard to shock.

"The advent of AIDS has cut down on promiscuity, but the trend is toward more intimacy and at a younger age. Although I mourn the loss of innocence, I see no way to turn the clock back." (Los Angeles Times, 23 July, 1993)

Sen. Daniel Patrick Moynihan: "In 1965, having reached the conclusion that there would be a dramatic increase in single-parent families, I reached the further conclusion that this would in turn lead to a dramatic increase in crime....The inevitable, as we now know, has come to pass, but here again our response is curiously passive. Crime is a more or less continuous subject of political pronouncement, and from time to time it will be at or near the top of opinion polls as a matter of public concern. But it never gets much further than that. In...words spoken from the bench, Judge Edwin Torres of the New York State Supreme Court, Twelfth Judicial District, described how 'the slaughter of the innocent marches unabated: subway riders, bodega owners, cab drivers, babies; in laundromats, at cash machines, on elevators, in hallways.' In personal communication, he writes: 'This numbness, this near narcoleptic state can diminish the human condition to the level of infantrymen, who, in protracted campaigns, can eat their battlefield rations seated on the bodies of the fallen, friend and foe alike. A society that loses its sense of outrage is doomed to extinction.' There is no expectation that this will change, nor any efficacious public insistence that it do so. The crime level has been *normalized*." (*The American Scholar*)

NBC Nightly News: "The Proportion of American adults who were single skyrocketed from 21 percent in 1970 to 41 percent in 1992." (16 July, 1992)

Dalma Heyn: "They began to fear that pleasure was not available to them—as though it was there for unmarried women but not for wives. They perceived the role of wife as a pointed renunciation of pleasure, a fact for which they didn't blame anyone." (*The Erotic Silence of the American Wife*, p. 113)

Dalma Heyn: "Connie never told a single one of her friends about feeling as if she were living in a cathedral rather than in a relationship, out of shame at seeming a misfit in marriage. Many of them, she learned later, felt the same way, but had systematically withheld from each other the truth about their uncertainty and isolation and disorientation, afraid of confirming their inadequacy or, even more damning, their unhappiness. They had become complicit in perpetuating the myth of their success and contentment as wives; colluding, in other words, in their collective silence about what they really felt and thought and knew." (*Ibid.*, p. 96)

Dalma Heyn: "Marriage is, remember, a male institution. Men created it, and men like it. Men need marriage more than women do and suffer far more profoundly outside it." (*Playboy*, April, 1993)

Judy Mann: "'No matter by which culture a woman is influenced, she understands the words *wild* and *woman* intuitively,' writes Clarissa Pinkola Estes. 'When women hear those words, an old, old memory is stirred and brought back to life. The memory is of our absolute, undeniable, and irrevocable kinship with the wild feminine, a relationship which may have become ghosty from neglect, buried by overdomestication, outlawed by the surrounding culture, or no longer understood anymore. We may have forgotten her names, we may not answer when she calls ours, but in our bones we know her, we yearn toward her; we know she belongs to us and we to her.'" (*The Difference*, p. 214)

Maggie Gallagher: "Research shows that children without fathers have lower academic performance, more cognitive and intellectual deficits, increased adjustment problems, and higher risks for psychosexual development problems. And children from homes in which one or both parents are missing or frequently absent have higher rates of delinquent behavior, suicide, and homicide, along with poor academic performance. Among boys, father absence has been linked to greater effeminacy, and exaggerated aggressiveness. Girls, on the other hand, who lose their father to divorce tended to be overly responsive to men and become sexually active earlier. They married younger, got pregnant out of wedlock more frequently and divorced or separated from their eventual husbands more frequently, perpetuating the cycle." (*Enemies of Eros*, p. 114)

Maggie Gallagher: "Although by 1995 criminologists were congratulating police forces for a modest drop in the crime rate, they were also warning, in the words, of Princeton's John Dilulio, 'this is the lull before the storm.' Forty million kids age ten and under are about to become teenagers, many of them 'fatherless, godless, and jobless.'....The evidence that young men and boys raised without fathers at home are significantly more likely to become criminals is now overwhelming. Violent crime continues unabated in large part because the proportion of young men raised without fathers continues to rise. Within a few years the boys of the baby boomlet, an astonishing and growing proportion of whom are growing up without fathers, will reach their crime-prone years." (*The Abolition of Marriage*, pp. 46f.)

Maggie Gallagher: " Crime and murder rates have jumped for both black and white young men, but the biggest jump has occurred among young black men—the same group that experienced the greatest degree of father absence and least likelihood of marriage." (*Ibid.*, p. 47)

Hillary Rodham Clinton: "The results of the National Survey of Children, which followed the lives of a group of seven- to eleven-year-olds for more than a decade, and other recent studies demonstrate convincingly that while many adults claim to have benefited from divorce and single parenthood, most children have not.

"Children living with one parent or in stepfamilies are two to three times as likely to have emotional and behavioral problems as children living in two-parent families. Children of single parent families are more likely to drop out of high school, become pregnant as teenagers, abuse drugs, behave violently, become entangled with the law....Further, the rise in divorce and out-of-wedlock births has contributed heavily to the tragic increase in the number of American children in poverty, currently one in five." (*It Takes a Village*, pp. 313f.)

David Blankenhorn: "Ronald J. Angel and Jacquiline I. Angel recently completed a careful review of current social science research findings regarding the impact of father absence on children's health. They conclude that 'the preponderance of evidence suggests that father absence results in fairly serious emotional and behavioral problems in children. Children in single-parent families suffer more psychiatric illness and are at a developmental disadvantage in comparison to children in two-parent families. These children have more problems at school, have less self-control, and engage in more delinquent acts than children with a father present. A mother with no husband may often be a poor disciplinarian, and her children may seek moral authority from others. Often that source is their peers, and children who grow up in the streets are unlikely to be exposed to the best role models. The evidence also indicates that fathers are important for a girl's sexual development and her ability to form relationships with men. Taken as a whole, then, the research we reviewed indicates that father absence places both girls and boys at elevated risk of emotional, educational, and developmental problems.'" (*Fatherless America*, pp. 255f.)

David Blankenhorn: "The *Post* cites a study by John Guidubaldi of Kent State University showing the harmful effects of fatherlessness. 'Children of divorce are more likely than children in traditional, intact families to engage in drug abuse, violent behavior, suicide and out-of-wedlock childbearing.'" (*Ibid*, p. 258)

Aaron Kipnis: "In the ghettos, an even higher percentage of fathers are exiled from the home and discouraged from having a presence in the family by social-welfare laws that threaten reduced aid to families with fathers. Young men in these communities are increasingly forming violent gangs. The absent father is one of many social causes of this phenomenon. Adolescent males inevitably search for some sort of masculine identity and male community wherever they can find it.

"Drug abuse among adolescent males is epidemic in our culture, and one factor many adolescent addicts share is an absent father." (*Knights Without Armor*, p. 54)

Patricia Pearson: "In Seattle, a therapist named Michael Thomas encountered the same gap between his schooling and his on-the-job experience. 'My initial work was with a child abuse agency,' he says. 'When you start listening to the children's stories, you start to realize that there's an awful lot more violence by women than any of us had been trained to expect.'...

"'These men are appeasers,' says the therapist Michael Thomas, referring to the battered husbands he counsels in Seattle. 'They always back down to keep things calm, to keep the conflict from escalating. In my experience, the women [in these particular marriages] have a lot of problems with anger control. They are much more likely to throw things, they're more likely to hit or kick when he's not looking or asleep or driving. He doesn't hit back because, number one, he's conditioned to believe that you never hit a woman. Two, he's afraid of losing his kids. Three, [our society] doesn't think of violence as mutual—it's always 'him' doing it to 'her.' So if he hits back, the attention shifts to him and he knows that he'll be up against the wall." (*When She Was Bad,* pp. 123, 129)

Patricia Pearson: "Women can operate the system to their advantage. Donning the feminine mask, they can manipulate the biases of family and community...in order to set men up. If he tries to leave, or fight back, a fateful moment comes when she reaches for the phone, dials 911, and has him arrested on the strength of her word: 'Officer, he hit me.' The tactic is reminiscent of well-to-do late-nineteenth-century American men having their wives committed to insane asylums—for a week or forever—solely on the basis of their say-so. Since a women had been stereotyped as fragile and prone to hysteria, it was possible to persuade authorities of their insanity. A century later, a confluence of social forces has created a parallel opportunity, but with the sexes reversed: Men can be committed to prison on the strength of stereotypes about *them.*

"With mounting pressure on North American police forces to disavow misogynistic attitudes and take the word of a women over a man, female psychopaths and other hard-core female abusers have an extremely effective means to up the ante and win the game....The most common theme among abused men is their tales not of physical anguish but of dispossession—losing custody of children due to accusations of physical and sexual abuse, and having criminal records that permanently shatter their integrity as loving men and decent human beings." (*Ibid*, pp. 142f.)

Patricia Pearson: "Consider such slogans, circulating in the early 1990s on bathroom walls: 'Dead men tell no lies.' 'Dead men don't rape!' 'The way to a man's heart is through his chest.' 'So many men. So little ammunition.' The individual man is not relevant; all men serve as symbolic targets. And this is true along a wide continuum, from permissibly sexist jokes about men to the applause garnered by women who kill. The message being conveyed is that women, being blameless, are entitled to victimize without consequence. It was in that context that Aileen Wuornos killed, and in that climate of sanctimonious wrath that she gained her sympathizers. As Candice Skrapec observed in 1993, in an essay about female serial killers, 'A woman's anger and need for empowerment will be directed at the power-brokers, those she has experienced as victimizing her. She will seek to punish them for being men.' With what result? 'The victim becomes the victimizer.'" (*Ibid.*, p. 232)

Maggie Gallagher: "[M]arriages in which both partners work full-time are far more prone to divorce." (*National Review*, 26 January, 1998)

Bryce Christensen: "Most researchers now agree that day care dramatically elevates the risk of infectious disease—especially respiratory illness and middle-ear infections....[Burton] White pronounced it 'a total disaster area, 'with no feasible way of turning it into a model industry.'" (*Day Care: Child Psychology and Adult Economics*, p. 44)

Judith Wallerstein and Sandra Blakeslee: "[W]e did not question the commonly held assumption that divorce was a short-lived crisis.

"But when we conducted follow-up interviews one year to eighteen months later we found most families still in crisis. Their wounds were wide open. Turmoil and distress had not noticeably subsided. Many adults still felt angry, humiliated, and rejected, and most had not gotten their lives back together. An unexpectedly large number of children were on a downward course. Their symptoms were worse than before. Their behavior at school was worse. Their peer relationships were worse. Our findings were absolutely contradictory to our expectations.

411

"This was unwelcome news to a lot of people, and we got angry letters from therapists, parents, and lawyers saying we were undoubtedly wrong. They said children are really much better off being released from an unhappy marriage. Divorce, they said, is a liberating experience.

"But that was not what we were hearing from our families....The children are not recovering, I said. The adults have not settled their problems....We also found, in this five-year follow-up, that the majority of children still hoped that their parents would reconcile....After the first five years they were intensely angry at their parents for giving priority to adult needs rather than to their needs....At the five-year mark, the majority of adults felt they were better off, but a surprisingly large number did not. Half the men and two-thirds of the women were more content with the quality of their lives. The rest, however, were either stalled or felt more troubled and unhappy than they had during the marriage. (*Second Chances,* pp. xvff.)

Judith Wallerstein and Sandra Blakeslee: "In our study, about 10 percent of the children had poor relationships with both parents during the marriage. This number jumped to a shocking 35 percent of children at the ten-year mark. These children were essentially unparented in the postdivorce decade. And in fact many of them were called upon to take care of their parents." *(Ibid.,* p. 200)

Judith Wallerstein and Sandra Blakeslee: " A quarter of the mothers and a fifth of the fathers have not gotten their lives back on track a full ten years after the divorce." *(Ibid.,* p. 202)

Judith Wallerstein and Sandra Blakeslee: "The years after divorce, close to one-half of the boys, who are now between the ages of nineteen and twenty-nine, are unhappy and lonely and have had few, if any, lasting relationships with young women." *(Ibid.,* p. 67)

Judith Wallerstein and Sandra Blakeslee: "In this study, however, almost half of the children entered adulthood as worried, underachieving, self-deprecating, and sometimes angry young men and women....Although boys had a harder time over the years than girls, suffering a wide range of difficulties in school achievements, peer relationships, and handling of aggression, this disparity in overall adjustment eventually dissipated. As the young women stood at the developmental threshold of young adulthood, when it was time to seek commitment with a young man, many found themselves struggling with anxiety and guilt. This sudden shock, which I describe as a sleeper effect, led to many maladaptive pathways, including multiple relationships and impulsive marriages that ended in early divorce." (*Ibid.*, p. 299)

Lynne Segal: "Virginia Woolf, Vera Brittain and many other feminists and pacifists recalling those days of war, were well aware that many women loved the war. They had excellent reasons for loving it: it liberated many women for the first time from the isolation and stifling shackles of the home." (*Is The Future Female?*, p. 171)

Peter G. Filene: "In public and in private, 'advanced' women attacked the conventional family as a kind of slavery, more subtle though no less oppressive than the bondage of blacks. Of course, the chains were not iron, but economic or psychological. And they were put on by choice rather than by birth. But they were chains nevertheless. According to feminists, the typical wife sacrificed her creative talents, her legal rights, and her personality either to the tedious rounds of child care and housework or, if she belonged to the privileged class, to the 'parasitism' of idle leisure. Whether in gingham or taffeta, marriage amounted to subjection—love and honor, perhaps, but mostly her obedience and his power. A half century after the Emancipation Proclamation, said the feminists, one-half of the American people remained unemancipated." (*Him/Her/Self*, p. 47)

Wini Breines: "Finally, we shall see that it was precisely the boys and young men who rejected the respectable route who were sexually attractive to many young, white, middle-class girls of the late 50s and 60s." (*Young, White and Miserable*, p. 40)

Barbara Ehrenreich: "[F]or women as well as men, sex is a fundamentally lawless creature, not easily confined to a cage." (Dust wrapper of Dalma Heyn's *Erotic Silence of the American Wife*)

David Bakan: "A female student in one of my classes once openly boasted to the class about how effectively she was raising her child born out of wedlock. Another female student deliberately planned to have, and had, a child out of wedlock. She said that she wanted a child but did not want a husband. Having a child, she said, was her destiny; but having a husband was not." (*And They Took Themselves Wives*, p. 4)

Arthur Evans: "Our hope in the midst of the present global crisis is the construction of foundations for a post-patriarchal civilization. One of the most important examples is the rise of the modern women's liberation movement. For some time now, feminist women have been in the forefront of challenging patriarchal attitudes and practices in regard to sex roles....

"Another promising sign is the gay liberation movement. At their best, lesbians and gay men have dramatically challenged the sexist role-playing that is at the very heart of the patriarchal psychosis and have succeeded in making an immense improvement in the quality of life for many gay people." (*The God of Ecstasy*, pp. 182f.)

Sandra Schneiders: "But once she has begun to see, begun the critical process of analysis, she will necessarily gradually be overwhelmed by the extent, the depth, and the violence of the institutional church's rejection and oppression of women. This precipitates the inward crisis which the feminist Catholic inevitably faces: a deep, abiding, emotionally draining anger that, depending on her personality, might run the gamut from towering rage to chronic depression." (*Beyond Patching*, p. 97)

Riane Eisler: "Furthermore, by social convention, the vast majority of divorces were filed by women." (*Dissolution*, p. 43)

Dr. Joyce Brothers: "American husbands are frequently more satisfied with their marriages than are their wives." (*Los Angeles Times*, 2 February, 1993)

Carol Cassell, Executive Director of the Institute for Sexuality Education and Equity and first Director of Education of Planned Parenthood: "The best sex takes place with two people who want to rip each other's jeans off. Do not give young people a double standard message. It is not normal to teach them to say 'no' when they want to say 'yes.'" (Quoted in *National Monitor of Education*, February, 1990)

Henrietta Furth, German feminist: "There has never yet been a time when motherhood was a life-filling vocation." (Quoted in Katherine Anthony, *Feminism in Germany and Scandinavia*, p. 197)

Editors of *Ms.*: "Sexuality is the area of our lives where the power balance has changed the most—and is likely to stay changed." (July, 1986)

Naomi Wolf: "Whether it is ready or not, 'society' no longer has the power to keep women in their place." (*Fire with Fire*, p. 52)

Naomi Wolf: "In most women, the original power feminist, with her brazen will intact, is not lost." (*Ibid*, p. 318)

Linda Bowles: "It isn't even close, the most abused, vilified, and sexually harassed Americans are white, heterosexual males. I don't know why they put up with it—and I wish they wouldn't." (*Liberator*, July, 1993)

Joycelyn Elders, former Surgeon-General: "Every girl should take a condom in her purse when she goes out on a date." (CBS' 60 Minutes, quoted in *Human Events*, August 28, 1993)

Dale Carlson: "I have heard many girls and women say that coming upon the ideas of the women's movement is like walking out of a small, dark room into the sun. To realize that other women feel constricted by the roles normally given to women, to know that women everywhere are at last demanding to choose their destinies instead of being handed the limiting roles of sex object, goddess (not much room to move on top of a pedestal), mother, wife, dependent servant, to understand that it's not just you, but all women, who are tired of feeling that it's a handicap to be born female—to be aware of these things brings an incredible measure of relief." (*Girls Are Equal Too*, p. 140)

Reuters dispatch: "[Shere Hite] says the 'holy family' model of Jesus, Mary and Joseph is 'an essentially repressive one, teaching authoritarian psychological patterns and a belief in the unchanging rightness of male power.' Hite argues that a family can be made up of any combination of people, heterosexual or homosexual, who share their lives in an intimate way." (Feb, 1994)

American Home Economics Association: "To help keep the concept of the family in step with the reality, the association has come up with a new definition of the family: 'Two or more persons who share resources, share responsibility for decisions, share values and goals and have commitment to one another over time.'" (*Los Angeles Times*, 20 July, 1979)

Helen Colton: "Marriage would have to guarantee a woman that she would retain the same autonomy of her personality that she had as a single woman. A legal reason for divorce could be: Deprivation of autonomy of personality. (*Sex After the Sexual Revolution*, p. 86)

Senator Daniel Moynihan: "By 1983 the poverty rate reached its highest level in 18 years....The principal correlate had been the change in family structure, the rise of the female-headed household." (*Family and Nation*, p. 95)

National Association of Elementary School Principals: "One-parent children, on the whole, show lower achievement in school than their two-parent peers....Among all two-parent children, 30 percent were ranked as high achievers, compared with only 1 percent of one-parent children. At the other end of the scale, the situation is reversed. Only 2 percent of two-parent children were low achievers—while fully 40 percent of one-parent children fell in that category....There were more clinic visits among one-parent students, and their absence rate runs far higher than for students with two parents, with one-parent students losing about 8 days more over the course of a year.

"One-parent students were consistently more likely to be late, truant, and subject to disciplinary action by every criterion we examined, and at both the elementary and secondary levels....One parent children were more than twice as likely as two-parent children to give up on school altogether." ("The Most Significant Minority: One-Parent Children in the Schools"; quoted in Moynihan, *Family and Nation*, pp.92f.)

Brae Canlen: "Hundreds of women from around the country—many of them white-collar wives who say they were also shafted by the court system—have written sympathetic letters to Betty [Broderick]. Some of them confide their own secret fantasies of killing their ex-husbands.

"A year before the murders, Betty wrote in her diary, 'If this is the way domestic disputes are settled in the courts, is there any wonder there are so many murders? I am desperate. What is a nice girl to do?'" ("No More Mrs. Nice Guy," *California Lawyer*, April, 1994; Betty Broderick shot and killed her ex-husband and his wife.)

Naomi Wolf: "The fathers' departure led directly to the girls' often shaky sense of sexual self-esteem. The boys lost their role models, but the loving parent of the opposite sex was still there to respond to them. Girls kept their role models, but just when the girls needed their fathers to be around to admire their emerging sexual identity from a safe distance—to be the dependable male figures upon whom they could innocently practice growing up—the fathers vanished." (*Promiscuities*, p. 19)

Eva Keuls: "The Athenian preoccupation with legendary tales of wives murdering their husbands was nothing short of obsessive....In vase paintings Clytemnestra frequently appears running with an ax toward a closed door....The theme of the murderous Danaids was one of the most, perhaps the most, widely dramatized motifs in Greek culture." (*The Reign of the Phallus*, p. 337)

Wini Breines: "Children were more important to women than husbands. A strikingly unromantic notion of marriage characterized women's attitudes. [Elaine Tyler] May points out that in her data, and in other studies done at the time [1950s], the women were 'much more likely to express their desire for children than their eagerness for marriage (a much higher proportion associated pleasure, love, and joy with having children than with getting married.'" (*Young, White and Miserable*, p. 54)

Rickie Solinger: "A 1958 study of residents in the Los Angeles Florence Crittenton Home [for unwed mothers] found 'dramatic evidence of severe emotional deprivation. Absent relationships with fathers appeared as a rather routine finding. In the Draw-A-Person Test almost all depicted the male parent as faceless with detached feet." (*Wake Up, Little Susie*, p. 91)

Shere Hite: "How traditional is the family as we know it? Since it is only about three thousand years old, the non-patriarchal families that preceded it may in fact have more right to be called 'traditional' families.

"It is as if we had no historical memory; as we have seen, the two-gender family has not always been the norm—mother-child societies were in existence before patriarchy, and now, an extremely large number of families are mother-child families in the West.

"Twentieth century Polynesian families, as documented by Margaret Mead, were found not to be at all like the nuclear family. There was little concept of 'private ownership' of children: children were cared for by the entire society." (*The Hite Report on the Family*, p. 359)

Lynette Triere: "It is no wonder that many unhappily married women mention a similar recurring wish: They wish their husband would die. In saying this, I don't mean to be lurid. It simply shows the depth of frustration for many of them." (*Learning to Leave*, p. 73)

Lynette Triere: "To be frank, money is a woman's ticket to freedom." (*Ibid.*, p. 167)

Juliet Mitchell: "The family as it exists at present is, in fact, incompatible with the equality of the sexes....Couples living together or not living together, long-term unions with children, single parents bringing up children, children socialized by conventional rather than biological parents, extended kin groups, etc.—all these could be encompassed in a range of institutions which matched the free invention and variety of men and women." ("Women: The Longest Revolution" in Betty and Theodore Roszak, *Masculine /Feminine: Readings in Sexual Mythology and the Liberation of Women*, pp. 172f.)

Miriam Schneir: "To move outside the reformist realm and try to effect fundamental changes in the structure of existing institutions, principally the family, is the dangerous yet exciting mission that today's radical feminists have undertaken." (*Feminism*, p. xix)

Barbara Ehrenreich, Elizabeth Hess and Gloria Jacobs: "Independence, even in straitened and penurious forms, still offers more sexual freedom than affluence gained through marriage and dependence on one man." (*Re-Making Love*, p. 196)

Stephanie Coontz: "To handle social obligations and interdependency in the 21st century, we must abandon any illusion that we can or should revive some largely mythical traditional family. We need to invent new family traditions and find ways of reviving older community ones, not wallow in nostalgia for the past or heap contempt on people whose family values do not live up to ours." (*The Way We Never Were*, p. 278)

Marie Enckendorff: "If ever there was a first and individual woman who...went voluntarily to the man and said: 'Protect me from the enemy and from hunger and let me believe in your gods, and I will serve you, bear your children, and you shall be my master.'—If that woman ever existed, who, out of fear of life and its inward and outward experiences, was glad to give herself, body and soul, to a fellow-creature, and bequeathed this position to her sex—she was in truth the mother of sin....The only ethical course for woman—also for her as a sex being—is the struggle for an independent human personality." (Quoted in Katherine Anthony, *Feminism in Germany and Scandinavia*, pp. 248ff.)

Betty Friedan: "The basis of women's empowerment is economic—that's what's in danger now." (*Newsweek*, 4 September, 1995)

Elizabeth Cady Stanton: "The true enemy of woman skulks behind the altar. The Bible is not the word of God. The Bible is the act of men written to keep women subordinate [and] written out of his love of domination." (Quoted in *Los Angeles Times*, 1 August, 1988)

Lynette Triere: "I came home with my ride who drives a little VW. And we came around the corner, and Rod's car was gone. I started screaming at the top of my lungs—'I'm free...I'm free!' My friend had never seen me act that way before, and he almost had an accident in front of the house, with me screaming and waving my arms. Then I stopped and looked at him and said very clearly, 'I'm OK now,' and he laughed. He knew what I'd been going through.

"I don't know an adjective to describe the emotion I felt. I really—for the first time in my life—felt free....I went in the house and I remember that happiness. I remember I felt like jumping up and down, and screaming and yelling, but I don't think I really did....At some point soon after leaving, the realization hits—I am free!...And as Beverly describes it, the feeling is wonderful. The sense of freedom regained is probably the most euphoric sensation a human being can experience." (*Learning to Leave*, p. 230)

Ira Reiss: "As I have said many times, to build pluralism we must firmly root out the narrow thinking about sex that exists in all of our basic institutions: family, political, economic, religious, and educational. We need to change our basic social institutional structure." (*An End to Shame*, p. 232)

419

Lord Raglan: "We may conclude by briefly considering whether what is described as marriage among the more primitive peoples has any claim to be considered as a permanent union. Among many savages there is no marriage ceremony whatever, and in many others the ceremony is of the simplest character, in which, as still in Scotland, the parties have merely to announce their union. Among some of the North American tribes unions are so temporary and informal that what some writers entitle marriage others describe as prostitution. In Persia it is still legal to contract a marriage for one day. It would be easy to adduce ample evidence to show that among the more primitive races the union of the sexes, whether we dignify it with the title of marriage or not, is in general anything but sacred and indissoluble." (*Jocasta's Crime*, p. 28)

Helen Colton: "No wonder that as women are freed financially, maternally, and sexually through having paid jobs, fewer children, and sexual equality, more of them declare their disinterest in being married. Let man live through the ignominy of putting in a sixteen- to eighteen-hour workday and then having to come to another human being for his sustenance for food, shelter, clothing, and pocket money, and he may begin to get some small idea of the rage women are feeling at the indignity of the marriage dole." (*Sex After the Sexual Revolution*, p. 86)

Betty Friedan: "But she still feels 'lazy, neglectful, haunted by guilt feelings' because she doesn't have enough work to do....It was not that too much was asked of them but too little....Society asks so little of women....I noticed that when these men were saddled with a domestic chore, they polished it off in much less time than it seemed to take their wives." (*The Feminine Mystique*, pp. 213, 238, 252)

Helen Colton: "As sex is separated from procreation, as women are freed from the bread-and-butter arrangement marriage is now for so many, as we have fewer children needing the protection of legally married parents, we may find ourselves caring less about a couple's pairing arrangements than we do about their right to pleasure. Increasingly, we will be living the philosophy of existence which makes hedonism (pursuit of pleasure) acceptable." (*Sex After the Sexual Revolution*, p. 92)

Mary Daly: "Feminism has a unique potential for providing the insight needed to undercut the prevailing moral ideology." (*Beyond God the Father*, p. 102)

Anne Wilson Schaef: "...I presented some of this material to a group of women seminary students. They in turn became furious with me. They did not like what I was saying at all! 'For centuries,' they said,' women have focused on primary relationships with men in order to establish identity and gain validation. We have given all of our energy to maintaining these relationships and none to taking care of our own intellectual and creative needs. We want this to stop! We want to start paying attention to our selves and our work—and we don't want to be told that we are "selling out" to the White Male System!'" (*Women's Reality*, p. 110)

Donna Mungen: "Despite the immediate mental anguish and strained relationships, many noncustodial mothers believe their choice helped contribute to the long-term well-being of their children, and to the improvement of their own lives." (*Ms.*, February, 1986)

Bruce Thornton: "Then we liberated Eros. We weakened those traditional social restraints as archaic, repressive impediments to the marriage of true hearts and minds. We dismissed them as puritanical inhibitions stifling the expression of our authentic selves. Guilt and shame were discarded as hurtful and hypocritical; no fault divorce reduced marriage to a lifestyle choice as changeable as a car or a job; reason was dismissed as the instrument of repression and neurosis. The result of this novel experiment? Look around you—venereal plagues, illegitimacy, weakening of the nuclear family, debasement of women, vulgarization of sex in popular culture, chronic dissatisfaction with our sexual identities—all testify to the costs of slighting Eros' dark power. A modern-day Medea drowns her two children because her boyfriend doesn't want them; a kindergarten beauty queen is raped and murdered; countless women are stalked and butchered by estranged and deranged boyfriends and spouses. We search everywhere for the answer except in the nature of eros itself and its potential for madness and violence. (*Los Angeles Times*, 14 Feb, 1997)

Linda Hirshman: "They force women into marriage with social pressures such as the withdrawal of welfare." *Los Angeles Times*, 25 September, 1996)

Betty Friedan: "Perhaps it is the least understood fact of American political life: the enormous buried violence of women in this country today." (*It Changed My Life*, p. 126)

Naomi Wolf: "Many women of our mothers' generation wrote critically about having been female in the shadow of the repressive hypocrisy of the fifties, and of 'finding themselves' by casting off that era's inhibitions." (*Promiscuities*, p. xix)

Janet Harris: "The chief difference between the viewpoints of black and white women, another student explained, is that black women "have not been dominated by black males." The black woman is the dominant figure in the home. She finds it easier to make a living, for she can always be a domestic, although her earnings are lower than white females and black males. (*A Single Standard*, p. 130)

Gustave Flaubert: "'Everything one invents is true, you may be sure of that,' wrote Flaubert to his mistress Louise Colet, while in the midst of writing his first and most famous novel. 'My poor Bovary, without a doubt, is suffering and weeping at this very instant in twenty villages of France.'" (Quoted in Dalma Heyn, *The Erotic Silence of the American Wife*, p. 13)

Rosie Jackson: "We have to try to undo the very mental processes that make us fall only too readily into maternal and care-taking positions. We (women as much as men) have to stop keeping woman in the position of the Mother (to adults as well as children) and to resist the fantasy of the Maternal which, as women, we are made to carry." (*Mothers Who Leave*, p. 284)

W. L. George: "The ultimate aim of feminism with regard to marriage is the practical suppression of marriage and the institution of free alliance." ("Feminist Intentions," *Atlantic Monthly*, vol. 2, No. 6; quoted in V. F. Calverton, *The Bankruptcy of Marriage*, p. 293)

Monica Sjöö and Barbara Mor: "Only when women give up our sexual autonomy and our right to be independent and creative, only when we give up ourselves and accept patriarchal male definitions and 'femininity' as passive, negative and receptive—only then will we be treated humanely." (*The Great Cosmic Mother*, p. 196)

Merlin Stone: "Within the very structure of the contemporary male religions are the laws and attitudes originally designed to annihilate the female religions, female sexual autonomy and matrilineal descent. (*When God Was a Woman*, p. 228)

Riane Eisler: "As Ehrenreich, Hess and Jacobs repeatedly note, what radically changed—and thus both directly and indirectly impacted the sexual relations between women and men—was that women at first tentatively, and then more determinedly, began to reclaim their own sexuality. And central to this was the reclamation of women's right to sexual pleasure—a reclamation that came hand in hand with women's reclamation of at least some measure of economic and political power. (*Sacred Pleasure*, p. 282)

Irwin Garfinkel and Sara McLanahan: "Moore and Burt have estimated that nearly 60 percent of all women on welfare in 1975 had been teenage mothers. Early childbirth is associated with lower education and higher fertility, both of which limit the development of skills and relevant experience and reduce earnings capacity." (*Single Mothers and their Children*, p. 23)

Irwin Garfinkel and Sara McLanahan: "Fairly good evidence indicates that girls who grow up in families headed by single women are more likely to become single parents themselves." (*Ibid.*, p. 167)

Lillian Faderman: "But they [lesbians] all agree that men have waged constant battle against women, committed atrocities or at best injustices against them, reduced them to grown-up children, and...a feminist ought not to sleep in the enemy camp." (*Surpassing the Love of Men*, p. 413)

Robert Briffault: "Wherever individual women enjoy, in a cultured society, a position of power, they avail themselves of their independence to exercise sexual liberty." (*The Mothers*, abridged by G. R. Taylor, p. 386)

Ira Reiss: "As the discussion proceeded, an American female college student who was spending the year in Sweden stood up and said, 'I find this discussion very upsetting! I think you have all lost sight of the value of saving sexual intercourse for marriage. Marriage is the proper place for starting sexual intercourse. It's not a matter of whether you are fourteen, sixteen, or any other age—it's a matter of being moral and waiting until you're married!'

"The Swedish parents were stunned into silence for a few moments. Swedes are not generally as confrontational or argumentative as Americans. Then one Swedish mother asked the American student, 'Do you know that in our country most women do not marry until they are over twenty-five years old? Are you proposing that our young women wait all those years for their first sexual intercourse?' The student responded, 'Yes, that is exactly what I am saying. Marriage is the only proper setting for sexual intercourse!' I thought to myself: 'Okay! Now we'll see some real verbal fireworks.' But the Swedish mother just looked at the American student, paused for a moment, and then calmly said: 'How Quaint!'" (*An End to Shame*, p. 62)

Ira Reiss: "For lesbians the broader societal influence was visible in the fusion for many women of lesbian identity with feminism. Sisterhood was often more important than erotic pleasures, and the bond to women and the freedom from men was primary. Lesbianism, in this sense, developed the 'male-free' potential of women." (*Ibid.*, p. 102)

Harriet Blacker Algrant: "Sexually, and in every other way, women were forced to become what men wanted them to be. Today's feminist is saying goodbye to all that! She wants to be free 'of the masochism which has so long characterized women of the western world.' For now, however, if women can only respect and enjoy their bodies the way men do theirs, they'll have truly come 'a long way, baby.'...A beginning is to understand what their sexuality is all about. Ms. Seaman puts forth the scientific and anthropologic evidence that women have an insatiable sex drive which has been deliberately curbed in order to build a stable society. It may well be, according to Dr. Mary Jane Sherfey, that the nymphomaniac may actually be the most normal and natural of women!...Single women have a happier and richer sex life than married women!...The economic liberation of women can only, therefore, make for better sex, for with economic independence, women will become freer to marry for love." (Publisher's cover letter for Barbara Seaman's *Free and Female*)

Charlene Spretnak: "Patriarchy is not 'natural'; it is a cultural choice." (*Women Respond to the Men's Movement*, ed. Leigh Hagan, p. 175)

Marilyn French: "Most basic of all is the power over one's own body—the right to be free of physical abuse, to control one's own sexuality, to marry when and whom one chooses, or not to marry, to control one's own reproduction, to have rights over one's own children,

and to divorce at will....The great good upheld by this book is pleasure."
(*Beyond Power*, pp. 125, 23)

Stephanie Coontz: "University of Chicago researcher William Julius
Wilson estimates that for every one hundred black women 20-24 in
1980, there were only 45 employed black men of the same age."(*The Way
We Never Were*, p. 251)

Lorraine Dusky: "When divorce was rare, English common law
automatically gave the children to the father." (*Still Unequal*, p. 336)

Stephanie Coontz: "A national survey conducted in 1989 found that
36 percent of single women polled had seriously considered raising a
child on their own." (*The Way We Never Were*, p. 186)

Phyllis Schlafly: "When a woman has a baby and a career, the
husband ranks third on her scale of priorities, and a poor third, at that,
because she's simply too exhausted for anything else even if she has any
extra time, which she usually doesn't.

"The lifestyle sections of newspapers have had many articles in
recent months about how men in their 20s and 30s are rejecting or
avoiding marriage. Is it any wonder? What man wants to risk a
financial/emotional commitment, buy a ring and assume a mortgage on
a house, when he will rank only #3 in the heart of the woman he loves?"
(*Phyllis Schlafly Report*, May, 1985)

Lynn Segal: "The turning point in the adoption of this new feminist
analysis of sexuality in Britain was when the Birmingham National
Women's Liberation Conference in 1978 passed (against such fierce
opposition that it terminated all future national conferences) the motion
to make 'the right to define our sexuality the over-riding demand of the
women's movement, preceding all other demands.' Men's sexual
domination of women, which prevented the emergence of women's self-
defined sexuality, was now being formally accepted as the pivot of
women's oppression." (*Is the Future Female?*, p. 85)

Jenny Teichman: "The father also had a right of custody which was
absolute as against the mother. Any action whereby a father attempted
to divest himself of the custody of his legitimate children in order to give
custody to the mother was void as contrary to public policy. It was not

until 1873 that this doctrine of the absolute custody rights of the father was formally abandoned." (*Illegitimacy*, p. 41)

Maggie Gallagher: "The evidence is now overwhelming that the collapse of marriage is creating a whole generation of children less happy, less physically and mentally healthy, less equipped to deal with life or to produce at work, and more dangerous to themselves and others. This evidence comes not from isolated studies but from hundreds of studies subsequently surveyed, critiqued, compared, and summarized by other scholars." (*The Abolition of Marriage*, p. 34)

Leontine Young: "The great majority of unmarried mothers come from homes dominated by the mother." (*Out of Wedlock*, p. 41)

George Bernard Shaw: "My own experience of discussing this question leads me to believe that the one point on which all women are in furious secret rebellion against the existing law is the saddling of the right to a child with the obligation to become the servant of a man." (Preface to *Getting Married; Prefaces*, p. 15.)

Black mother describing black father: "I don't need that man." (Brenda Scott, *Children No More*, p. 158)

Maggie Gallagher: "Demographers estimate that up to 65 percent of all new marriages now fail." (Citing Teresa Castro Martin and Larry Bumpass, "Recent Trends in Marital Disruption," *Demography*, 26 (1989): 37-51; *The Abolition of Marriage*, p. 5)

Constance Ahrons: "Today, record numbers of women have options for the first time in their lives. One enormous option is to leave a marriage that doesn't meet their needs. As we have previously seen, two-thirds to three-quarters of divorces in Western society are initiated by women. (*The Good Divorce*, p. 35.)

Bishop Spong: "Little did people realize what a taste of economic power would do to women's yearnings for independence." (*Living In Sin?*, p. 59)

Judy Mann: "In recent years, much of the anti-feminist drumbeat has been the attempt to regulate women's reproductive freedom....Somewhere in adolescence, our daughters are silenced....They become uncomplaining and compliant. They learn to wait. Carol

Gilligan and her associates describe how girls drive their perceptions of reality underground. The work of these researchers evokes a powerful image of a turbulent subterranean river in women's psyches while their surface behavior adapts to the social imperatives to 'be nice' and not to be 'rude' or 'disruptive.'" (*The Difference*, pp. 12f.)

Index

A

abolishing prostitution, 184
AFDC, 56, 71, 128, 164, 178, 202, 209, 211, 299, 313, 367, 387
affirmative action, 311, 314
Allred, Gloria, 28
Angel in the House, 37, 50, 52, 188, 189, 387
Arendell, Terry, 17
Asherah, 92, 102, 122
assets of the marriage, 27, 28, 31, 42, 285, 357, 380

B

Bacchae, 238
Backup System, 49, 126, 157, 210, 235, 302, 328, 344
bargaining power, 25, 26, 42, 43, 55, 66, 73, 86, 101, et passim
Bettelheim, Bruno, 88
Bhutto, Benazir, former Prime Minister of Pakistan, 340, 341, 409
Biller, Henry, 18
Birmingham National Women's Liberation Conference, 85, 453
black females, superiority of, 6, 138, 139, 141, 323
Blankenhorn, David, 20, 44, 47, 76, 87, 208, 396, 436, 437
Book of Common Prayer, 39, 67
Boulding, Elise, 88
Boyle, Fr. Gregory, 354
bribing women to behave themselves,, 164
Briffault's Law, 14, 34, 48, 63, 82, 99, 128
Brothers, Dr. Joyce, 39, 140, 318, 442
Brown, Joan, 219, 222

C

casual sexual adventures, 358
cheating on spouses, now an equal-opportunity sport, 367, 385
child abuse mostly committed by mothers, 178
child support, 35, 36, 44, 58, 70, 71, 72, 78, 79, 90, et passim
childhood, 1, 2, 61, 97, 110, 127, 181, 192, 431
Chopin, Kate, 360
Christian Gnosticism, 104
civilization, artificiality of, 11
civilization, built on female chastity, 137, 262, 263, 266
civilized society, a man's world, 35, 175, 355, 384
Clark, Marcia, 32, 54, 60, 74, 155, 156, 200, 283, 344, 361
classificatory system, 124, 125, 163
Columbus, 185

coming white underclass, 100, 248, 387
compulsory heterosexuality, 85, 87
Confucius, 53
confusion of authority and power, 363
Coontz, Stephanie, 128, 140, 141, 158, 183, 184, 186, 187, et passim
Cosmopolitan, 26, 183, 247, 378, 432
Courtwright, David, 157, 210, 211, 212, 217, 335, 336, 337, 356
couvade, 89
custody, mother, 13, 16, 18, 19, 30, 31, 36, 43, 59, 76, 110, et passim

D

Daddy's Little Parcel, 303
Dash, Leon, 4, 260, 261
deadbeat dad, 13, 167, 212, 371, 374
Descriptive System, 125
Diner, Helen, 34, 103, 419
Dionysus, 68, 69, 84, 132, 165, 238, 244, 245, 269
divorce in mid 19th century, 163
Doll's House, 164
double standard, 45, 57, 131, 149, 153, 154, 157, 158, 159, et passim
double standard increases the number of prostitutes, 364
Durant, Will and Ariel, 149, 195

E

Ehrenreich, Hess and Jacobs, 20, 23, 37, 39, 45, 48, 49, 55, 68, 81, 84, 87, 96, et passim
Eisler, Riane, 55, 56, 62, 63, 79, 103, 104, 105, 118, 122, et passim
El Saadawi, 241, 403
Elders, Joycelyn, 154, 246, 314, 433, 443
enforced virginity, 305
enormous potential counterforce, 47, 106, 107, 129, 136, 146, 175, 285, 319
Evans, Arthur, 5, 104, 193, 237, 238, 264, 269, 332, 380, 405, 406, 441
exogamy, 88, 196, 197, 203

F

Faderman, Lillian, 87, 451
Faludi, Susan, 24, 25, 26, 27, 28, 183, 247, 3et passim2
fatherhood, a social invention, 1, 2, 4, 5, 6, 11, 19, 24, 34, 35, 41, 43, 61, 75, 78, 84, 102, 103, et passim
fatherless children, iv, 16, 17, 18, 86, 113, 128, 133, 192, 210, 278, 295, 313, 322, 330
fatherless homes, pathology of, 12, 71, 192, 411, 426

fathers more responsible, 162
Feldman, Sandra, 17, 256, 257, 258
female headed households, 11, 46, 127, 181, 222, 223, 251, 361
female kinship system, 1, 3, 7, 8, 10, 12, 24, 33, 37, 39, 49, 56, 59, 60, 61, 62, 63, 64, 69, 70, 72, 78, 79, 80, 81, 83, 86, 93, 102,et passim
female sexual disloyalty, 26, 113, 233, 290, 308, 312, 379
feminine mystique, 47, 82, 89, 90, 101, 126, 164, 170, 188, 243, 277, 301, 308, 326, 327, 329, 356, 362, 387
Feminine Mystique, 6, 28, 34, 36, 72, 73, 75, 89, 90, et passim
Finkelhor, David, 179, 180
first law of matriarchy, 20, 190, 196, 197, 232, 351, 401
Fisher, Helen, 175
Fiske, John, 2
Forehand, Rex, 31, 429
free and joyous love, 73, 81, 82, 142, 152, 202, 282
free love, 104, 405
French, Marilyn, 35, 164, 165, 167, 234, 271, 359, 420, 452
Freud, Sigmund, 72, 117, 143, 165, 166, 180, 196, 216, 262, 263, 407
Freud's question What does a woman want?, 117, 165
Friedan, Betty, 6, 28, 34, 36, 38, 40, 43, 47, 48, 50, 51, 52, 59, 72, 73, 81, 89, 90, 101, et passim
Fugitive Slave Law, 372

G

Gallagher, Maggie, 12, 32, 69, 76, 95, 155, et passim
Gates, Daryl, 209
Gelles, Richard, 178
Gelles, Richard and Murray Straus, 53, 54, 178, 179
Gilder, George, 25, 43, 46, 47, 82, 83, 84, 173, 211, 237, 258, 259, 260, 347, 348, 351
Goldberg, Steven, 6, 53, 96, 176, 236
Golden Bough, 106

H

Hamburg, David, 169
Harris, Janet, 322, 450
Hartman, David, 30, 192
Harvey, Brett, 189, 190, 193, 197, 417
Hawthorne's Scarlet Letter, 113
Hayward, Frederic, 371, 376
Heard, Gerald, 192, 193, 242, 269, 332, 333
Heilbrun, Carolyn, 72, 114, 115, 431
hero, an inevitable development, 115, 242, 333
Hewlett, Sylvia, 34, 35, 156, 175, 176, 193, 208, 209, 308, 309, 370, 376, 377, 378, 383
Heyn, Dalma, 24, 34, 48, 54, 56, 62, 67, 68, 70, 81, 96, et passim
Hite, Shere, 39, 244, 348, 410, 443, 445
Hoggett, Brenda, 21, 22, 63, 65, 86, 131, 158, 218, 223, 224, 315
Horn, Wade, 60, 61
hypergamy, 23, 54, 90, 111, 216, 217, 343, 344, 345

I

Ibsen, Henrik, 56, 77, 78, 148, 164, 166, 167, 399
idolatry, 122
increasingly younger criminals, 169
"Is this all?", 157, 158

J

Jamieson, Kathleen Hall, 84
Janus, Sam, 23, 24, 378
Joint Custody, not a cure, 150, 168
judicial weakness of character, 232

K

kept woman, 63, 163, 242, 350
Killing the King, 103
Koedt, Anne, 20, 22, 215
Kurgans, or Indo-Europeans, 239

L

Landers, Ann, 14, 15, 254, 289, 302, 364, 365, 367, 385, 433
Lee, Madeline, 45
legal shell of a marriage, 34, 383
Legitimacy Principle, 20, 57, 98, 172, 198, 258, 336
Lerner, Gerda, 57, 128, 166, 167, 236
Liberator, 57, 324, 431, 443
loyalty of wives, 8

M

male, greater vulnerability of the, 143
Mann, Judy, 7, 99, 100, 128, 133, 320, 394, 397, 410, 435, 455
Mansbridge, Jane, 56
marriage contract, 13, 22, 24, 29, 35, 65, 66, 120, et passim
marriage is an economic institution,, 151, 174, 341
masks, 47, 48, 50, 51, 54, 81, 176, 188
matriarchy, 3, 5, 6, 8, 9, 11, 20, 22, 24, 25, 26, 27, 30, 34, 35, 41, 48, 58, 60, 61, 62, 67, 68, 71, 80, 83, 85, 91, 95, et passim
Mead, Margaret, 1, 2, 11, 56, 87, 174, 175, 297, 329, 338, 341, 387, 408, 445
mentors for fatherless boys, 370
Messalianism, 104
Miles, Rosalind, 34, 92, 93, 94, 95, 96, 103, 106, 107, 241, 260, 320, 321, 403, 410
Mill, John Stuart, 19, 83, 201
Miller, Stuart, 161, 168, 373
Mitchell, Brian, 52
"Mommy and I are one," 243
Money Card, 23, 30, 33, 127, 137, 138, 149, 150, 188, 205, 224, 252, 281, 339, 380
Mother Goddesses, 94
Moynihan, 9, 11, 147, 410, 422, 431, 434, 443, 444

Mulder, Thomas, 58, 59, 60, 61, 62, 137, 202
Murray, Charles, 53, 186, 210, 219, 387
Mutilated Beggar, 10, 19, 35, 49, 59, 79, 112. 158, 163, 192, 226, 230, 273, 281, 311, 316, 325

N

naturalness of female kinship system., 4
Navy study reveals that 65% of enlisted women become pregnant on sea duty, 171
Nayo, Lydia, 297, 298, 299, 300, 301, 302, 313, 314
Nehru, 184
neoteny, 127, 208
Noland, Robert, 4, 5, 6, 11, 49, 78, 88, 95, 125, 129, 145, 147, 185, 202, 219, 227, 231, 245, 339, 366
Novello, Antonia, 5, 6

P

paidomorphy, 127, 192, 208
patriarchal revolution, 108, 236, 265
patriarchal system, the greatest of all human creations, 7, 14, 15, 20, 21, 25, 32, 35, 37, 43, 46, 48, 52, 54, 63, 72, 77, et passim
patriarchy, 2, 6, 7, 8, 9, 10, 20, 21, 22, 23, 26, 38, 40, 41, 43, 47, 49, 57, 58, 60, 64, 67, 68, 70, 72, 75, 76, 78, 79, et passim
patriarchy, benefits to women, 2, 6, 7, 8, 9, 10, 20, 21, 22, 23, 26, 38, 40, 41, 43, 47, 49, 57, 60, 64, 67, 68, 70, 72, 75, 76, 78, 79, 82, 83, 85, 86, 88, 89, 95, 97, 98, 99, 100, et passim
Pirani, Alix, 38
Pollitt, Katha, 187, 188, 189, 193
Pope John Paul II, 313
Popenoe, David, 18, 75, 76, 156, 204, 208. 355, 409, 416, 426, 431
Promiscuity Principle, 71, 172, 198, 220, 339
putting sex to work, 107, 111, 245, 265

R

Raglan, Lord, 49, 195, 196, 447
raising of men's consciousness, 168
Reed, Evelyn, 37, 38, 199, 202, 237, 277, 401. 409, 419, 422
Reiss, Ira, 54, 55, 87, 179, 180, 405, 415, 425, 433, 447, 451, 452
Rich, Adrienne, 32, 47, 65, 73, 86, 107, 146. 211, 283, 344, 360, 361, 397, 420
Richmond-Abbott, Marie, 176, 177, 293, 367
Rivers, W. H. R., 203
Rothman, Barbara, 124, 125, 126, 127, 128
Russell, Diana, 179, 180, 381, 401

S

Sand, George, 159, 160, 418, 425
Sanger, Margaret, 130, 218, 276, 397, 405

Satin, Joseph, 75
Schlafly, Phyllis, 50, 51, 323, 433, 453
Seaman, Barbara, 34, 39, 67, 118, 119, 121, 128, 143, 144, 244, 375, 383, 404, 405, 418, 452
Seri Indians, 167, 203
sexual law-and-order, 22, 23, 34, 38, 45, 59, 108. 112, 121. 192, 247, 277, 296, 326, 329, 362, 375
sexual loyalty, 25, 29, 38, 42, 43, 72, 81, 90, 101, 131, 141, 150, 155, 163, 175, 177, 190, 199, 217, 221, 225, 226, 234, 248, 272, 290, 331, 339, 346, 365, 367, 379
sexual revolution, 41, 57, 75, 87, 104, 107, 108, 109, 110, 113, 126, 137, 141, 197, 208, 230, 236, 263, 269, 277, 296, 317, 319, 330, 365, 366, 389
Shalala, Donna, 181, 373
Shaw, George Bernard, 128, 454
Sherfey, 84, 118, 121, 144, 331, 392, 452
Sjöö and Mor, 20, 88, 89, 90, 101, 102, 125, 126, 148, 243, 244, 351
Smith, Lynn, 17, 410
Spong, Bishop, 39, 40, 41, 42, 44, 92, 93, 94, 95, 96, 97, 98, 100, 101, 107, 108, 109, 110, 111, 112, 122, 206, 303, 304, 306, 307, 309, 310, 455
Steinem, Gloria, 45, 49, 59, 291, 336, 337
Stokes, Gail, 173, 174
Stone, Merlin, 128, 147, 262, 265, 269, 380, 381, 450
Sumner, William Graham, 317, 333

T

Thatcher, Margaret, 47, 224, 225, 345
Tocqueville, Alexis, 113
Toffler, Col. Patrick, 50, 51
Triere, Lynette, 31, 32, 33, 62, 63, 129, 272, 273, 275, 278, 279, 280, 281, 283, 346, 386, 446, 447
troth, giving versus pledging, 39, 305
Tucker, William, 44, 203

U

underclass, 44, 100, 171, 191, 288, 328, 337, 362

V

van Buren, Abigail, 57, 227, 294
Vanzi, Max, 169
Vico, Giambatista, 332

W

wall, 123, 318, 348, 368
Wallerstein, Judith, 31, 56, 97, 98, 112, 119, 136, 162, 175, 176, 193, 369, 393, 408, 414, 427, 439, 440
War Against Patriarchy, 8, 51, 53, 59, 60, 135, 136, 143, 155, 297, 316, 331
war between the two kinship systems, 102, 269, 383
Ward, Janie Victoria, 140, 318, 327
Washington, D.C, 250
Weitzman, Lenore, 27, 28, 29, 186, 272, 296, 337, 379, 380

White House Conference on *Families*, 64
white males have all the stuff, 308
Whitehead, Barbara Dafoe, 76, 78, 156, 390, 391, 393, 394,
    414, 417, 418, 421
Williams, Walter, 250
Wolf, Naomi, 10, 267, 304, 305, 331, 395, 442, 444, 450
woman as a moral minor, 229
women's bargaining power, 42, 43
women's divorce-proneness, 117
women's hatred of patriarchy, 98
women's sexual loyalty, 101
women's sexual revolution, made possible by women's
    economic independence, 137
world historic defeat of the female sex, 145

Y

Yos, Nancy, 252
Young, Leontine, 2, 314, 404, 408, 416, 454